UNIVERSITY TEACHING

GARLAND STUDIES IN HIGHER EDUCATION
VOLUME 13
GARLAND REFERENCE LIBRARY OF SOCIAL SCIENCE
VOLUME 1123

GARLAND STUDIES IN HIGHER EDUCATION

This series is published in cooperation with the Program in Higher Education, School of Education, Boston College, Chestnut Hill, Massachusetts.

PHILIP G. ALTBACH, *Series Editor*

UNIVERSITY TEACHING
INTERNATIONAL PERSPECTIVES

EDITED BY
JAMES J.F. FOREST

GARLAND PUBLISHING, INC.
A MEMBER OF THE TAYLOR & FRANCIS GROUP
NEW YORK AND LONDON
1998

Library of Congress Cataloging-in-Publication Data

University teaching : international perspectives / edited by James J.F. Forest.
      p.   cm. — (Garland studies in higher education ; v. 13.
Garland reference library of social science ; v. 1123.)
    Includes bibliographical references (p.   ) and index.
    ISBN 0-8153-2460-X (alk. paper)
    1. College teaching—Cross-cultural studies.   2. Learning—Cross-
cultural studies.   3. Universities and colleges—Administration—Cross-
cultural studies.   I. Forest, James J.F. II. Series: Garland reference library
of social science ; v. 1123. III. Series: Garland reference library of social
science. Garland studies in higher education ; vol. 13.
LB2331.U78   1998
378.1'2—dc21   97-49898
                                                    CIP

Printed on acid-free, 250-year-life paper
Manufactured in the United States of America

SERIES EDITOR'S PREFACE

Higher education is a multifaceted phenomenon in modern society, combining a variety of institutions and an increasing diversity of students, a range of purposes and functions, and different orientations. The series combines research-based monographs, analyses, and discussions of broader issues and reference books related to all aspects of higher education. It is concerned with policy as well as practice from a global perspective. The series is dedicated to illuminating the reality of higher and postsecondary education in contemporary society.

Philip G. Altbach
Boston College

Contents

Preface

The primary scope of this book is to address the question of what is going on in the world of university teaching. University and college teaching and the assessment and reward of teaching are among the most important topics in higher education worldwide, and increasing in importance. However, surprisingly little has been done towards collaboratively presenting the growing wealth of quality research on university and college teaching from around the world. A cross-cultural perspective in research on higher education helps us extract from a set of different social arrangements that which, if not universal, is at least true in a large number of cases. Even when a researcher attempts to enhance our understanding of a single nation and its uniqueness, this is often best accomplished through comparison with other national contexts. Thus, this book offers for consideration several comparative and international perspectives on teaching in postsecondary education.

Additionally, under the conviction that faculty in one country can learn a great deal from the experiences of their colleagues in other parts of the world, this volume incorporates an international collection of engaging case studies on various topics of college and university teaching. This collection of essays and case studies is not meant to provide a comprehensive overview of university teaching and learning around the world. Such a task would require more than a dozen volumes for the English-speaking nations alone. Rather, the intent of this volume is to contribute a diverse set of perspectives on the many dimensions of university and college teaching, including preparation, assessment, reward, and the cultural and social influences that reside within each of these dimensions. However, while the book provides a considerable richness in diversity of topics and authors, a main concern is to provoke the reader to observe the many commonalities in the thinking and approaches towards college teaching that pervade higher education systems worldwide, and from these shared elements derive the insights needed to address the challenges of today's higher education environment.

THE ORGANIZATION OF THE MATERIAL
The chapters of this volume are loosely grouped under four categories: issues of instruction; research and perspectives on student learning and assessment; the training and development of current and future university teachers; and institutional policy, structure and organization. The first two chapters of the volume provide comparative perspectives on university teaching from

two markedly different approaches. W. Alan Wright's research involves an international survey of 331 instructional developers, while David Watkins presents his research on what students in different countries perceive to be "good teaching." This is followed by James Forest's general overview of several dimensions of university teaching encountered by faculty worldwide.

Section 2 begins with Noel Entwistle's essay on the usefulness of research on student learning, incorporating concepts derived from research on student learning, carried out mainly in Europe and Australasia. France Mugler and Roger Landbeck provide a discussion on learning conditions and strategies of students in a distance learning environment, and Kari Smith contributes her observations on the benefits of using portfolios in classroom assessment. Further perspectives on student learning are provided in chapters by Ted and Patricia Panitz and by Kyle Smith, Seyda Türk Smith, and Iain K.B. Twaddle.

Returning to focus on faculty issues, Graham Gibbs and Michael Herrick each provide their own thoughts and research on how to improve the preparation of faculty for classroom teaching. This section is rounded out with John Dwyer's discussion of how one university in Canada developed a university practicum to train graduate students—our professors of the future—in the art and skill of teaching.

The final section of the volume provides an international collection of perspectives and studies on institutional policies, structures and organizational attributes which impact university teaching, beginning with Margaret Robertson's observations on the growing use of benchmarks in evaluating teaching. Terry Hyland discusses the relationship between work-based learning and professional higher education in British universities, followed by Tronie Rifkin's observations on the changes in Denmark brought by the introduction of a 3-year baccalaureate degree structure. Rifkin notes that the pressures of this new expedited system have the effect of convincing both faculty and students that productivity and efficiency of the system are more important than the quality of the learning produced by their efforts. Howard Fergus presents the organizational history, policy implications and future directions of distance teaching and learning in the West Indies, and Sheila Vance and Glenda Crosling discuss various methods of integrating writing skills development into the curriculum of most any discipline. Yung Che Kim's discussion of the relationship between student activism and college teaching in South Korea leads us to the conclusion that policies and methods of college teaching simply cannot completely ignore the moral or social realities or conditions that students face. And this section ends with a chapter from Marcela Mollis and Daniel Feldman on the role of contested academic appointments at the University of Buenos Aires, addressing the issue of how institutional policies impact the culture of academic departments in ways that affect teaching.

It is hoped that this international collection of perspectives will be useful in enhancing our understanding of the multiple dimensions that reside under the general rubric of university teaching. Obviously, a volume such as this must be limited in scope and breadth and cannot address the somewhat overwhelming multitude of topics or dimensions of university teaching and learning worldwide. Indeed, as every cultural context is unique, readers are encouraged to explore further the issues raised by these authors, particularly in the context of their own academic surroundings. Additionally, many of the concepts and suggestions presented in this volume are not tied to any particular culture or groups of cultures; thus it is important to recognize the value of comparative studies in these areas.

WHERE TO GO FROM HERE?

It is feasible that many readers of this volume might question how we can synthesize these authors' work to form a collective approach to understanding and enhancing university teaching. This is not the intended outcome of presenting these chapters together as a collection. Each author in this volume, from various corners of the world, has provided us with their own perspective about this important topic. Indeed, this collection of chapters covers a broad spectrum in terms of focus, orientation, and narration. However, there are several commonalities, the most general of which is that they are all concerned with some aspect of university teaching. Indeed, the entire volume reflects a commitment to recognizing and improving our understanding of teaching in universities worldwide. This in turn is an effort to reflect on the global pervasiveness of the belief in university teaching and learning as a means for personal, social and economic development. In these chapters, authors have presented case studies of student learning, of teaching development programs for faculty and graduate students, and of institutional polices and structures that can impact—either positively or negatively—on university teaching and learning. Many of the authors have also offered research-based suggestions on ways to enhance university teaching efforts in ways that promote both teacher and student learning.

Certainly, a cross-national perspective helps to establish the validity of generalizations that are derived initially from studying something in only one country. One approach for future studies in university teaching could look at nations as components of larger international systems—in this case, the increasingly globalized world of higher education. Seeing the nation as a context in which events take place helps us to recognize how we can learn from our colleagues in other nations and how they approach dilemmas in university teaching in different ways. However, searching for commonalities is not the only suggestion for future research in this area. Comparative and international approaches should seek not only the similarities but also the differences in the way things work in different national settings.

Many differences in theoretical and practical approaches to particular situations are rooted in cultural and social contexts, and this raises a number of questions for future research. For example, consider Kari Smith's discussion of using portfolios as a tool for assessing learning in her classrooms. One immediate question that comes to mind is whether portfolio assessment is applicable outside the particular historical, cultural, and political context of Israel. Are portfolios a useful learning assessment tool for countries that have capitalist economies or those characterized by Western culture, which places a relatively higher value on self-direction?

This collection of perspectives is thus intended mainly as an introduction to the possibilities in terms of bringing an international flavor to the discussions of teaching and learning that occur with great frequency at departmental meetings, at academic conferences, and in the halls of legislatures. It is nowhere suggested that a comparative perspective can solve local problems. It is, however, proposed that looking internationally, one may find similar problems, and by learning how others address those problems we gain new insights for forming our own strategies. University teaching and learning is a phenomenon which exists worldwide. Thus, looking beyond our traditional boundaries provides us with a rich resource of knowledge, just waiting to be explored.

ACKNOWLEDGMENTS

In closing, I sincerely commend and thank the contributors for their diligence, hard work, and patience in this project. As well, the warm reception that many of them offered me upon being approached for their contributions will always be greatly appreciated. I owe a considerable debt of gratitude to Professor Philip G. Altbach, my guide through the labyrinth of academe and the General Editor of the *Garland Series in Higher Education*. And finally, to all college and university teachers—and particularly those who put a little extra time, heart and soul into their work—I offer my deepest respect.

James JF Forest
July 1997

About the Contributors

GLENDA CROSLING is a lecturer at Monash University in Melbourne Australia and is responsible for the language and learning program in the Faculty of Business and Economics, on the Clayton Campus. She has considerable experience in developing programs to enhance tertiary literacy in the university setting and has developed a popular discipline-specific program, "Legal Language for Commercial Law." She has published articles on writing and non-English-speaking students, on the culture of law in business degrees, and co-authored with Helen Murphy the book *How to Study Business Law: Reading, Writing and Exams* (2nd ed. Sydney: Butterworths, 1996).

JOHN DWYER is the author of *Virtuous Discourse: Sensibility and Community in Late Eighteenth-Century Scotland* (Edinburgh, 1985) and *The Age of the Passions* (forthcoming). He has edited several books and composed numerous articles on Scottish culture and the eighteenth-century Enlightenment. As a university administrator, Dr. Dwyer has been the Placement Director for York's Business School, the Personal Assistant to York's Vice President (External), the Associate Director of York's Centre for the Support of Teaching and, most recently, the Associate Director of University Advancement at McMaster University. As a teacher, Dr. Dwyer has taught at Edinburgh University, North Island College, University of British Columbia, Simon Fraser University and York University. While at York University, he was a member of the Faculty of Graduate Studies and had responsibility for supervising graduate students enrolled in York University's Teaching Practicum.

NOEL J. ENTWISTLE is Bell Professor of Education and Director of the Centre for Research on Learning and Instruction at the University of Edinburgh. He is the coordinating editor of the internationally circulated journal *Higher Education*.

DANIEL FELDMAN is Adjunct Professor of Didactics at the School of Philosophy and Letters at University of Buenos Aires; and researcher in Contents, Curriculum and Teaching Practice at the Research Institute of Education (Instituto de Investigaciones en Ciencias de la Educacion, IICE) at the University of Buenos Aires.

HOWARD A. FERGUS is Senior Lecturer/Resident Tutor, School of Continuing Studies, University of the West Indies; he has been Speaker of the Montserrat Legislative Council since 1974 and deputizes as Governor of the Island periodically. A lifelong career educator, Dr. Fergus has taught at several levels. He has research interests in both history and education, in which he has published widely. Recent works include "The Challenge of Educational Reform in Micro States: The Case of the Organisation of Eastern Caribbean States" *Prospects* Vol. 31, No. 4 (UNESCO, 1991), and *Montserrat: History of a Caribbean Colony* (London: Macmillan, 1994). He is currently writing a book, *A History of Education in the British Leeward Islands, 1834-1956*.

JAMES JF FOREST is Technology Specialist for the National Center for Urban Partnerships, where he directs a strategic planning and development initiative for the Ford Foundation involving Internet-based collaboration between schools, communities, and higher education institutions in Puerto Rico, South Africa, and the United States. He is also Research Associate for the Boston College Center for International Higher Education. He holds degrees in Foreign Service, International Development Education, and Higher Education Administration, and has authored several publications and conference presentations on international and comparative higher education, technology in educational organizations, and university teaching.

GRAHAM GIBBS is Co-Director of the Center for Higher Education Practice at the Open University, England. The Center develops and runs distance learning programs for teachers in higher education, worldwide. He is the Convenor of the International Consortium for Educational Development, a network of national higher education organizations, and has been a consultant to universities in many countries.

MICHAEL HERRICK is currently a consultant to the Ministry of Education in Muscat, Oman, where he assists in the development of a teacher training center. From 1992-1996, under a CIDA-funded University of Manitoba contract with the University of Botswana, he was instrumental in setting up an academic staff training unit titled the Higher Education Development Unit. Until 1992 he was an associate professor in the Faculty of Education at Saint Mary's University, Halifax, where he taught methodology and curriculum development. During 1986-1989 he was director of Saint Mary's CIDA-funded Canada/China Language and Cultural Program which exchanged instructors with Beijing Normal University and operated an English/French language teaching center in Beijing and orientation centers in five Canadian universities. Dr. Herrick holds degrees in English, Curriculum and Instruction, and Human Resources Development.

TERRY HYLAND has worked in schools, further, adult and higher education since 1971 and has taught in a number of post-school teacher education institutions before taking up his present post as Lecturer in Continuing Education at the University of Warwick in April 1991. His principal research interests are in vocational and professional education and the post-school curriculum, and he is author of a recent book, *Competence, Education and NVQs: Dissenting Perspectives* (London: Cassell, 1994).

YUNG CHE KIM is a professor in the Department of Psychology, Keimyung University, in Korea. He has served as Dean of Student Affairs, Dean of Academic Affairs, and Dean of the Graduate School of Education at Keimyung University. He has authored more than a dozen books, and has held several nationally prominent roles in Korean higher education, including specialist member of the Presidential Commission for Education Reform and university accrediting member of the Korean Council for University Education.

ROGER LANDBECK is Director of the Centre for the Enhancement of Learning and Teaching at the University of the South Pacific. Previously, he worked in a center devoted to improving learning and teaching in Griffith University, Brisbane, Australia. Dr. Landbeck has taught at universities in in England and Africa in the fields of physics and science education, in addition to working in curriculum development in secondary school science in England.

MARCELA MOLLIS is Professor of History of Education and Comparative Education at the University of Buenos Aires. She is currently running a program on Comparative Higher Education titled "Quality Evaluation of Higher Education: The Case of Argentina and Canada," at the Research Institute of Education (IICE/ UBA). She has been a Japan Foundation Fellow at Nagoya University in Japan and a Ford Foundation Fellow at Harvard University. She has published the results of her research in Brazil, Mexico, Japan, Spain, and the United States.

FRANCE MUGLER is Senior Lecturer in Linguistics at the University of the South Pacific (USP), a regional university that serves 12 Pacific island nations and whose main campus is in Suva, Fiji. She has done research on the sociolinguistic situation in Fiji in general and Dravidian languages in particular, Pacific languages in education, and student learning at the USP.

PATRICIA PANITZ has taught for ten years as an adjunct professor at Cape Cod Community College, using collaborative learning extensively in courses on English composition and developmental English. She has served as a consultant to the New Bedford Junior High Schools and has made presentations on collaborative learning at the Lilly New England conferences in 1995 and 1996.

THEODORE PANITZ has taught at Cape Cod Community College for 21 years, using a collaborative learning format in courses on engineering, mathematics, and developmental mathematics. He has been an instructor at Parkersberg Community College and the Illinois Institute of Technology and has served as a consultant to the New Bedford Junior High Schools on cooperative learning techniques. He has made numerous presentations at conferences on the subject of collaborative learning.

TRONIE RIFKIN conducted the study upon which her chapter is based as a Fulbright Scholar in Denmark during the 1993-94 academic year. She has recently received her Ph.D. in Higher Education from the Graduate School of Education and Information Studies at UCLA and is currently the assistant director of the ERIC Clearinghouse for Community Colleges at UCLA. Her research interests include international higher education, faculty issues, and perspectives on teaching in higher education, academic ethics, and community colleges.

MARGARET ROBERTSON is Senior Lecturer in Education at the University of Tasmania. Her background is in psychology and geography, and she has a wide range of teaching experience with undergraduate teacher education students and graduate students and lecturers in higher education. She has taught in Australia, New Zealand, Malaysia, United Kingdom, and Finland. Her research experience is primarily in the field of visual-spatial perceptions. She has given a number of papers at international conferences based on her postdoctoral research in the field of environmental perceptions. Many of these findings contribute to her views on teaching and learning, especially with respect to the role of personal contexts. Her research has attracted interest and collaborative projects with colleagues in Germany and Finland where her methodology on environmental perceptions is being applied in different cultural and teaching contexts.

KARI SMITH is chair of the Department of Education, Oramim School of Education of the Kibbutz Movement, Haifa University, Israel. Her main teaching and research interests are in language teaching, general teacher education, and educational assessment procedures at all levels of education.

KYLE D. SMITH is associate professor in the Division of Social/Behavioral Sciences and Social Work at the University of Guam. Dr. Smith received his Ph.D. in social psychology from the University of Washington in 1987. He has taught a variety of courses in psychology, statistics, and research methods in the mainland United States, Turkey, and Micronesia. His research interests include cultural factors in emotion and moral concepts.

SEYDA TÜRK SMITH received her bachelor's degree in psychology from Istanbul University and her Master's and Doctorate in social psychology from the University of Washington. Her teaching specialties include developmental psychology, organizational behavior, and research methodology. Dr. Türk Smith's current research focuses on cultural factors in self-concept and their relation to styles of child-rearing.

IAIN K. B. TWADDLE received his Ph.D. in clinical psychology from the University of Windsor in Ontario. He teaches courses in clinical psychology and history and systems of psychology. His research interests include the sociopolitical underpinnings of mental health care systems.

SHEILA VANCE is a language and learning lecturer at Monash University (Melbourne, Australia). She is responsible for language and learning programs in all faculties at the Peninsula Campus and has collaborated extensively with discipline-based lecturers (including Arts, Business, Computing, Education, and Nursing) in the development and delivery of discipline-specific literacy programs. She has published articles on writing development and integrated writing programs and has a strong interest in discipline-specific writing and composing strategies.

DAVID WATKINS is Professor of Education at the University of Hong Kong, where he has taught for eight years. Previously he has held academic posts in Australia and New Zealand and has also taught courses in China and the Philippines. He is the author of several books, chapters, and articles primarily in the area of student learning and self-concept from a cross-cultural perspective. He is currently the East Asian representative on the Executive Committee of the International Association of Cross-Cultural Psychology.

W. ALAN WRIGHT is the founding Executive Director of the Office of Instructional Development and Technology at Dalhousie University, Nova Scotia, Canada, where he is responsible for a comprehensive teaching improvement program and oversees Instructional Media Services. Dr. Wright has earned degrees from Mount Allison University (New Brunswick), as well as from McGill University and the Université de Montréal in his native Québec. He has a vast experience in a variety of educational milieux, and his current activities in instructional development include research and writing, speaking at conferences, and presenting faculty workshops in college and university settings. He is the author (with associates) of *Teaching Improvement Practices: Successful Strategies for Higher Education* (Anker Publishing, 1995).

Issues of Instruction

CHAPTER 1

Improving Teaching by Design
Preferred Policies, Programs and Practices
W. Alan Wright

The matter of improving teaching must rank as a top priority in universities and colleges around the world if they are to successfully fulfill their missions as institutions of higher learning. What is more, successful teaching enhancement requires the on-going commitment of members of the academic administration and the professoriate as well as instructional and staff developers. At the institutional level, constant attention to teaching improvement policies, programs and practices is required to ensure the status and quality of college and university teaching.

A wide variety of strategies may contribute to a comprehensive approach to improving teaching on a given campus. Although local conditions, climate and cultures often prevail in matters of educational improvement and innovation, the academic community should nonetheless establish priorities when pursuing instructional development goals. Priority items for the instructional development agenda on a given campus should take into account the experience and opinions of the professoriate and professionals in the field of faculty development. This chapter examines five key elements of an overall design for teaching improvement. The first concerns the value of teaching in personnel decisions; the second concerns the leadership of academic administrators in the realm of teaching enhancement; the third involves mentoring, consultation and other programs for new instructors; the fourth regards programs directly supporting teaching innovation; and the fifth concerns faculty workshops and institutes with specific reference to the teaching dossier or portfolio.

The key elements of this design to enhance university teaching spring from three sources—the results of an international survey of 331 instructional developers, an analysis of the responses of the same survey completed by of over 900 faculty, department heads or chairs and deans, and the experience of directing the instructional development program at Dalhousie

University in Nova Scotia, Canada. All respondents were asked to rate their confidence, on a scale of one (low confidence) to ten (high confidence) in each of 36 items in terms of its potential to improve teaching. In the data analysis the 36 teaching improvement activities were rank ordered according to their mean ratings on the 10-point scale. The faculty/staff developers represented 331 different institutions in the United States, Canada, the United Kingdom, and Australasia. The majority of the 906 faculty, deans and chairs surveyed work at 7 universities (5 anglophone and 2 francophone) in Atlantic Canada, while the others are employed either at a university in Quebec, Canada or one in California, U.S. Table 1 shows the comparative rank order of the items for: 1) the faculty developers' group; 2) the group of faculty, deans and heads; and 3) Dalhousie University respondents (faculty, deans and heads).

Not included in the table are the results of the same survey, completed at a meeting of university presidents and vice-presidents in Atlantic Canada. The senior administrators—representing 13 institutions—ranked several items in a similar fashion to other campus groups. Notably, they also rated the importance of consideration for teaching in personnel practices at the top of their list and ranked workshops, mentoring programs and instructional leadership on the part of deans and heads as among the top ten of 36 items relating to teaching improvement. The main differences between their rankings and those of the other campus groups were that 1) they did not favor reduced workloads and grants to professors attempting to improve their teaching, and 2) they rated the importance of their own leadership roles in improving teaching higher than did the deans, professors and instructional developers.[1]

Before examining individual components of a faculty development program, let me emphasize the fact that the instructional developers responding to our survey stressed the importance of a comprehensive approach to the problem of enhancing teaching. It is difficult, in their judgment, to evaluate certain instructional development policies in isolation. Comments from faculty developers in four countries serve to illustrate this concept:

> The combined effect or "mix" of initiatives is more important than any one item listed. The potential of any one initiative to improve teaching may vary greatly depending on how many other initiatives exist on a given campus.
> (United States)

Table 1

Survey Responses

"Rate each item to indicate the confidence you have in its potential to improve the quality of teaching in your university." (Scale: 1 = least confident; 10 = most confident)

Teaching Improvement Practice[2]	International Faculty Developers[3] (n=331)		Faculty, Heads & Deans[4] (n=906)		Dalhousie Univ. (Faculty, Heads & Deans)[5] (n=295)	
	Rank	Mean	Rank	Mean	Rank	Mean
Recognition of teaching in tenure and promotion decisions	1.	8.24	1.	7.94	1.	8.02
Deans/Heads foster importance of teaching responsibility	2.	7.94	2.	7.65	2.	7.80
Deans/Heads promote climate of trust for classroom observation	3.	7.47	10.	6.41	9.	6.51
Mentoring programs and support for new professors	4.	7.38	7.	6.92	5.*	6.90
Grants to faculty to devise new approaches to teaching	5.	7.31	9.	6.51	10.	6.27
Workshops on teaching methods for targeted groups	6.	7.30	3.	7.15	4.	7.08
Deans/Heads praise and reward good teaching	7.	7.29	6.	7.11	3.	7.33
Hiring practices require demonstration of teaching ability	8.	7.21	4.	7.14	7.	6.83
Consultation on course materials with peers (formative)	9.	7.20	8.	6.84	8.	6.54
Temporary workload reduction for course improvement/revision	10.	7.13	5.	7.12	5.*	6.90

* denotes tie

No one teaching improvement practice is crucial in itself. The important issue is comprehensive, holistic, continuing support for teaching and lecturing excellence.
(United Kingdom)

It is impossible to say what is the one strategy for the improvement of teaching; rather it seems a combination of factors are helpful. These are quite varied in approach.
(Canada)

No one strategy, on its own, is likely to improve the quality of teaching. What is required is an integrated program which consistently and across a broad front raises the profile and status of teaching. (Australia)

Notwithstanding the need for a comprehensive approach to instructional development, instructional developers and faculty alike have identified preferred practices, programs and policies via our international surveys. The items which follow should be considered carefully by all members of the academic community concerned with maximizing the impact of instructional development programs.

PERSONNEL DECISIONS

Academics worldwide emphasize the prime importance of valuing university teaching in institutional personnel decisions. It follows that those responsible for teaching improvement programs should consider the status of teaching in university procedures and policies with regards to hiring, contract renewal, salary increases and merit pay, as well as tenure and promotion. One American academic responding to our survey put it bluntly:

Money talks! As long as research is more important to tenure and promotion than teaching, that's where people will put their effort.

Faculty in Atlantic Canada, in research universities and liberal arts colleges alike, emphasize the importance of rewarding teaching. Many of them took the initiative to comment on this matter when responding to our teaching improvement practices survey. Some faculty bemoaned the fact that research is much more prized than is teaching.

The best incentive is to know teaching is important and to have it a significant part of the evaluation process for tenure and beyond.

Unless we reward and recognize teaching at least as equal to research, all efforts will have minimal impact.

Teaching should be given equal value as research in all career decisions.

The main barrier to excellent teaching is the pressure to excel at research. We work hard, more than 50 hours per week, but prioritize our time as 1) research, 2) teaching, 3) administration.

It is my perception so far that anything goes at this University in teaching, whereas success in research has rewards (grants, promotion, recognition). If new and not-so-new faculty perceive that teaching *counts*, they are intelligent enough to make it good. But the University *must reward* this effort with merit pay, promotion and proper recognition.

As a scientist who is also expected to teach, I have limited time for "teaching research"; if I do not publish papers and obtain external funding for my research, I will not continue to be employed at the University, no matter how good a teacher I am. This situation is *not* ideal, but *is* universal in my discipline.[6]

Other faculty members decry the fact that teaching performance makes a difference only in cases when it is done poorly, claiming rewards for outstanding teaching performance.

On souligne toujours les personnes qui enseignent mal, mais on souligne pas les personnes qui enseignent bien.

Reward system must recognize excellence and improvement in teaching, not just adequate teaching. Evaluation should not be punitive, but supportive.

It is critical that the reward system require "good +" teaching as a minimum for promotion and tenure. Senior administrative support is only symbolic. Has to impart at Department/Senior faculty level.

Not only does ensuring tangible recognition for teaching accomplishment take an important place in an overall plan to improve university pedagogy, but many academics believe that it is a pre-requisite for any instructional development program to succeed.

I have tended to rank reward and recognition highly in terms of the development of good teaching. This is based on the conviction that the incentive to use workshops, libraries and other resources is driven by the perception that teaching is a valued and important activity, and that the attainment of a high level of competence as a teacher will be 'rewarded' in one way or another.

Exhortation, talk, conferences, committees, meetings don't help. The University must put money or (equivalently) faculty *time* into making improvements. Also that time and effort must be rewarded with promotion, money, recognition of some form.

Obviously, many of the suggestions would have to be implemented for a real improvement in teaching. Some real "carrots" would go a long way in the present climate.

Almost as important as recognition for teaching in tenure and promotion decisions (in the view of many instructional developers and other academics) is the need to hire professors with attention to their proven ability or potential as teachers. As the survey responses in Table 1 show, hiring practices which require a demonstration of teaching ability rank among the top ten items for the potential to improve teaching for all categories of our respondents. One Canadian faculty developer put it this way:

We need to recognize the importance of teaching and adjust our hiring practices and expectations accordingly. Applicants should be required to demonstrate teaching abilities.

Many faculty colleagues in universities in Atlantic Canada agreed:

People either love to teach or it's something that gets in the way of other interests. Hire as many of the former type as possible.

Exiger démonstration des capacités pédagogiques à l'embauche.

On a les professeur-e-s que l'on mérite. Tout se joue à l'embauche. Le candidat au poste de professeur devrait être évalué avant l'embauche.

Some faculty do not believe that all new hires can aspire to excellence in both research and teaching. They think academia should face the inevitable, hiring for strength in *either* teaching or research.

Should hire faculty based on teaching or research as a primary consideration. They can then focus on their duties instead of being torn apart between two disciplines.

Consider hiring faculty mainly on their ability to teach with less responsibility for administration and research. In other words, hire people to do what they do well and let it be clear that *teaching* is of equivalent value (salary and promotions, etc.) to research.

Finally, some faculty feel it is unfair to scrutinize teaching abilities before hiring the *inexperienced* professor.

> Many new faculty have *not* taught a great deal and to require demonstration of teaching ability (other than to give one lecture as part of an interview) would be difficult and may rule out faculty who *will develop* (but have not yet demonstrated) good teaching abilities and skills.
>
> I agree with respect to hiring of experienced personnel—but not to neophyte appointments.

The controversy concerning the notion of 'streaming' new professors into careers accenting research or teaching notwithstanding, many academics are convinced that we must place more emphasis on teaching abilities during the interviewing and selection process.

LEADERSHIP OF DEANS AND HEADS

Instructional developers and faculty, as well as academic administrators themselves emphasize the critical role department heads, chairs and deans play in raising both the status and the quality of teaching in higher education. More specifically, some twelve hundred academics responding to our questionnaire rated the role of deans and heads in fostering the importance of teaching responsibilities second only to recognition for teaching in tenure and promotion decisions (in terms of potential impact on quality). As the survey responses in Table 1 show, praise and reward for good teaching and promoting a climate of trust for classroom observation constitute additional means which deans and heads can call upon in an effort to improve university pedagogy.

A faculty member in the health sciences field at a mid-sized research university stresses the notion that heads and directors have a greater role to play in teaching improvement than do senior administrators.

> I don't think rhetoric by senior administration will help faculty who need to see rewards of good teaching or consequences of poor teaching. Those who need to emphasize importance of teaching are directors/unit heads who have regular contact with faculty.

Other Canadian faculty members underline the need for deans to reinforce quality teaching while putting the accent on "learning effectiveness" and finding a balance between teaching and research:

It's not what the deans say, but how they reinforce good teaching with perks. We need to develop a "learning effectiveness" model—not "teaching effectiveness."

Administrators and Rank and Tenure committees have to praise and reward good teaching and not put so much importance on research, research, research.

NEW FACULTY DEVELOPMENT: MENTORING AND CONSULTATION

The third essential area of activity in an overall scheme to improve the quality and status of university teaching involves programs for new instructors, mentoring plans for new and junior faculty and consultation services. As the survey responses in Table 1 show, mentoring and other means of support for beginning faculty are thought by instructional developers and faculty to have very high potential to enhance teaching in higher education. Though not limited to involvement of junior faculty, consultation on course materials with peers achieves, potentially, similar goals to mentoring.

Structured instructional development programs generally include well-received orientation to teaching events for new faculty. An instructional developer in a mid-sized university in Ontario, Canada, describes the interest in her center's services:

> Over the summer, new faculty contact our office with practical issues about their teaching roles. In addition to these private consultations, the New Faculty Workshop held at the beginning of September is always popular and helpful to beginning faculty.

Our experience at Dalhousie University supports the need for an orientation program for new faculty. Evaluations of orientation activities over the last eight years have been favorable. New professors have commented as follows:

> Excellent day—invaluable for encouragement as much as for facts and resource identification.

> Terrific source of information to 'get started.' Thank you.

> Very useful—saved a lot of time and trial and error discovery.

I really appreciated meeting the resource people and hearing them emphasize their availability should help or information be needed. I am in a better position to teach from than I would be otherwise. It was a good idea to have various other support groups besides those having directly to do with teaching. They all have something to do with teaching one way or another. It was good to have the opportunity to meet other new faculty members.

Though orientation or induction activities are useful, they should be followed by 'new' or 'junior' faculty development plans. Mentoring is a favored means of developing the beginning instructor. According to a comprehensive review of mentoring practices in higher education in the United States (Luna and Cullen, 1995), the approach has numerous benefits:

Faculty career development, better teaching, quality research, and improved leadership skills can be positive outcomes of mentoring. (p. 71)

Though faculty developers often promote interdisciplinary mentoring, many senior faculty prefer discipline-based plans. Comments submitted by our survey respondents serve to illustrate these points.

I believe teaching effectiveness requires a sincere interest on the part of the faculty member. Peer assistance can be successful, immensely helpful, and I like the idea of new faculty being invited to sit in on lectures of faculty with reputations for being able to teach effectively.

Assist young faculty *early* via co-operative activities.

Scholarly activities and enthusiasm for the subject are the basis of good teaching, not techniques. Disciplinary-based mentoring programs are excellent ways of introducing new scholars.

Orientation activities and a mentoring program lie at the heart of a comprehensive junior faculty development program and a successful junior faculty development program can have positive impact on faculty careers. (For a full account of such a program see Milton Cox, 1995).

SUPPORT FOR IMPROVEMENT INITIATIVES

A fourth element of a successful instructional development plan involves ongoing programs of support for faculty making improvements to courses and teaching. The potential of grants to faculty to devise new approaches to teaching obtains a very high confidence rating from faculty developers internationally, while deans, heads and faculty express relatively less confidence in this approach to improving teaching. On the other hand, as the survey responses in Table 1 show, faculty, deans and heads favor temporary workload reductions for course improvement and revision while faculty developers express relatively less confidence in this teaching improvement practice. The problem with both schemes, of course, is one of resource allocation—as resources dwindle, few are the optimistic academics anticipating additional funds for teaching innovation and reduced workloads for course revision. Yet many faculty responding to our survey, particularly those in a mid-sized research university, expressed great frustration with the lack of time to improve teaching and the competing demands on their time:

> One of my main constraints when it comes to teaching is *time*. In a system which still values research more than teaching, your professors cannot put 100% into teaching. My teaching would be better if I had more time.

> Just give a bit more time to read, rearrange, re-think, and be prepared and up-to-date. We are overloaded and have no time to think!

> The largest hurdle to being more involved in teaching is the time factor. We are doing more clerical work with less staff.

> Free up time from other demands to recognize the importance of developing teaching.

Ironically, many faculty report that they cannot ("despite my best intentions") even find time to attend workshop activities designed to help them enhance their teaching. Although there is no simple solution to the scarcity of resources on campus, administrators and faculty developers should be mindful of the fundamental need to support teaching improvement by individual faculty as an on-going institutional priority.

WORKSHOPS AND INSTITUTES

The fifth and last component among the preferred instructional development practices is workshops on teaching for targeted groups. Workshops for faculty are the 'bread and butter' activities of instructional development offices or centers. But deans, heads and faculty (taken as a group) express even greater confidence in the potential of workshops than do the faculty developers themselves. (See Table 1)

A faculty member in a university in the United States recognizes the importance of campus instructional development activity:

> Our center does an excellent job. They regularly sponsor workshops, speakers and classes for us.

A faculty developer in the United States described her university's "most successful teaching improvement initiatives" as "on-campus workshops provided by outsiders and faculty forums—informal discussions among faculty concerning teaching issues." Workshops have also formed an integral part of our instructional development program at Dalhousie University over a period of eight years. Hundreds of positive comments on 'participant response forms' collected at the conclusion of dozens of workshops assess these activities as having a practical impact on the quality of teaching.

Despite their popularity, isolated workshops of one to three hours on a topic of interest to university teachers likely have little tangible impact on the quality of teaching on campus. Many academics recognized the benefits, however, of the extensive workshops, or institutes on teaching improvement. These events last one, two, or even several weeks. (For an account of the benefits of workshops and institutes, see Eison and Stevens, 1995.)

The "Recording Teaching Accomplishment Institute" is a successful example of an event of this kind. This week-long workshop held at Dalhousie University brings faculty from a variety of disciplines and institutions together to develop their teaching portfolios. Participants come from Canada, the United States and the Caribbean. The purpose of the Institute is to support professors in the creation of a ten-page document describing their teaching approaches, accomplishments and aims. (For more information on how to develop a teaching dossier or portfolio see O'Neil and Wright, 1995.) The Institute offers a judicious mix of presentations, workshops, individual reflection and writing, 'expert' and peer consultations, and meetings in a social setting. Although participants are inevitably proud of the portfolios they assemble in only five days, emphasis is not totally on product. Process is important to organizers and participants alike. The Institute affords professors time to reflect on their teaching, to clarify goals, to benefit from the perspectives of other academics and, perhaps, to commit to writing for the first time a philosophy of teaching. The participant comments which follow express the many benefits of the institute format:

I found the experience enriching and the end product one of the most valuable documents of my work; past, present and for the future. I should have done this years ago.

I had fun working on my dossier and it was a very satisfying process. It made me think about who I really was as a teacher. It is good to "know" oneself. Developing this dossier was very rewarding and many of my friends are waiting to read it and start their own.

Excellent opportunity to take a consolidated time frame and think about nothing else. I recognize that the dossier still needs some work and updating. I intend to use the dossier as way to "show" my teaching effectiveness and areas to work on.

Mentoring, sharing, exchange and review of our teaching is important. I found the mentoring with staff and conferences with peers to be vital.

Benefits are those of self-reflection, self assessment, analysis, and setting goals for the future. It provides my future teaching with a higher foundation to work from and a higher ceiling to aspire to.

Longer workshops and institutes allow both the instructional developer and the faculty participants to see a project through to completion, to explore pedagogical ideas in some depth, to gain a sense of achievement and professional progress.

CONCLUSION

This chapter has dealt with a number of policies, practices and programs which are favored by professional faculty developers, faculty, deans and heads. Several of the approaches described here relate closely to the eight "characteristics of cultures that support teaching and its improvement" identified in a major Higher Education Report or "integrative study" titled "Taking Teaching Seriously: Meeting the Challenge of Instructional Improvement" (Paulsen and Feldman, 1995). Three of the eight characteristics correspond directly to the approaches highlighted in this chapter. These involve the demonstration of effective teaching when interviewing and hiring new faculty, the leadership of department chairs who support teaching and its improvement, and the rigorous evaluation of teaching in tenure and promotion cases (pp. 121-122).

Two other characteristics identified in the Paulsen and Feldman study overlap with the programs which are featured in this chapter. The Report lists "frequent interaction and collaboration among faculty and a sense of community among faculty regarding teaching-related issues" and a "faculty development program or campus teaching center" as key elements of an institutional environment supportive of teaching. Orientation, mentoring and consultation (as discussed above) overlap with the former, while workshops and institutes (also discussed above) are prime features of instructional development programs as developed by centers. It is interesting to note that while our international survey of more than 300 instructional developers rated the presence of a campus center very highly, over 900 faculty, deans and heads rated the presence of such a center far down the list of ways and means of improving teaching. Yet the faculty, deans and heads rated many of the activities normally organized by centers as having an important role to play in the improvement of teaching!

Additional characteristics listed by Paulsen and Feldman may be implied in this chapter but are not treated per se. They involve "an expanded view of scholarship and scholarly activities" and "shared values about the importance of teaching between administrators and faculty" (p. 121). The identification of support for faculty initiatives to improve teaching by temporarily reducing workloads or subsidizing innovation and change as discussed above specify concrete ways and means of demonstrating campus adherence to the values emphasized by Paulsen and Feldman.

The eighth characteristic from Paulsen and Feldman concerned the "unambiguous commitment and support by senior administrators to teaching and its improvement" (p. 121). While this commitment is no doubt necessary, our survey respondents placed more emphasis on the role of heads, chairs and deans than they did the role of vice-presidents, presidents, and provosts. (There may be some ambiguity here, of course, if one considers the deans as senior administrators.)

In an era of dwindling resources, what can faculty, instructional developers, deans, directors and unit heads do to enhance the quality and the status of teaching in a given institutional setting? They can make a concerted effort to improve university teaching by design. On the one hand, they should assess the campus teaching culture, enumerating strengths and noting weaknesses. On the other hand, they should work towards the creation of a model which gives every consideration to incorporating preferred programs, policies and practices as identified by their academic colleagues internationally. Drawing on a thorough knowledge of both the local environment and the research findings of the broader academic milieu, campus leaders can formulate an approach to teaching improvement which promises to make a significant impact in their university community.

ACKNOWLEDGMENTS
Graham Skanes of Memorial University of Newfoundland and Roger Barnsley of St. Thomas University (New Brunswick) participated in the design of the original survey instrument as used with university presidents and vice-presidents. Carol O'Neil, of the Office of Instructional Development and Technology, Dalhousie University, made significant contributions to all stages of the survey research and analysis. Financial assistance for the survey of staff developers in the United Kingdom was offered by the Staff and Educational Development Association's small grant scheme. The Professional and Organizational Development Network provided support for the survey of instructional developers in the United States.

NOTES

1. Various aspects of this research were originally reported by Alan Wright and Carol O'Neil in the publications listed in the References. The comments of the survey respondents have not previously appeared, nor has Table 1.
2. There were 36 items ranked in the survey. Using the results from the International Faculty Developers survey as a base, a comparison is made with results of the survey of 906 Faculty, Deans and Heads and those respondents from Dalhousie University.
3. The 331 Faculty Developers responding to the survey represent 165 universities in the United States, 82 in the United Kingdom, 51 in Canada and 33 in Australasia. This list represents 10 of the top 12 Preferred Practices of Developers. The items omitted here concerned a "Center to promote effective instruction" (ranked 3rd by Developers but only 22nd by Faculty, Heads and Deans and "Senior Administrators give visibility to teaching improvement activities" (ranked 11th by Developers but only 14th by Faculty, Heads and Deans).
4. The top 8 of the 10 items listed here were ranked among the 10 Preferred Practices by Faculty, Heads and Deans. Those indicated as 9th and 10th are ranked *relative to* the top 8. Of the complete list of 36 items, these two items were ranked 11th and 15th by this group.
5. The top 9 of the 10 items listed here were ranked among the 10 Preferred Practices by Dalhousie University Faculty, Deans and Heads. The item listed as 10th is ranked *relative to* the top 9. Of the complete list of 36 items, this item was ranked 15th by the Dalhousie group.
6. The quotations throughout this chapter are taken from our international surveys of instructional developers as well as faculty, heads and deans. The faculty quoted in this chapter come from a variety of fields including, among others, biology, earth sciences, law, mathematics, management, medicine, pharmacy, psychology, sociology and political science.

REFERENCES

Cox, M. (1995). The development of new and junior faculty. In W.A. Wright (Ed.), *Teaching improvement practices: successful strategies for higher education* (255-282). Bolton, MA.

Eison, J., & Stevens, E. (1995). Faculty development workshops and institutes. In W.A. Wright (Ed.), *Teaching improvement practices: successful strategies for higher education* (206-236). Bolton, MA.

Luna, G., & Cullen, D.L. (1995). *Empowering the faculty: mentoring redirected and re-newed* (1995 Report Three: ASHE-ERIC Higher Education Reports). Washington, D.C.: The George Washington University, Graduate School of Education and Human Development.

O'Neil, M.C., & Wright, W.A. (1995). *Recording teaching accomplishment: A Dalhousie guide to the teaching dossier.* (5th ed.) Halifax, NS: Dalhousie University, Office of Instructional Development and Technology.

Paulsen, M.B., & Feldman, K.A. (1995). *Taking teaching seriously: meeting the challenge of instructional improvement* (1995 Report Two: ASHE-ERIC Higher Education Reports). Washington, D.C.: The George Washington University, Graduate School of Education and Human Development.

Wright, W.A. Teaching improvement practices in Canadian universities. In Rogers, P. (Ed.), *Teaching and learning in higher education* (STLHE) (bulletin), 18, 5-8.

Wright, W.A., & O'Neil, M.C. Improving Teaching: Priorities for Dalhousie University. *Focus on university teaching and learning. Office of Instructional Development* (bulletin), 6, 1.

Wright, W.A., & Associates. (1995). *Teaching improvement practices: successful strategies for higher education.* Bolton, MA.

Wright, W.A., & O'Neil, M.C. (1995). Perspectives on improving teaching in Canadian universities. *The Canadian Journal of Higher Education, xxiv-3,* 26-57.

Wright, W.A., & O'Neil, M.C. (1994). Teaching improvement practices: New perspectives. *To improve the Academy,* 13, 1-37.

CHAPTER 2

A Cross-Cultural Look at Perceptions of Good Teaching

Asia and the West

David Watkins

In most Western countries in recent years there has been increasing pressure placed on universities to publicly demonstrate that the funding they receive is justified by the quality of learning outcomes their students achieve. This emphasis on accountability has largely come about by the ever-increasing financial demands of the tertiary sector due to a worldwide trend to expand the percentage of the population going on to higher education. This expansion has also caused problems for tertiary teachers as they now have to cope with larger numbers of students—representing a wide range of abilities, interests, motivations and age-groups—than ever before, while *per capita* resources decrease (Cooke, 1996). This situation has placed more attention on the teaching competence of university lecturers.

In the U.S., Canada, the U.K., Australia and New Zealand, as well as many European countries, external authorities—at the behest of their respective governments—are increasingly assessing institutional goals, processes and outcomes (Cooke, 1996). Universities in return have often set in place mechanisms to evaluate and (typically less successfully) to reward teaching quality and to establish centers whose role is to improve teaching at their campus. Much of this latter work is based on recent developments in research in cognitive psychology (Bereiter, 1990; Ramsden, 1992).

While these changes can be seen as worthwhile advances toward a higher level of teaching accountability, it must be remembered that they are based on Western conceptions of what constitutes good teaching. However, of course, it is not only Western countries that are concerned with the quality of university education. This issue is of major concern to developing countries, which often do not have great economic resources and view quality higher education as a necessity for economic development (Altbach & Selvaratnam, 1989). This chapter examines the cross-cultural validity of Western conceptions of good teaching and how it impacts teaching in a non-

Western culture. First, qualitative research into conceptions of learning and teaching in different cultures will be reviewed. Then comparative research into how students from two Western and five non-Western countries perceive good and bad lecturers will be presented. Finally, the extensive attempts to improve university teaching in one non-Western but highly developed country—Hong Kong—will be discussed.

CONCEPTIONS OF TEACHING AND LEARNING
Western Conceptions
Current views of teacher education emphasize the need for the teacher to be a 'reflective practitioner' (Clark & Peterson, 1986; Wittrock, 1986). This is more than just the latest fad, for it is based on a major shift in cognitive psychology since the early 1980's. No longer is the human learner seen as a passive information storage system, but rather as an active, self-determining agent who selects information from his or her environment and then constructs new knowledge in terms of what that individual already knows (Biggs & Telfer, 1987; Shuell, 1986).

Research into how Western school and university teachers perceive their role indicates that many espouse a 'teaching as the transmission of knowledge' conception (Biggs & Telfer, 1987; Samuelowicz & Bain, 1992; Trigwell, Prosser & Taylor, 1994). According to this conception, it is basically the teacher's job to know her subject and then to impart that knowledge accurately and clearly to her students. If the learning outcomes are unsatisfactory, it is the students' fault due to their lack of ability, motivation, etc. Teachers expressing this view generally have a quantitative conception of teaching, seeing it as a matter of the amount of knowledge absorbed and they evaluate accordingly.

More experienced, expert teachers tend to espouse a qualitatively different conception of both teaching and learning (Biggs & Telfer, 1987; Marton, Dall'Alba & Beatty, 1994; Wittrock, 1986). In line with current views of cognitive psychology, high quality learning is seen as requiring active construction of meaning and the possibility of conceptual change on the part of the learners. It is the teacher's role to facilitate that occurrence by engaging them in appropriate learning activities (Shuell, 1986).

The former approach to teaching is likely to encourage a relatively superficial approach to learning with corresponding low levels of learning outcomes (Ramsden, 1992; Trigwell et al., 1994). The latter approach is likely to encourage understanding and intrinsic motivation, leading to higher levels of learning outcomes if assessed appropriately (Biggs & Telfer, 1987; Cole, 1990).

Unfortunately the majority of high school teachers in the U.S. (Shavelson & Stern, 1981) and most Western university teachers (Biggs, 1989) appear to utilize the former approach. As Radloff and Sampson (1988) commented of the Australian tertiary scene:

> The typical view of the tertiary teacher has been that of didactic lecturer. The traditional mode of instruction has been that of the one person talking and the many listening. Many students perceive their role as passive listeners and recorders of the lecture content . . . they write much and understand little.

Non-Western Conceptions

Cross-cultural researchers have long questioned the assumptions that Western educational and psychological constructs, theories and measuring instruments are appropriate for non-Western subjects (Enriquez, 1977). Fortunately in recent years there has been a flurry of research in non-Western cultures which, while generally supporting the validity of the above Western views, do indicate that some modifications may be necessary.

Regarding conceptions of learning, content analysis of written responses to the question "What do you mean by learning?" by 333 Nepalese Master's students (Watkins & Regmi, 1992) found that the view of learning as rote memorization for examination purposes commonly held by Western students was held by few of the Nepalese. While Western research has consistently supported a hierarchy of conceptions of learning from the superficial to changing as a person (Marton et al., 1994), the Nepalese research also questioned the existence of such a hierarchy. The responses indicated that for these Nepalese students the conception of learning for character development emerged at a much lower cognitive level, perhaps due to cultural and religious beliefs rooted in Hindu philosophy.

This latter finding also supports research with teachers both in Hong Kong and China (Gao, 1996; Lo & Siu, 1990), that the ability of teachers to foster responsibility and good moral conduct in their students was seen as a sign of a good teacher. Indeed in traditional Chinese culture, the concepts of teaching and educating were not distinguished, and they share the same Chinese character *jiao*. The aims of *jiao* are not related only to the delivery of knowledge and the fostering of cognitive abilities but also, more importantly, to the cultivation of humanity and morality. In the first chapter of the book *Zhong Yong (The Doctrine of the Mean)*, Confucius said that "What Heaven has conferred is called The Nature. To follow what is nature is The Way. To cultivate and clarify The Way is called *jiao*."[1] Han Yu, one of the most outstanding scholars and educators in the Tang Dynasty, illuminated Confucius' views in his book *Shi Shou (On Teachers)* and said: "What is a teacher? A teacher is the one who shows you the way of being human, teaches you knowledge and enlightens you while you are confused."[2] Confucius also argued that "When the personal conduct of a man is upright, the people will be attentive even if he does not issue orders; however, if his personal conduct is not upright, even if he issues orders, they will not be followed."[3] Confucius was careful to put his ideas into practice and was honored as the *wang shi shi biao* (a model teacher for ten thousand generations). His way of cultivating students by his exemplary role is regarded as the best way of teaching and educating. Many teachers in Chinese societies today follow these ideals, even if unaware of their Confucian roots, and regard good teaching as involving not only educating students from the intellective or academic perspective, but also in terms of conduct and morality. A good teacher should not only perform well in teaching and learning but also perform well in other aspects of life, the so called *wei ren shi biao*. One Chinese science teacher interviewed in recent research explained this as follows:

> Many physics teachers, including myself, restrict our target to knowledge teaching. However, teaching should be far more than knowledge delivery. It should include educating and cultivating students. Teach them how to be a person. That's the so called *jiao shu yu ren*.
> (Gao, 1996, interview record 1.7)

In addition, research with Japanese (Hess & Azuma, 1991; Purdie, Hattie, & Douglas, 1996), Hong Kong, and Chinese students (Kember, & Gow, 1991; Marton, Dall'Alba, & Tse, 1996; Watkins & Biggs, 1996) indicates that many of the better students tend to combine the processes of memorization and understanding to promote higher order learning outcomes in ways not appreciated by Western educators. How the teaching promotes this view is not fully understood but seems to involve much use of repetition to develop basic skills. However, this repetition should always be embedded in meaning, and the skills thus developed provide the student something with which to be creative (Watkins & Biggs, 1996).

However, Gow, Kember, and Sivan (1992) found from semi-structured interviews with 39 Hong Kong lecturers that there were two predominant conceptions of teaching: knowledge transmission and learning facilitation. This supports the findings of Western studies reported above. Kember and Gow (1994) developed a questionnaire to tap these two orientations to teaching whose validity was supported by factor analysis. They showed that departments at a Hong Kong university whose lecturers tended to espouse a learning facilitation rather than a transmission view of teaching were more likely to have students who reported that they were trying to understand what they were learning. In a recent review of the conceptions of university teaching research, Kember (1996a) argues that a transitional category—which he labels student-teacher interactions—is the conceptual link by which lecturers can change from a transmission to a learning facilitation view of teaching in both Western countries and Hong Kong.

PERCEPTION OF GOOD AND POOR LECTURERS

The research presented in the above discussion is based on university lecturers' views of teaching. But on what basis do students from different countries evaluate their teachers? Marsh (1986) proposed an 'applicability paradigm' which would be an indicator of similarities between perceptions of teaching effectiveness in different settings. My colleagues and I used this approach to compare perceptions of good and bad teachers in seven different countries (Lin, Watkins, & Meng, 1994).

This paradigm requires students in these different settings to choose one of the worst and one of the best lecturers who has taught them and then evaluate each on an instrument which combines items from the Student Evaluation of Educational Quality (SEEQ; Marsh, 1981) and the Endeavor (Frey, 1973) questionnaires. The perceptions of teaching effectiveness in the different settings can then be assessed by comparing the perceived appropriateness and importance of the items, which items were best able to discriminate between the good and poor teachers, and the characteristics of these teachers and their classes. The instruments are based on a multidimensional view of teaching effectiveness including:

- scales assessing the students' perception of the value of what they learned in the course;
- the extent and quality of group interaction in the class;
- the extent of individual rapport with the teacher;
- the fairness of the assessment;
- the workload;
- the organization and planning of the course; and
- the clarity of the teacher's presentation.

The subjects of this research were students from leading universities in two Western countries and five non-Western countries:

Table 1

Countries Surveyed

Australia (n=158)	China	(n=367)
New Zealand (n=119)	Hong Kong	(n=87)
	Nepal	(n=297)
	the Philippines	(n=77)
	Taiwan	(n=371)

Of the non-Western group, Hong Kong, Taiwan, and China all share a common culture based on Confucian beliefs. However, the educational practices of both Hong Kong and Taiwan are strongly influenced by the U.K. and the U.S., respectively, and particularly by Western attitudes regarding economic development. Both have thriving economies and well-established and expanding university systems. Higher education in China has undergone drastic changes in the last fifteen years, powered by economic and social reforms. There is now much more Western influence due to student and faculty exchange programs, but the teaching is still fairly traditional in form. The Philippines has had a long tradition of higher education, modeled first after Spain and then the U.S. However, its higher education system is better known for its quantity than quality (Gonzalez, 1989). Nepal is one of the world's poorest countries and its few universities have poorly paid staff with little incentive to do research or improve their teaching. Both Australia and New Zealand are geographically and culturally similar countries with high Western standards of living and established university systems based on that of the U.K.

As the questionnaires to be used in this research were both developed in the U.S. it was first necessary to test the reliability and within-construct validity in each of the seven countries. In China and Taiwan a Chinese translation was used but the original English version was used in the other five countries (as English was the medium of instruction in all five). The median alphas for the scales of the instruments were a very pleasing 0.85 or better in six of the seven countries. The exception was Nepal where the median alpha of 0.74 could be considered to be moderate. Factor analysis and multitrait-multimethod analyses supported the convergent and discriminant validity of the instrument's scales and their underlying factor structure but did indicate more of a general teaching effectiveness factor in several of the non-Western countries than suggested by Marsh's multidimensional model (see Watkins, 1994, for further details).

Appropriate Items
The students were asked to indicate which of the 55 questionnaire items were inappropriate in their educational context. The Hong Kong students indicated the highest percentage of inappropriate items (5.8%) followed by Australia and Nepal (both 3.6%), New Zealand (3.4%), Taiwan (2.0%), the Philippines (0.8%), and China (0.2%). Every item was considered appropriate by at least 80% of respondents from each country. Moreover, in all seven countries the items most frequently judged as inappropriate were those which involved the value of feedback from examinations and whether examinations were fair. This probably reflects different assessment practices in the different campuses (e.g. end of year examinations versus continuous assessment where feedback is more likely).

Most Important Items
The respondents in each country were also asked to indicate which 5 of the 55 items were most important for differentiating between their chosen 'good' and 'bad' lecturers. In all seven countries the two most important items concerned whether the teaching style held their interest and whether the lecturer's explanations were clear. But there were indications of differences according to country. Whereas the Nepalese were quite concerned that their teachers allowed them to share ideas in class, the Australian, New Zealand, Chinese, and Taiwanese respondents considered the lecturer's enthusiasm and the interest they could generate in the students as far more important. Both the Hong Kong and Filipino students cared more about the learning outcomes they achieved.

We then examined the similarity in the pattern of the most important items across the seven campus settings. Following the method of Marsh (1986), an objective index of similarity was obtained by calculating the correlation coefficients between the frequency of the importance rating of each of the 55 items between each of the pairs of countries. An index of the similarity between each of the country responses and the overall pattern was also obtained by correlating the country response to the overall responses for the overall sample (weighted so each country contributed equally). A matrix of similarity indices was then constructed (see Table 2).

Table 2

Cross-Campus Similarity in Patterns of Items Judged to be
Most Important in the Seven Countries (after Lin, et al., 1994)

	Tot	Au	NZ	Nep	Phi	HK	Twn	Chi
Total	-							
Au	.84	-						
NZ	.82	.86	-					
Nep	.54	.26	.21	-				
Phi	.64	.46	.57	.21	-			
HK	.76	.65	.63	.47	.56	-		
Twn	.82	.58	.63	.29	.58	.52	-	
Chi	.91	.72	.66	.39	.53	.60	.71	-

Note: Au = Australia; NZ = New Zealand; Nep = Nepal; Phi = Philippines;
HK = Hong Kong; Twn = Taiwan; Chi = China.

It can be seen that the Chinese responses were most representative of the overall pattern (a similarity index of 0.91). The Australian, New Zealand, and Hong Kong patterns were also fairly representative of the overall pattern with similarity indices of 0.76 or above. The least similar to the overall pattern were the Nepalese and Filipino respondents with indices of 0.54 and 0.64, respectively. This latter findings was supported by the country similarity indices with Nepal and the Philippines showing least similarity to the other five countries or indeed to each other.

As expected the two Western countries with very similar cultural, geographical, and educational systems—Australia and New Zealand—were found to have the most similar pattern of importance ratings (index of 0.86). Perhaps more surprisingly the three Chinese culture countries were much less similar to each other (with indices of 0.52 between Hong Kong and Taiwan; 0.60 between Hong Kong and China, and 0.71 between China and Taiwan. As can be seen from Table 1 the correlations between these Chinese culture countries and the two Western countries tended to be if anything slightly higher than among each other.

Differentiating between 'Good' and 'Poor' Lecturers
In all seven country samples it was found that relative to the 'poor' the 'good'

lecturers were those who tended to hold the students' interest and give clear explanations. To see if students in each country tended to use the same basis for differentiation of teaching effectiveness we then calculated another set of similarity indices. In each country the mean difference between each subject's ratings of their 'good' and 'poor' lecturer was calculated for each of the 55 items. Each item was then ranked according to the size of these differences for each country. The Spearman rank order correlations between the ranks of these 55 items for each pair of seven countries were then calculated. The resulting correlations are shown in Table 3.

Table 3
Correlations between the 55 Items Ranked According to their Degree of Differentiation between "Good" and "Poor" Teachers across the Seven Countries (after Lin et al., 1994)

	Au	NZ	Nep	Phi	HK	Twn	Chi
Au	-						
NZ	.88	-					
Nep	.80	.71	-				
Phi	.73	.78	.62	-			
HK	.89	.90	.80	.83	-		
Twn	.80	.84	.70	.80	.89	-	
Chi	.77	.76	.65	.72	.82	.83	-

Note: Au = Australia; NZ = New Zealand; Nep = Nepal; Phi = Philippines; HK = Hong Kong; Twn = Taiwan; Chi = China.

Clearly, there was considerable cross-country agreement about what distinguishes good from poor teachers (mean correlation of 0.79 and a range of 0.62 to 0.90). A closer examination of Table 2 shows that there was slightly more agreement between the respondents from Hong Kong and each of New Zealand (0.90), Australia (0.89), and Taiwan (0.89) rather than China (0.82); Taiwanese responses were as similar to New Zealand (0.84) and Australia (0.80) as to China (0.82); and Chinese responses were somewhat more like those from Hong Kong (0.82) and Taiwan (0.83) than those from New Zealand (0.76) and Australia (0.77). As expected the degree of agreement between the latter two country's subjects was high (0.88).

Characteristics of 'Good' and 'Poor' Lecturers

A further perspective on cross-cultural differences in students' perceptions of teaching effectiveness was gained by examining characteristics of the lecturers and the classes they taught (Australian data were not obtained on these variables so could not be included in this analysis). In each country, the respondents reported that the 'good' teachers tended to give higher grades than the 'poor'. However, statistically significant (p <0.01) differences were found between perceptions of the 'good' and 'poor' teachers between the six country samples on the remaining variables. In all but Taiwan and China there was no age difference between the teachers. However, in Taiwan the better teachers were thought to be younger but in China older. New Zealand and Nepal were the only countries where class size seemed to make a difference. Surprisingly, perhaps, it was the teachers of larger classes who were rated more highly in both these countries. Finally, the 'good' lecturers were more often reported to be teaching their major subjects by the Hong Kong, New Zealand, and Filipino respondents.

Based on the apparent cross-cultural similarities found in this study, it is reasonable to suggest that efforts to improve teaching in one country may be usefully adopted by another. Thus, it is useful to examine more closely the teaching improvement initiatives of one country. For this discussion, Hong Kong was chosen, as it is both non-Western and highly developed—unlike most of its Asian neighbors. The two initiatives described below are seen as broad enough to be useful for higher education institutions in both Western and non-Western university settings.

UNIVERSITY TEACHING IN HONG KONG

Hong Kong is currently a British colony of some 5.5 million people which is to be reincorporated into the People's Republic of China under a 'one country two systems policy' in July, 1997. It is a city with a 95% Chinese population which has achieved rapid modernization through capitalist economic means.

Hong Kong's higher education system has grown rapidly, following a government decision in 1989 to virtually double the number of available degree places by 1995. In 1994-95 it was estimated that enrollment had reached 58,000 (18% of the relevant age cohorts). It was estimated that another 25,000 were attending overseas universities at that time (Postiglione, 1996). Hong Kong now has 10 degree granting institutions, six of which have gained university status. There has also been a major change in the nature of academic work with much more emphasis being placed on research and postgraduate students who, for example, have gone from a handful to one-third of the student body at the University of Hong Kong (UHK). In the past, the majority of academics at Hong Kong's two oldest universities—UHK and the Chinese University of Hong Kong—were recruited from overseas and were often expatriates. As tertiary education has expanded, and the take-back by China approaches, the percentage of ethnic Chinese staff is also rising rapidly.

The Hong Kong government has been an enthusiastic supporter of the world trend to more closely scrutinize educational institutions, particularly in cost-benefit terms. In 1994, and again in 1996, the government conducted a Research Assessment Exercise for university academics. Each department had to rate each of its teachers as a 'researcher' or a 'non-researcher' based on their publication rate, and the validity of these classifications was checked by an external assessment team. While it was made clear that was there no disgrace in being placed in the 'non-researcher' category, a portion of departmental funding at UHK is based on the percentage of 'researchers', so it is not surprising that there is considerable pressure to publish, particularly for those not on tenured contracts (a situation which is becoming increasingly common).

This emphasis on research has been rightly criticized as leading to a possible neglect of teaching quality. Indeed the Hong Kong government has responded by proposing a Teaching Assessment Exercise which was carried out in early 1996. Each university has been encouraged to establish centers for improving university teaching and to set up a formal system of course evaluations. While quality assurance by means of external examiners and student evaluations predominate, some universities advocate the use of teaching portfolios. Moreover, considerable funds have been set aside for applied research designed to improve university teaching. For example, in 1994 large grants were awarded to two major cross-institutional projects—the Action Learning project, and the Evaluation of the Student Experience project—which are described further below. Another U.S.$20 million has been set aside for Teaching Development Grants in the 1995-98 triennium.

The Action Learning Project
This project utilized the method of action research associated with critical theory to improve university teaching in Hong Kong. Kember and McKay (1996) characterize action research in the following terms: it is concerned with social practice, it empowers participants to decide on topics, it aims towards improvement, and involves a reflective, cyclical process of system-

atic inquiry. Through involving teachers in the selection of topics and the research process itself, it is argued that action research overcomes the criticism of much educational research as being irrelevant for classroom practice. The role of the faculty developer is to act as a 'critical friend' (Stenhouse, 1975), encouraging academics to start projects and providing advice when requested, but leaving the focus of the research up to the lecturers to choose.

The project put forward by an inter-institutional team was awarded almost U.S.$2 million by the University and Polytechnic Grants Committee (UPGC) in Hong Kong to enhance faculty development throughout the territory's institutions. The research base of the project was the consistent finding that there was no justification for the widely held view that Hong Kong students are inherently or culturally likely to rely on rote memorization. As described by Watkins and Biggs (1996), there are contextual factors such as the assessment system, the medium of instruction, the workload, and the teaching style, which encourage a superficial approach to studying. These are all factors which are under the control of individual university teachers. The aim of this project was to improve the quality of student learning through actively engaging lecturers to evaluate and modify these aspects of their courses. It was postulated that involvement in action research projects would develop an awareness of the salience of such aspects of teaching and thus create an academic climate where the need for monitoring and possible change was accepted. The characteristics of the project were described by Kember (1996b) as follows:

> To date the project has awarded grants to over fifty teams of academics from all seven universities in Hong Kong. Each of these subprojects involves action research into aspects of their own teaching. Preliminary analyses of an evaluation questionnaire sent to those involved in these sub-projects found that 87% of the respondents agreed that the project has led to an improvement in their teaching while 75% and 68%, respectively, believed that the project had led to an improvement in their students' learning approaches and outcomes (Kember, 1996b).

Evaluation of the Student Experience Project
This three-year inter-institutional project was funded by a U.S.$1.3 million grant from the UPGC in Hong Kong. Its primary aims were first to explore Hong Kong student's experience of tertiary education and then to develop methods and instruments for evaluating that experience. It was proposed that

this would allow teachers and institutional managers to better tailor their services and provision for students. Teaching and learning were seen to be the central—but not the exclusive—focus of the project. A central, underlying notion is that if universities are to provide high quality education, they must obtain evaluative feedback from students and other interested parties about the process and output of the educational experience (Armour, 1995). Moreover, it is argued that there are a wide range of reasons for obtaining evaluative feedback, a wide range of interested parties, and a number of different possible recipients of the feedback data.

While tertiary education quality indicators have been developed in many countries, all too often they seem to have been based on easy-to-get data such as unit costs or staff-student ratios. Too often this has led to oversimplified cost-benefit analyses which ignore the cognitive and affective benefits of being a student. This project was designed to develop for the first time in Hong Kong and perhaps elsewhere in the world, indicators of quality based on factors that are demonstrated by research to enhance the student experience in five key areas: assessment, workload, medium of instruction, the course experience, and the classroom experience. This project has to date developed to where the initial research studies are now being written up. The next stage—implementing the newly developed battery of instruments to more adequately evaluate the quality of higher education throughout Hong Kong universities—will commence soon, and promises to be both exciting and informative.

CONCLUSIONS

Western conceptions of what constitutes good teaching seem to have a high degree of cross-cultural validity. However, Western educators may benefit from an understanding of how the effective Chinese and Japanese teachers use repetitive strategies as a means to enhance student understanding. As well, the Asian view that a good teacher—at whatever education level—should also be a good moral guide could perhaps also benefit Western lecturers and their students. Not surprisingly, though, well-developed Western instruments designed to assess student evaluations of tertiary teaching (such as the SEEQ) have proven to have commendable reliability and validity in a range of non-Western universities. Therefore they may well be worth employing in attempts to monitor the quality of teaching in such countries (after modifications for local conditions if necessary). While Marsh and Roche (1994) claim that such instruments should also play a predominant role in the improvement of teaching effectiveness, a better approach would be to focus the lecturers' attention on the impact that their assessment and teaching methods have on the quality of their students' learning outcomes.

In addition to presenting an important cross-cultural perspective on these issues, this chapter has sought to explain two higher education initiatives in a non-Western culture which can inform both non-Western and Western higher education institutions. The Action Learning Project in Hong Kong appears to have convinced many professors here of the level of impact that their assessment and teaching methods have on the quality of their students' learning outcomes. This project could serve as a useful example to lecture development centers everywhere. While the coordination and evaluation of such a large scale project required a significant amount of funding, the encouragement of lecturers to become "researchers of their own students' learning" (Ramsden, 1992) needs only a little effort and direction. It may also enable committed teachers to fulfill institutional requirements for research publications.

As well, the Evaluation of the Student Experience Project provides Hong Kong higher education with the promise of developing an instrument battery capable of assessing the quality of a university's performance along genuinely educational principles, rather than a reliance on only simple economic indicators. It is foreseeable that at least some of these instruments may prove appropriate to assess the university experience in other countries as well. The least we can do is try. As the world itself grows increasingly more interdependent, academic institutions and its members would be remiss if they did not broaden the scope of their understanding of these important issues to include the perspective of multiple cultures.

ACKNOWLEDGMENTS

The writer would like to thank Gao Ling Bao for advice on traditional Chinese views of teaching and David Kember for providing copies of several as yet unpublished manuscripts.

NOTES

1. The extract is from Tsai Chih Chung (1994), *The wisdom of Confucius*, translated by Mary Ng En Tzu. Singapore: Asiapac Books, p.64.
2. From Liu Zhen (1973), *The way of being a teacher in China*. Taipei: Chung Hwa Book Co., p.754.
3. See *The Analects*, Chapter 13. The extract is from Tsai Chih Chung (1994), *The sayings of Confucius*, translated by Lun Yu, Singapore: Asiapac Books, p.134.

REFERENCES

Armour, R.T. (1995). *Evaluation of the student experience project: interim report to University Grants Commission.* City University of Hong Kong: Hong Kong.

Altbach, P.G. & Selvaratnam, V. (Eds.) (1989). *From dependence to autonomy: The development of Asian universities.* Dordrecht: Kluwer.

Bereiter, C. (1990). Aspects of an educational learning theory. *Review of Educational Research,* 60(4), 603-624.

Biggs, J.B. (1989). Approaches to the enhancement of tertiary teaching. *Higher Education Research and Development,* 8(1), 7-25.

Biggs, J.B. & Telfer, R. (1987). *The process of learning.* Sydney: Prentice-Hall of Australia.

Clark, M. & Peterson, P. (1986). Teachers' thought processes. In M. Wittrock (Ed.), *Handbook of research on teaching* (3rd edition) (pp.255-296). New York: Macmillan.

Coles, N.S. (1990). Conceptions of educational achievement. *Educational Researcher,* 19, 2-7.

Cooke, B. (1996). Valuing teaching. *Teaching Matters,* 1(1), 2-4.

Enriquez, V. (1977). Filipino psychology in the third world. *Philippine Journal of Psychology,* 10, 3-17.

Frey, P.W. (1973). A two-dimensional analysis of student ratings of instruction. *Research in Higher Education,* 9, 69-91.

Gao, L.B. (1996). A validity study of the Teachers' Conception of School Physics Teaching Questionnaire. Unpublished manuscript, University of Hong Kong.

Gonzalez, A. (1989). The Western impact on Philippine higher education. In P.G. Altbach & V. Selvaratnam (Eds.), *From dependence to autonomy: The development of Asian universities.* Dordrecht: Kluwer.

Gow, L., Kember, D. & Sivan, A. (1992). Lecturer's views of their teaching practices: Implications for staff development needs. *Higher Education Research and Development,* 11(2), 135-149.

Hess, R.D. & Azuma, H. (1991). Cultural support for schooling. *Educational Researcher,* 20(9), 2-12.

Kember, D. (1996a). A reconceptualisation of the research into university academics' conceptions of teaching. As yet unpublished manuscript, Hong Kong Polytechnic University.

Kember, D. (1996b). Private communication.

Kember, D. & Gow, L. (1991). A challenge to the anecdotal stereotype of the Asian student. *Studies in Higher Education,* 16, 117-128.

Kember, D. & Gow, L. (1994). Orientations to teaching and their effect on the quality of student learning. *Journal of Higher Education,* 65(1), 58-74.

Kember, D. & McKay, J. (1996). Action research into the quality of student learning. *Journal of Higher Education,* 67(5).

Lin, W.Y., Watkins, D. & Meng, Q.M. (1994). A cross-cultural investigation into students evaluations of university teaching. *Education Journal,* 22(2), 291-304.

Lo, L. & Siu, T. (1990). Teacher's perception of a good teacher. Paper presented at the Annual Conference of the Hong Kong Educational Research Association, City University of Hong Kong.

Marsh, H.W. (1981). Students' evaluations of tertiary instruction: testing the applicability of American surveys in an Australian setting. *Australian Journal of Education,*

25, 177-192.

Marsh, H.W. (1986). Applicability paradigm: Students' evaluations of teaching effectiveness in different countries. *Journal of Educational Psychology,* 78, 465-473.

Marsh, H.W. & Roche, L. (1994). *The use of students' evaluation of university teaching to improve teaching effectiveness.* Canberra: Australian Government & Publishing Service.

Marton, F., Dall'Alba, G. & Beatty, E. (1994). Conceptions of learning, *International Journal of Educational Research,* 19, 277-300.

Marton, F., Dall'Alba, G. & Tse, L.K. (1996). Memorizing and understanding: The keys to the paradox? In D. Watkins & J. Biggs (Eds.), *The Chinese learner: Cultural, psychological, and contextual influences.* Hong Kong / Melbourne: Comparative Education Research Centre; Australian Council for Educational Research.

Postiglione, G. (1997). The future of the Hong Kong academic profession in a period of profound change. In P.G. Altbach (Ed.), *The international academic profession: Portraits of fourteen countries.* Princeton: The Carnegie Foundation for the Advancement of Teaching.

Purdie, N., Hattie, J. & Douglas, G. (1996). Student conceptions of learning and their use of self-regulated learning strategies: A cross-cultural comparison. *Journal of Educational Psychology,* 88(1), 87-100.

Radloff, A. & Sampson, J. (1988). Promoting intelligent behaviour in students: The role of the tertiary teacher. Paper presented at Seminar on Intelligence, Australian Council for Educational Research, Melbourne, August 24-26.

Ramsden, P. (1992). *Learning to teach in higher education.* London: Routledge.

Samuelowicz, K. & Bain, J. (1992). Conceptions of teaching held by academic teachers. *Higher Education,* 22, 229-249.

Shavelson, R. & Stern, P. (1981). Research on teachers' pedagogical thoughts, judgements, divisions, and behavior. *Review of Educational Research,* 51, 455-498.

Shuell, T.J. (1986). Cognitive conceptions of learning. *Review of Educational Research,* 56, 411-436.

Stenhouse, L. (1975). *An introduction to curriculum research and development.* London: Heinemann.

Trigwell, K., Prosser, M. & Taylor, P. (1994). Qualitative differences in approaches to teaching first year university science, *Higher Education,* 27,75-84.

Watkins, D. & Biggs, J.B. (Eds.) (1996). *The Chinese learner: Cultural, psychological, and contextual influences.* Hong Kong/Melbourne: Comparative Education Research Centre/Australian Council for Educational Research.

Watkins, D. & Regmi, M. (1992). How universal are student conceptions of learning? A Nepalese investigation. *Psychologia,* 35, 101-110.

Wittrock, M. (Ed.) (1986). *Handbook of research on teaching* (3rd edition). New York: Macmillan.

CHAPTER 3

University Teachers and Instruction
Important Themes for a Global Discussion

James JF Forest

This chapter lays out a discussion of several themes and issues faced by university teachers throughout the world. Beginning with a narrative description of a typical university teacher, the notion is introduced that university teaching is a truly international activity, and thus a comparative perspective is useful for identifying and addressing shared concerns. Dimensions of university teaching activity chosen for discussion in this chapter include: gender and diversity among faculty and students; communication and language; faculty attitudes and behaviors; instructional methods; the impact of new technology in teaching and learning; and the evaluation of teaching. While these are just a few of the many issues faced by faculty worldwide, the overall intent of this discussion is to illustrate concerns which faculty in one country are likely to share with their colleagues in another part of the world, as well as demonstrate the value of looking at these issues from a comparative perspective.

SAM: A PORTRAIT OF A UNIVERSITY TEACHER

A phone rings, an electronic buzzing that breaks the silence of a room where the air is heavy with concentration. A man in his late fifties, startled, glances away from the computer screen in front of him and looks toward the direction of the sound. All he sees are stacks of papers and books, some higher than others, presenting a topographic landscape that reminds him of his trip last summer to the Andes. The phone rings again. The man squints and peers closer at his private range of mountains, and sees a phone cord dangling out from beneath a stack of looseleaf binder notepaper. He digs for the receiver.

His wife is calling to ask that he stop by the market on his way home from work and pick up some coffee for tomorrow morning's usual breakfast routine. She sounds exhausted, and he asks how her day at the courthouse went. She had to try two juvenile cases and hear testimony in a divorce case, all before her lunch meeting with an old friend, one of her former law professors. It's not easy being the first female of her graduating class to make circuit judge.

The conversation lasts only a few moments, and the phone receiver is returned to its cave beneath 'Mount Graded Essays.' Sam is a professor at one of the most prominent colleges in the region. He returns to his computer screen to finish reading an e-mail message from one of his graduate students. He takes pride in his work and in his career, and is very conscientious in responding to the student's request for guidance. He then reads a few more of his messages, and then turns to a small stack of papers to the left of his computer. It is time to begin preparing for this afternoon's class, and he reviews the lecture notes he prepared the night before. He is reminded that one of the articles in the day's required reading list is a considerably thick and complex piece, and he makes a note to take extra time in the day's lecture to help clarify some of the author's points.

Sam tells his friends that he likes to teach, and feels that he does it well. His student evaluations have been consistently positive in general, although most everything he now knows about teacher he has had to learn on the job, through trial and error. His graduate training, like that of most of his colleagues, focused almost entirely on the discipline content and on developing research skills, with barely any exposure to methods or theories of classroom teaching and learning. However, over time, he had learned to draw on his students' evaluations and the advice of his peers, and now had developed what he feels to be an adequate personal theory of teaching—in other words, knowing what works for him and his students.

Sam paused for a moment of reflection. His students—how they have changed over the years. Surely he, too, had changed, but it seemed to him that the students who now sat in his courses had different issues, even different languages, than the students of just ten years ago. He had tried to adjust the content of his courses appropriately, to make the subject more relevant to his increasingly diverse audience.

Another thought crept in about his classroom—the department was changing the standard student evaluation forms which had been used for years, in response to recent pressures from the administration to "provide better measures of teaching effectiveness." How, wondered Sam, would this be possible? Were we not supposed to train students to think, analyze, solve problems, and strive for truth, or should we instead encourage them to excel at performing small, measurable tasks?

Sam reflected on the seemingly constant demands that he struggled to meet in his chosen profession. For example, he was expected to keep up with research in his field, to publish and attend conferences, as well as maintain some level of involvement in the campus community. Sam had met the requirements for tenure years ago, and enjoyed a relatively comfortable position in comparison to those poor new recruits, who faced not only a tough road getting into the profession, but as well a declining willingness on the part of the public to stay out of the college classroom and let the professor do his or her job unimpeded. The department and institutional administrators were in the middle of all this, and usually sided with the demands of those who held the purse strings—the students, parents, and their representatives in the legislature.

Sam looked up from his pensive reflection, searching for the tiny clock on his computer screen. Almost time for class—just a few more moments to focus on these lecture notes and get charged up for the task at hand.

A COMPARATIVE PERSPECTIVE

Ponder Sam for a moment, and then see if you can determine what country this professor works and lives in. Japan? Brazil? Could this be Professor Samuel Yankovich of Israel, or perhaps Professor Kim Sam Yeung of Korea? Is this Samson Johanssen of Stockholm, or Samuel Adams of Boston? Perhaps this is Professor Sammy Davis, of Australia? Truth is, "Sam" could be a professor in one of several countries. While there are certainly many differences in teaching environments and cultures across national and geographic boundaries, there are also a great deal of similarities shared by faculty around the globe. As Altbach (1992) observed, "universities worldwide share a common culture and reality. In many basic ways, there is a convergence of institutional models and norms." Indeed, there are often more differences in approaches to teaching across campus than across countries. For example, teaching Shakespearean drama or sociology differs considerably from teaching journalism or vascular surgery. At the same institution, one may find several faculty committed to collaborative learning, several other faculty who view the classroom as a stage in which to perform, and still other faculty whose discipline requires specialized guidance in a laboratory or computer room. Concern over teaching in the university is a truly international phenomenon, in dimensions beyond the comparative perspective of the academic profession. Indeed, as British scholar W.H. Taylor (1993) observes, "the young need to be educated to realize how much of their lives will be determined by transnational forces."

However, one should be cautious not to downplay the importance of culture in higher education—a Confucian approach to teaching and learning is significantly different from a traditional Western modernist approach. Students in Malaysia have significantly different approaches to classroom interaction and individual learning than their counterparts in North America, and thus require markedly different approaches to classroom interaction. A lecture in Germany is not quite the same—and does not quite mean the same to its audience—as a lecture in Argentina. Indeed, culture and language play a prominent role in teaching and learning in higher education. However, as Kohn (1987) observed, cross-national research can be useful for discovering "social-structural regularities that transcend the many differences in history, culture, and experience that occur among nations." Indeed, it is this complex web of both similarities and differences across so many cultures and languages that provide a rich—and largely untapped—resource for expanding our understanding of university teaching. For example, in the absence of appropriate cross-national evidence, we would be unable to determine whether traditional Western interpretations of the very term "teaching" are applicable outside the particular historical, cultural and political contexts of the West. As well, a comparative approach is not new to academe—as Brown (1992) observes, "the inheritance of all the main scholarly traditions—Asian, Judaeo-Christian, Islamic—is that knowledge is for sharing trans-nationally, at least among the community of scholars."

Comparative research studies in higher education have emerged over recent decades to show that academics throughout the world perform many of the same kinds of tasks, and are faced with very similar kinds of challenges in their work. We know that worldwide, there are more males than females in the faculty ranks—this has been true throughout the history of the academic profession, with the exception of a small number of disciplines like nursing or education, where men have been the historic minority. We know that the lecture is by far the most common method of instruction in classrooms. We know that tenure exists in many corners of the world, and is often defined in much the same way in Hong Kong or in Sweden as it is in Canada or Australia.

A recent survey by the Carnegie Foundation for the Advancement of Teaching sought to collect data on the similarities and differences shared by faculty in 14 countries: Australia, Brazil, Chile, England, Germany, Hong Kong, Israel, Japan, Korea, Mexico, the Netherlands, Russia, Sweden, and the United States.[1] Nearly 20,000 usable survey responses were returned—although the response rate varied considerably for each country, the survey administrators were confident that the data collected were reasonably representative of each country's academic profession. The study collected data from comparable institutions worldwide, although the final report omits information collected from the community colleges and technical and vocational programs due to comparability problems.

The Carnegie survey, the first of its kind, was structured around a set of themes which the survey administrators were convinced would be applicable for faculty in all the 14 countries surveyed. These themes, as presented in their initial technical report, included professional activity, satisfaction with working conditions and institutional governance, and the role of higher education in society. The survey results revealed a number of striking similarities about how faculty worldwide view their professional responsibilities vis-à-vis classroom instruction. For example, a majority of faculty in all countries surveyed agreed that "student opinions should be used in evaluating the teaching effectiveness of faculty" (Boyer, Altbach, & Whitelaw, 1994). At the same time, a majority of all faculty surveyed indicated that better ways of evaluating their teaching were sorely needed. This and other cross-national studies, particularly in the field of organizational socialization, generally seem to agree on the notion that higher education institutions and faculty worldwide clearly pursue similar goals and are faced with similar problems. Thus, a discussion of teaching-related issues shared by faculty worldwide is useful not only for enhancing our understanding of university teaching, but also for helping to identify the academic profession in a more global light.

Problems and Issues Shared Cross-Nationally by University Teachers
There are a number of issues that college and university teachers around the world must grapple with. The themes chosen for discussion in the remainder of this chapter include:
- gender and diversity among faculty and students;
- issues of language in instruction;
- faculty attitudes and behaviors;
- instructional methods;
- the impact of technology in teaching and learning; and
- the evaluation of teaching.

Beneath the rubric of each of these themes, a brief overview is presented of issues and research that university teachers in large parts of the world may find both applicable and useful. As described above, the overall intent of this discussion is to illustrate concerns which faculty in Malaysia are likely to share with their colleagues in Germany or Mexico, as well as demonstrate the value of looking at these issues from a comparative perspective. While a comprehensive discussion of all possible issues, similarities, and differences is well beyond the scope of this chapter, readers are encouraged to explore any of these themes further, or perhaps more importantly, to identify and elaborate those themes where barely any comparative information is yet available.

DIMENSIONS OF GENDER AND DIVERSITY

As many scholars have observed, there is nothing more fundamental to social organization than gender (Schlegel, 1996). While there are culturally-specific concepts and norms for how gender or racial identity impacts social interaction and structures, it may generally be said that diverse backgrounds and perspectives have always had some influence on classroom teaching and learning experiences. As Clinchy (1990), Gilligan (1982) and others have observed, women learn in markedly different ways than men. As well, several recent studies of the academic profession have indicated that women and minority faculty approach their classroom duties differently than many of their colleagues. For example, a recent survey of research on women and minority faculty in the United States revealed that these academics tend to have a stronger teaching orientation than their male counterparts (Olsen, Maple & Stage, 1995). Tierney and Bensimon (1996) speak of "doing Mom's work" when discussing the female faculty's tendency to approach teaching in a more nurturing fashion than male faculty. Goodwin and Stevens' (1993) research suggests that female professors might place greater value or importance on, or be more interested in, enhancing students' self-esteem and in encouraging student interaction and participation in class than their male colleagues.

In general, what little we have come to know about this issue underscores the potentially positive impact of increasing diversity within the faculty ranks. However, as with most things, there is another perspective. Feldman (1993a, 1993b) notes that there is little evidence of gender differences in students' evaluations of professors. As well, according to a recent study by Goodwin and Stevens (1993), male and female professors seem to share similar views about what constitutes "good" teaching, and about the appropriate outcomes of "good" teaching. Thus, perhaps it is not so much the diversity of faculty that is most important, but rather, its relationship to the diversity of students in their classrooms.

Recent decades have seen a significant rise in the number of women and minority faculty in higher education classrooms. In the United States, more women than men currently enroll in higher education, and the percentage of women is very high among Hispanic and African American students. As student populations become more diverse, and the classroom audience thus becomes less homogeneous, the university teacher is faced with a new and important set of challenges. In "Conducting Discussions in the Diverse Classroom," authors Knoedler and Shea (1992) explore three cognitive frameworks and ways to make classroom discussions more inclusive of all students. They point out that every student in the classroom has a different style of thinking and learning. Obviously, teachers who approach their class with the assumption that their preferred teaching techniques and choice of readings and lecture topics are adequate to ensure widespread student learning—without regard to the diversity of students' learning preferences—is bound to run into trouble.

As shown by scholars in the field of cognitive development, learning is student-specific, and thus teachers must broaden their approach to teaching to address a wide range of culturally-infused learning styles. Higher forms of justification, more complex and comprehensive measures of rationalizing beliefs and actions, are a product of both environment influences and interpersonal interaction. If student learning is indeed the goal of teaching activities, then the need is great for faculty to incorporate an understanding of their students' diverse backgrounds and approaches to the material, preferably before the course is halfway through the semester.

Of course, increasing the percentage of women and faculty of color in the department is one important way to address this issue. Certainly, these faculty are in high demand by the increasing numbers of women and minority students, who seek them out as mentors and role models. Verdugo (1995) observes the important role of Hispanic faculty in representing to minority students "a group who have overcome numerous obstacles in acquiring an education and thus are not only exemplars of the benefits of an education but also transmitters of this highly esteemed cultural value." Women and minority university teachers have also helped to introduce new perspectives and literature into the college curriculum, which further addresses the issue of inclusion of diverse perspectives in the university classroom. However, this particular achievement has in most cases been the result of a long and sometimes frustrating struggle, and institutions in time of retrenchment have often been inclined to first close courses in fields which have a relatively high presence of women and minority faculty (Gumport, 1993; Slaughter, 1993).

In general, women and minority faculty provide an invaluable resource for female and minority students, both in and out of the classroom. However, the extra pressures and workload which accompanies the responsibilities of role modeling and mentoring are rarely recognized or rewarded by academic departments. As institutions strive to be more inclusive in their administrative structures and proceedings, women and minority faculty are asked to sit on several departmental committees. However, as they are often the only women or minority faculty, they find themselves sitting on considerably more institutional committees than their white male counterparts. As well, there are likely to be few mentors of the same gender or ethnicity in their department who can to show them "through the ropes." Also, as mentioned previously, the rise in women and minority students in higher education creates a high demand on these faculty as mentors and role models. This often results in these faculty members taking on an unequally large share of student advising in their departments. This "hidden workload" (Tierney & Bensimon, 1996) that women and minority faculty must bear undoubtedly affects their experiences in the academic workload, and in many places contributes to their diminished presence within the faculty ranks. Unfortunately, research studies have indicated that minority faculty are less likely to be tenured than Caucasian female faculty who, in turn, are less likely to be tenured than Caucasian males (Carter & Wilson, 1992).

These trends have encouraged a new and growing field of literature on what the academy must do to retain women and minorities, and on what these faculty must do in order to survive (Johnsrud & Des Jarlais, 1994). In *Lifting a Ton of Feathers: A Woman's Guide to Surviving in the Academic World*, Paula Caplan (1993) suggests several coping mechanisms for women faculty to consider in successfully navigating the male-dominated world of academe. The author's suggestions include networking, handling sexist comments, and looking for mentors, all of which could make a woman academic's job less stressful and increase her chances for success. Lynne Welch's edited volume, *Perspectives on Minority Women in Higher Education* (1992), also offers a wide range of observations and useful recommendations for both faculty and administrators to work together in improving the academic work conditions of women and minority faculty.

More research along these lines will undoubtedly be useful in improving the experiences of women and minority faculty, which translates directly into higher percentages of them remaining in the academic profession—an important goal, considering the rising numbers of women and students of color throughout higher education. These and other dimensions of gender and diversity impact classroom teaching and learning in complex ways, and in virtually any cultural setting. Thus, there is considerable need for this research cross-nationally as well as locally. How academic departments address this increasingly important issue will have considerable impact on the future of higher education.

DIMENSIONS OF LANGUAGE

New student populations are coming to higher education classrooms, and are bringing new languages with them. In addition to the spoken languages of peoples whom have been historically excluded from higher education, students are bringing their own ways of communicating with each other into the classroom. For example, a teacher at an urban college in New York, tells the story of a group of students in her history class who, when asking questions in class, would consistently use phrases that students in the classroom seemed to clearly understand, but that she found completely foreign. Once the teacher understood the meaning of these phrases, she was able to more appropriately answer their questions. The point here is that students in any particular course may not be speaking the same language as their teacher— an important issue to grapple with in any classroom settting. Perhaps foreign language training should be a required component of graduate education, or incorporated into faculty development programs. Overall, the burden resides with the individual teacher to learn and use the kinds of language that will most effectively communicate the message to his or her students.

Imagine what would happen if Professor Bean were to go to Guatemala and teach a course in American History. Let's say that Professor Bean can understand and speak some level of Spanish, at least enough to get around town. However, his students grew up speaking Spanish on the streets, with indigenous dialects that one does not often find in a Spanish textbook of any kind. Obviously, Professor Bean will encounter some difficulty in the classroom, and thus he has taken it upon himself to enroll in a course or two at the local embassy to prepare himself. Now, imagine that instead of Guatemala, Professor Bean has taken a job at a community college in urban Detroit, where the student population is markedly different from Bean's former Ivy League crowd, and who tend to use different words and phrases to communicate various messages. Where is Professor Bean to turn in seeking an understanding of the language used by his students? Regardless of where you live and teach, generational gaps exist and new words are introduced to describe new social fads. To be successful, college teachers must strive to stay abreast of the uses of language that their students relate with.

But there is another, more common and complex dimension to language in our college classrooms—understanding and making accessible to others the language of academe. At a recent conference of educational researchers, the speaker in one of the sessions referred to "the aesthetic of postmodernist epistimology" as if he were referring offhand to something as common as a cup of coffee. In retrospect, it might have been quite useful if someone had made a scene. Perhaps someone should have stood up, interrupted the speaker, and called for a show of hands throughout the auditorium of who really understood what he had meant.

University teachers are no different from their students in a number of dimensions—we are all mere humans, plugging away through life as best we can, and we are forever struggling to make meaning of an increasingly incomprehensible world. Yet we often seem to make our world less accessible to others by using complicated terms to describe phenomena that relatively few would understand regardless of whatever terms we used. College and university teachers are trained in the language of research, and yet we must find ways to express our ideas to individuals with markedly different levels of preparation. This is a challenge for university teachers both within and outside the university classroom, but the former arena is arguably where the need for attention is most crucial.

This is definitely not, however, a call to "dumb down" the vocabulary one uses in presenting his or her ideas. Nor is it implied that today's students are unable or unwilling to broaden their vocabulary or comprehension skills. Rather, echoing the observation of many recent scholars, academics should be encouraged to focus their writing—as well as their speaking—for a larger audience than the typical academic journal, faculty conference, or lecture hall. In particular, university teachers must strive to understand their audience's level of familiarity with the topic discussed, and meet them halfway in terms of the vocabulary used in the discourse.

There is yet another dimension to the issue of language in higher education. The proliferation of specialized fields of study has also led to the introduction of countless new terms into the academic vocabulary. Things were much simpler in the old days, when monarchs and religions dictated all that we were supposed to know, thereby limiting the scope of our confusion. Today, the proliferation of knowledge and perspectives has created a fundamental ambiguity in our attempt to understand the world around us. Conventional wisdom no longer supports a singular content, research method, or a singular description of an historical phenomenon. And yet, students often come to college and university classrooms seeking not ambiguity, but clarity and understanding. Thus, the language that college and university teachers rely upon in the classroom is of utmost importance, regardless of whether in South Africa, Hawaii, Israel or Sweden. Clarity of message and purpose has never been more important.

DIMENSIONS OF ATTITUDE AND BEHAVIOR

Years ago a Swedish relative of mine came to visit me while I was in college, so I took him to my political science class one afternoon. Some of the students in our class disagreed with the professor's point of view on the particular subject of the day, and ten minutes into the lecture, my cousin was shocked to see students actually speaking up in class. As he later explained to me, talking to the professor in his native college environment was quite unusual, except for tutoring sessions held in private. Certainly, culture plays a significant role in the attitudes and behavior one can expect to find in a university classroom. In some cultures, eye-to-eye contact between teacher and student is largely a taboo, while in other cultures, a student who avoids eye contact with his or her student may be seen as shifty and dishonest. Students in Japan are rumored to be considerably more polite and attentive in class than the typical American student. Faculty who go abroad to teach are sometimes given a reasonable level of preparation on what attitudes and behavior to expect in their foreign classrooms, but all too often faculty are forced to discover these differences on the job.

For more than 50 years, research on teaching has involved teacher observations, rating scales, questionnaires, and personality inventories—while attempting to systematize this research into categories such as teacher styles, behaviors, characteristics, competencies and methods (Ornstein, 1995). The results of many of these studies—sometimes written in the form of recommendations or rules for teachers to follow—tended to focus on isolated teacher behaviors and methods, and held little regard for what those behaviors or methods meant in relation to the realities of the classroom (Ornstein, 1995).

Issues of teacher and student attitude and behavior in university classrooms present several challenges to faculty throughout the world. Human personality traits are not bound by geography or a colored flag. In every corner of the world you can find some students—as well as some faculty—who are confrontational by their very nature, and others who are passive. An aggressive or hyperactive teacher may frighten a more calm and soft-spoken student, and vice versa. Beneath the general topic of personal attributes, there are a number of important issues worth exploring, including the relationship between teacher personality traits and teaching effectiveness; developing and understanding a personal philosophy of teaching; and the influence of reward structures on attitudes and behaviors.

Teacher Personality Traits and Teaching Effectiveness

Despite a growing number of research efforts, relatively little is known for certain about the relationship between teacher personality and teacher effectiveness. Some scholars have explored personality traits of academics to determine whether personal values and beliefs impact a professor's teaching abilities. Feldman (1986) reviewed the research that relates the perceived effectiveness of teachers with their personality traits, as the latter are determined by teachers' own responses, gained primarily from self-reported personality inventories and related means of obtaining self-descriptions. He found "no studies in which perceived teaching effectiveness was compared with teachers' general values or general interests." However, another study on the degree of relationship between observed faculty personal characteristics and teaching effectiveness suggested that "the improvement of teaching effectiveness may depend more on changes related to personality factors than on those involving classroom procedures." (Sherman and Blackburn, 1975)

Rosenshine's (1971) research illustrated a positive association between businesslike, task-oriented behaviors (such as stating objectives, brisk pacing, and use of factual questions) and student achievement in basic-skill subjects such as reading and mathematics. According to this research the better teachers are those who are aware of their classroom behaviors and actively seek to use their behaviors to augment the learning experiences of their students. In another study (Murray, Rushton, & Paunonen, 1990), 29 personality traits of 46 psychology instructors were systematically compared with the instructor's teaching effectiveness ratings in six different courses. Their study found that personality traits were significantly related to teaching effectiveness, and specific traits were differentially effective, depending on the course. In addition, role flexibility–arguably a personality trait as well–was shown to play an important role in an instructor's teaching performance. Perhaps most striking, however, was their finding that "the compatibility of instructors to courses is determined in part by personality characteristics." As addressed later in this chapter, the issue of compatibility is an important consideration for developing new perspectives towards the evaluation of teaching.

Lecturing is the most common form of instruction in colleges and universities worldwide. Thus, a quick look at personal attributes which complement effective lecturing seems appropriate here. William Ekeler (1994) has compiled a helpful list of personal attributes (p. 91-2), in which the author maintains that an effective lecturer is one who:

- Is well-organized;
- Likes people, and is not irritated at questions in the classroom;
- Portrays enthusiasm, and is charismatic, dynamic and highly motivated;
- Has a sense of humor and occasionally pokes fun at self (which breaks down the damaging appearance of pompous superiority than can accompany classroom instruction);
- Is self-aware (of gait, posture, hands, clothing, etc.); and
- Believes in oneself and in the material.

Other attributes for effective lecturing are more related to behavior. Making eye contact, being well-rested before the lecture, never reading from a book, using emotion-enhancing words and moving about the classroom to avoid remaining in a stationary position are all important attributes of an effective lecturer,

According to the research literature, many of the personal attributes related to effective teaching are related in some way to verbal aptitude—how one uses his or her voice in the classroom matters considerably. According to Murray (et al.,1990), an animated teacher is comparatively more successful at "eliciting and maintaining student attention." As he puts it, "behaviors aimed at structuring material or stimulating independent thought can be expected to be successful only to the extent that student attention has already been effectively engaged." For example, a professor at Temple University uses role playing and storytelling to enliven his course on law and society, and his course lectures are frequently interrupted by people playing the roles of characters whose actions are used to illustrate legal disputes (Cage, 1995). In speaking on verbal aptitude, Ekeler (1994) notes that most criticism from students include monotone voice, inability to speak loudly or project one's voice, mumbling, speaking too rapidly or too slowly, and so forth.

In general, research studies on teaching and learning in higher education have found several important attitudinal and behavioral characteristics of both students and teachers that can enhance or inhibit learning. Faculty should be encouraged, perhaps through teaching development workshops or peer consultation, to gain an objective understanding of what their classroom behaviors and attitudes may be (or may appear to be to the classroom audience). If it is discovered that certain personality traits may be inhibiting student learning, the good news is that there are several resources available in print that can help address these issues in a positive and useful manner.

Developing and Understanding a Philosophy of Teaching

A university teacher's sense of self is an important topic of discussion. Just as their individual strengths can facilitate learning, their fears and misperceptions can become barriers to improved teaching. A faculty's attitude toward classroom instruction is important in their classroom interactions with students. Faculty who love to teach are usually received more favorably by their students than faculty who appear wholly uninterested in their teaching. To be sure, students can tell the difference. Certainly, a great many teachers seem to love teaching outright. In the United States, Elaine El-Khawas' (1991) recent study on senior academics' preferences found that, contrary to what much of the popular media would have us believe, most senior faculty are productive, contributing members of the academic professions, who are particularly active and interested in teaching undergraduates.

Louis Schmier (1996), who has made an art of describing the beauty and rewards that he has found in teaching at a small college in Georgia, observes that "good teachers . . . come as lovers of learning, as classroom stimulates rather than barbiturates. . . Their classes are loving and nurturing worlds of adventure—worlds of growth, transformation, and discovery." A teacher's philosophy of teaching plays an important role in their approach to their classroom duties. For many faculty, the creation of knowledge—or the development of new cognitive awareness—is viewed as either an exchange of fact and theory between teacher and student, or as an act of internal growth, under the guidance of the sage. There are faculty who prefer to transmit the canon to the students—the "empty vessel" perspective of teaching and learning. There are others who insist that, since knowledge can only be constructed from within, the teacher must play the role of "expert guide," or focus his or her efforts toward "shaping" or "growing" the student's cognitive abilities (Fox, 1983). The debate over which approach has more legitimacy rages on, but it is not a debate confined to national, geographic, or even disciplinary boundaries—a teacher's philosophy of teaching undoubtedly colors his or her relations with students in most any context or culture. Further research in this area—particularly comparative and cross-cultural studies—can be useful for determining the extent to which certain philosophies of teaching affect students in different ways.

A Final Note on Attitudes and Behaviors: Reward Structures in Academe

Reward structures often influence attitudes and behavior, but to varying degrees. For several decades now, research productivity has been the 'coin of the realm' in many corners of higher education. A recent study of faculty in the United States found that "faculty with the least amount of student contact hours earn the highest salaries," and that "the more refereed publications a faculty member publishes, the higher his or her salary." (Fairweather, 1993) Obviously, faculty responsibilities and rewards at a research university differ considerably from those at a community college or polytechnic. However, as Sowell (1990) states, "Money talks in academia as elsewhere, and what money says on most campuses is 'do research'." Among faculty in highly industrialized nations, research does indeed seem to be the most important component in an academic career. The Carnegie international survey of the academic profession revealed that a majority of faculty in almost all of the countries surveyed feel that their personal interests either "lean towards research" or "lie primarily in research." An emphasis on rewarding research may have considerable implications for how faculty feel about the value of their teaching.

As Lewis (1996) and other have observed, intrinsic motivation often plays a prominent role in faculty's commitment to teach. Indeed, few countries offer a high level of economic rewards for teaching. In his landmark *Scholarship Reconsidered* (1990), Boyer suggests that members of the higher education enterprise should revisit these reward systems and develop a shared vision of intellectual and social possibilities—a new vision that acknowledges and rewards what he calls "the scholarship of discovery, of integration, of application, and of teaching." With regard to the reward of teaching alone, there are several possible approaches to consider.

Prominent teaching award programs, like the Robert Foster Cherry Awards at Baylor University, are one way to reward good teaching and may have some role in promoting good teaching throughout the institution. However, while some institutions find it useful to recognize excellent teaching, other researchers question their impact on promoting effective teaching throughout the institution. For example, Australian scholars Anwyl and McNaught (1993) undertook a longitudinal study in Australia to determine what effects, if any, institutional teaching award programs might show in overall improvements in college teaching. The authors found that recognizing and rewarding excellent teachers does not equate with recognizing and rewarding *excellent teaching*. The authors also found that the criteria used to reward excellent teachers varied between institutions in their study, thus undermining the usefulness of these teaching award programs across a wide array of institutions. Still, if attitudes and behaviors are influenced to some degree by reward systems, then rewarding good teaching or good teachers is certainly a more recommended option than doing nothing at all.

There is another point of view, however, on the importance of emphasizing and rewarding teaching in higher education. The way in which academic activities are rewarded plays a prominent role in how faculty go about doing them. Academics are rational human beings, unlikely to engage in activities that would potentially jeopardize their chosen career goals. As teaching routines become more important for promotion and tenure, we will more likely see less–instead of more–willingness to question the presumptions upon which we base our use of these routines, as well as the presumptions upon which we base our evaluation of the effective use of these routines. Academics may be discouraged from exploring new ideas for teaching and learning in higher education–by the same logic as their aversion to controversial or "illegitimate" research topics–when the decisions they make about their teaching may undermine their career goals and job security. Thus, initiatives that emphasize the importance of effective teaching and learning must take caution that their approach to rewarding teaching does not also limit the potential choices a teacher may make about methods, course materials, and other aspects to their classroom experiences. In general, the kinds of potential effects that reward structures may have on attitudes and behaviors toward university teaching must be further studied before conclusive recommendations may be made along these lines.

DIMENSIONS OF INSTRUCTIONAL METHODOLOGY

A large body of research on college and university teaching focuses on the collection of accepted routines which faculty rely on in the classroom. Such routines include issues of method, time, physical space and tools, and evaluation procedures. Issues of method refer broadly to the type of instruction preferred by the teacher, whether it be lecture, group discussions, laboratory assignments, or whatever. There are a limited number of these methodological routines, many of which have struggled to gain legitimacy within the academic profession. There are some methods which, based largely on ideological grounds, a number of academics hold strong criticism for, such as the extensive use of drama and humor in the classroom. Issues of time include the predictable nature of today's courses. They meet a certain number of hours each week, at the same time and on the same day of the week, in the same classroom, etc. As well, time-related routines in college teaching include how a professor begins and ends class periods.

University teaching is perhaps the most difficult and complex activity within the academic profession. From textbook selection to classroom management and organization, to giving and grading exams, teaching requires a considerable commitment of time, energy and skill. Thus, it comes as no surprise that a good deal of research on university teaching is dedicated to helping the teacher achieve these multiple tasks more effectively. While addressing the wide range of perspectives available on this issue is well beyond the scope of this discussion, it may be useful to explore a few kinds of instructional methods that effectively enhance learning in many different contexts.

The Elusive Search for 'Best Practice' in University Teaching

The instructional methods adopted by university teachers are often influenced by their attitudes and philosophy toward teaching, in addition to various social, environmental and other conditions. Often, teachers will choose the techniques with which they are more familiar—if their undergraduate and graduate learning experiences involved mostly lectures, chances are high that they will adopt the lecture for their own classrooms. Role models play a similar role in affecting one's choices of instructional methods. As mentioned previously, institutional norms, evaluation activities and reward structures may play an important role in an instructor's choice of method. Other factors that may influence a teacher's choice of method in instructing a particular class are contextual, including availability of textbooks or other reading materials and resources. Above all, the appropriateness of method to student population (in terms of both quantity and diversity), course subject and physical context of a course is crucial.

Chickering and Gamson (1987) summarized years of study on effective college teaching in *Seven Principles for Good Practice in Undergraduate Education,* which has set the standard for research and discussion on this topic for the past two decades. They concluded that good teaching:

1. Encourages contacts between students and faculty
2. Develops reciprocity and cooperation among students
3. Uses active learning techniques
4. Gives prompt feedback
5. Emphasizes time on task
6. Communicates high expectations
7. Respects diverse talents and ways of learning

Within eighteen months of its original publication, 150,000 copies of the article had been distributed by the Johnson Foundation, which had supported its development. Without doubt, this has become the most popular resource on the subject to date. However, as Angelo (1993) and others have suggested, these principles are inherently limited, and useful only as companions to other approaches to evaluating good teaching. As McKeachie, Pintrich, Lin, and Smith (1986) have pointed out, most research of this sort does not result in the discovery of new teaching strategies, or the one "best" method of instruction or a magic elixir for fostering student learning and motivation, but it can help college faculty conceptualize teaching and learning in useful ways.

While there is certainly no shortage of scholars who provide research-based suggestions for effective teaching practices, this discussion highlights only a small handful of methods that can enhance university teaching.

Employing Effective Group Assignments

Assigning effective group assignments and activities can be a powerful tool for developing students' higher-level cognitive skills. Michaelsen (1994) offers several guidelines for designing appropriate questions, forming groups and establishing a grading system to support individual preparation and team development. He suggests that effective group assignments require:

- an understanding of the course concepts;
- a level of difficulty that requires collaborative (over individual) effort;
- ensuring that groups perform activities that groups do well (e.g., identifying problems, formulating strategies) while minimizing time spent on activities that individuals could do more efficiently alone (e.g., creating a polished document);
- giving students the opportunity to apply the course concepts to realistic problems; and
- work that is interesting or fun; and
- a tangible output that can be effectively evaluated.

A more thorough discussion on group assignments and collaborative learning is offered in the chapter by Ted and Patricia Panitz in this volume.

Encouraging Classroom Discussion

Classroom discussions can produce benefits for students along the same lines as effective group assignments. Bane's (1925) pioneering work on comparing lectures and discussions introduced a measure of 'delayed recall' to determine long-term learning. This scholar's work showed clearly that, while there was little difference between his groups on the tests immediately following the course, there was a considerable superiority for students in the discussion group on the measure of delayed recall. Effective discussions hinge on instructors' learning to become more comfortable with control issues and with their ability to guide students (and themselves) through the minefield of interpersonal interactions, especially those in multicultural classrooms (Frederick, 1994).

Collaborating with Colleagues
Academics are largely autonomous, and are usually rewarded only for their work as independent researchers or teachers, as opposed to collaborative research or teaching. However, interest in team teaching, faculty collaboration, and interdisciplinary education is increasing (Austin & Baldwin, 1991; Klein, 1990). Faculty collaboration and team teaching can amplify the energy of a classroom, particularly when the instructors have organized the material (and their presentation of it) in ways that highlight their collective as well as individual strengths. As well, team teaching can play an important role in presenting students with useful models for working together effectively and respecting diversity of opinion and perspective (Smith, 1994).

Assigning Problem-Solving Exercises
Guenter (1994) promotes fostering creativity through problem solving exercises. The latter author believes that by assigning problem-solving activities that promote critical thinking, teachers help students develop creativity by providing avenues for intrinsic motivation (motivation from within the student). Effective teachers must adamantly discourage "killer statements"— statements that cut down an idea before it has a chance to grow ("that's been tried before," "that's ridiculous/impossible . . ."). According to Guenter, when students "own" a problem, intrinsic motivation for creative problem solving is best enabled.

Seeking Feedback from Students
Demonstrating respect for and interest in student opinions and perceptions is a powerful tool for engaging them more in the learning process. Cross and Angelo (1988) recommend "One Minute Papers" as a quick and effective way to collect written feedback about a course or a specific class session, particularly in large lecture classes. Here, the instructor asks students to write a brief answer to the following two questions: "What was the most important thing you learned in today's class?" and "What question or questions that you have from today's class remain unanswered?" Another technique that is useful is to allow for anonymous, open-ended teaching evaluations at various points throughout the course, and then make adjustments to meet the

concerns expressed in these reports. In general, seeking feedback from students about the course direction or discussion encourages students to be more active participants in the classroom learning experience.

Organizing the Classroom Experience

The most common form of academic writing involves opening our discussion with a brief summary of what will be said, presenting the main arguments, and then closing the discussion with a concluding summary of the discussion's highlights. We often use this same structure in many areas of academic work, including the course syllabus we design or grant proposals we write. Applying the same organization to each class we teach can help students considerably in constructing their understanding of the material and how the ideas and concepts presented relate to one another. In addition to summarizing the main points of the lecture, it is also useful to leave time for questions and clarifying concepts at the end of the class session.

Clarifying Concepts

According Decyk (1994), using examples to teach concepts helps students to organize new ideas in their mind through association with more commonly known knowledge. She maintains that it is no coincidence that *Webster's Dictionary* offers many examples of the words it provides definitions for. Just as important, the author observes, teachers must encourage students to create their own examples to defining concepts and problems, within a set of reasonably established parameters.

Promoting Inquiry

According to Hansen (1994), effective teachers use different questioning techniques to promote creative and critical thinking and cooperative learning. Asking questions, and then asking for further clarification, or for connections to other pertinent materials, is a very valuable skill for teachers. According to King's (1994) work on inquiry as a tool in critical thinking, what teachers tell their students to do with the material greatly affects how they think about it. Thus, teachers should show students how (and encourage them) to ask their own questions, which helps make the learning experience more their own responsibility, which in turn helps to make the classroom into a "community of learners."

Developing an Effective Speaking Style

Although this was mentioned in the previous discussion on attitudes and behaviors, a teacher's use of voice is critical enough to bear further emphasis. As Lowman (1994) observes, "teachers who have developed a personal style of public speaking—whether flamboyant, whimsical, sardonic, or quietly intense—that students find engaging and energetic are more likely to be seen as exemplary than those whom students view as dull and lifeless." Additionally, according to Guenter (1994), "an instructor who smiles and demonstrates a sense of humor is a key catalyst for creativity in the classroom." I would argue that developing an effective speaking style is just as important for a college teacher as developing a competent base of disciplinary knowledge.

Using Experiential Learning Exercises

Field trips help students to see things as they really are: complex and imperfect, and not as they might be idealized in a textbook; In his article, "Classroom Without Walls" (1993), Harvard educator Harold Howe states that normal school routines "inoculate kids against learning through experience." Field trips provide students with an opportunity to get involved in the learning process, which promotes active learning through student participation. As research on cognitive development have shown, participation plays an important role in fostering student motivation for learning.

Establishing Learning Contracts

Learning contracts are useful tools for the teacher and the student to come to terms with what each expects from the course. Students may desire a guarantee that the activities they will perform in the course will help to foster the knowledge they desire. They may seek recognition from their professors that their efforts have been of high quality, and they may also seek to establish a relationship between themselves, their teacher, and their fellow classmates that includes mutual trust, respect, and collegiality. Teachers may desire a written agreement from the student that he or she will complete their assignments on time and in the format requested. They may also seek to ensure by some form of signed agreement that the student knows and understands what is expected for successfully completing the course. These contracts offer an effective strategy for structuring the teaching and learning environment to benefit both the learner and the teacher. Additionally, learning contracts provide a means through which students can set goals, which they are then motivated to achieve. According to Perry (1991), providing students with a perception of control over the learning environments and experiences can provide a powerful motivating factor for effective learning.

Final Comments on Methods of University Instruction
In general, teaching methods—or routines—have not changed dramatically since the first institutions of higher education at Bologna and Paris, perhaps a reflection of the organizational theory that where there might be uncertainty, individuals choose imitation. Recent questions raised over teaching behaviors and methods in terms of student cognition have generated interest but mostly have not been well-received by most faculty members, the majority of whom are comfortably secure in their chosen routines of classroom activity. However, the vast amount of research on teaching and learning in higher education also holds many diverse opinions on how to induce effective learning. This is not a bad thing, as we are provided with a rich banquet of approaches from which to choose that which best suits our personal tastes. Of course, this diversity also may create a problem for those seeking the formula for "best practice." The introduction and rapid expansion of technology in the classroom has added another dimension to this dilemma. Although teachers may be provided the opportunity of using new and fancy gadgets, there is still scarce research on how to use these new tools effectively in enhancing student learning.

DIMENSIONS OF TECHNOLOGY AND UNIVERSITY TEACHING
The growing influence of technology in our lives is an important issue to grapple with in university teaching. A fair amount of the recent literature on teaching and learning in higher education seems mostly directed towards developing new routines, adding to the collection of teaching routines a teacher may chose from, without questioning the underlying presumptions of the uses of routines in college teaching. Very recently, technology and distance learning initiatives have begun to change the direction—albeit slightly—of discussions and policies toward teaching. However, the bulk of these initiatives are concerned with new ways of packaging the same old routines, such as lectures on video tape or in real-time Internet transmissions. Technology offers university teachers the opportunity to explore new ways of promoting learning. As Neil Rudenstine, President of Harvard University, observed, "there is a very close fit between the structure and process of the Internet, and the main structures and processes of university teaching and learning." (1997, p. 5) As well, the enormous growth seen this decade in the use of technology for global communication and information shar-

ing can influence university teaching and learning in many ways, particularly in terms of teacher-student interaction.

Students often appreciate the type of access to their teacher offered by e-mail messages (provided the professor responds to them in a timely manner). The professor has an electronic record of their conversations. The Internet links scholars and students together to discuss issues specific to their field. Students can communicate with other students regardless of geographic boundaries—Carlos, a biology student in Spain, can share his thoughts and questions with Kris, a medical student in Canada. In virtually every discipline and field there are websites, newsgroups and listservs to explore and retrieve an overwhelming amount of information. There are links to the Library of Congress (and thousands of other libraries) and to most U.S. government agencies. One can find information on countless professional organizations, institutions, research subjects and, increasingly, commercial products worldwide. We now have online access to up-to-the-minute satellite data on orbits, scientific experiments, the movement of comets, or planetary alignments, as well as access to tens of thousands of Civil War era newspapers and recently de-classified documents from the Nixon era.

Students and professors can turn to these resources for the very latest information and perspectives on a world of topics. Teachers can create simulations of reality that are almost as compelling as reality itself. Students can create learning spaces on the Internet where they and fellow learners can grapple with problem solving. However, the existence of these technologies, whether inside or outside the classroom, is not in itself a recipe for enhanced student learning. What students need in order for these technologies to enhance their learning can be expected to change markedly as they progress through their courses. First year students need substantial guidance, as they are not yet likely to be experienced in how to use these resources for productive learning—entertainment is the more common focus. Thus, providing them with technology and access to information sources is not enough—first year students need substantial "how to use this stuff to learn" guidance, as well as a curriculum designed to take such needs into account. On the other hand, senior students are generally more self-sufficient in their approaches to learning and can make good use of technology-assisted independent learning courses. For example, advanced students in physical sciences courses can reap tremendous rewards through the use of computers, which help perform accurately controlled experiments and can track every step a student makes in the experiment to help identify where help is needed.

New developments in technology and telecommunications and the growing importance and accessibility of information are influencing both the representation of knowledge "content" and the facilitation of knowledge "reproduction." Students no longer rely on a printed text for their sources of information. Indeed, we now have a generation of college-bound students who have been exposed from birth to rapid, entertaining video images. As Sacks (1996) and others have observed, this does not bode well for the makers of college textbooks. Indeed, publishing houses throughout the world face an alarming decline in the number of books they can sell, and the resulting increases in book price (to meet the bottom line of expenses at the publishing firm) have forced the industry into a supply-cost-demand spiral which has already seen several casualties. Smaller firms are being bought up or closed altogether, the opportunities to publish one's work are growing fewer, and there is a noticeable dissatisfaction from both students and professors at the rising costs of items at their local bookstore.

Simultaneously, technology presents new dilemmas with regard to copyright issues, knowledge distribution and reward for creativity. Anyone with an Internet connection can host their own website, and the number of sites has been growing exponentially every week. While a good deal of information available on the Internet is useful and timely, individuals in various corners of the world are taking advantage of this new, relatively free medium to promote their own views, however falsely based. For educators, this presents a new responsibility of teaching students how to judge analytically the sources of their information and to seek multiple perspectives on issues before deciding for themselves what is fact and what is fantasy. This also has other implications for the college teacher seeking new and inventive ways to encourage students to develop their thinking and analysis skills. The savvy teacher must begin to look online for the most up-to-date information resources, and we are already seeing required URLs[2] listed on many course syllabi.

Technology also presents new dilemmas for the professor. Plagiarism has never been easier—in fact, the selling and distribution of 'college-level' term papers through the Internet is a booming market. The amount of information being offered on the World Wide Web, both academic and otherwise, offers the unethical student a world of opportunities. The information is in electronic form. No need to photocopy or re-type the article out of some library journal, now you can simple "cut-and-paste" right into your word processor, slap your name on it, and in fifteen minutes you're ready to go out on the town with your friends. Certainly, a college or university professor who suspects plagiarism of their students can call them out, challenge them to defend the argument in their paper or to more thoroughly demonstrate that the product is truly theirs. However, identifying one of these "cut-and-paste" jobs is becoming increasingly difficult, as a simple visit to any of the more sophisticated online term paper warehouses will demonstrate. Unfortunately, if one were to hazard a guess, strikingly few college or university professors are Internet-savvy enough to know where to locate potential sources of these sorts of papers, although chances are their students are no stranger to them.

The presence of technology in the university classroom is still relatively new, and as such many professors have successfully avoided dealing much with it. However, as new generations of students who have become familiar with technology at increasingly earlier stages of their lives, teachers who are not competent in things technological run the risk of appearing outdated, which undermines their authority as a bearer of knowledge or facilitator of learning. Thus, we are seeing a rise in faculty development seminars and conference presentations that address various issues of integrating technology and the university teaching environment. As well, a new and important field of research on the effectiveness of technology in enhancing student learning will benefit faculty worldwide. Certainly, how university teachers respond to the challenges and opportunities of new technologies will have a considerable effect on the course of higher education in the next decade.

DIMENSIONS OF EVALUATING TEACHING EFFECTIVENESS

Ernest Boyer (1990) calls for redefining the term *scholarship* to incorporate the importance of effective teaching and college classroom interaction. However, the term *effective teaching* has yet to find a common definition in many academic circles. Indeed, anyone who carries out research on teaching effectiveness quickly runs into the problem of evaluating the outcomes of teaching (McKeachie, 1990). How do classroom processes affect learning outcomes? Students react differently to the same teacher, and yet the majority of current teaching assessment methods throughout the world rely on student evaluations. According to a recent international survey of the academic profession by the Carnegie Foundation for the Advancement of Teaching, teaching evaluation by students and by department peers is quite common in most countries (see Table 1).

Table 1

"By Whom Is Your Teaching Regularly Evaluated?"
(more than one response could be selected)

	YOUR PEERS IN YOUR DEPARTMENT	THE HEAD OF YOUR DEPARTMENT	MEMBERS OF OTHER DEPARTMENTS AT THIS INSTITUTION	SENIOR ADMINISTRATIVE STAFF AT THIS INSTITUTION	YOUR STUDENTS	EXTERNAL REVIEWERS
Australia	28%	64%	6%	11%	74%	6%
Brazil	53	51	15	28	54	5
Chile	30	64	26	23	51	4
Germany	30	44	6	8	59	2
Hong Kong	23	70	7	23	76	24
Israel	24	45	7	7	85	7
Japan	42	43	10	41	37	5
Korea	18	29	9	70	12	8
Mexico	37	62	23	55	57	10
The Netherlands	49	29	7	7	79	17
Russia	32	76	14	21	62	6
Sweden	20	26	11	7	96	9
United Kingdom	16	64	7	13	67	21
United States	49	78	16	34	91	7

Source: Boyer, Altbach, & Whitelaw, (1994). *The Academic Profession: An International Perspective.* Princeton, NJ: The Carnegie Foundation for the Advancement of Teaching.

Further, as reflected in Table 2, faculty in most countries surveyed agreed that students should be involved in evaluating their teaching.

Table 2

"Student Opinions Should Be Used in Evaluating the Teaching Effectiveness of Faculty"

	Agree	Neutral	Disagree
Australia	79%	11%	10%
Brazil	83	8	9
Chile	71	17	12
Germany	67	17	16
Hong Kong	73	13	14
Israel	70	16	14
Japan	50	28	23
Korea	64	21	15
Mexico	78	13	9
The Netherlands	71	18	12
Russia	65	24	11
Sweden	86	9	6
United Kingdom	78	12	10
United States	73	12	15

Source: Boyer, Altbach, & Whitelaw, (1994). *The Academic Profession: An International Perspective.* Princeton, NJ: The Carnegie Foundation for the Advancement of Teaching.

As the survey did not collect information on whether faculty used their student evaluations in a conscientious effort to improve their teaching, this is one area where further research would be incredibly useful for defining the term "effective teaching."

McKeachie (1990) observed that "despite faculty doubts about the ability of students to appreciate good teaching, the research evidence indicates that students are generally good judges—surprisingly so, in view of the fact that most research on student evaluation has been carried out in introductory classes, in which one would expect the students to be less able to evaluate them than in more advanced classes." However, evaluation instruments tend to favor teachers adept in observable or measurable teaching behaviors, while teachers who stress abstract or divergent thinking often do not fare well on such evaluations. These and other issues often confound the usefulness of the relationship between evaluation and reward of effective teaching.

In general, methods of assessing teaching performance have changed very little over the last several decades, and the notion of assessing teaching is common throughout the world. According to the Carnegie survey data, with the exception of Japan and Germany, over 65% of faculty in all the countries surveyed indicated that their teaching is evaluated in some form or another. The evaluation of teaching bears particular relevance for the development of policies and procedures which identify and reward effective teaching. Academic reward structures in the post-war years increasingly favored sponsored research over teaching, and scholars rose to the pinnacle of their professions primarily by means of their research and not necessarily by their teaching prowess. Quality in research was shown to be much easier to assess than quality in teaching. How can you measure the effectiveness of a teacher in fostering inquisitiveness, or of the effectiveness of a minister in increasing faith? (Stuart and Whetten, 1985) Presented with the difficulty of quantifying the long term impact of a teacher on a student, several researchers have made assumptions about the maximum number of students a professor can effectively instruct, and then treated faculty/student ratios as indicators of the quality of education (Stuart and Whetten, 1985). As others have observed, a faculty/student ratio provides fairly unimportant information in terms of assessing the quality of one's teaching or student learning (Forest, 1995).

Policymakers throughout the higher education landscape are paying closer attention to the assessment and improvement of classroom activities, largely in response to public concerns over skyrocketing costs and corporate complaints of underprepared graduates of higher education institutions.

Buzzwords like 'accountability' and 'benchmarks' have become commonplace in legislative subcommittees on higher education. Around the globe, faculty are feeling increasing pressure to justify what they spend their time doing in and outside the classroom, under the guise of a public concern that students be better equipped to handle the challenges of modern society. Thus, it may come as no surprise that faculty throughout the world feel that better ways are needed to evaluate teaching performance (Boyer, Altbach and Whitelaw, 1994).

However, there is little widespread agreement on how teachers directly affect student cognitive development or the construction of knowledge. A recent article (Forest, 1997) addresses this issue with a new way of looking at the assessment of teacher-student classroom interaction, in which a new sharing of responsibility for providing "opportunities for learning" is presented. What is offered here is a relatively new paradigm—learning as a product of multiple forces surrounded by ambiguity. This framework views learning as the result of a combination of influences, including the instructor (and his or her chosen routines), the learner, and the environment.

The Opportunity for Learning Moments
Bowen (1980) describes learning as having at least three dimensions—knowing and interpreting the known (scholarship and criticism), discovering the new (research and related activities), and bringing about desired change in the cognitive and affective traits and characteristics of human beings (education). The creation of knowledge is an event, which does not take place in a vacuum. Most scholars have come to agree that learning and teaching occurs with frequency outside the traditional classroom—indeed, many would argue that practically every waking moment is a potential learning opportunity. The environment in which learning moments take place assumes considerable importance when considering current initiatives for measuring the effectiveness of one's teaching. As well, the process of learning involves teacher and learner personalities, teacher and learner preparation, skills and aptitudes. Variations in any of these three elements can produce remarkably diverse results in terms of student evaluations. But just how much do any of these three really impact student learning? On this subject, there is plenty of empirical research but little widespread agreement.

It is proposed that a fourth element—chance—is also part of the combination of influences involved in the creation of knowledge. The perspective provided in this discussion is adapted from literature on organizational leadership. In their groundbreaking study, *Leadership and Ambiguity*, Cohen and March (1986) offered a new and vastly different paradigm for viewing the role of leadership in organizational decision making. Their notion of ambiguity in how decisions are made—or rather, how problems, solutions, and participants mix randomly together, while the problems solved depend on a whole host of complex and random activity—lends itself nicely to a discussion on how the creation of knowledge may occur. Four elements—teacher, student, environment, and chance—are described as influences of opportunities for learning. A poor showing in any one of these dimensions can seriously inhibit the opportunity for learning moments to occur. Each of these elements is described briefly below, followed by a visual representation of how they interact to provide opportunities for learning.

Dimensions of a Teacher's Contribution to Learning Moments

The combination of teacher preparation, attitudes, behavior, and teaching method is integral to the success of a teacher's work with students. As mentioned previously in this chapter, gender and racial or ethnic diversity may play a role in how the teacher relates to his or her students, and vice versa. Behaviors such as making eye contact, moving about the classroom, and projecting one's voice effectively are all useful when lecturing. A university teacher's attitude toward instruction is important in their classroom interactions with students, as is their philosophy of teaching—particularly, whether knowledge is seen as transmitted or constructed. Institutional reward structures may influence how a faculty member approaches their teaching responsibilities. And without question, an instructor's choice of teaching method has considerable impact on most any classroom learning experiences, particular in terms of how comfortable the instructor is with their choice of method.

Dimensions of a Student's Contribution to Learning Moments

There are many dimensions to how a student contributes to his or her learning. For example, the learner's prior knowledge plays a critical role in comprehension and knowledge acquisition (Schallert, 1991) as well as the construction of what Perry (1985) calls "personal meaning." What the student knows provides the platform upon which a teacher can help the student build a more complex understanding of the material. According to Astin (1984), students do better academically if they are involved in campus life. Motivation and interest in the subject matter are additional dimensions of a student's contribution to a learning moment. Extrinsic motivation—the economic or status rewards for achieving a higher degree—may influence markedly different approaches to learning than intrinsic motivation. According to Pintrich and Garcia (1991), students who are encouraged to set goals and are given license to regulate their own attainment of those goals tend to focus more of their attention and energy on their learning. Decades of research have confirmed that socioeconomic class effects learning in various ways throughout the world, including parental support and pre-college preparation. Gender and racial or ethnic diversity may play a role in how the student responds to the teacher.

Yet another dimension is a student's personal learning style. Some students will learn if they are given the opportunity to take risks and discover on their own, but they also need constant support from the teacher (Moore, 1994). Some students may need concrete examples from audiovisual presentations, whereas others may benefit more from reading a good textbook (Carskadon, 1994). How a student best learns is, for the most part, individually dependent on a wide range of variables specific to that student. Complexities notwithstanding, research on student cognitive development, as well as other research discussed earlier in this chapter, can provide useful tools for gaining a more comprehensive understanding of the many dimensions of a student's contribution to a learning moment.

Dimensions of a Physical Environment's Contribution to Learning Moments
The element of physical environment—including trust between student and teacher, and between students—is also important for the opportunity for a learning moment to present itself. According to McKeachie (1990), the question of whether small classes were more effective than large classes was probably the first major question that research on college teaching tried to answer. Among the first investigators of class size were Edmondson and Mulder (1924), whose comparison of students in two classes (one large, the other small) found relatively equal performance on learning assessments, although students reported a preference for small classes. Further studies–such as Macomber and Siegel's (1957, 1960) experiments at Miami University–determined that the effect of class size on learning depends on what the teacher does in that classroom. Glass and Smith's (1979) meta-analysis of class size research, which takes into account more basic outcomes of retention, problem solving, and attitude differentiation as criteria for learning, shows that small classes are indeed more favorable. Issues of physical space and tools also include the size and layout of the classroom, chairs, blackboard, pens, reading and homework assignments, exams, door, and clock. As well, research on experiential learning demonstrates how field trips can provide new and

inventive ways for students to get more involved in their learning process (Classrooms without Walls, 1993). The kinds of resources upon which students and their teachers can rely surely has a considerable impact on their teaching and learning experiences.

Ambiguity and the Dimension of Chance
Cohen and March's (1986) study of university organizations yielded a surprisingly new perspective—one which they gave the term "organized anarchies." They presented a theory called "the garbage can process," where "problems, solutions, and participants move from one choice opportunity to another in such a way that the nature of the choice, the time it takes, and the problems it solves all depend on a relatively complicated intermeshing of the mix of choices available at any one time, the mix of problems that have access to the organization, the mix of solutions looking for the problem, and the outside demands on the decision makers." (p. 90)

In their discussion, the authors refer to a "flashpoint" or "decision moment" to describe the event where a problem, a solution, and participants come together with a choice opportunity to produce an outcome of some sort. As they explain,

> Although we think of decision making as a process of solving problems—a process which involves problems and choices to be made—that is often not what happens. Problems are worked upon in the context of some choice, but choices are made only when the shifting combinations of problems, solutions, and decision makers happens to make action possible. (p. 90)

The notion of a "flashpoint" can also be applied to describe a moment where an individual experiences cognitive development—also referred to in this discussion as a learning moment.[3] Rather than a "garbage can," perhaps we can look at learning moments within the context of chemical reactions that occur in the atmosphere when elements—under the influence of gravitational and other forces—collide, creating increasingly complex elements. The construction of knowledge is an event which does not take place in a contextual vacuum. Most scholars have come to agree that learning and teaching occurs with frequency outside the traditional classroom—indeed, many would argue that practically every waking moment offers a potential learning opportunity. In a sense, a classroom is simply one of any number of environments in which learning moments can occur—not too dissimilar from the decision moments described by Cohen and March. While a moment of knowledge construction can occur virtually anywhere and anytime, this discussion is concerned exclusively with the implications of this perspective in terms of activities within college and university classrooms.

Ambiguity and Teaching

Classroom teaching is perhaps the most difficult and complex activity within the academic profession. While a college teacher strives to encourage students to learn the material, to learn to think critically and analytically, and to create knowledge for themselves, the results of their labor are often ambiguous and hard to pin down. Learning is inherently an individual achievement—no two individuals in an classroom have identical views toward the material or identical preparation, or achieve identical 'outcomes', or even learn at the same pace. Thus, for a learning moment to be possible, each individual must be presented with the right mix of teacher, learner, and environment. However, even when this mix is present, there is never a guarantee that a learning moment will occur—thus, the fourth element, chance. As Figure 1 illustrates, the intersection of all four elements described above lead to the opportunity for a learning moment to occur.

Figure 1
Diagram of a Learning Moment

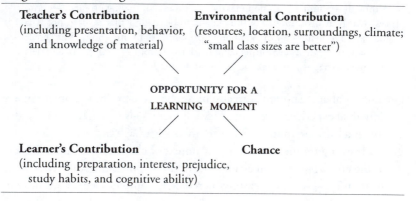

Teacher's Contribution	Environmental Contribution
(including presentation, behavior, and knowledge of material)	(resources, location, surroundings, climate; "small class sizes are better")

OPPORTUNITY FOR A
LEARNING MOMENT

Learner's Contribution	Chance
(including preparation, interest, prejudice, study habits, and cognitive ability)	

Summary and Policy Implications for Evaluating Teaching

Rather than looking at the activity of learning in traditional ways, we may consider that the *opportunity* for learning occurs at the intersection of four main elements—teacher, learner, environment, and chance. The influence of each of these elements varies from situation to situation, yet a poor showing in any of them can almost certainly cause difficulties for the achievement of student learning in the college classroom. Thus, in assessing the effectiveness of higher education institutions, we must look at questions of how well the instructor, student, and institution work together to provide the opportunity for learning. Obviously, the fourth element, chance, is well beyond our control. However, in general, this approach is a clear departure from traditional methods of evaluation teaching and learning in higher education.

College teachers are merely humans, plugging away through life as best we can, struggling to make sense and meaning of an increasingly complex and incomprehensible world. The creation of knowledge—or the development of new cognitive awareness—has been traditionally viewed as either an exchange of fact and theory between teacher and student, or as an act of internal growth, under the guidance of the sage. While it is true that the actions of a teacher can influence the potential for learning, this theory argues that the level of this influence is minimal at best. Under the framework outlined herein, the best we can do in an ambiguous situation is identify and create the most opportunities for learning moments to occur.

Many scholars and practitioners have questioned whether teaching or learning can really ever be meaningfully assessed—indeed, how does one measure what one does not entirely understand? Granted, when faced with things as complex as how students learn, we opt for more easily measurable indicators of productivity, such as how many bodies are in that teacher's classroom, and how those bodies respond to items on a teaching evaluation form. These approaches to assessing faculty productivity are rooted in faulty assumptions of the teaching-learning interaction and of how knowledge is constructed. If the true purpose of evaluation is to encourage the enhancement of student learning in university classrooms, then it seems more useful to evaluate the effectiveness of all elements that are involved in providing opportunities for learning moments to occur.

CONCLUDING REMARKS

This chapter has taken a rather abbreviated view of some of the many issues that university teachers worldwide grapple with in their professional lives. A conscious effort has been made to present the material in a manner that does not rule out applicability in different cultural or geographic contexts. Obviously, there are a number of areas in which we have learned a good deal about university teachers and their teaching. However, there is much that we have yet to learn, particularly in the comparative sense. As Kerr (1990) observes, "we live in a world where . . . the worldwide advancement of learning has become the single most influential factor affecting the human condition." In modern societies, the elements of rationalized formal structure are deeply ingrained in, and reflect, widespread understandings of social reality (Meyer and Rowan, 1978). Comparative studies, such as the Carnegie international survey discussed in this chapter, help us to understand how academics, in the broadest sense, view the social reality of their work–their responsibilities to their professions, to society and to themselves.

Our world is rapidly becoming more interdependent and inextricably linked, and the distribution of information has achieved dimensions never previously conceived of. Internationalization in higher education has become a driving force in university policy discussions in many small states around the world. Rising costs and increased social demand for access to higher education have compelled governments in these regions to take a fresh look at funding arrangements, international linkages and joint ventures (Crossley and Louis, 1994). Our understanding of the academic responsibility of teaching needs to encompass an international dimension in order for our students–and our colleagues–to adequately address the demands of this increasing global interdependence.

Academics are intelligent, rational decision-makers. A good number of them would be willing to change their approach to teaching, if they believed it would benefit their students and themselves. As the Carnegie survey and other studies of the academic profession have affirmed, most university teachers take a great deal of pride in their work, as well they should. As Stanley Hauerwaus (1988) points out, "teaching is a way to enhance our society through knowledge and wisdom. The moral authority of the teacher derives from this commitment and is the reason why the society as a whole feels betrayed when it is not honored." Teaching is arguably one of the most vital activities that members of any society can perform. With a renewed interest in and commitment to this aspect of academic work and life, we will surely achieve Boyer's (1990) vision of a profession that is "intellectually vibrant and more responsive to society's shifting needs."

NOTES

1. Egypt also participated in the Carnegie survey data collection, but for political reasons has not yet released their data to the Carnegie Foundation. Thus, they are omitted from the discussion here.
2. URL is the widely-used acronym for "Universal Resource Locators"—the text string that indicates a location of an online information resource. Common beginnings for URL text strings include: http://www.something.edu, or gopher:// or ftp:// something.edu.
3. The notion of learning moments as applied in the current discussion is not to be confused with related research on the "critical moment in learning" (Palmer, 1993, *Change* 25,6). For more discussion on learning moments, see Bowen, Howard R. (1980). *Investment in Learning.* San Francisco, CA: Jossey-Bass Publishers.

REFERENCES

Altbach, P.G. (1992). Patterns in higher education development: Towards the year 2000. In Altbach, P.G. & Morsy, Z. (Eds.) *Higher education in international perspective.* New York: UNESCO/Advent Books.

Angelo, T.A. (1993). A "Teacher's Dozen": Fourteen general, research-based principles for improving higher learning in our classrooms. *AAHE Bulletin,* 45 (8).

Anwyl, J., and McNaught, C. (1993). Awards for teaching excellence at Australian universities. *Higher Education Review,* 25 (1).

Astin, A.W. (1984). Student involvement: A developmental theory for higher education. *Journal of College Student Personnel* 25 (4) (July), p. 297-308.

Austin, A. & Baldwin, R. (1991). *Faculty Collaboration: Enhancing the quality of scholarship and teaching.* (ASHE-ERIC Higher Education Report No. 7). Washington, DC: George Washington University.

Bane, C.L. (1925). The lecture vs. the class discussion method of college teaching. *School and Society,* 21, p. 300-302.

Bowen, Howard R. (1980). *Investment in Learning.* San Francisco, CA: Jossey-Bass Publishers.

Boyer, E.L., Altbach, P.G., & Whitelaw, M.J. (1994). *The academic profession: An international perspective.* Princeton, NJ: The Carnegie Foundation for the Advancement of Teaching.

Boyer, E.L. (1990). *Scholarship reconsidered: Priorities of the professoriate.* Princeton, NJ: Carnegie Foundation for the Advancement of Teaching.

Brown, L. (1992). Higher education and the reality of interdependence. *International Journal of Educational Development*, 12 (2), p. 87.

Cage, M.C. (1995). Mixing the outrageous with the educational. *Chronicle of Higher Education,* (May 24, 1995), p. A19.

Caplan, P.J. (1993). *Lifting a ton of feathers: A woman's guide to surviving in the academic world.* Toronto: University of Toronto Press.

Carskadon, T.G. (1994). Student personality factors. In Prichard, K.W. & Sawyer, R.M. (Eds.), *Handbook of College Teaching: Theory and applications.* Westport, CT: Greenwood Press.

Carter, D. & Wilson, R. (1992). *Minorities in higher education.* Washington, DC: American Council on Education.

Chickering, A.W. & Gamson, Z.F. (1987). Seven principles for good practice in undergraduate education. *AAHE Bulletin*, 39, p. 3-7.

Classrooms without walls. (1993). *Earthwatch*, (March-April), pp. 9-12.

Clinchy, B.M. (1990). Issues of gender in teaching and learning. *Journal of Excellence in College Teaching*, 1, p. 52-67.

Cohen, M.D. & March, J.G. (1986). *Leadership and ambiguity: The American college president* (2nd edition). Boston, MA: Harvard Business School Press.

Cross, K.P. & Angelo, T.A. (1988). *Classroom assessment techniques: A handbook for faculty.* Ann Arbor, MI: National Center for Research to Improve Postsecondary Teaching and Learning.

Crossley, M. & Louis, P. (1994). The changing role of the small state in higher education: A comparison of national and regional initiatives in the Caribbean and the South Pacific. *Compare*, 24(2), p. 11

Decyk, B.N. (1994). Using examples to teach concepts. In Halpern, D. & Associates, *Changing college classrooms: New teaching and learning for an increasingly complex world.* San Francisco: Jossey-Bass.

Edmondson, J.B., & Mulder, F.J. (1924). Size of class as a factor in university instruction. *Journal of Educational Research*, 9, 1-12.

Ekeler, W.J. (1994). The lecture method. In Prichard, K.W. & Sawyer, R.M. (Eds.), *Handbook of college teaching: Theory and applications.* Westport, CT: Greenwood Press.

El-Khawas, E. (1991) "Senior faculty in academe: Active, committed to the teaching role" *Research Briefs*, Vol. 2, No. 5 (Washington, D.C.: American Council on Education, Div. of Policy Analysis and Research)

Fairweather, J.S. (1993). *Teaching, research and faculty rewards, A summary of the research findings of the faculty profile project.* Penn State University: NCTLA.

Feldman, K.A. (1993a). College students' views of male and female college teachers: Part I—evidence from the social laboratory and experiments. *Research in Higher Education*, 33, p. 317-75.

Feldman, K.A. (1993b). College students' view of male and female college teachers: Part II—evidence from students' evaluations of their classroom teachers. *Research in Higher Education*, 34, p. 151-211.

Feldman, K.A. (1986). The perceived instructional effectiveness of college teachers as related to their personality and attitudinal characteristics: A review and synthesis. *Research in Higher Education*, 24 (2).

Forest, J.J.F. (1997). Teaching and ambiguity. *Teaching in Higher Education*, 2 (2), p. 181-185.

Forest, J.J.F. (1995). Turning the mirror on ourselves: Current research on teaching in higher education. *International Higher Education*, 2 (Fall).

Fox, D. (1983). Personal theories of teaching. *Studies in Higher Education*, 8, p. 151-163.

Frederick, P.J. (1994). Classroom discussions. In Prichard, K.W. & Sawyer, R.M. (Eds.), *Handbook of college teaching: Theory and applications.* Westport, CT: Greenwood Press.

Gilligan, C. (1982). *In a different voice: Psychological theory and women's development.* Cambridge, MA: Harvard University Press.

Glass, G.V. & Smith, M.L. (1979). Meta-analysis of research on class size and achievement. *Educational Evaluation and Policy Analysis*, 1, p. 2-16.

Goodwin, L.D. & Stevens, E.A. (1993). The influence of gender on university faculty members' perceptions of "good" teaching. *Journal of Higher Education*, 64(2).

Guenter, C.E. (1994). Fostering creativity through problem solving. In Halpern, D. & Associates, *Changing college classrooms: New teaching and learning for an increasingly complex world.* San Francisco: Jossey-Bass.

Gumport, P. (1993). The contested terrain of academic program reduction. *Journal of Higher Education,* 64 (May-June), p. 283-311.

Hauerwaus, S.M. (1988). The morality of teaching. In A.L. Deneef, C.D. Goodwin and E.S. McCrate (eds.) *The academic's handbook* (Durham, NC: Duke Press), 19-28

Hansen, C.B. (1994). Questioning techniques for the active classroom. In Halpern, D. & Associates, *Changing college classrooms: New teaching and learning for an increasingly complex world.* San Francisco: Jossey-Bass.

Johnsrud, L.K. & Des Jarlais, C.D. (1994). Barriers to tenure for women and minorities. *Review of Higher Education,* 17(4), p. 335-353.

Kerr, C. (1990). The internationalisation of learning and the nationalism of the purposes of higher education: Two 'laws of motion' in conflict? *European Journal of Education,* 25 (1).

King, A. (1994). Inquiry as a tool in critical thinking. In Halpern, D. & Associates, *Changing college classrooms: New teaching and learning for an increasingly complex world.* San Francisco: Jossey-Bass.

Klein, J.T. (1990). *The fifth discipline: The art and practice of the learning organization.* New York: Doubleday.

Knoedler, A.S. & Shea, M.A. (1992). Conducting discussions in the diverse classroom. *To improve the academy,* 11, p. 123-135.

Kohn, M.L. (1987). Cross-national research as an analytical strategy. *American Sociological Review,* 52 (6), p. 713-31.

Lewis, L. (1996). *Marginal worth: Teaching and the academic labor market.* New Brunswick, NJ: Transaction Publishers.

Lowman, J. (1994). Professors as performers and motivators. *College Teaching,* 42 (4), p. 137-141.

Macomber F.G. & Seigel, L. (1957a). A study of large-group teaching procedures. *Educational Research,* 38, p. 220-229.

Macomber F.G. and Seigel, L. (1957b). *Experimental study in instructional procedures.* (Progress Report No. 2) Oxford, OH: Miami University.

Macomber F.G. and Seigel, L. (1960). *Experimental Study in Instructional Procedures.* (Final Report) Oxford, OH: Miami University.

McKeachie, W.J. (1990). Research on college teaching: The historical background. *Journal of Educational Psychology,* 82 (2), p.189-200.

McKeachie, W.J, Pintrich, P.R., Lin, Y. & Smith, D.A. (1986). *Teaching and learning in the college classroom: A review of the research literature.* Ann Arbor: University of Michigan, National Center for Research to Improve Postsecondary Teaching and Learning.

Meyer, J.W. & Rowan, B. (1978). Institutionalized organizations: Formal structure as myth and ceremony. *American Journal of Sociology,* 83, 2, p. 340-363

Michaelsen, L.K. (1994). Team learning: Making a case for the small-group option. In Prichard, K.W. & Sawyer, R.M. (Eds.), *Handbook of college teaching: Theory and applications.* Westport, CT: Greenwood Press.

Moore, W.S. (1994). Student and faculty epistemology in the college classroom. In Prichard, K.W. & Sawyer, R.M. (Eds.), *Handbook of college teaching: Theory and applications.* Westport, CT: Greenwood Press.

Murray, H.G., Rushton, J.P. & Paunonen, S.V. (1990). Teacher personality traits and student instructional ratings in six types of university courses. *Journal of Educational Psychology,* 82 (2). p. 250-261.

Olsen, D., Maple, S.A., & Stage, F. (1995). Women and minority faculty job satisfaction. *Journal of Higher Education*, 66 (3).

Ornstein, A.C. (1995). The new paradigm in research on teaching. *Educational Forum*, 59 (Winter), p. 124-129

Penner, J.G. (1984). *Why many college teachers cannot lecture.* Springfield, IL: Charles C. Thomas.

Perry, R.P. (1991). Perceived control in college students: Implications for instruction in higher education. In Smart, J. (Ed.), *Higher Education: Handbook of theory and research* (Vol. 7, pp. 1-56). New York: Agathon Press.

Perry, W.G. (1985). Different worlds in the same classroom: Students' evolution in their vision of knowledge and their expectations of teachers. In Gullette, M.M. (Ed.) *On teaching and learning.* Cambridge, MA: Harvard-Danforth Center for Teaching and Learning.

Pintrich, P.R. & Garcia, T. (1991). Student goal orientation and self-regulation in the college classroom. In Maehr, M. & Pintrich, P.R. (Eds.), *Advances in motivation and achievement: Goals and self-regulatory processes.* 7, 371-401. Greenwich, CT: JAI Press.

Rosenshine, B. (1971). Teaching behaviors related to student achievement. In Vestbury, L. (Ed.), *Research into classroom processes: Recent developments and next steps.* New York: Teachers College Press.

Rudenstine, N.R. (1997). Special address. In O'Reilly & Associates, *The Harvard conference on the Internet and society.* Cambridge: Harvard University Press.

Sacks, P. (1996). *Generation X goes to college: A journey into teaching in postmodern America.* Chicago: Open Court.

Schallert, D.L. (1991). The contribution of psychology to teaching the Language Arts. In Flood, J., Jensen, J.M. & Squire, J.R. (Eds.), *Handbook of research on teaching the English Language Arts* (pp. 30-39). New York: Macmillan.

Schlegel, A. (1996). Gender issues and cross-cultural research. In Inkeles, A. & Sasaki, M. (Eds.), *Comparing nations and cultures: Readings in a cross-disciplinary perspective.* Englewood Cliffs, NJ: Prentice Hall.

Schmier, L. (1996). *Random thoughts: The humanity of teaching.* Madison, WI: Magna Publications.

Sherman, B.R. & Blackburn, R.T. (1975). Personal characteristics and teaching effectiveness of college faculty. *Journal of Educational Psychology,* 67(1), p. 124-131.

Slaughter, S. (1993). Retrenchment in the 1980s: The politics of prestige and gender. *Journal of Higher Education,* 64 (May-June), p. 250-282.

Smith, B.L. (1994). Team-teaching methods. In Prichard, K.W. & Sawyer, R.M. (Eds.), *Handbook of college teaching: Theory and applications.* Westport, CT: Greenwood Press.

Sowell, T. (1990). On the higher learning in America: Some comments. *The Public Interest,* 99, p. 68-78.

Stuart, A. & Whetten, D.A. (1985). Organizational identity. *Research in Organizational Behavior,* 7, p.263-295

Taylor, W.H. (1993). "Educating British children for European citizenship. *European Journal of Education,* 28(4), p. 439.

Tierney, W. & Bensimon, E.M. (1996). *Promotion and tenure: Community and socialization in academe.* Albany, NY: State University of New York Press.

Verdugo, R.R. (1995). Racial stratification and the use of Hispanic faculty as role models: Theory, policy, and practice. *Journal of Higher Education,* 66(6).

Welch, L (Ed).(1992). *Perspectives on minority women in higher education.* New York: Praeger Publishers.

Perspectives on Student Learning and Assessment

CHAPTER 4

Improving Teaching Through Research on Student Learning

Noel Entwistle

INTRODUCTION

Current movements towards quality assurance in higher education have led to attempts to define high quality teaching, in order to rate both departments and individual faculty members. Emphasis on the teacher, and the performance aspect of teaching, rather than the learner and the overall context within which learning takes place, perpetuates a long-standing perception about the function of teaching in higher education. Teaching does not cause learning in the direct way that is often assumed. In higher education, in particular, much of a student's learning takes place in private, through the effort to make sense of new ideas and to develop and practice new skills. Teaching contributes to this activity, but so do many other components of the overall learning environment.

This chapter looks at teaching from the learner's perspective and asks what aspects of teaching contribute to effective and high quality learning. It introduces a coherent set of concepts derived from research on student learning, carried out mainly in Europe and Australasia. It is not claimed that this particular set of concepts, or the conceptual model built from them, is definitive. There are other alternative, and equally valuable, descriptions based on other theories, concepts, and research findings (see, for example, Biggs, 1993a; Janssen, 1996). The ideas presented here, however, are intended specifically to encourage a re-conceptualization of the relationship between teaching and learning. The guiding principle is that learning outcomes depend on an interaction between the characteristics of the student, the teaching style and methods of the teacher, and the policies and practices of the department and institution. This three-way interaction is represented visually in Figure 1, introduced towards the end of the chapter. However, looking at that conceptual overview just now may help to indicate both the range of concepts to be discussed and the general line of argument to be followed.

We look first at the concepts derived from the characteristics and experiences of students, before moving on to look at the way teaching and institutional policy and practice may influence the quality of student learning. Descriptions of student characteristics draw on constructs used by traditional psychologists to describe individual differences. These constructs are based on a belief that human behavior is predictable and can be explained in terms of traits which, while they may change over time, do have a marked consistency. Psychologists tend to down-play the effects of the environment on behavior, including study behavior. In contrast, a newer set of constructs has emerged from research on student learning which emphasize that study behavior is strongly influenced by the specific academic context within which learning takes place.

The traditional psychological constructs will be discussed here, only briefly. Much more emphasis will be put on the more recent concepts derived from research on student learning, which will underpin the subsequent discussion of teaching in higher education. The newer concepts are, however, linked to the psychological concepts in ways suggested by Table 1.

Table 1

Concepts Describing Student Characteristics

Traditional psychological constructs	Concepts from research on student learning	
Prior knowledge		
Intellectual abilities	Epistemological level	Conception of learning
Personality	Learning style	Approach to learning
Motivation	Learning orientation	
	Work habits	Approach to studying
	Study methods	Forms of understanding

STUDENT CHARACTERISTICS

The student characteristics introduced here have all been shown to be associated with differences in academic performance. In the earlier research, the more general psychological constructs were used to explore the existence of relationships with study behavior and academic success or failure, but more recent work has demonstrated the limitations of this way of thinking about study behavior. In particular, the psychological research does not lead to direct implications for teaching, and the focus on the individual does not do justice to the marked effects of the learning environment.

The concepts for this discussion will be introduced in the order which reflects the top half of Figure 1 (see p. 105). Student characteristics will be explored first in terms of psychological constructs, and then using concepts derived from research on student learning. This will be followed by discussions on intellectual traits, personality and motivation, and finally, work habits of students.

Prior Knowledge, Intellectual Abilities, and Epistemological Level
One of the founding fathers of modern educational psychology, David Ausubel, stressed the crucial importance in teaching of checking on prior knowledge—what students bring to a course.

> The most important single factor influencing learning is what the learner already knows. Ascertain this and teach accordingly (Ausubel et al., 1978, p. 163).

Building knowledge on an insecure base is one of the main causes of early difficulty in studying, and yet academic staff are often unaware of important gaps in students' prior knowledge or of their serious conceptual misunderstandings (Entwistle et al., 1991). In higher education, faculty members are often lecturing to groups with widely different levels of prior knowledge, which creates problems in knowing at what level to pitch the teaching. Knowing the variation in prior knowledge can help to overcome that difficulty.

Differences in ability are well-known influences on the quality of work students produce. While the term 'ability' is widely applied by faculty to explain academic success, it is used in its everyday sense. Psychological research has sought to clarify the nature and structure of intelligence, with a continuing debate about the value of describing a general ability factor 'g.' While this general factor underlies a good deal of intelligent behavior, in academic work specific abilities are often equally important to success. (Gustafsson & Balke, 1993). The specific abilities most frequently identified are those which underpin science and engineering on the one hand (analytic skills including convergent, logical-mathematical thinking and spatial ability), and those which relate to languages and the humanities on the other (synthetic skills involving, for example, divergent thinking and linguistic ability) (Hudson, 1968; Cooley & Lohnes, 1976). Although other forms of intelligence have subsequently widened the range of abilities described (Gardner, 1984; Sternberg, 1987), the broad distinction between analytic and synthetic abilities represents a useful starting point in thinking about influences on student learning.

Departments usually have a good idea of the general intellectual level of incoming students either through Scholastic Aptitude Test (SAT) scores or from the grades obtained at the end of secondary education. Such scores and grades do not, however, give information either about specific aptitudes which may be important in individual areas of study, or about the quality of the students' thinking. These latter qualities are by no means fixed—abilities develop, and higher education is intended to encourage such development. Investigations of such developmental trends in higher education have led to the idea of *epistemological* levels (see Gardiner, 1994, pp. 12-15).

In an influential study, Perry (1970) interviewed students in successive years of study and reported a recurring developmental pattern. His epistemological scheme suggested that students progress through various stages of thinking—from what he called *dualism*, through *multiplicity*, to *relativism*, and finally to *commitment*. Dualism implies the existence of right or wrong answers to every question and, in the early stages of their course, students often expect faculty to provide the 'right' answers which they can learn and reproduce in tests and examinations. Having realized that there is, in fact, almost always more than one way of looking at a given situation, students seem to conclude that any one opinion (and particularly their own) is as good as any other (multiplicity). Only gradually are they ready to accept that conclusions rest on interpretations from objective evidence, with different interpretations justifiably being drawn, in many instances, from the same body of evidence (relativism). This degree of uncertainty disturbs many students sufficiently to impede academic progress (which depends on using relativistic thinking). Only a minority of students in Perry's study were able to take the final step and demonstrate personal commitment. This final stage may be seen in the attempts which some students make to develop coherent, individual perspectives on the discipline, with a commitment to the particular forms of interpretation which develop through them.

Although the existence of some such developmental sequence might be taken to be self-evident, many courses seem to take little account of the developmental levels of the students. It cannot be expected, for example, that students in the early years of a degree course will readily use relativistic thinking. And yet that type of thinking is so routine to academics that they often fail to appreciate the difficulties which many students face as they are confronted with apparently contradictory theories or interpretations from lecturers which can differ markedly from those they meet in their reading.

Personality and Learning Style

The term 'general ability' describes a range of related cognitive skills. In the emotional and affective areas of behavior, the term 'personality' has been used with a similarly broad coverage, although no single, integrative dimension of personality has been found. Instead, there are five traits which are currently thought to cover this area—extroversion, emotionality, conscientiousness, agreeableness, and intellectual openness, each with their opposite pole (Snow et al., 1996). Early research on the influence of personality on academic performance suggested an advantage for students low in extroversion and emotionality and high in conscientiousness. However, it was subsequently found that these relationships with extroversion and emotionality were not general: they depended on ability level, gender, and subject area (Snow et al., 1996). More recently, it has been argued that descriptions of individual differences based on studies carried out within the higher education context itself are likely to show stronger, and more readily interpretable, relationships with academic performance (Entwistle, in press).

An early study by Heath (1964), which has interesting parallels with Perry's work, followed up students throughout their university careers and sought to describe not only the main personality differences, but also developmental trends in those differences. Three personality types were identified—*non-committers* who were seen as cautious, anxious and disinclined to take risks, *hustlers* (competitive, dynamic, but insensitive), and *plungers* (impulsive, emotional, and individualistic). Over time, these distinctive differences were found to follow a developmental trend towards an ideal type— the *Reasonable Adventurer*—which integrated the most positive features of the separate personality types. The description of the Reasonable Adventurer also helps us to see how the two most distinct forms of thinking (analytic and synthetic) become integrated in academic study.

> In the pursuit of a problem, (the Reasonable Adventurer) appears to experience an alternation of involvement and detachment. The phase of involvement is an intensive and exciting period characterized by curiosity, a narrowing of attention towards some point of interest. . . . This period of involvement is then followed by a period of detachment, an extensive phase, accompanied by a reduction of tension and a broadening range of perception. . . . Here (the Reasonable Adventurer) settles back to reflect on the meaning of what was discovered during the involved stage. Meaning presumes the existence of a web of thought, a pattern of ideas to which the 'new' element can be related . . . the critical attitude.

We see, therefore, in (the Reasonable Adventurer) a combination of two mental attitudes: the curious and the critical. They do not occur simultaneously, but in alternation. (Heath, 1964, pp. 30-31)

These two 'mental attitudes' reappear in the literature under a different guise—as learning styles. A learning style represents a preference, often with a strong feeling tone, for a particular way of learning. Many researchers have found a dichotomy in style between global and articulated thinking (Witkin et al., 1977), contrasting thinking which is impulsive and intuitive with that which is cautious and logical. Torrance and Rockenstein (1988) have suggested that these styles are associated with contrasting intellectual functions of left and right brain hemispheres, hence justifying the existence of a strong dichotomy. They describe the thinking functions of the left hemisphere as verbal, analytical, and abstract thinking, and those of the right as non-verbal, spatial, concrete, analogic, intuitive, and aesthetic (echoing the distinctive intellectual abilities mentioned earlier). There is, however, evidence of a third style—integrated—which brings together the other two, as in the Reasonable Adventurer. Such integration is inevitable, in fact, if the styles represent hemispheric functions. The hemispheres do not act in isolation: they are linked, and information passes readily between the two halves of the brain, leading necessarily to some degree of integration.

A series of research studies by Pask (1976, 1988) brings the idea of learning styles closer to the context of higher education. His ideas developed out of naturalistic experiments, designed to mimic certain everyday learning situations. Students were asked to discover the principles of classification of sub-species of imaginary animals and then to 'teach-back'—explaining what they had come to understand. Pask found that the students tackled the task, and described their understandings, in two quite different ways. Some of them looked for the 'broad picture' (holist), while others tried to build up their understanding in small steps, bit by bit (serialist). The ways in which students tackled this particular task, to some extent, generalized into fairly consistent preferences for learning—their learning style. The full defining characteristics of these two styles are shown in Table 2.

Table 2
Defining features of learning styles (derived from Pask, 1976)

	Prefers step-by-step, tightly structured learning
Serialist	Focuses on the topic in isolation
	Concentrates on details and evidence
leading to	Adopts cautious logical stance, noting objections
Improvidence	May fail to seek analogies or to use own experience
	May fail to make connections with related ideas
	Prefers personal organization and a broad view
Holist	Tries to build up own overview of topic
	Thrives on illustration, analogy and anecdote
leading to	Actively seeks connections between ideas
Globetrotting	May fail to give sufficient attention to details
	May be over-ready to generalize / reach conclusions
Versatile	Can alternate readily between each style and so adapt to material presented in either style

Pask (1988) went on to demonstrate that allocating students to learning materials written in the opposite style to their own severely dislocated their learning, while matching materials to their own style facilitated learning, although to a less marked extent. As teachers are likely to teach in the ways they prefer to learn (Entwistle, 1988), the possible effects of contrasts in teaching style on student learning need to be borne in mind.

Links between learning style and areas of academic specialization have also been established (Hudson, 1968; Witkin et al., 1977), with science students tending to rely more on the serialist style and holistic thinking being used more in the humanities (Entwistle & Ramsden, 1983). But, of course, the difference between subject areas is only a matter of degree or balance. In all subject areas, both ways of thinking exist and are necessary. Science depends, particularly at its leading edge, on intuition and imagination, while evidence has to be used effectively to support arguments within the humanities. Still, the influence of stylistic preferences do affect the way people teach and learn, and so are important to the developing argument here.

Motivation and Attitudes to Courses
Another important psychological construct which affects academic success is 'motivation.' This term is used to explain the differing amounts of effort that students put into their work and implies that behavior is either 'driven'

by needs or 'pulled' towards goals. Again, no single global form of motivation has been suggested—rather, psychologists have sought to describe different types of motivation. The distinction between *intrinsic* and *extrinsic* motivation is the most fundamental (Entwistle, 1987). It indicates whether the effort derives from an interest and concern with the learning material itself, or from the rewards and punishments associated with the activity. Another important distinction is between *achievement motivation* and *fear of failure*. The former is a competitive drive which feeds on success and feelings of satisfaction and self-confidence, while the latter is more reactive, deriving from a lack of confidence and an awareness of the consequences of failure.

Differences in personality and motivation have been found in interviews with students and seemed to have influenced their study methods and even their perception of higher education.

> Some students are stable, confident and highly motivated by hope for success, while others are anxious, uncertain of themselves, and haunted by fear of failure, and yet both groups are capable of high levels of academic performance. The interview data take the differences even further. Students of differing personality and motivational types not only tackle their academic work in different ways but, from their descriptions of their university experience, they evidently perceive themselves to be in differing environments (Entwistle et al., 1974, p.393).

These differences in perception of the learning environment, deriving from individual differences, have become an important recurring theme in the more recent research on student learning, as we shall see.

The differing forms of motivation can also be seen reflected in students' *attitudes to courses* and their reasons for choosing particular courses in higher education. Yet, interviews with students also serve to warn against a too ready acceptance of psychological views on the stability of motivational traits. Not only do students have mixed motives, but their goals change as they progress through higher education—experience modifies both their expectations and their academic targets. From extensive interviews with students, Beaty has suggested that students develop a *study contract* of their own which reflects their current study goals (Beaty et al., 1997). Contracts are 're-negotiated' on the basis of experience, but at any one time their reasons for taking a particular course can be classified in terms of their general *learning orientation*. This broad concept summarizes differences in students' aims, their concerns, and the type of interest they have in the course in terms of four main orientations—vocational, academic, personal, and social (see Table 3). But perhaps the most marked influence on the way they subsequently study comes from whether their interest in the course is *intrinsic*—in the content of the course itself—or *extrinsic*—in the other benefits the course might bring.

Table 3
Learning Orientations: Aims, Concerns, and Interests
(adapted from Beaty et al., 1997)

Orientation	Interest	Aim	Concerns
Vocational	Intrinsic	Training	Relevance of course to future career
	Extrinsic	Qualification	Recognition of qualification's worth
Academic	Intrinsic	Intellectual interest	Choosing stimulating lectures
	Extrinsic	Educational progression	Grades and academic progress
Personal	Intrinsic	Self-improvement	Challenging, interesting material
	Extrinsic	Proof of capability	Feedback and passing the course
Social	Extrinsic	Having a good time	Facilities for sport and social activities

Beaty is quick to stress that these are *analytic categories*—they do not describe individuals or types. The categories can be used to describe differences between students, but no individual can be expected to fit readily into any single category. Rather, it is the relative strength of each category, and the balance between them, which describes the individual. This warning about the use of descriptive categories applies to all qualitative research on student learning and needs to be kept firmly in mind in thinking about the implications of the research findings.

Work Habits and Study Skills
This section introduces some of the earliest research on student learning which examined the ways in which students organized their studying, and the relative strength of their study skills. Although this research does not describe psychological traits, as such, the methodology used implies consistency in the ways in which students work, and the studies investigated how different methods of studying were related to academic achievement.

While students tend to develop somewhat idiosyncratic ways of studying, most successful students report, in interviews, methods which are well-organized and systematic, although the actual systems used vary widely (Small, 1966). Much of the research in this area has been carried out using questionnaires and, in this research too, organized studying came out as one of the factors which most consistently correlated with academic performance (Biggs, 1987, 1993b). When students are asked how long they spend in classes and independent teaching studying, in Britain at least, a consistent pattern is found. Although there are large individual differences, on average students spend some 40 hours a week working, no matter what the subject area. If the classtime hours are long, then independent study time is correspondingly reduced (Entwistle & Entwistle, 1970).

Psychologists have looked at the general cognitive skills believed to underpin study activities, and investigated whether these skills can be developed through systematic training. The main emphasis in this research has been on the degree of elaboration used in studying. In other words, it has asked whether the material to be learned has been accepted as it stands, or worked on to see how it relates to other topics and to previous knowledge. Weinstein (1988) has described the specific types of skill which students need to develop, including information processing (e.g., reasoning, and the elaboration of ideas through the use of images or analogies) and selecting main ideas (identifying the key points in lectures or in a book). She also identified the importance of time management, concentration, self-testing, and test strategies, and demonstrated that systematic training in these skills can improve subsequent academic performance.

Recent theoretical work has been stressing the importance of *metacognitive awareness*—encouraging students to think about their ways of learning in relation to what is required by teachers (Brown, 1987), to monitor and regulate their own studying (*self-regulation)*, and to recognize their own strengths and weaknesses, adjusting their learning strategies accordingly (Pintrich & Garcia, 1994; Meyer, Cliff, & Dunne, 1994; Vermunt, 1996). This theoretical orientation departs from an emphasis on the training of specific skills, and replaces it with a way of thinking about studying and learning which has a broader focus and greater transferability into a range of future learning situations. It also leads to an alternative to skills training, which will be discussed later on.

CONCEPTS DERIVED FROM RESEARCH ON STUDENT LEARNING

So far, we have described characteristics of students in terms of individual differences identified by psychologists and somewhat related concepts emerging from research on student learning. The psychological constructs describe consistencies in human behavior, as we have seen. We now move on to a group of concepts which point up more strongly the influence of teaching, assessment, and the learning environment in general. Being based on interviews with students, these concepts have a greater ecological validity than the psychological constructs, although they are less firmly established. The ecological validity, however, allows staff and students to grasp the meaning of the terms from their own experience, rather than facing technical terms which seem less relevant to their main concerns.

Much of the research evidence presented in this and subsequent sections is derived from the rigorous qualitative analysis of interview transcripts. The initial purpose of this research was to try to understand the experience of higher education from the student's perspective. The concepts were used to describe that experience but, in the interviews, students also commented on the reasons why they were studying in particular ways. These comments began to change the focus of the research towards the influences of particular types of teaching and assessment on the quality of the student's learning.

CONCEPTIONS OF LEARNING, AND APPROACHES TO LEARNING AND STUDYING

The most general concept which has emerged from this qualitative research is that of *conception of learning* (Säljö, 1979; Marton & Säljö, 1997), which shows a developmental trend not dissimilar to the progression from dualism to relativism in Perry's scheme (Marton et al., 1997).

Students differ in whether they see learning as mainly a matter of memorizing and *reproducing* knowledge in ways acceptable to the teacher, or as a process of *transforming* the incoming information and ideas as they extract personal meaning from it. The full hierarchy of conceptions identified in the research studies is shown in Table 4.

Table 4

A hierarchy of conceptions of learning
(adapted from Marton & Säljö, 1997)

Learning is seen as involving	
A quantitative increase in knowledge	*Reproducing*
Memorizing what is required	
Acquiring facts and procedures for subsequent use	
Abstracting meaning for yourself	
An interpretative process aimed at understanding reality	
Developing as a person	*Transforming*

The conception of learning, together with the reasons for studying (learning orientation), substantially affects the ways in which students tackle everyday academic tasks. A whole series of research studies has used qualitative analyses of interview transcripts to explore learning and studying both in naturalistic experiments and in everyday studying (Marton et al., 1997). The starting point was an investigation into how students went about reading (Marton & Säljö, 1976). Students were asked, individually, to read an academic article and were told that they would be asked questions on it afterwards. It became clear from the transcripts that students had interpreted this instruction very differently, and their ability to answer questions about the meaning of the text depended on how they had decided to tackle the task. Some students had sought a thorough understanding of the author's message, while others had relied on 'question-spotting'—learning just those pieces of information expected to come up in the test. This distinction was gradually refined through qualitative analysis to produce a descriptive concept with two categories—deep and surface *approaches to learning*.

In the deep approach, the intention to extract meaning leads to active learning processes which concentrate on both ideas and evidence, in ways reminiscent of Perry's description of relativistic reasoning and also of the alternation between 'the curious and the critical' found in Heath's Reasonable Adventurer. In the surface approach, the intention is to cope with the task in a minimalist fashion, which deflects attention from any underlying meaning and leads to the concentration on isolated aspects of the text and too great a reliance on rote learning.

Table 5
Defining features of approaches to learning and studying

Surface Approach	*Reproducing*
Intention—to cope with course requirements	**by**

Studying without reflecting on either purpose or strategy
Treating the course as unrelated bits of knowledge
Memorizing facts and procedures routinely

Finding difficulty in making sense of new ideas presented
Feeling undue pressure and worry about work

Deep Approach	*Transforming*
Intention—to understand ideas for yourself	**by**

Relating ideas to previous knowledge and experience
Looking for patterns and underlying principles

Checking evidence and relating it to conclusions
Examining logic and argument cautiously and critically

Becoming actively interested in the course content

Strategic Approach	*Organizing*
Intention—to achieve the highest possible grades	**by**

Putting consistent effort into studying
Finding the right conditions and materials for studying
Managing time and effort effectively

Being alert to assessment requirements and criteria
Gearing work to the perceived preferences of lecturers

The original naturalistic experiment used a realistically complex text, but it was not part of the syllabus. Subsequent interviews have asked students about their experiences of everyday studying. Again, the distinction between deep and surface approaches came out remarkably clearly (Entwistle & Ramsden, 1983), and can be seen in the responses of electrical engineering students who had been asked about their ways of studying (Entwistle et al., 1989).

Interviewer:

Tell me something about how you are tackling this course, and how you work on the problem sheets you are given.

Surface Approach:

I suppose I'm mainly concerned about being able to remember all the important facts and theories that we've been given in the lectures. We are given an awful lot of stuff to learn, so I just plough through it as best I can. I try to take it all down in the lectures, and then go over it until I'm sure they won't catch me out in the exams . . . . (With the problem sheets) the first step is to decide which part of the lecture course the problem comes from. Then I look through my notes until I find an example that looks similar, and I try it out. Basically, I just apply the formula and see if it works. If it doesn't, I look for another example, and try a different formula. Usually it's fairly obvious which formula fits the problem, but sometimes it doesn't seem to work out, and then I'm really stuck.

Deep Approach:

It is not easy, you know. There is a great deal to cover, and I am not satisfied unless I really understand what we're given. I take quite full notes, but afterwards I go through them and check on things which I'm not clear about. I find that working through the problem sheets we're given is a good way to test whether I know how to apply the theory covered in lectures, and I do that regularly. Once you realize what lies behind the problems—that's the physics of it and what makes it a problem—then you can do them. You get a kick out of it too, when it all begins to make sense. Applying the right formula is not difficult, once you know you are on the right lines.

(adapted from Entwistle et al., 1989)

The interviews on everyday studying have also drawn attention to the pervasive influence of assessment procedures on learning and studying. Ramsden found it necessary to introduce an additional category—*strategic approach*—in which the intention was to achieve the highest possible grades, by using organized study methods and good time-management (Entwistle & Ramsden, 1983). This approach also involved an alertness to the assessment process. As one student commented in an earlier study:

I play the examination game. The examiners play it, so we play it too
.... The technique involves knowing what's going to be in the exam
and how it's going to be marked. You can acquire these techniques
from sitting in a lecturer's class, getting ideas from his point of view,
the form of his notes, and the books he has written—and this is separate to picking up the actual work content (Miller & Parlett, 1974).

This extract suggests a student who had two distinct focuses of concern
within the lecture—the academic content and the demands of the assessment system. The interest in the content is typical of a deep approach, but
the alertness to assessment requirements is typically strategic.

Whereas the distinction between deep and surface approaches was derived from analyses which focused on extracting meaning from text, the strategic approach, together with its opposite—the *apathetic approach* (Tait &
Entwistle, 1996)—indicates how students act in everyday study situations.
They are therefore better described as *approaches to studying.*

Other researchers have subsequently found equivalent differences in the
way students tackle a wide range of academic tasks (Marton et al., 1997),
suggesting that these differing approaches to learning and studying are of
wide significance and applicability (also see Biggs, 1987, 1993b). Table 5
draws together the defining features of the three main approaches, as they
have been described in a wide range of studies. In the deep approach, as we
have seen, the student is essentially *transforming* the learning material in the
process of making sense of it, while a student adopting a surface approach
is simply *reproducing* what has been presented by the lecturer. In the strategic approach, the emphasis is on *organizing* time and effort effectively to meet
the perceived assessment requirements and to maximize the reward in terms
of grades (see, also, Becker et al., 1968).

The widespread use of these categories in staff development activities has
brought with it some serious over-simplifications and misunderstandings.
Sometimes, there has been a tendency to treat approaches to learning as traits
describing students, rather than as categories describing students' reactions
to a particular task in a specific learning context. In practice, students do
develop study habits which lead to a reliance on one or other approach, and
so to a certain consistency, but the context still has an important influence.
Students do not use the same approach across all courses, or even on all topics
and tasks within the same course (Entwistle & Ramsden, 1983). Moreover,
time constraints prevent students being able to adopt the deep approach consistently, even when that is the approach they prefer. Adopting a deep ap-

Table 6

Contrasting conceptions of teaching

Teacher focus	
Information transfer	• conveying information and covering the syllabus • making sure that necessary knowledge and skills are acquired • maximizing the general level of performance of the class
Conceptual understanding	• developing conceptual understanding and employment-related transferable skills
Conceptual change	• awakening and maintaining students' interest in the subject • encouraging students to think independently and imaginatively • helping students to develop personal and social skills, and a broader perspective on their future life and vocation
Student focus	

proach involves a substantial investment of time, and students have to tread a wary path between their academic interests and the time pressures created by deadlines and backlogs of work. Listing the defining features of each approach also invites over-simplification. Those features serve as general guidelines, but the approach needs to be re-interpreted, to some extent, within each area of study or discipline. A deep approach will always imply the intention to understand, but the ways of thinking involved in reaching understanding, and the balance between them, will vary across subject areas. The deep approach may, on occasions, require the use of memorization—of terms or other details—but such memorization is within an overall framework through which understanding is being sought. Within the surface approach, however, memorization tends to focus on lecture notes and specific pieces of information *in isolation,* with the intention of being able to reproduce them in the form they were originally learned without elaboration or re-structuring. Memorization can thus be part of the alternation between different ways of thinking needed for thorough understanding, particularly in the scientific areas of study, but on its own it is characteristic of a limited approach to learning which is inappropriate as the main way of learning within a degree course.

It is logically impossible to adopt, simultaneously, a deep and a surface approach, but a combination of deep and strategic approaches is commonly found, while surface and apathetic approaches also go together. The combination of deep and strategic approaches to studying can be clearly seen as students prepare for essay examinations (Entwistle & Entwistle, 1997), with one student commenting:

The more I have done exams, the more I'd liken them to a performance, like being on a stage . . . having not so much to present the fact that you know a vast amount, but having to perform well with what you do know. . . . Sort of, playing to the gallery . . . I was very conscious of being outside what I was writing. (p. 150)

Later on, we shall examine the effects of assessment on approaches to learning in more detail, seeing how the perceived demands of the assessment procedures influence approaches to learning and learning outcomes.

Influences of Teaching on Learning
The research which introduced the idea of the strategic approach to studying (Entwistle & Ramsden, 1983) also began mapping out the various influences of teaching on learning. Since then, additional aspects of teaching, assessment, and the learning environment as a whole, have been shown to affect the quality of student learning. However, this area of research is less fully developed than that on student learning itself, with much left to be done. The following sections have to rely, to some extent, on development work to fill the gaps left by research studies.

This section concentrates on how the individual faculty member can influence learning through teaching, while the subsequent one outlines the influences of assessment procedures and other policies and practices which are, to a greater extent, under the control of departments or institutions. Specifically, this section introduces the ideas of conceptions of teaching and approaches to teaching, styles and methods of teaching, and the selection and organizing of content.

CONCEPTIONS OF TEACHING AND APPROACHES TO TEACHING

Just as students were found to differ in what they believe learning to require of them, so academic staff have been shown to differ in what they understand teaching to involve. Faculty members develop what Fox (1983) described as 'personal theories of teaching.' In his study, when lecturers were asked "What do you mean by *teaching?*", four basic conceptions emerged.

There is the 'transfer theory' which treats knowledge as a commodity to be transferred from one vessel to another. There is the 'shaping theory'—moulding students to a predetermined pattern. Thirdly, there is a 'traveling theory' . . . (where there are) hills to be climbed for better viewpoints, with the teacher as . . . an expert guide. Finally, there is the 'growing theory' which focuses more attention on the intellectual and emotional development of the learner. (p. 151)

Fox went on to argue that the particular theory espoused by a lecturer would affect not only the choice of teaching methods and the style of presentation but also attitudes towards innovative teaching and training programs. Contrasting theories of teaching are rooted in well-established belief systems. It cannot be a surprise, therefore, that attempts to introduce radical innovations are often vigorously opposed by people who have more conservative views on teaching. In one study, for example, lecturers who endorsed traditional teaching methods, angrily denounced the experimental introduction of innovative methods in one area of the curriculum (Mahmoud, 1989).

Ramsden (1992) describes theories of teaching in terms of three progressively more sophisticated conceptions—teaching as telling, as organizing student activity, and as making learning possible. These distinctions have been developed further by Prosser et al. (1994). Their conceptions of teaching again have three main divisions—transmitting information, helping students to acquire the concepts of the discipline, and helping students to develop and change their own conceptions. But underlying these conceptions of teaching are two contrasts. Firstly, there is a distinction between viewing teaching from the perspective of staff and institution, or from that of the student. And then there is a related contrast between seeing teaching as transmitting information, or as encouraging learning. In the small-scale study reported by Prosser and his colleagues, just under half of the science lecturers in their sample saw teaching as transmitting information, a quarter were in the second category, while less than one in ten saw teaching as helping to develop students' own conceptions.

Several other studies have suggested similar ways of describing conceptions of teaching (e.g. Samuelowicz & Bain, 1992), which can be summarized through the set of categories presented in Table 6. These categories show a strong parallel with the conceptions of learning presented earlier in Table 4. The emphasis on information transfer implies a reproductive conception of learning, while a concern for awakening interest indicates a transformational conception. Trigwell and Prosser (1996a) see conceptions of teaching as forming a 'nested hierarchy,' in which the encouragement of transformational learning subsumes the emphasis on information transfer. The ability to integrate the student focus with the teacher focus is certainly a more complete view of teaching, but it is also possible to see the extreme categories as indicating contrasting teaching styles, with only a minority of 'versatile' teachers being able to achieve full integration.

The research on student learning showed how students' conceptions of learning led to equivalent approaches to learning and studying. It is reasonable, therefore, to anticipate that lecturers will also show coherence between their conceptions of learning, their conceptions of teaching, and their approaches to teaching. Edited extracts from the interview of one of the science lecturers (described above) can be used to illustrate these expected connections.

Conception of learning

The kind of learning we want to have in education is a process of invention, rather than a process of ingestion of information. If you're really going to learn something, then you have to invent it for yourself. It doesn't matter that someone three or four hundred years ago was the first person to invent this, the fact that you're engaged in the same sort of inquiry as they were, doesn't take away from you the act of invention on your part.

Conception of teaching

I like to make a distinction between having something as a presence and something somewhat removed from that, as a concept. Lectures provide a presence that a book doesn't, and you can utilize that in the lecture by a directly engaging question. The lecturer can actually engage (the student) in that question, in a much more interactive mode. Teaching also has a theatrical element to it. I suppose I'm saying that the function of the lecture is to bring inquiry to life, the inquiry that learning is.

Approach to teaching

Students learn, over the years, to get into *lecture mode* very readily. What they'll do is walk into a lecture theater, and it's automatic— most of the brain shuts down, and all that's left active is this very narrow channel which connects the eye to the hand. The whole basis for my style of lecturing is to defeat that lecture mode, to give another dimension an opportunity to operate. I'm constantly challenging the students in the lecture to think something through for themselves. I think that generates a certain sense of . . . I think intrigue is a good word, but wonderment is another one, appreciation is another one, and understanding is related to that. (And) in my preparation I actually have to create this (situation) every time, rather than just remember (the content). (The lecture) is a conversation in which there's active listening involved. (Prosser, personal communication)

Running through this extract is the lecturer's conviction that learning, and teaching, involve the active construction of meaning, and that conviction is then expressed through the teaching methods adopted. These connections may seem to be logically inevitable—they certainly emerge as empirical relationships in recent analyses (Trigwell et al., 1994; Trigwell & Prosser, 1996b). It does seem, however, that some teachers who have a student-centered view of teaching are constrained by external pressures to adopt teaching approaches which rely more on information transfer, and that may well be a developing trend as economy becomes the watchword in higher education. In interviews, even lecturers rated as excellent are now expressing concern with the current institutional climate they are experiencing.

(Their) multiple roles led to a feeling of being overburdened, and exhausted from (trying) to find a balance between the effort and attention required for good teaching and the demands of their other roles. . . . Administrative structures were seen to get in the way of the teaching process; there was an overemphasis on 'accountability,' and administrators were seen as watchdogs rather than supporters of teaching. (Andrews et al., 1996, p. 88)

It is reasonable to expect that an approach to teaching intended to create conceptual change will actively encourage students to develop a deep approach. Already, it has been shown that students who habitually adopt a deep approach prefer teaching which is challenging and encourages independent thinking (Entwistle & Tait, 1990). And there are close connections, too, between students' approaches to studying and the way they perceive their teaching and learning environment as a whole (Meyer, 1991). The aspects of teaching found most likely to encourage a deep approach can now to be elaborated more fully.

Styles and Methods of Teaching
A more general analysis of the effects of various methods of teaching on learning has already been published (Entwistle, 1992). Here, we shall illustrate these effects by concentrating on the ways in which different lecturing styles

and practices influence students' approaches to learning, but with discussion classes being briefly considered as well.

Although the use of lectures has been heavily criticized in the research literature (see, for example, Gardiner, 1994), it is still the most common form of teaching in higher education. In spite of the criticisms, it can still be argued that a *good* lecture is the most appropriate way of introducing a topic and providing a conceptual map of the subject. It can also be used to increase student motivation and to convey a distinctive way of thinking about the discipline (Brown & Atkins, 1988). However, a review of the literature indicated that most lectures were ineffective, presenting too much detail and too little illustrative material, and offering few opportunities for active involvement by the students (Gardiner, 1994). Direct observations of lectures have also produced an unflattering description of lecturing styles. For example, Brown and Bahktar (1983) identified five distinct categories based mainly on the way information was organized and presented. Some lecturers produced ineffective, disorganized presentations (described in two categories—*amorphous* and *self-doubters*). A stylistic difference could be seen between *oral* lecturers who wove intricate verbal webs but lacked clear structure or audio-visual support (possibly holists), and *information providers* who followed their notes closely in providing a tedious amount of detail (serialists). Finally, there were the *exemplary* lecturers (versatile) who had a clear set of objectives, avoided too much detail in the lectures (providing handouts or recommended reading for that purpose), and used audio-visual aids to enliven their presentations.

When students are asked about their experiences of lectures, either in interviews (Hodgson, 1997; Ramsden, 1992, 1997) or through evaluation questionnaires (Marsh, 1987), a clear picture emerges of what constitutes 'good lectures' from the student's perspective. They are described in terms of seven main categories—level, pace, structure, clarity, explanation, enthusiasm, and empathy. And of these, the comments of students suggest that it is the 'three E's'—explanation, enthusiasm, and empathy—that are the most likely to support a deep approach to learning.

The quality of the explanation affects the extent to which students are encouraged, and find it easy, to make sense of the topic in their own way. Explanations can also be used to model the distinctive forms of argument and use of evidence adopted in the discipline. Brown and Atkins (1988) emphasize the value of evoking intellectual curiosity through the use of problems or paradoxes and show how good explanations depend on being well-suited both to the topic and to the students' existing knowledge, and on the extensive use of examples, analogies, metaphors, and personal anecdotes. Combining a supporting framework within the lecture (serialist) with many links to related ideas (holist) is recognizably a versatile style of lecturing.

The enthusiasm shown by the lecturer communicates itself to students and arouses interest. Some lecturers may even create a 'conversion experience' through the "vicarious experience of relevance" (Hodgson, 1997), which shifts the student from a surface to a deep approach. Finally, students comment on the lecturer's perceived concern with them as learners—concern about potential difficulties in the subject matter and about the progress they are making. In the literature, such concern is described as 'empathy.' It is also shown by the readiness to answer questions and to provide opportunities for discussion (Brown & Atkins, 1988). However, there may be a more fundamental aspect of empathy. Teaching depends on being able to put oneself in the position of the learners—to recognize what is needed to help bridge the gulf between initial incomprehension and the subsequent dawning of understanding.

There can, however, be too much emphasis placed on techniques of teaching. A very recent study by Andrews et al. (1996) has found that lecturers rated by their senior colleagues as 'excellent' had consistent views about the nature of teaching and yet had quite different methods of achieving their goals.

> The professors emphasized a balance between process and content (in their teaching): however, mastery of content was assumed as a starting place for the process to truly begin. They considered specific techniques of teaching to be subordinate tools, to be used as situations dictated . . . . Most importantly, excellent teachers seem to want to facilitate a meaningful approach (deep) to learning rather than a reproducing (surface) approach . . . . (They also make) use of self-reflection to develop a model (either formal or informal) for teaching within a particular context; they then attempt to 'live the model,' and be authentic to and congruent with their model . . . . (pp. 98, 101, 86-87)

Thorough preparation and organization were seen by these lecturers as crucial, balanced by flexible implementation, but central to their practice was a concern to keep the subject alive for their students, to reveal their way of thinking about the subject, and to have a relationship with the students which demonstrated respect and concern for the learning taking place.

Turning now to discussion classes, the literature typically emphasizes the over-riding importance of allowing students time to talk. All too often discussions are dominated by the tutor who feels obliged to correct every error and drive the discussion in predetermined directions (Jaques, 1985). Freedom to talk, however, by no means guarantees good learning, as undirected student discussion often becomes anecdotal or irrelevant. A very recent study (Anderson, 1997) has shown how the most effective tutors provide a climate within which students become relaxed and ready to contribute and then challenge the students to think more clearly and guide them towards a deeper understanding of the topics they are discussing.

> Tutors in their dual roles as 'gatekeepers' for a discipline and guides to the less expert have to lead students towards ways of construing particular topics or problem situations in an appropriate fashion. This might be perceived as a *constraining* function. Yet, tutors are, at the same time, *enabling* novices to gain new framing perspectives on topics and so develop their abilities. They are assisting students to gain the knowledge and ways of acting needed for them to participate more fully in academic life . . . (p. 197).

This description indicates how tutors can support and shape understanding, but Anderson also stresses the importance of the *moral order* of discussion classes. Students had

> a clear expectation that tutors . . . would act to re-direct a discussion which had gone "a bit astray" . . . "to correct" or "to clarify" student contributions to the discussion . . . . (But they also) assumed that any 'corrective' teaching actions would be carried out in a socially sensitive manner which would not threaten the student's public face of competence . . .(being used) solely for the *purpose* of enhancing students' understanding (p. 196).

Selection and Organizing of Content

In a wide range of studies and commentaries on teaching in higher education, the importance of the selection of content, and its organization into a coherent sequence, is stressed (e.g., Leinhardt & Greeno, 1986). The content chosen for a course, or within a lecture, has a direct and immediate impact on the quality of learning, in two main ways—the volume of material which is included in the syllabus and the extent to which the material chosen is perceived as interesting and relevant by the students.

An important balance has to be struck by a lecturer between coverage and thoroughness. There is often a view expressed that all the required material has to be 'covered' in the lecture course (Entwistle et al., 1989). This can lead to a hurried and inadequate treatment of topics. While lecturers may feel comfortable that these topics have been 'covered,' students find it difficult to understand what has not been thoroughly explained. Coverage does not ensure learning; rather, it may prevent it. Here, the term 'thoroughness' is being used to indicate the need for full explanations which draw on a variety of examples and illustrations (Brown & Atkins, 1996), not an emphasis on specific detail. In the sciences, in particular, the volume of material included in lecture courses often increases year by year. Keeping up to date with new developments expands syllabuses, but little material is dropped. Where students feel that they are being 'bombarded' by a seemingly endless flow of new and detailed information, a surface approach is almost inevitably adopted as a coping ploy (Entwistle et al., 1989).

In planning a lecture course, it is crucial to consider the best ways of evoking and maintaining interest, since this is the essential motivating force behind a deep approach to learning. Relevance is all too often taken for granted by staff. It is essential to help students perceive relevance by justifying the importance of topics at the start of a course, and explaining the importance of new topics, as they are introduced. Various techniques can also be built into the course to maintain interest, just some of which are: introducing professional experiences; posing and thinking through problems; and bringing to life major breakthroughs in the discipline in story form (Brown & Atkins, 1988).

Decisions about the way topics are ordered are also important in generating and maintaining interest. Lecturers often look for a logical order in terms of traditional ways of treating a topic. But what is logical within a formal treatment of a topic may not be the best way to generate interest. Ausubel (1985) stressed the importance of finding an order which has a pedagogical logic. Generally speaking, practical or professional examples illustrating major concepts or principles make a firmer starting point than abstract definitions of ideas. However, Ausubel believes that some 'ideational scaffolding' is necessary, after evoking initial interest, and suggests the use of an *advance organizer* to provide a conceptual framework into which subsequent material can be fitted. An organizer should be more than an initial overview; it should provide a principle, or a series of related principles, to which details or examples presented subsequently can be readily related. Thereafter, explicit linking statements to show how the lecture or course is developing, and regular short summaries, help students to make connections as they build up their own understanding (McKeachie, 1994).

INSTITUTIONAL POLICIES AND PRACTICE

This next section explores another series of influences on the quality of learning—*policy on teaching*—which is less under the control of the faculty member, although some elements of individual control generally remain. Again, the literature on student learning is being used to identify the aspects of institutional policies and practice which are known to influence approaches to learning and studying, and through them, learning outcomes. This section highlights workload, freedom of choice, study skills support, library provision, learning materials, course design and objectives, and departmental teaching ethos. It begins, however, with the most important of these departmental characteristics—the nature of the assessment procedures, together with the feedback provided to students on their work and academic progress.

Assessment Procedures and Feedback to Students

There are several studies which show how students' perceptions of assessment procedures affect their studying. Gibbs (1981), for example, describes how first-year psychology students had ignored important background reading, because they had been led to believe, falsely, that their practical reports were more influential on their overall marks. Another example comes from changes in the form of a medical examination which led students to concentrate on learning theory rather than spending time on the wards, because they believed that ward assessments were generally favorable. This innovation had the opposite effect to what had been intended (Newble & Jaeger, 1983).

The form of the examination has also been shown to affect the approach to learning adopted by students. Multiple-choice tests are generally seen by students as requiring little more than rote learning, and so they are likely to encourage a surface approach to learning. This perception of multiple-choice tests and other similar test procedures seems to be accurate. Gardiner (1994) reviewed several research studies, all of which indicated that faculty do not generally produce tests which necessitate the use of higher-order thinking. In a study where a direct comparison was made between multiple choice testing and essay-type examinations, it was found that multiple-choice testing shifted the class as a whole towards higher scores on the surface approach (although the rank order of scores remained much the same) (Thomas & Bain, 1984). Of course, multiple-choice tests *can* be designed to test higher-

order thinking, and questions set in essay examinations *can* lead to reproductive learning, if they focus too directly on the information presented in
lectures (Entwistle & Entwistle, 1997).

Students adopting a strategic approach are particularly aware of the relationship between forms of assessment and ways of studying. Such students
vary their approaches to studying to meet the perceived requirements of the
different techniques of assessment they meet. As one student said about the
short-answer tests which were regularly set in his department:

> I hate to say it, but what you've got to do is have a list of the 'facts'—
> you write down ten important points and memorize those, then you'll
> do all right in the test . . . . If you can give a bit of factual informa-
> tion—so and so did that, and concluded that—for two sides of writ-
> ing, then you'll get a good mark. (Ramsden, 1997, p. 198)

That same student had a very different strategy for dealing with the more
demanding essay examinations which came at the end of the year and
achieved a First-class degree.

Students need to have prompt and regular feedback on their academic
progress, not just in the form of grades, but also through detailed comments
on the quality of their work. Effective learning depends crucially on knowing precisely what may be wrong and how to overcome deficiencies. And
yet assessment arrangements often fail to provide early enough indications
about progress, and the comments made by faculty on assignments can be
seen by students as demoralizing or incomprehensible (Hounsell, 1987).

Workload and Choice
The deep approach to learning takes time. When discussing work habits
earlier, it was noted that students in different subject areas, on average, spent
about the same amount of time working. If there is a large amount of contact time, then there will be correspondingly less time spent on independent
studying. In the applied sciences in particular, contact hours tend to be high,
and students comment on the difficulties this creates for them. They tend
not to read books, or discuss their work. They concentrate on completing
assignments in an effort to cope with what many of them see as unreason-
able demands from staff (Entwistle et al., 1989).

Evidence for a statistical relationship between perceived workload and approaches to learning came from a large-scale survey of British universities
(Entwistle & Ramsden, 1983). A heavy workload was associated with a sur-

face approach to learning. In the same study, it was also found that 'freedom in learning'—opportunities to choose course units and assignments—seemed to encourage a deep approach. Given that interest has been shown to underpin the deep approach, this relationship with choice is almost inevitable.

Study Skills Support

As student intakes into higher education become more heterogeneous, the importance of systematic study skills support is becoming more generally accepted—at least in the rhetoric of quality management. Actual provision is, however, lagging seriously behind this rhetoric, in spite of the growing emphasis on developing transferable skills (Gardiner, 1994).

Students are often expected by staff to have developed the necessary study skills while at school, but studying in higher education involves a different set of activities—taking lecture notes, taking part in discussions, writing essays, producing laboratory reports, taking examinations but, above all, studying independently without the direct support of a teacher. Advice on study skills is often presented as a series of instructions—a 'recipe book' approach (Nisbet, 1988)—which implies that there are 'right' and 'wrong' ways of studying. Suggestions on these ways of working are drawn from personal experience and also from psychological research, some of which is of dubious applicability to the context of higher education (Gibbs, 1981). Such advice is not only too dogmatic in tone, but it is often perceived by students as being unrealistically demanding of time, and too general to be applied within specific courses of study.

Recent efforts at supporting effective studying have moved the emphasis away from the 'recipe book' approach, focusing instead on developing metacognitive awareness—helping students to understand their own strengths and weaknesses, and monitoring the success of the methods they are using (Biggs, 1987; Ramsden & Martin, 1987; Meyer, Cliff, & Dunne, 1994). Workshops of this kind involve students in comparing and contrasting their own ways of studying (Gibbs, 1981), or draw on the student learning literature to explain what is involved in a deep, strategic approach to studying (Tait & Entwistle, 1996). 'Learning to learn' courses do foster awareness of the need to develop study skills, but it generally proves easier to shift students away from a surface approach, than to increase the use of deep approaches. Students apparently perceive a deep approach to be both more difficult and more risky (Norton & Dickins, 1995). Moreover, students have to be persuaded that spending time on improving their study skills is a good, medium-term investment of their time, and that can only be done by building skills training into curricula and ensuring that staff reinforce its importance through their attitudes and comments.

Library Provision and Learning Materials
The opportunities students have for effective independent studying depend on the availability of appropriate learning materials. Adequate library provision is the most obvious and crucial need, but so also is the choice of textbooks which encourage a deep approach to learning. All too few textbooks provide explanations and illustrations designed to encourage understanding. Again, detailed coverage of the syllabus often seems to take precedence over thorough explanation (Eizenberg, 1988).

Some attempts have been made to replace lectures by resource materials from which students learn on their own—indeed, distance learning depends on the production of such materials. Learning materials have the advantage that students can return again and again to topics which cause them difficulty, while the quality of the explanations provided can be refined by discussion with several colleagues (Verduin & Clark, 1991). However, these materials inevitably lack the 'presence' provided by face-to-face teaching.

Technology-based learning materials potentially offer even greater advantages, both through almost instantaneous access to reference materials, and through the use of hypermedia techniques which allow progressively more detailed explanations and illustrations to be provided (Laurillard, 1993, 1997). What is still far from clear, however, is the type of technology-based learning materials which will foster deep approaches to learning in the different subject areas. Surprisingly little research has been carried out on this so far. Work will also be needed to discover just how much of a student's curriculum can be presented in this way without affecting the important social and personal aspects of studying.

Learning materials are also routinely supplied through lecture handouts, although these are variable in purpose and quality. Handouts generally provide copies of all the overheads presented during lectures, the additional details needed to supplement the overviews provided in the lectures, and the references which students are expected to follow up in subsequent work. But if deep approaches to learning are to be encouraged, then handouts also need to provoke thinking, by asking open-ended questions and by setting specific tasks which encourage both thinking and additional reading. Through extensive development work in schools, Perkins and his colleagues at Harvard have developed a 'teaching for understanding' framework (see Perkins &

Blythe, 1994). Their approach depends on the provision of *understanding performances*—tasks which necessitate the demonstration of understanding. Perkins argues that it is through working on a succession of such understanding performances that students develop the habit of seeking personal understanding.

Course Design and Objectives

Until quite recently, course design in traditional British universities might well be carried out by a single faculty member, who would submit just a course outline of the topics to be covered together with an indicative reading list. Course design is increasingly being seen as the work of a course team, and the scrutiny of new courses, together with the review of existing courses, is being carried out in a more thorough and systematic manner. Course design now usually starts from the specification of learning goals, objectives, and outcomes. Ideally, course design should also take into account the anticipated variations among the students who will be taking the course—variations in prior knowledge, epistemological levels, and learning orientations—before justifying the methods of teaching in relation to these differences and the course objectives. The course design would also be expected to show how the assignments and methods of assessment to be used take into account the varying strengths of students as well as covering the whole range of expected learning outcomes.

Unfortunately, emphasis on course approval procedures may lead to excellent documentation and rhetoric but may not significantly affect the quality of the actual teaching. Effective course monitoring procedures are needed which go beyond statistical evidence on pass rates to judge the extent to which the teaching is encouraging high quality learning. Feedback questionnaires have been designed recently which probe the experience of students in this way, and provide information to faculty which can be used to generate active reconsideration of the whole rationale of teaching provision (Ramsden, 1991).

DEPARTMENTAL TEACHING ETHOS

Departments give differing emphases to teaching and research. In Britain at least, research is currently bringing much greater financial reward both to departments (through current funding policy) and to individual faculty members (through promotion opportunities). While the accepted wisdom in universities is that high quality research and good teaching necessarily go together, studies of this link suggest that the relationship is near zero

(Feldman, 1987; Ramsden & Moses, 1992). The skills of research and effective teaching are so different that this lack of relationship at lecturer level is almost inevitable (Gardiner, 1994), while departments whose policies direct effort and reward towards research outputs are unlikely to give equal encouragement to teaching. There are, however, important exceptions, where departments with outstanding research reputations, nevertheless are equally concerned about providing excellent learning opportunities for students. In those circumstances, the research activity will most certainly strengthen and enliven the teaching. The research evidence, however, suggests strongly that this is the exception rather than the rule.

In a previous section, the very different conceptions of teaching held by faculty members were discussed, with a distinction being made at the extremes, between teaching as transmitting information and teaching as supporting student learning. Such differences can be seen between departments as well, leading to the idea of *departmental teaching ethos*. So far, very little research has been directed at describing such differences and their influences on learning, but in one recent Australia study, there was

> some evidence . . . that a department which sees teaching as being about transmission of information is more likely to have students adopting a surface approach to learning, while a department that sees teaching as being about changing students' understanding is more likely to have students adopting a deep approach. (Lublin & Prosser, 1994, p.40)

There is also accumulating anecdotal evidence from the reports of quality assessors in Britain to suggest that there are marked variations in the emphasis departments put on teaching (see, for example, SHEFC, 1996). Assessors talk to departmental staff, collectively, about their teaching strategies. In some departments it is clear that this topic has been regularly debated and a consensus view has emerged, with staff sharing an enthusiasm for teaching and being well informed about pedagogical principles. In other departments, it is equally evident that such discussions do not take place, and that the professional enthusiasms of staff are directed single-mindedly towards their research interests.

The attitudes of senior faculty, and particularly those of the Departmental Head, are very influential in developing the teaching ethos. Those attitudes will affect the reward system which operates within the department, and the way resources are distributed. Departmental staff receive clear signals about what activities 'count,' and the effort they put into teaching is controlled in that way by the academic managers. In Britain, elaborate policies are in place to ensure that all staff are appraised on a regular basis. Such appraisal generally leads to an action plan, but it is still rather unusual for that plan to specify professional development activities to improve teaching. As Gardiner (1994) comments in the American context,

> Clearly, our casual approach to developing and sustaining our new colleagues—and renewing and upgrading the skills of senior faculty—must be directly responsible for much of the low-quality student experience portrayed by the research and the low-quality educational results many of our societal stakeholders decry. (p. 141)

The failure to build a proper reward system for excellent teaching, while increasing the pressures to attract research grants and publish extensively, explains the way faculty currently thinks about teaching. The lack of effective initial training in teaching means that most lecturers lack the background which could provide both a language through which to discuss any problems, and the self-confidence to think critically about their ways of teaching. As it is, opportunities for educational development activities are rarely sought, or taken. Where innovations are introduced, they are often minor changes incorporated into approaches to teaching which retain their previous characteristics. Even faculty who have a student-oriented conception of teaching may feel inhibited from converting their convictions into their teaching practice without substantial support from their department, and encouragement from central management. And they may still lack a satisfying rationale for any changes they envisage.

THE LEARNING ENVIRONMENT

So far, we have explored the many factors which have been shown, separately, to influence the students' approaches to learning and studying, and the quality of learning outcomes. But these factors never operate in isolation, they operate synergistically to create what can be called a *learning environment*. Biggs (1993a) has emphasized the importance of looking at learning environments from a 'systems' perspective, while Eisenberg (1988) has argued that every component within the learning environment must be designed to support the required approaches to learning. He comments that:

> Inappropriate approaches are simply induced: just one piece in the jigsaw that is out of place (mismatched or misperceived) may inter-

fere with the relation between the learner and the content. (p. 196)

Ensuring that each element within a learning environment contributes towards the overall teaching aims of the department is extremely difficult, if not impossible, but it represents an ideal which can be used to guide reviews of current teaching policies and practice.

While it is the overall learning environment which determines the quality of learning, that relationship is still not a direct one. Biggs (1993a) has described a 3-P model (presage, process and product) which indicates how the outcome of learning (product) depends on presage variables—the initial knowledge and other characteristics of the learner—and process variables or the learning environment experienced by the learner. In our review, the emphasis has been on the individual student's *perception* of the learning environment, which is a product of the student's past educational history and the whole range of individual differences described earlier. As Meyer (1991) has argued, the learning in higher education depends on effective *study orchestration*—the match between the students' approaches to studying and their perceptions of those aspects in the learning environment. Relationships between teaching and learning are not direct, they are mediated by the learner's own abilities and goals. If we are to provide a comprehensive picture of the teaching-learning process, therefore, this level of complexity must be represented in our descriptions and models.

A CONCEPTUAL OVERVIEW OF THE TEACHING-LEARNING PROCESS
The research on student learning described in this chapter has made use of a wide variety of concepts, all of which contribute towards an understanding of the student's learning strategies and the learning outcomes which derive from them. Bringing them together within Figure 1 provides a conceptual overview of the research, which has similarities to Biggs' 3-P model but also indicates the links which exist between student characteristics, teaching, and teaching policies.

In Figure 1 strategies and outcomes are placed at the center—the target of the explanations which are built up from the concepts and research findings. Around the top of the shaded 'diamond,' there are *student characteristics*, moving from prior knowledge on the left to study skills on the right. The four components shown on the left make up some of the main influences on approaches to learning (shown within the diamond), although attitudes to the course and motivation also have an important influence on whether a deep or surface approach is adopted. Approaches to studying—

Figure 1

A conceptual overview of the teaching-learning process

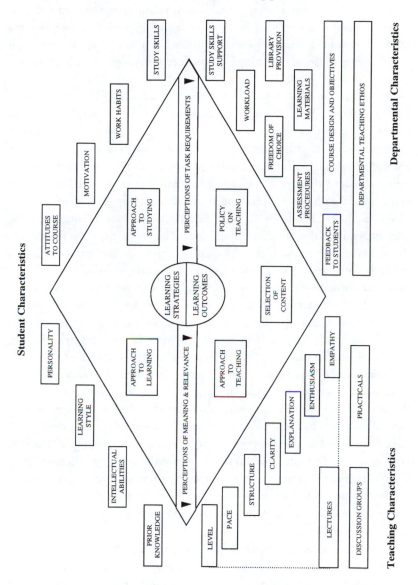

strategic or apathetic—again are affected by attitudes and motivation, as well as by academic self-confidence deriving from ability and prior knowledge, but they are more closely related to work habits and study skills.

Across the center of the diagram are shown the student's perceptions of the learning environment, which act as a lens through which the learning environment is seen and interpreted. Cognitive and personality differences, as well as approaches to learning, influence the *perceptions of meaning and relevance* seen in the teaching, while approaches to studying, together with the characteristics underpinning them, affect *perceptions of the task requirements.*

At the bottom left-hand of the diagram, the *teaching characteristics* which influence approaches to learning are shown in detail, but only for lecturing, where the research evidence is strongest. Similar influences are, however, likely to be found with other teaching methods, such as discussion groups and laboratory classes. The positioning of the lecturing components, which reflect the individual lecturer's *approach to teaching,* is intended to indicate vertical links with student characteristics. Thus, the level at which the lecture is pitched depends on the prior knowledge of the students, while the pace depends on their intellectual abilities. The way the topic is structured, the clarity of presentation, and the quality of the explanations—the lecturing style—will depend on the lecturer's own learning style, and the reaction of students will depend on the match with their own preferred ways of learning. Finally, personality will affect the extent to which a lecture is presented enthusiastically, and contributes to the appearance of a lecturer's empathy with the audience. Again the students' reactions to the lecturer's style of teaching will depend, at least, on their own personality and learning style.

Selection of content is placed at the bottom center of the shaded diamond to indicate its importance, and that it is initiated by faculty members but depends also on institutional approval. Below that, and to the right, *departmental characteristics,* as well as institutional influences, are described which have been found to affect approaches to learning and studying. The overall policy on teaching is unpacked to show some of the strongest effects on learning. Assessment procedures, and the feedback provided to students on the quality of the work, have been shown to have the strongest overall effects on approaches to both learning and studying, but they also influence attitudes and motivation.

As was shown earlier, freedom of choice and workload both have some impact on learning (more freedom—deep; heavy workload—surface), while study skills support has its expected effect, but only if that support has been carefully designed. Library provision and learning materials provide the essential means through which teaching can be converted into learning, through the effort and study skills of the individual student. More general influences on the quality of learning come from the course design and associated learning objectives, while the departmental teaching ethos acts both indirectly through its effect on individual faculty members and directly through established departmental policies and procedures.

CONCLUSION

This conceptual overview has been provided to encourage reflection on the current situation. Some of that thinking would need to be carried out at institutional level by institutional managers, but its message is directed more particularly at departments and individual faculty members. The research findings cannot produce generalized, specific advice about 'best practice.' Indeed, the idea that there can be such a thing as 'best practice' is a myth, given the range of institutional missions, professional requirements, disciplines, teaching styles, and student intakes (Dahllöf, 1991). *Good* practice will occur where the learning environment has been thoughtfully designed to achieve the specific objectives of a course in ways which suit most of the students. What the research most clearly *does* establish, however, is a distinctive way of thinking about teaching which radically differs from that inherent in much current practice (Hounsell, 1997).

Of course, some faculty members will find an analysis derived from research findings entirely unconvincing, believing that it cannot take account of the 'realities' of the teaching situation. It is one of the paradoxes of higher education that faculty, who rely extensively on research findings within their own discipline, are reluctant even to consider the research on teaching. The lack of professional training in teaching does make them defensive towards suggestions about improvement, and the claim that the research is unrealistic is such a reaction, at least in part. The research studies have looked at learning and teaching in a wide variety of actual contexts. If the findings are an accurate portrayal of these situations, then the conceptual overview derived from them cannot be wholly idealistic. It becomes unrealistic, perhaps, when all the influences on learning are brought together within the overview, and the implications of the interactive and mutual dependent system are taken into account. While the research does not demand wholesale change, it does invite a thorough reconsideration of current arrangements.

Attempts to improve the general quality of teaching in universities depend, in part, on a change in the reward system, and in the attitudes of senior management, both at institutional and departmental levels. Only then can educational development activities become accepted, and indeed valued. Their potential value can be seen in a recent Canadian study which tracked the changing conceptions and teaching practices of an experienced colleague who had taken part in a series of discussions on teaching (Amundsen et al., in press). His conception of teaching was seen most clearly through the metaphors he used to describe his role as a teacher. Initially, he saw himself as the concert pianist striving to give a perfect performance, then as the conductor orchestrating and controlling learning activities, and finally as a participant in a live jazz session with interaction and extemporary performance. In his initial conception, he sought to introduce changes, but in a piecemeal manner which proved ineffective. The discussion group gave him the confidence and insights to 're-invent' himself as a teacher, by bringing his teaching into line with his own feelings about teaching and learning.

It seems that educational development activities, as with workshops on learning to learn, have to focus on raising awareness and changing existing attitudes and conceptions of teaching. Only with a broad and integrative perspective on the ways in which teaching affect learning can faculty see effective ways of modifying their own practice.

Ideally, in any institutional review, the whole teaching-learning environment should be kept in focus when considering ways of improving the current situation. In practice, it will rarely be feasible to alter several aspects of the learning environment at the same time, but there will always be *some* steps which can be taken to improve the current situation. Viewing the learning environment as an interactive system allows the whole picture to be considered and the probable interactions between the various components to be borne in mind. Such an overview should encourage the development of a coherent strategy designed to achieve planned *evolutionary* change over time. At present, strategic plans for developing effective teaching and learning environments are rarely found.

REFERENCES

Amundsen, C., Saroyan, A., & Frankman, M. (in press) Changing methods and metaphors: a case study of growth in university teaching.

Anderson, C.D.B. (1997). Enabling and shaping understanding through tutorials. In F. Marton, D.J. Hounsell, & N.J. Entwistle (Eds.), *The experience of learning* (2nd ed.). Edinburgh: Scottish Academic Press.

Andrews, J., Garrison, D.R., & Magnusson, K. (1996). The teaching and learning transaction in higher education: a study of excellent professors and their students. *Teaching in Higher Education, 1*, 81- 103.

Ausubel, D.P. (1985). Learning as constructing meaning. In N.J. Entwistle (Ed.), *New directions in educational psychology. I. Learning and teaching.* London: Falmer Press.

Ausubel, D.P., Novak, J.S., & Hanesian, H. (1978). *Educational psychology: A cognitive view.* New York: Holt, Rinehart & Winston.

Beaty, L., Gibbs, G., & Morgan, A. (1997). Learning orientations and study contracts. In F. Marton, D.J. Hounsell, & N.J. Entwistle (Eds.)' *The experience of learning* (2nd ed.). Edinburgh: Scottish Academic Press.

Becker, H.S., Geer, B., & Hughes, E.C. (1968). *Making the grade: The academic side of college life.* New York: Wiley.

Biggs, J.B. (1979). Individual differences in study processes and the quality of learning outcomes. *Higher Education, 8* , 381-394.

Biggs, J.B. (1987). *Student approaches to learning and studying.* Melbourne: Australian Council for Educational Research.

Biggs, J.B. (1993a). From theory to practice: A cognitive systems approach. *Higher Education Research & Development, 12,* 73-86.

Biggs, J.B. (1993b). What do inventories of student's learning processes really measure? A theoretical review and clarification. *British Journal of Educational Psychology, 63,* 3-19.

Brown, A. (1987). Metacognition, executive control, self regulation, and other more mysterious mechanisms. In F.E.Weinert & R. H. Kluwe (Eds.), *Metacogniton, motivation, and understanding* (pp. 65-116). Hillsdale, N J: Lawrence Erlbaum.

Brown, G.A., & Atkins, M. (1988). *Effective teaching in higher education.* London: Methuen.

Brown, G.A., & Atkins, M. (1996). Explaining. In O.Hargie (Ed.) *Handbook of Communication Skills.* London: Routledge.

Brown, G.A., & Bahktar, M. (1983). *Styles of lecturing.* Loughborough: Loughborough University Press.

Cooley, W., & Lohnes, P.R. (1976). *Evaluation research in education.* New York: Irvington.

Dahllöf, U. (1991). Towards a new model for the evaluation of teaching. In U.Dahllöf, J. Harris, M. Shattock, A. Staropoli, & R. Veld (Eds.), *Dimensions of evaluation.* London: Jessica Kingsley.

Eisenberg, N. (1988). Approaches to learning anatomy: Developing a program for pre-clinical medical students. In P. Ramsden (Ed.), *Improving learning: New perspectives* (pp. 178-198). London: Kogan Page.

Entwistle, N.J. (1987). Motivation to learn: Conceptualizations and practicalities. *British Journal of Educational Studies, 25,* 129-148.

Entwistle, N.J. (1988). *Styles of learning and teaching.* London: David Fulton.

Entwistle, N.J. (1992). *The impact of teaching on learning outcomes in higher education.* Sheffield: Universities' and Colleges' Staff Development Unit.

Entwistle, N.J. (1997). Understanding academic performance at university: a research retrospect. In D. Shorrocks-Taylor & V. Varma (Eds.), *Directions in Educational Psychology.* London : Whult.

Entwistle, N.J., & Entwistle, A.C. (1996). Revision and the experience of understanding. In F. Marton, D.J. Hounsell, & N.J. Entwistle (Eds.), *The experience of learning* (2nd ed.). Edinburgh: Scottish Academic Press.

Entwistle, N.J., & Entwistle, D.M. (1970). The relationships between personality, study methods, and academic performance. *British Journal of Educational Psychology, 40,* 132-141.

Entwistle, N.J., Macaulay, C., Situnayake, G., & Tait, H. (1989). *The performance of electrical engineers in Scottish higher education.* Edinburgh: University of Edinburgh, Center for Research on Learning and Instruction.

Entwistle, N.J., & Ramsden, P. (1983). *Understanding student learning.* London: Croom Helm.

Entwistle, N.J., & Tait, H. (1990). Approaches to learning, evaluations of teaching, and preferences for contrasting academic environments. *Higher Education, 19*, 169-194.

Entwistle, N.J., Thompson, J.B., & Wilson, J.D. (1974). Motivation and study habits. *Higher Education, 3*, 379-396.

Entwistle, N.J., Wall, D., Macaulay, C., Tait, H., & Entwistle, D.M. (1991). *School to higher education: Bridging the gap.* (Interchange Report No. 2). Edinburgh: Scottish Office Education Department.

Feldman, K.A. (1987). Research productivity and scholarly accomplishment of college teachers as related to their instructional effectiveness: A review and exploration. *Research in Higher Education, 26*, 227-298.

Fox, D. (1983). Personal theories of teaching. *Studies in Higher Education, 8*, 151-163.

Gardiner, L.F. (1994). *Redesigning higher education.* (ASHE-ERIC Higher Education Reports). Washington: George Washington University, Graduate School of Education and Human Development.

Gardner, H. (1984). *Frames of mind.* London: Heinemann.

Gibbs, G. (1981). *Teaching students to learn: A student-centered approach.* Milton Keynes: Open University Press.

Gustafsson, J-E., & Balke, G. (1993). General and specific abilities as predictors of school achievement. *Multivariate Behavioral Research, 28*, 407-434.

Heath, R. (1964). *The reasonable adventurer.* Pittsburgh: University of Pittsburgh Press.

Hodgson, V. (1997). Lectures and the experience of relevance. In F. Marton, D.J. Hounsell, & N.J. Entwistle (Eds.), *The experience of learning* (2nd ed.). Edinburgh: Scottish Academic Press.

Hounsell, D.J. (1987). Essay writing and the quality of feedback. In J. T. E. Richardson, M.W. Eysenck, & D. Warren-Piper (Eds.), *Student learning: Research in education and cognitive psychology* (pp. 109-119). Buckingham: Society for Research in Higher Education / Open University Press.

Hounsell, D. J. (1997). Understanding teaching and teaching for understanding. In F. Marton, D.J. Hounsell, & N.J. Entwistle (Eds.), *The experience of learning* (2nd ed.). Edinburgh: Scottish Academic Press.

Hudson, L. (1968). *Frames of mind.* London: Methuen.

Janssen, P. J. (1996). Studaxology: The expertise students need to be effective in higher education. *Higher Education, 31*, 117-141.

Jaques, D. (1985). *Learning in groups* London: Croom Helm.

Laurillard, D. (1993). *Rethinking university teaching: A framework for the effective use of educational technology.* London: Routledge.

Laurillard, D. (1997). Learning formal representations through multimedia. In F. Marton, D.J. Hounsell, & N.J. Entwistle (Eds.), *The experience of learning* (2nd ed.). Edinburgh: Scottish Academic Press.

Leinhardt, G., & Greeno, J. (1986). The cognitive skill of teaching. *Journal of Educational Psychology, 78* (2), 75-95.

Lublin, J., & Prosser, M. (1994). Implications of recent research on student learning for institutional practices of evaluation of teaching. In G. Gibbs (Ed.), *Improving student learning: Theory and practice.* Oxford: Oxford Brookes University, Oxford Center f Staff Development.

Mahmoud, M. (1989). Contrasting perceptions of an innovation in engineering education. *European Journal of the Psychology of Education, 4*, 453-468.

Marsh, H. (1987). Students' evaluations of university teaching: Research findings, methodological issues, directions for future research. *International Journal of Educational*

Research, 11 (3).

Marton, F., Beaty, E., & Dall'Alba, G. (1993). Conceptions of learning. *International Journal of Educational Research, 19,* 277-300.

Marton, F., Hounsell D.J., & Entwistle, N.J. (Eds.). (1997). *The experience of learning* (2nd ed.). Edinburgh: Scottish Academic Press.

Marton, F., & Säljö, R. (1976). On qualitative differences in learning. I. Outcome and process. *British Journal of Educational Psychology, 46,* 4-11.

Marton, F., & Säljö, R. (1997). Approaches to learning. In F. Marton, D.J. Hounsell, & N.J. Entwistle (Eds.), *The experience of learning* (2nd ed.). Edinburgh: Scottish Academic Press.

McKeachie, W. (1994). *Teaching tips* (9th ed.). Lexington, MA: D.C. Heath.

Meyer, J.H.F. (1991). Study orchestration: the manifestation, interpretation and consequences of contextualised approaches to studying. *Higher Education, 22,* 297-316.

Meyer, J.H.F., Cliff, A. F., & Dunne, T. T. (1994). Impressions of disadvantage: II— Monitoring and assisting the student at risk. *Higher Education, 27,* 95-117.

Miller, C.M.L., & Parlett, M. (1974). *Up to the mark: A study of the examination game.* London: Society for Research in Higher Education.

Newble, D.I., & Jaeger, K. (1983). The effect of assessments and examinations on the learning of medical students. *Medical Education , 17,* 25-31.

Nisbet , J.D. (1988). Beyond the study skills manual. In P.J. Hills (Ed.), *Study courses and counselling: Problems and possibilities.* London: Society for Research in Higher Education.

Norton, L., & Dickins, T.E. (1995). Do approaches to learning courses improve students' learning strategies? In G. Gibbs (Ed.), *Improving student learning through assessment and evaluation.* Oxford: Oxford Brookes University, Oxford Center for Staff Development.

Pask, G. (1976). Styles and strategies of learning. *British Journal of Educational Psychology, 46,* 128-148.

Pask, G. (1988). Learning strategies, teaching strategies and conceptual or learning style. In R.R. Schmeck (Ed.), *Learning strategies and learning styles.* New York: Plenum Press.

Perkins, D., & Blythe, T. (1994). Putting understanding up front. *Educational Leadership, 51* (5), 4-7.

Perry, W.G. (1970). *Forms of intellectual and ethical development in the college years: A scheme.* New York: Holt, Rinehart & Winston.

Pintrich, P.R., & Garcia, T. (1994). Self-regulated learning in college students: Knowledge, strategies, and motivation. In P. R Pintrich, D.R. Brown, & C.E. Weinstein (Eds.), *Student motivation, cognition, and learning* (pp. 113-134). Hillsdale, NJ: Lawrence Erlbaum.

Prosser, M., Trigwell, K., & Taylor, P. (1994). A phenomenographic study of academics' conceptions of science learning and teaching. *Learning & Instruction, 4,* 217-232.

Ramsden, P. (1991). A performance indicator of teaching quality in higher education: The Course Perceptions Questionnaire. *Studies in Higher Education, 16,* 129-150.

Ramsden, P. (1992). *Learning to teach in higher education.* London: Kogan Page.

Ramsden, P. (1997). The context of learning in academic departments. In F. Marton, D.J. Hounsell, & N.J. Entwistle (Eds.), *The experience of learning* (2nd ed.). Edinburgh: Scottish Academic Press.

Ramsden, P., & Martin, E. (1987). Learning skills or skill in learning? In J.T.E. Richardson, M.W. Eysenck, & D. Warren-Piper (Eds.), *Student learning: Research in education and cognitive psychology.* Buckingham: Society for Research in Higher Education / Open University Press.

Ramsden, P. & Moses, I. (1992). Associations between research and teaching in Australian higher education. *Higher Education, 23,* 273-295.

Säljö, R. (1979). *Learning in the learners' perspective. I. Some common-sense conceptions.*
(Report 76). Gothenburg: University of Gothenburg, Department of Education.

Samuelowicz, K., & Bain, J.D. (1992). Conceptions of teaching held by academic teachers. *Higher Education, 24,* 93-111.

SHEFC (1996). *Annual report on quality assessment* . Edinburgh: Scottish Higher Education Funding Council.

Small, J.J. (1966). *Achievement and adjustment in the first year at university.* Wellington:
New Zealand Council for Educational Research.

Snow, R.E., Corno, L, & Jackson, D. (1996). Individual differences in affective and cognitive functions. In D.C. Berliner & R.C. Calfree (Eds.), *Handbook of educational
psychology.* New York: Macmillan.

Sternberg, R.E. (1987). The triarchic theory of human intelligence. In J.T.E. Richardson,
M.W. Eysenck, & D. Warren-Piper (Eds.), *Student learning: Research in education and
cognitive psychology.* Buckingham: Society for Research in Higher Education /Open
University Press.

Tait, H., & Entwistle, N.J. (1996). Identifying students at risk through ineffective study
strategies. *Higher Education, 31,* 97-116.

Thomas, P. R., & Bain, J.D. (1984). Contextual dependence of learning approaches: The
effects of assessments. *Human Learning, 3,* 227-240.

Torrance, E.P., & Rockenstein, Z.L. (1988). Styles of thinking and creativity. In R.R.
Schmeck (Ed.), *Learning strategies and learning styles.* New York: Plenum Press.

Trigwell, K., & Prosser, M. (1996a). Changing approaches to teaching: A relational perspective. *Studies in Higher Education,* 21, 275-284

Trigwell, K., & Prosser, M. (1996b). Congruence between intention and strategy in university science teachers' approaches to teaching. *Higher Education,*32, 77-87

Trigwell, K., Prosser, M., & Taylor, P. (1994). Qualitative differences in approach to teaching first year science. *Higher Education, 27,* 74-84.

Verduin, J.R., & Clark, T.A. (1991). *Distance education.* San Francisco: Jossey-Bass.

Vermunt, J.D. (1996). Metacognitive, cognitive, and affective aspects of learning styles
and strategies: A phenomenographic analysis. *Higher Education, 31,* 25-50.

Weinstein C.E. (1988). Assessment and training of student learning strategies. In
R.R.Schmeck (Ed.), *Learning strategies and learning styles* (pp. 291-316). New York:
Plenum Press.

Witkin, H.A., Moore, C.A., Goodenough, D.R., & Cox, P.W. (1977). Field-dependent
and field-independent cognitive styles and their educational implications. *Review of
Educational Research, 47,* 1-64.

CHAPTER 5

"It's Just You and the Books"
Learning Conditions and Study Strategies of Distance Learners at the University of the South Pacific

France Mugler and Roger Landbeck

INTRODUCTION

This chapter examines the extent to which the learning conditions of distance education students influence the strategies they adopt in their studies, the consequences for the quality of learning students are able to achieve, and ways in which this can be improved. It is based on a pilot study of students enrolled in distance education courses at the University of the South Pacific (USP), a regional institution unique in the vastness of the geographical area spanned by its member countries and the linguistic and cultural diversity of its student body.

THE UNIVERSITY OF THE SOUTH PACIFIC

The University of the South Pacific is a regional institution which has served the people of twelve island nations in the Pacific for over 25 years. It offers a wide range of undergraduate and postgraduate programs, as well as pre-degree certificates and diplomas.

The twelve member countries of the USP are Cook Islands, Fiji, Kiribati, Marshall Islands, Nauru, Niue, Solomon Islands, Tokelau, Tonga, Tuvalu, Vanuatu, and Western Samoa. The main campus is in Fiji's capital, Suva, where most of the face-to-face teaching is conducted through programs run by three schools: the School of Pure and Applied Sciences, the School of Social and Economic Development, and the School of Humanities. Suva's Laucala Bay campus also houses various research institutes, as well as support units such as a library, a computer center, a media center, etc. The Alafua campus in Apia, Western Samoa, is home to the School of Agriculture, while the Pacific Languages Unit and most of the Department of Law are located in Port Vila, Vanuatu.

Formal education was introduced to the Pacific as a result of European contact and colonization. Current educational systems to a great extent still bear the imprint of this nineteenth-century imported Western education, and are generally exam-driven and teacher-centered. This is the case from primary school all the way up to the tertiary level, including USP, where the dominant teaching mode in on-campus courses is the lecture, and where most courses have a final exam whose weight must normally be between 40% and 60% of the total course assessment.

EXTENSION STUDIES AT USP
University Extension and the USP Centers
From its inception in 1968, the USP was conceived as a dual mode institution, offering both face-to-face and distance education. The USP's traditional commitment to distance learning stems from the early realization that not every potential student would be able to study full-time on campus, given the great distances and limited economic resources of the South Pacific region.

Courses offered by academic departments are administered centrally through University Extension (UE), in Suva, and locally through a USP Center in 11 of the 12 member countries.[1] The Centers advise and enroll students, run local tutorials, forward students' assignments to UE in Suva for marking, and channel marked assignments back to students.[2] In their Center, students take final examinations which are prepared by their lecturers on campus. Each Center has a library and some have science laboratories.

While not all courses or programs are available through the Extension mode, it is possible to complete some certificates, diplomas, and Bachelor's degrees in some disciplines entirely by distance learning. Extension courses were first offered in 1971, and enrollments have grown steadily since, overtaking on-campus numbers in 1984. In 1995, Extension accounted for nearly 62% of total enrollments (see Table 1).

Table 1
The Growth of Extension Enrollments

	Extension	On-campus
1971	154	671
1984	2,197	2,002
1995	5,419	3,357

(Based on USP Statistics 1995, p. 29)

Students who enroll for an Extension course are given a course package which typically includes an Introduction and Assignment Booklet, a Study Guide, a textbook or Coursebook (which may be in two volumes), and a Reader (i.e. a collection of readings specially compiled for the course). Some course packages also contain audio cassettes and a few have video tapes. All materials except for textbooks and some of the readings are normally developed at USP.

Besides the local tutorials organized by each Center, tutorials are run by satellite from Suva (and Vila), generally once a week. This enables the lecturer in charge of the course to communicate verbally with students in the various countries of the region. Scheduling can be tricky, since the USP region spans not only different time zones but also the international dateline, which means that when it is 4pm in Fiji, it is 6pm in the Cook Islands, and that Monday in Vila is Sunday in Western Samoa. Technical problems can cut off a particular country from the satellite network, sometimes for weeks. Another limitation is that access to tutorials of any kind is restricted to students who live in or near their country's Center. Some Centers also arrange peer tutorial groups, in which students taking the same course are put in touch, then left to themselves to organize regular meetings in which they discuss the course.

The Environment: Distance and Diversity

The enormous distances in the region and the diversity in lifestyles and economic conditions lead to considerable variety in the learning conditions of Extension students. The twelve member countries are spread over 32 million square kilometers of ocean, and a student's home may be thousands of kilometers from the administrative center for Extension studies—University Extension, in Suva—and even hundreds of kilometers or more from his or her country's USP Center.

While many Extension students live in or around their country's capital—usually the site of their USP Center—others live in remote rural areas or isolated outer islands. A student whose home is in downtown Apia is a short walk away from the Western Samoa USP Center. But someone who lives on one of the islands in the Vava'u group is over 300 kilometres from the Tonga Center in the capital, Nuku'alofa, while the most remote settlement in Kiribati is 3,500 km from the country's capital on Tarawa. If the USP Center in Port Vila, Vanuatu is "only" 1,000 km away from UE in Suva, those in Honiara (Solomon Islands), Majuro (Marshall Islands), and Rarotonga (Cook Islands) are over 2,000 km away. An assignment from

Nauru will make a return trip of nearly 4,500 km before it goes back, corrected and marked, to the student.

The USP region is made up of over 300 inhabited islands—and thousands of uninhabited ones—scattered over thousands of miles of ocean. It is traditionally divided into three broad cultural areas, Melanesia, Polynesia, and Micronesia, each of which is itself rich in cultural and linguistic diversity. While a nation like Niue is a single island with a nearly homogeneous population and one indigenous language, others are made up of dozens of islands and scores of languages, such as Vanuatu, which has the highest language density in the world, with over a hundred languages for a population of about 150,000. Located at the heart of the most linguistically rich area of the world, the USP region itself is home to over 200 languages.

English, the ex-colonial language of many of the member countries and the medium of instruction at USP, is a second language for nearly all students, and a third or even fourth language for some. Except in multiethnic Fiji—where it plays a role as a lingua franca, particularly in urban areas—English has very limited functions in the region, essentially as the official language of instruction throughout the school system, and as official or co-official language of government and of the media. This means that the students' exposure to the language in which they have to acquire their tertiary education is restricted, leading to problems both in comprehension and expression.

The economies of the South Pacific also vary widely. While Nauru, thanks to its phosphate, has one of the highest per capita incomes in the world, Tokelau has one of the lowest. Fiji has a relatively diversified economy, but many of the other countries have to rely on a combination of tourism and subsistence agriculture and fishing. This is often supplemented by remittances from nationals who have migrated to Pacific Rim countries, such as New Zealand, Australia, Canada, and the United States. Some of the smaller countries would have great financial difficulties without these contributions, and limited economic opportunities are the major cause of emigration, which is sometimes so massive as to amount to depopulation. About three times as many Niueans live in New Zealand as in Niue, for instance. In most of the countries of the region a high percentage of the population lives on the margins of the cash economy.

For many students, large distances, isolation, and limited economic resources and infrastructure result in transportation difficulties and, in particular, a relatively long turn-around time from when an assignment is mailed to the Center to when it comes back marked to the student. Many isolated students are unable to attend local or satellite tutorials. Although many have access to a tape recorder, so that they can use any audio materials which may be part of their course package, resources such as books or newspapers are often extremely scarce. Some homes do not have electricity and studying must be done by the light of a kerosene lamp. Often the student has no private space for studying. Family, community, religious, and work obligations often take precedence over studying. While members of the family may support in principle an individual's decision to study, they may be unable to provide assistance or even to understand the students' difficulties and needs. The isolated student is unable to get academic or psychological support from the informal networks that are such a source of strength to students in more populated and accessible areas.

THE STUDY

The work reported in this chapter is part of a study of USP students' conceptions of learning and approaches to study, using a phenomenographic research method pioneered by Marton (1981). The method consists of conducting semi-structured interviews which prompt students to reflect on the way they study and on what they think the process of learning is about. The first part of the research project was conducted with a random sample of students in a linguistics course on the main campus in Suva (Landbeck & Mugler, 1994, 1995, 1996). An analysis of interview transcripts revealed the difficulty of the transition from high school to university, the influence of assessment on study strategies, and a wide range of conceptions of learning, similar to those identified among students in other parts of the world (Marton & Saljö, 1976; Saljö, 1979; Van Rossum & Schenk, 1984; Watkins & Regmi, 1990, 1992; Nagle & Marton, 1993; Marton, Dall'Alba, & Kun Tse, 1993). These conceptions go from an increase in knowledge, memorizing and reproducing, to applying knowledge, understanding, seeing things in a different way, and changing as a person (Marton, Dall'Alba, & Beaty, 1993).

Because of the importance of distance learning at USP, the project was then expanded, and in 1995 a series of similar interviews was conducted with 24 Extension students from different parts of Fiji. The original interview schedule, adapted from previous phenomenographic studies, was further modified to focus on some of the specific features of distance learning (see Appendix 1).

The 24 students interviewed were selected randomly from enrollment lists, and re-selection was used to ensure a rough balance between the sexes and an age range representative of the population of Extension students at USP. The sample includes 10 males and 14 females. Ages range from 19 to 47, with 8 students between 19 and 24, 6 between 29 and 32, and 10 between 35 and 47. The majority (15) are teachers (see Appendix 2). Interviews were conducted in three towns on the Western Side of the main island of Viti Levu, and in the two main towns on the second largest island, Vanua Levu.

The number of students interviewed was partly determined by the availability of the students for interviews, the time available to the interviewer in each location, and the total number needed to provide useful data, similar to the number used in phenomenographic studies in different fields (e.g., Prosser, Trigwell, & Taylor, 1995; Bain & Samuelowicz, 1992).

The project has now been expanded to the rest of the USP region, and to date interviews have been conducted in Vanuatu, the Solomon Islands, Western Samoa, Tuvalu, and Kiribati. The last interviews will take place in Tonga in early 1997. Since the regional interviews conducted so far are very recent and have not been transcribed, only the results of the Fiji study are reported here.

LEARNING CONDITIONS

The conditions in which distance learners in the South Pacific study are described above in general terms. One of the goals of the interviews was to explore what it is like for students to study by Extension. The transcripts give an insight into some of the problems students face and how they try to solve them. Two major issues emerge: tutorial support and access to resources.

Tutorial Support

The University Extension organizes tutorials in a number of towns in Fiji, such as Lautoka and Labasa.[3] In most subjects there may be two tutorials a semester, while a course with large enrollments may meet every week.

Students are nearly unanimous in wishing that they had more tutorials or that they could attend the ones offered. Unfortunately access to tutorials is limited: some students live too far from where they are held, others are too busy to attend. Some complain that they receive notices about tutorials too late or not at all. There aren't enough tutorials; they're too short; they're too late. No one complains that they are too long or that there are too many. Tutorials held at the beginning of the semester help "get things rolling," and those held a few weeks before final exams are also particularly appreciated. Although not all tutorials are helpful—one tutor "just gave the answers and that's all" (LJ, p. 2)—some not only help clarify content and provide guidance for further study but also "keep things interesting," allow students to find out who else in their area is taking the course, and help break down the feeling of isolation expressed by the leitmotif, "it's only you and the books" (SI, p. 1).[4]

In addition to the organized tutorials, spontaneous study groups often form among people taking the same course, meeting sometimes regularly, sometimes on an ad-hoc basis. In these groups students discuss readings and assignments, exchange ideas, go over the self-assessment questions together and prepare for final exams (see below). Not only do these peer tutorials help students to understand the content of their courses better, they also provide much needed psychological support:

> You feel like studying because we are in a group and they are doing something more the same as you are doing . . . . Through their support we work together and seek each other's help . . . . I feel that if I had my friends to work with I would do better (CS, p. 2).

Several of the students interviewed have had the experience of studying full-time on campus, and they contrast this with studying by Extension:

> We just have to rely on what's in the book . . . . When you are in the university environment, you know your mates, after, you're learning in the room and after, I mean, outside the room, with all your mates (CD, p. 3).

The Fiji Center has experimented with organizing peer groups. One student suggests that they are less successful than those that form spontaneously because "people are new and then, you know, ideas don't flow like that, because if there are people whom we know, it becomes very easy" (SD, p. 2).

Many of the students interviewed are teachers, and networks that are already established with colleagues turn out to be useful to them as Extension students. Teachers who have already taken the course can answer questions and share resources. A student describes the workings of such a network:

> Sometimes I just come out and find resources from teachers or members, I mean, other students who have done this course, and I get the resource from them and I try to do my . . .

> [Interviewer: How do you locate these teachers who have done the course?]

Yes, sometimes I ask one or two of my friends whether they have and then they ask in their schools or sometimes, yeah, in the schools mostly, and they tell me the name of the teacher and then I go and I approach the teacher and ask for their materials and they are willing to give. [Interviewer: Yes, sure. And did you have much contact with the other school teachers?]

Yes. Here, the secondary school is quite near, so I've made friends with the secondary school teachers and meet them often and also when we attend workshops or teachers' workshops or seminars or something, or bazaars, then we are able to make contacts and we become friends and we ask (RL, p. 4).

No matter how useful peer study groups or individuals are, the absence of a tutor is often a source of anxiety:

Here, when you write through Extension, you just don't have any idea what to do, you read the question and whatever comes into my mind, I just write that down. I don't know whether it's right or wrong because there is no one to guide me . . . . We don't have any guidance from our lecturers . . . . We may be discussing things which may not be required (VM, pp. 3-4).

Another source of insecurity related to the absence of face-to-face contact with a lecturer is the kind of feedback given on marked assignments. This is one of the only kinds of personalized guidance the student can get from the marker. Good feedback is very helpful, but inadequate feedback leaves the student frustrated and completely at sea:

Most of the assignments didn't have any comments . . . only the mark . . . sometimes you had to spend so many hours looking for the answer, and you've got nothing to show whether it's a good answer, except you guess by the marks, I suppose, but you got no help to show you what was good and bad (VK, pp. 3-4).

About a third of the students interviewed do not work in groups—a few because they prefer studying alone, but most because they know no one else or find out only at exam time who else is taking the course.[5] Students who do not have access to a peer group often look for an individual who can help if they run into difficulty. This can be a relative, a friend, a colleague, or a superior, such as a head teacher or a former teacher. Some of these individuals are very generous with their time and knowledge, and some try to help in spite of not feeling competent in the discipline:

> I have another teacher from my school. Normally we discuss, but we are not sure whether our discussions, I mean, our answers are right or not (KD, p. 3).

In spite of their academic shortcomings, such people obviously provide valuable psychological support to the isolated student. But some have no one at all:

> I don't think there was any moment last time I did Extension that I could ask any question to any person (LJ, p. 3).

The absence of a lecturer is nearly always the first difference interviewees mention between on-campus and Extension studies, one that most see as a clear disadvantage. Some students evidently consider Extension studying second best and go quite far in idealizing studying on campus—one saying it would be "a dream come true" (SI, p. 4):

> On campus there is someone to guide us on every step . . . . I think it would be better if I would be on campus, as a full time student . . . . I would be helped all the time (FR, pp. 2-3).

> You have got tutors, all the assistance you need, access to library books . . . and if you have any difficulties, the problem is rectified there and then (MA, p. 2).

But while learning on your own is difficult, some students find that Extension studying also has its advantages: the possibility of working at your own pace, and a feeling of responsibility and accomplishment:

> [Extension] gives us lots of time to do research work and find out things for ourselves (SA, p. 1).

> It's more or less what you can do on your own, like the effort and the initiative has to come from within me . . . we find ample time to allocate to our studies (BN, pp. 1-2).

> It's quite interesting in the sense that, like, I'm here, being my own tutor and student at the same time . . . . If I do wrong at least I'm learning instead of relying on somebody (NS, pp. 1-2).

Thus, Extension seems to suit best students who already are independent learners, while others have great difficulty coping, both academically and psychologically, with the isolation and lack of guidance.

Access to Resources

In Fiji the University has established mini-libraries at selected secondary schools (e.g., in all the locations of the interviews except Savusavu). These libraries contain a very limited selection of books related to some of the Extension courses. Students complain that there are "no good libraries" or that libraries are "not fully equipped," that there are not enough materials and on some subjects, no materials at all. The lack of access to books is often mentioned in the same breath as the absence of tutors or fellow students as the two most obvious disadvantages of studying by Extension rather than on campus (see, e.g., MA, p. 2 above):

> We cannot travel to Labasa, so we miss the tutorials and we don't have any tutorials in Savusavu and not even any text materials. And some books which we need as reference, we are not able to find them in Savusavu . . . . I was just thinking that if I have to take the 200 level [second year courses] it would be very hard for me to do it, because I can't find anything here (KT, p. 3).

> Actually, in Lautoka we hardly have some materials here. See, if you are living in Suva, you have a lot of materials and bookshops (SI, p. 10).

Another student summarizes some of the differences between on-campus and Extension studies:

> When you go to USP and you enroll for the on-campus program, you have a lot of resource materials, you have access to resource materials. But through Extension mode, if you have to get faced with any problem, there's only you on your own, because the students who take other similar units are probably very far away or are reluctant to discuss, and then we don't have any resource materials to back up, we don't have a library. Well, the USP at the moment has put up the mini-libraries but does not have enough materials (VK, p. 2).

Some students make up for these limitations by building up their own book collection or consulting resources available from colleagues, and one student mentions going to the USP library in Suva during school holidays. Over half the students interviewed do not mention using resources beyond their course package, or say outright that they do not use any. What this means is an almost complete dependence on the course package, whose quality is crucial.

In short, the learning conditions of Extension students in Fiji vary quite widely. While some have a certain amount of tutorial support, contact with peers, and access to resources, others are extremely isolated and deprived. In fact, some students in Fiji who live only a couple of hundred kilometers from the capital are much more isolated than students in other USP member countries who live near a Center and therefore have access to local and satellite tutorials, to tutors and other students, and to books and other resources. Many students are very enterprising and ingenious in devising ways of making up for the serious limitations they face, but they can only do so much and it is often not enough.

STUDY STRATEGIES
Approaches to Study during the Semester
The assignment booklet and study guide in each course package give advice about how to study. The assignment booklet contains a timetable which lists due dates for assignments and tests and suggests how long to spend on each unit—usually one week. The study guide is a road map to the course and directs students to read specific sections in a textbook and often also in a reader. Self-assessment questions appear at regular intervals in the text to enable students to test their understanding of the material. Most assignment booklets also include a sample final examination from a previous year.

Most students say that they try to study regularly through the week and weekend, to follow the study guide directions closely, including the timetable, and to work steadily through the material from the beginning of the course. But with family obligations and work commitments, most soon fall behind. They find themselves having to put in many more hours to complete the assignments and many do not catch up before the final examination.

> Sometimes for two or three days I cannot do any studies, and then if I have time, I do studies for one or two days per week because, like, now I'm also married, I have a daughter now and it is very difficult for me to study at home because if I'm there with my books, so she comes around (a full-time teacher, FR, p. 1).

> Well, from the beginning, roughly I give about 45 minutes to one hour

per day, and then before the assignments I make it about 3, 4 hours per day (SD, p. 7).

Sometimes I have difficulty coping with the times, like I may be one week or two weeks behind the schedule and sometimes even I've been late with my assignments (KD, p. 7).

A common pattern of study is to read through each unit several times in order to understand the text, and most students identify the "main points" by either highlighting the text or writing notes or both. The notes are mostly written in their own words except when they are not sure about the meaning of the text. It is difficult for many students to explain how they know which points are important. One says it is what she thinks is needed for the course, another "something that is new to me . . . something requiring me to understand further" (MA, p. 4). All say they use their notes to review for the examinations at the end of the course, which saves having to read the material again. This form of note taking seems to have been learned in high school.

A few students mention the need to read with a dictionary, which is often necessary, especially since the language of instruction, English, is not their first language. This means that understanding complex concepts can take a long time. The self-assessment questions in the text are reportedly very helpful for helping students gauge their understanding of the material:

If you are, you know, faithful to yourself, so you don't look at the answers, you can find out about your understanding (EV, p. 6).

The following quotes illustrate the range of variation in approaches to study that can be found among a relatively small group of students. The first two are from students who appear to be studying the course in detail:

I will first look at the Study Guide. I look at the program. Sometimes it says . . . 'read so and so a book', so I read that book, you know, the Study Guide would tell me 'read this page', so I'll read that page, 'go back to the Study Guide when you finish reading after making short notes, come back to the Study Guide where it says, ok, do this, do that', and when you finish all that, for example all that is required for that particular unit, if you finish, then it might say 'Unit Two, read this and then go on to Unit Three' and there it says 'begin Assignment One, so now I should be able to do Assignment One (MT, p. 4).

The first thing I do is to go through the requirements, what I'm supposed to do when my assignments are due and all, and I list it out in front when they are due . . . . But the actual learning of the material, well, I sit and read and during my reading I make, I underline important things, things I think is important to me. Then our book always have questions there . . . so I look at the questions first . . . . If I find a statement that's important I will highlight it, that remains in my mind (IT, pp. 19-20).

Many students are very strategic in their approach to study. They focus on the material that is relevant to completing a given assignment and doing only what is necessary to pass the course. Other material is ignored. Some would prefer to study the material more thoroughly but do not consider that possible, given time constraints:

I mean, most of the time I look at the assignment and the first assignment is based on such unit, so those units I read first (NG, pp. 4-5).
I study till late and then I usually wake up at 4 o'clock in the morning to study and I make shortcut races to town on Saturdays and all that so I can study on Saturdays and Sundays, as long as I find time because I cannot, and most of the time I'm behind in my assignments and because of this, this is really difficult (MT, p. 2).

Here is a candid account of an extreme example of this strategic approach:

It's written clearly what to do . . . but if I don't have time I skip. In most of the time we have to leave it until the end of the course when the exam is nearing . . . . Most of the courses I didn't have time to read, you know, there is a Reader. I have never read any of that because I don't have time . . . . I look at the assignments first and I see what topics do I have to read (CD, pp. 7-8).

His general view of Extension studying is that "Extension is just cram and go and sit for your exam" (2), a view reiterated at various stages of the interview:

You don't learn much, I tell you the truth, you don't learn much. You only do to pass that exam. Extension, I think it means to pass a unit . . . . This [course name] I didn't learn anything. But I know I'll pass the exam even though I haven't learned much (4).

This student articulates most clearly the advantages of the face-to-face mode, in this case a six-week Summer School, over studying by Extension:

The courses that I did through Extension, I forgot most of the materials and I'm pretty sure that the materials that I did in my Summer School, I won't forget for a long time and I think similar to courses that are run full-time. People don't forget, they apply that. I think, well, the two reasons that I said, that there is a lecturer teaching you, and you sharing your knowledge with a lecturer and other students who are doing (6).

He is well aware, then, of the difference in quality of learning, at least for him, between the two modes. This extremely strategic approach may seem cynical, but obviously it works, insofar as he has successfully passed courses thanks to it. At the same time, this is someone who is quite concerned about learning and is very clear about what genuine learning is:

You can't apply that knowledge to your place, I mean, why do you study? To apply that knowledge (4).

What is the most extreme about this student may be his candor, rather than his approach, which is echoed by others in the sample. It is clear from the interviews that this strategic approach is not a result of low-level conceptions which equate learning with memorizing and reproducing information, but of the various constraints which face most Extension students and the observation that such an approach often leads to success in passing courses.

Preparation for Exams
In this section we present a typical scenario of a student preparing for final examinations, told in the first person. It is a composite based on the answers of the majority of students interviewed and is told as much as possible in the students' own words.

I've found out that there's never enough time to go over all the course materials all over again before the exam. In fact, usually by the time I should start preparing for my exam, I'm behind with my studies anyway and I find myself trying to catch up. So I have to rely very heavily on the notes that I've taken during the semester—notes about the main points, maybe some definitions—and I reread the summaries I've written.

But the most important thing that I do is to go over the sample exam that is included at the end of the assignment booklet. These samples are very useful because they give us a good idea of what to expect on the exam. Sometimes the tutors will also give us an idea about the format of the exam. It's good to know what to expect because then you're a bit more confident. Also, I try to get a couple more past years' exams from friends who are studying on campus.

Then I get together with some of my friends who are taking the same course and we discuss these past papers. We look at how many sections there are, for instance, and the types of questions that come up. Sometimes the questions are phrased differently but we know that the lecturers expect the same answers. Then we might discuss the questions first, exchange ideas, and then each person in the group is assigned to look at a question or several questions and work out the answers, so that as a group we end up doing the whole paper. Sometimes we write up the answers fully, other times just in point form. That depends on the subject, or just on the way some people prefer to prepare.

Some of the details of this exam preparation vary: one student does try to reread all the course materials, another goes carefully over her assignments and the marker's feedback, others sporadically refer to the Study Guide or the readings if they find their notes unclear or their summaries too sketchy; some students use only the sample exam provided while others try to collect two or three more; some students write full answers to the sample exam(s), others merely write outlines in point form; most study in groups if they can, but many cannot, and a few prefer to prepare alone.

Three general points about exam preparation are worth noting. First, the students' various other commitments mean that they are nearly all behind in their studies, almost from the word go, and the pressure of time is naturally heaviest before exams: there's never enough time to study and there's certainly not enough time to prepare for exams. The second is the reliance on peer groups, which may be the preferred way of studying of many students, and is probably reinforced by time pressures and the isolation of distance learning. Finally, there is the frequency of mention of exams in the context of the discussion on memorization:

> Sometimes we have to memorize too, I should admit it too, because some of the concepts, some of the definitions, I mean those definitions are coming in the exams and we have to write those definitions, so the main thing is, we have to memorize (MT, p. 14).

Students memorize because they think that they have to, not because it is the only way they know how to learn, and—contrary to what some lecturers seem to think—certainly not because they are convinced that it is the best way to learn. On the contrary, they are well aware of the two major drawbacks of memorization: it does not lead to long-term retention or to understanding and, therefore, genuine learning:

As soon as we finish with the exam, then it goes away . . . . Because some of this memorizing only helps to pass exams. It doesn't help later in our life, unless you understand the thing (RL, p. 12).

There are instances that people learn things, like they cram it, for the purpose of examination, you know, just to pass exams . . . . When it comes to actual day life . . . people don't actually understand it, what it really is, how to apply it (EV, p. 14).

One would memorize to pass through the exams and then the same situation is put into real life, they will not be able to do it. There is no theoretical knowledge of things. Whereas when you understand things you will tend to do or put that situation in real life and you'll know where to work (MA, p. 1).

An interesting relationship between memorization and understanding surfaces in many interviews: if you understand something, then it is easy to memorize it and the knowledge stays with you; on the other hand, if you don't understand something and yet are forced to display your "knowledge" of it, then you are forced to memorize, but you forget the material very quickly and you can't use it in real life.

There are times when you don't understand, then we memorize it. I would say it is bad learning, just trying to say it again and again without knowing what it is, and just being able to say the word without knowing the meaning of the word (CS, p. 18).

What you can understand, you can, it helps you in your exam and after the exam. If you memorize, it's only for the purpose of the exam, and I'm sure after the exam you will forget everything. So that's the problem with, I think, the Extension and full-time, I mean, the courses, Extension courses, you know. You have to memorize quite a lot because we don't understand (CD, p. 9).

These observations are fairly damning, and while the link between memorization and exams is not made only by Extension students, the last quote makes it clear why the particular conditions Extension students have to study in magnify their reliance on memorization. Memorization doesn't lead to understanding, but it can often lead to passing courses. If exams are designed in such a way that you can pass them in spite of not understanding the material, then why not memorize? In the words of one student:

When I was memorizing I thought I was expected to memorize—from the examination point of view (IT, p. 17).

RECOMMENDATIONS

The learning conditions revealed by this study affect the way students learn as follows:

- The lack of resources and isolation lead to a complete or near complete reliance on the study materials in the course package.
- The time pressures from a variety of commitments lead to concentrating on work required for assessment.
- The lack of tutorial support leads to uncertainty and a lack of understanding of the material.

It is, admittedly, very difficult to reproduce for Extension students the on-campus experience of being part of a community of learners, with access to resources and academic staff. Neither can the cut and thrust of academic debate be easily reproduced at a distance. The strategies students use are a result of their learning conditions and their observations about what "works." It is difficult to see how the quality of learning can improve if two factors remain the same: the learning conditions of students and the design of instructional materials and assessment instruments.

The following recommendations go some way towards improving these factors. However, this analysis of current learning conditions suggests that it would be prudent to stop and take a more realistic view of the kind of university education that can be effectively provided through distance education in the South Pacific.

Reliance on Study Materials

If students are forced to rely heavily, or even exclusively, on the study materials, then these should be designed in such a way as to encourage learning with understanding. Unfortunately, many course writers hold conceptions of teaching that stress the importance of transmitting information, which does not promote learning, and getting them to modify their conceptions is slow and difficult. Small steps can be taken to provide more questions and activities that require students to interact and think about the materials.

The reader often provided with the course—which some students admit not having read—is often limited in scope and comprehensiveness, and could contain a greater variety of readings, such as chapters from other texts, journal articles, and extracts from newspapers and magazines, to give students a feel for the wide variety of printed resources. If these readings are necessary to complete assignments, then they have more of a chance to be read.

Audio tapes can be used creatively to bring the course alive and compensate to some extent for the lack of a tutor. In a course in Educational Psychology the lecturer realized that students could not experience tutorials because of their isolation and had difficulty with a research project. She designed an audio tape of excerpts from several tutorials and asked a series of questions of the type that would be asked in a face-to-face tutorial. The students were able to get a feel for the atmosphere of a live tutorial. She also recorded a series of discussions she had with an on-campus student as they worked through the steps of a research project. Of these tapes one student says, "the cassettes are very helpful, as if we are talking to the tutor himself [sic]" (SA, p. 10).

TV coverage is growing all over the Pacific and there is scope for educational programs, including the use of quality video programs from other distance education providers. The growth of video players, even in the most isolated countries, means that it would be possible to disseminate programs more widely. This requires adequate financial resources and governments should be prepared to assist as part of their policy to improve learning opportunities for the population.

Concentration on Assessment

If students are forced to concentrate on assessment and can pass some courses by just "cramming" without learning, then assessment items that test "real learning" must be developed—and this is just as true for on-campus as for Extension courses. Assessment, more than any other factor, determines the nature of learning, and at present, in a variety of disciplines, there are not nearly enough examples of items that enable students to learn with real understanding, particularly on final exams. The tendency to rely on rote memorization is exacerbated for Extension students, as we have seen, but it is also worsened, for all students, by the weight of final exams, which for nearly all courses, is anywhere from 40% to 60% of the total course grade. One of the major arguments against decreasing the weight of final exams, particularly for Extension courses, is that students cheat on assignments. While cheating undoubtedly does occur, good assessment design can not only encourage learning with understanding, it can also minimize the opportunity to cheat.

Lack of Tutorial Support

Compensating for the lack of tutorial support is not easy. The informal groups that already exist should be encouraged and it should be possible for lists of students' addresses in the same town or area to be published so that they can contact one another and form a study group.

Improved feedback on assignments would decrease the uncertainty of students about their work. Audio tapes could be used to give more personal feedback to students. A blank tape could be supplied by the student with each assignment—or it could be included in the course package—and the marker would record comments and return the tape with the marked assignment. This is no more time-consuming than writing comments that are detailed enough to provide useful feedback.

Although these suggestions could improve the experience of students, the learning conditions of many are so extreme that the question arises, "is it realistically possible to provide a University education through the distance mode in the South Pacific?"

Some argue that the Internet is rapidly making physical distance irrelevant. In the developed world it is becoming increasingly possible to participate in top quality courses from universities around the world. But the cost of equipment and communications connections is prohibitive for most Pacific nations, where some students do not even have electricity. It is now possible to communicate by e-mail to nearly all the USP Centers, and one can imagine students typing up their assignments on computer and e-mailing them for marking to Suva, for instance. But serious infrastructure problems remain: there are only three telephone lines in and out of Tuvalu, for example, and e-mail messages can only be sent or received once a day at best—when the lines are not down. Electronic communication, like satellite tutorials, is only a solution for students who live in or near the capital. The problems of isolation remain for many students. Far from opening opportunities of learning to the less developed countries, the gap between 'haves' and 'have-nots' may well be getting wider.

Students taking courses through distance providers like the Open University in the United Kingdom and the University of New England in Australia not only have access to a wide variety of resources (e.g., public libraries, bookshops, other educational institutions, audio and video tapes, educational TV), they have far greater tutorial support than their fellow students in the South Pacific. In addition, those institutions insist on regular residential schools which provide the important face-to-face contact, interaction with fellow students, and access to excellent library facilities. USP runs similar

Summer Schools, but it can offer only a limited number of such courses in only some of the countries of the region, and thus only reaches relatively few students. Moreover, a Summer School, or other face-to-face, component is very rarely required in a given program.

It may be argued that if a true University education is to be provided, an on-campus experience is essential. The University could offer a limited number of well-designed first year Extension courses in a new degree program which would start with a "foundation" year, possibly in Arts and Social Sciences, to avoid having to provide laboratory facilities for Science courses. The new foundation program of study would lead into the present degree majors. This would mean radical rethinking of degree programs both on and off campus, but in the end it would mean a better use of limited staff resources and provide a much better overall learning experience for students. It would also be necessary for regional governments to be more flexible and generous with their scholarships to enable more students to come to campus.

For the present it's still "just you and the books" most of the time. One can only admire the ingenuity and dedication of those students who achieve some success in their studies, given the conditions they have to try to learn in. We owe it to them to make the experience much better.

NOTES

1. Tokelau does not have its own Center and is served through the USP Center in Apia, Western Samoa. In addition to its Center in Vila, Vanuatu has a Sub-Center in Luganville, on Santo, the largest island of the group.
2. Some marking is also done locally, by "markers" appointed by the relevant teaching department.
3. In an effort to decentralize, the USP Center in Fiji (or "Fiji Center") has recently been relocated from the capital Suva, site of the main campus, to the town of Lautoka, on the Western Side of Viti Levu.
4. Students quoted are referred by the coded initials listed in Appendix 2 (e.g., here, LJ and SI). The number refers to the page of the interview transcript. Transcripts have not been edited for grammatical mistakes or idiosyncrasies.
5. One student suggests that the Center should circulate the class list at the beginning of the semester so that students can set up peer tutorials themselves, and that those would be sufficient, without the presence of a tutor or lecturer.

REFERENCES

Bain, J., & Samuelowicz, K. (1992). Conceptions of teaching held by academic teachers. *Higher Education* 24, 93-111.

Landbeck, R.C., & Mugler, F. (1994). Approaches to study and conceptions of learning of students at the USP. Report from the Center for the Enhancement of Learning and Teaching. Suva, Fiji: The University of the South Pacific.

Landbeck, R.C., & Mugler, F. (1995). The meanings of learning for students at the University of the South Pacific. Paper presented at the Sixth EARLI Conference (European Association for Research in Learning and Instruction), 26-31 August, University of Nijmegen, Holland.

Landbeck, R.C., & Mugler, F. (1996). The transition from high school to university at the University of the South Pacific. In G. Gibbs (Ed.), *Improving Student Learning: Using Research to Improve Student Learning* (pp. 76-85). Oxford: Oxford Centre for Staff Development.

Marton, F. (1981). Phenomenography—describing conceptions of the world around us. *Instructional Science* 10, 177-200.

Marton, F., Dall'Alba, G., & Beaty, E. (1993). Conceptions of learning. *International Journal of Educational Research* 19, 277-300.

Marton, F., Dall'Alba, G., & Kun Tse, L.K. (1993). The paradox of the Chinese learner. Occasional Paper 93.1. Educational Research and Development Unit. Royal Melbourne Institute of Technology.

Marton, F., & Saljö, R. (1976). On qualitative differences in learning: 1. Outcome and process. *British Journal of Educational Psychology* 46, 4-11.

Nagle, A., & Marton, F. (1993). "Learning, knowing and understanding. Qualitative changes in student teachers' views of the relationship between some educational phenomena during the first term of pre-school teacher education in Uruguay." Paper presented at the Fifth EARLI Conference, Aix-en-Provence, 31 August-5 September.

Saljö, R. (1979). *Learning in the learner's perspective. 1. Some common sense conceptions* Reports from the Department of Education, University of Gothenburg, No. 76.

Prosser, M., Trigwell, K., & Taylor, P. (1995). A phenomenographic study of academics' conceptions of science learning and teaching. *Learning and Instruction* 4, 217-231.

USP Statistics (1995). Planning and Development Office. Suva, Fiji: University of the South Pacific.

Van Rossum, E.J., & Schenk, S. (1984). The relationship between learning conception, study strategy and learning outcome. *British Journal of Educational Psychology* 54, 73-88.

Watkins, D., & Regmi, M. (1990). An investigation of the approach to learning of Nepalese tertiary students. *Higher Education* 20, 459-469.

Watkins, D., & Regmi, M. (1992). How universal are student conceptions of learning? A Nepalese investigation. *Psychologia* 25, 101-110.

APPENDIX 1

The Interview Schedule

What are you studying by Extension at the moment?

What are you aiming to do with your studies?

How long have you been studying by Extension?

Have you studied any courses since leaving high school?

What is it like to study by Extension?

What do you think are the differences between studying by Extension and studying on campus?

How do you study?

How do you read? Any special way? As you read, what are you trying to do?

Do you make notes? What kind of notes, why those kind, what are you going to do with them?

How do you prepare for the final exam?

What help do you get with your studies, e.g., visits from USP staff, local tutors?

What books, libraries, other resources can you use?

What about fellow students, are you able to meet with them? If so what would you do when you meet?

Can you give me an example of something you have learned recently?

Think about "learning" for a moment. What thoughts come into your mind when you hear that word? What do you mean by "learning"?

How do you know if you have learned something?

What do you mean by "understanding"?

How do you know if you have understood something?

Do you think it is possible to memorize something without understanding it?

Is memorizing different from understanding?

Are you happy with the way you learn?

What do you think would make you an even better learner?

Extension Students Interviewed

	code	sex	age	occupation	place of residence
1	AB	M	32	teacher	Rakiraki
2	SD	F	42	teacher	Lautoka
3	BN	M	45	teacher	Lautoka
4	KD	F	39	teacher	Lautoka
5	SA	F	23	teacher	Rakiraki
6	VM	F	32	teacher	Labasa
7	NG	F	24	teacher	Rakiraki
8	VK	M	35	teacher	Sigatoka
9	SI	F	19	unemployed	Lautoka
10	NS	F	29	bank teller	Sigatoka
11	MT	M	47	educ. officer	Labasa
12	EV	M	23	bank teller	Sigatoka
13	IT	F	38	teacher	Lautoka
14	RL	M	23	teacher	Sigatoka
15	PN	F	40	teacher	Sigatoka
16	CD	M	29	teacher	Lautoka
17	LK	F	31	teacher	Savusavu
18	FR	F	29	teacher	Labasa
19	KT	F	23	bank teller	Savusavu
20	CS	M	24	teacher	Savusavu
21	MA	M	37	salesman	Sigatoka
22	LJ	F	23	teacher	Rakiraki
23	DG	M	44	business	Rakiraki
24	CR	F	39	librarian	Rakiraki

CHAPTER 6

Portfolios as an Alternative Assessment Practice in Higher Education

Kari Smith

> How we assess students says far more about us and what we value, than we might wish. (Knight, 1996)

INTRODUCTION

The use of portfolios for assessing student learning in higher education is an increasingly talked-about—but not so often used—practice. This chapter illustrates the usefulness of portfolios in higher education, specifically for teacher training programs, by drawing on personal experiences with portfolios in a variety of courses. Since 1993 I have used portfolios as the main assessment practice in pre- and in-service training of secondary school teachers at Oranim School of Education of the Kibbutz Movement in Israel, a small training college. This paper presents several case studies, each with a different story to tell. The students' opinions about the use of portfolios in their courses are used to illustrate the learning process they went through when compiling the portfolios. Advantages and disadvantages are discussed, alongside the main problems we—the students and I—encountered. The paper concludes with a general discussion on the place of portfolios in teacher training and higher education in general.

BACKGROUND

From my extensive experience teaching in school and in higher education, I have found that assessing learners is an integrated part of my work. Moreover, this part has a major influence on the students' attitude toward the subject matter I teach, and toward me as a teacher. However, perhaps most importantly, my assessment of students plays a crucial role in their present and future lives. This is a heavy responsibility to carry, and for years I have felt that the widely used practice of learner assessment in the form of tests—

often as an appendix after the course had been completed—did not agree with my views on learning or teaching. I have had considerable difficulty accepting the notion that the work put into the learning process and the learning product could be measured by only one test, of my or any other design, and timed by me or by an external body which did not know my students. I struggled with a feeling that was later so well worded by Tomlinson and Saunders:

> There is something inherently inhuman in the attempt to reduce human capacity to a set of criteria statements. (1995)

Thus, I began to look for alternative assessment methods which could reflect learning as a developmental process in which the learner and the tutor carry on a learning/teaching dialogue (Vygotsky, 1978) leading to an outcome which represented the individual learner's achievements. Recent literature on educational assessment criticizes the psychometric test, claiming that it does not reflect what really happens in the classroom (Elliott, 1991; Archbald, 1991; Wolf, et al., 1991; Moss, 1992; Shoamy, 1989; Birenbaum, 1994; and Nevo, 1995, among others), and that it narrows the curriculum to the teaching of only what would be on the exam. Gipps (1994) describes a current "shift in practice from psychometrics to educational assessment, from a testing culture to an assessment culture" (p.158). Educational assessment is meant to represent reflective learning, comprehension and application, in contradiction to the often shallow, rote learning which is often produced by a traditional examination.

The question we as educators have to ask ourselves is simply, "Why do we assess?" Do we want the assessment of learning to serve as the basis for accountability for the institution—do we want it to serve accreditation purposes—or do we want it to promote and encourage the learning process? (Gipps, 1994) While it is important to encourage accountability for institutions and programs, the assessment of learning—particularly in current, widely used standardized forms—should not play a primary role in the evaluation and accountability of a college or university. The most important purpose for the assessment of learning is to promote learning—to develop an active and reflective learner—in addition to serving as evidence of the learning process and learning achievements.

THE PORTFOLIO AS AN ALTERNATIVE ASSESSMENT TOOL

The portfolio is one of a variety of instruments suggested for alternative assessment purposes, alongside exhibitions, individual and group projects, learner diaries, self-assessment, and others. A portfolio is, as I use it, "a collection of samples of biographies of students' work collected over a period of time." (Smith, 1996) Although various uses of portfolios are being implemented in education—mostly as a learning and assessment tool for formative purposes—there is still apprehension towards using it as a certification tool. It is often recommended that portfolios be used alongside more standardized forms for learner assessment (Koretz, Stecher, Klein, McCaffrey, and Deibert, 1993). This has been done successfully by myself and other teachers of English as a foreign language in Israel (Smith, 1995). Portfolios can be put to a variety of uses, from pure learning-promotion reasons to pure accountability reasons. Gottlieb (1995) describes a "cradle approach" to portfolio applications, moving from an informal learning device for the student to a formal accountability tool for the institution. In my personal experience, the portfolio has been used as a learning and assessment device, and it has not yet been used for accountability purposes in my institution.

In order to describe the reasons for choosing portfolios as the assessment practice in my courses, it is necessary to explore more closely the definition of portfolios provided earlier in the chapter—a collection of samples of biographies of students' work collected over a period of time.

A Collection

Any assessment of the learner must be based on samples of the learning process and outcomes—it is impossible to incorporate everything a course covers into any form of assessment, whether it be a test or portfolio. It is, however, important that more than one sample is collected, and that the learner is involved in choosing the samples which will ultimately reflect his or her own learning achievements. Thus, there is a section in the portfolios I collect from my students which is purely optional, providing the learner with the choice of what entries to include in their portfolio. The assigned portfolio entries reflect the course content and are all based on individual or group projects from the course. There are also assignments that I see as essential evidence of learning in my course. These assignments reflect the core of the course, and I want all course participants to experience working with them. This is the compulsory part of the portfolio.

Portfolios thus represent samples of work chosen by the learner and the teacher, entries which represents both my choice as the course teacher and also individual choices made by the learner. The portfolio includes samples representing the course content—some work accomplished by all learners, others individualized, representing a specific learner only. The result provides course validity, a basis for comparison, and individualization.

Biographies of Work

The portfolio contains the biographies of the entries—that is, the progressive drafts and revisions of each assignment—which is, in my opinion, crucial when discussing educational assessment. The learners do not have only "one shot" at the assignment (nor are they assessed based on one attempt). They are invited to open up a learning dialogue with the teacher, which in turn leads to individualized teaching. The learners give me a draft of the assignment, which I then comment on and return to them—no grades are given, but instead guidelines for revision and improvement are offered. The comments are made in a personal, informal way, and the learners may ask me to comment on as many versions as they desire—usually about two or three. All versions are included in the portfolio together with the final product. These are the biographies of the assignments which serve as evidence for the learning process of the student. The dialogue with the tutor is individualized and focused on the needs of the individual learner. The achievements are assessed based on the final product, but in concert with the cumulative portfolio entries that serve as evidence of the learning process.

Collected over a Period of Time

The portfolio is a collection of problem solving or research assignments, and it is important that the learners are given adequate time to work on these. Therefore, the completed portfolio should be handed in and assessed summatively at the end of the course. The various entries are, however, assigned and worked on throughout the course, and there is constant formative assessment of the students' work and learning. A portfolio which is handed in at the end of the course, presenting only one version of the assignments, is decidedly not of the same quality as a portfolio which contains revised versions of the learning tasks. The time element is an important factor in compiling a representative portfolio.

ASSESSMENT OF THE PORTFOLIOS

If the learner portfolios are to be used for assessment purposes and not only to promote learning, the assessment criteria have to be clearly understood by the assessor and carefully explained to the learners. An integrated part of the assessment criteria is the learner's self-assessment, which takes the form of *reflections* on the various entries. Self-assessment is a major component of alternative assessment (Shoamy, 1989; Ediger, 1993; Elliott, 1991; Harris and McCann, 1994; Gipps, 1994). Through self-assessment, the students learn about themselves as learners and can make decisions regarding their own learning. Self-reflection is the process the learner goes through in order to arrive at the assessment, and requires distancing oneself from the task we are working on, looking at the approach chosen, the effort put into it, and the quality of the final product.

Self-reflection is largely an attempt to look at our own work with the eyes of somebody else, but with having much more information than anyone else about our abilities, reasons for choices made, amount of work put into the assignment, and level of satisfaction with the assignment. Self-reflection is not a simple task to undertake, but it is an essential characteristic of metacognitive learners who are capable of managing their own learning (Haller, Child and Walberg, 1988). Moreover, Rowe (1988) claims that "metacognitive awareness is a prerequisite for academic and real life success." (p. 229) Reflection has thus become an integrated part of the portfolios I work with, and it is incorporated in each and every entry. The learners are asked to reflect on and assess the process they went through while working with the entry, the ups and downs they had, the effort they put into it, what they learned (or what they did not learn) from the assignment, and their level of satisfaction with the outcome. In addition, they are asked in the concluding assignment of the portfolio project to reflect on the portfolio as a learning and assessment tool.

The importance of this self-reflection component is perhaps even more significant in that I work with students who will someday become—or already are—teachers. Schon's (1983) introduction of the concept *reflective teaching*—based on Dewey's (1916) classic work on *reflectivity*—only emphasizes the need to encourage my students to recognize the importance of ongoing reflections in their personal work. Thus self-assessment is not only viewed as part of the assessment criteria of the portfolio but also as a means for training to learn and teach effectively. The trainees assess their portfolio work through their reflections. They are also asked to grade their portfolios independently of their teacher's grading, based on the criteria outlined below, which they have been familiarized with from the onset of the course.

Assessment Criteria
Each entry in the portfolio is given a specific weight in terms of numbers, as the trainees must be given a number (percentage out of a hundred) as their final course grade. This was found to be a feasible means for offering an al-

ternative assessment approach within the present institutional system of numerical grades. As well, the use of numbers also provides a means for moving away from an overall impressionistic marking of the portfolios, by instead attempting to break the project down into smaller, more measurable parts. A common argument against the use of portfolios is that the subjective, often unreliable grading of portfolios is a serious problem, particularly if used for accreditation purposes. By setting clear standards and having more than one grader, I aim at increasing the reliability of the tool. The entries are graded according to the following standards:

1. *Revision*—the use the learner has made of the learning dialogue with the tutor. Did the learner take my comments into consideration in revising the assignment? How far did the learner choose to take this dialogue?
2. *Level of learning outcome*—what were the learner's achievements as compared to fixed criteria for each assignment?
3. *Reflections*—did the learner reflect on the assignment? How serious are the reflections? Are the learners capable of distancing themselves from their own work and examining the process and the outcome from a more objective perspective?
4. *Layout*—is the entry presented in a clear and aesthetic form?

In addition to the assessment criteria related to each entry, the portfolio as a whole is assessed based on its completeness—whether it includes all the required entries, an introduction, a conclusion, a table of contents, a list of references, and so forth.

From my experiences with portfolios in higher education, I have learned that the assessment criteria must be clearly spelled out and presented to the learners at the beginning of the course. By the time students get to higher education, they are (unfortunately) so accustomed to being assessed on the basis of standardized tests and examinations, that it may be difficult for them to accept a different approach. Thus, at present, portfolio assessment is best served by being translated into the assessment terminology which the learners are familiar with.

CASES REPRESENTING USES OF PORTFOLIOS

For the last three years portfolios have become an integrated part of my work in teacher training. The Oranim School of Education of the Kibbutz Movement in Israel is a rather small training college, yet unique in its approach to teacher training. At the university division of the college, where I work, the trainees graduate with a B.A. or B.SC. degree in the respective disciplines, along with a teaching certificate for secondary school. Their teacher education training is not, as in most other universities, an addition which follows their degree program but instead is integrated with their studies from the beginning. For the first four years, students take courses within their specific disciplines for three days a week, and education courses for the remaining two days. In their final year they teach in a school for at least ten hours a week, and take courses related to their teaching two days a week. In these final courses, the trainees discuss their work experiences in a didactic seminar related to their discipline. As well, they also meet with novice teachers of other subjects in a course called "classroom situations," where the trainees use their own and their colleagues' cases as the basis for professional development. The teacher trainees also take a course in "educational assessment," in which they discuss and experience alternative assessment approaches as learners, with the purpose of enhancing their teaching skills.

Oranim also offers an in-service training center, where experienced teachers come in for knowledge and skills enhancement, advanced certificates and retraining. These veterans participate in various courses one day per week for a year or sometimes in more intensive courses which meet more frequently, but for only one semester. One of the most popular courses in recent years has been a course on "alternative educational assessment." Two cases presented in this chapter are taken from courses I teach at the university division—methodology of teaching of English as a foreign language, and educational assessment for novice teachers with a mixed subject population. The third case comes from my experience teaching an in-service course for school principals.

In recent years, portfolios have been used in all my courses as a learning promotion and assessment tool. For the following cases, the framework of each course is briefly described followed by a short explanation of the portfolio outlines used. Problems met will be identified, and examples of learners' and my reflections of the projects are included.

Case 1: English Language Teaching Methods
This course is the major educational course which English teachers-to-be take in the third year of their training. The course runs eight hours per week for a whole year—one hour per day, four days a week at Oranim, with one four-hour day spent at the schools. Portfolios are a compulsory part of the trainees' requirements in the more theoretical aspect of the course, and a dialogue journal related to their practical experience is required in the practical component of the course. An action research project provides the link between

these two components of the course. The intensity of the course in terms of time and requirements makes this a major part of the teacher training program.

The portfolio assignment, which carries a weight of 50% of the course grade, is presented to the trainees at the beginning of the year, at which time they are given a short introduction to the rationale behind portfolios as an assessment practice.

The outline of assignments provided (see Table 1) reflects the topics dealt with in this course. Compulsory entries involve reflection on various assigments regarding the teaching of reading comprehension, grammar, and literature. These represent the basics of teaching English as a foreign language in Israel. Optional entries are related to other issues discussed in the course, such as their own language learning experience, test administration, the ideal teacher, using a blackboard, vocabulary and dictionary work, vocabulary teaching, developing oral skills, and so forth.

Table 1
Portfolio Outline of Topics for 3rd-Year English Language Teaching Methodology

---

Compulsory entries: 50 points
Introduction to the portfolio
Grammar project
Reading project
Literature project
Your reflections on this portfolio project

Optional entries: 50 points, Choose four
Your language learning experience, what was positive/negative?
What is learning/teaching?
How can we bridge the gap from elementary to secondary language teaching?
How would you teach new vocabulary?
How would you promote the oral/aural skills in your pupils?
Efficient use of the board: a model
Visual aids in language teaching
Teaching language in heterogeneous classes
Whole language teaching: how can we implement it?

After the topics have been dealt with in class, the trainees decide which ones they will work on more in depth and include in the portfolio and then open a *learning dialogue* with me on these. The learning dialogue takes on mostly a written form, but involves weekly one-on-one discussion during the two

weekly hours I have set aside for personal tutorials. These meetings are meaningful to me as the course teacher in understanding and learning about (and
from) the trainees, and they prove to be helpful to the students in developing the ability to reflect on their own work. The portfolios are handed in at
the end of the year—by that time I have become familiar with the biographies of the various entries, so the portfolio itself is really a collection of the
trainees' work which I have seen and read several times.

As a learning tool the portfolio proves to be an excellent means to promote learning in-depth on assignments the trainees found interesting. Some
extracts from students' comments illustrate this.

> The portfolio forced me to be a serious learner; there was no way of just doing an
> assignment and to forget it.

> I appreciate the fact that I didn't have only one shot at an assignment. I know I never
> succeed the first time. The portfolio gave me the opportunity to learn from my mis-
> takes.

The fact that the learners were asked to reflect on their activities helped
them clarify their weaknesses and strengths as teacher trainees, as well as their
roles as teachers.

> I never realized that it is so complicated to teach English grammar. As a native speaker
> I never really thought of it. I have a problem here when I shall teach grammar to Is-
> raeli children.

> Teaching English is not like teaching math. Via English, I teach about the world . . .
> yes, in fact, about life. I am not just a teacher, I am an educator. This was new to me.

As an assessment tool the portfolio reduced much of the tension related to
assessment, and the learners felt that the portfolio enabled them to present
themselves at their best. The students' self-assessment of the portfolios correlated well with my assessment, and in this course there are few cases of wide
gaps between the two raters (the student and the course teacher).

> This portfolio is like an album which I make up after a wonderful trip. Each entry is
> a snapshot of experiences I had as a learner during this year, and I had the possibility
> to choose the "pictures" which I wanted to represent me. I even had the chance to
> work in the laboratory to improve the shots before they were put in the album.

> This is me at my best. I could never show you this in a test.

There were, however, problems the trainees brought up which I shall have
to take into consideration in the future.

> The portfolio was too much work. I never got things really finished. There was always something I could improve.

> There were too many requirements for the portfolio . . . other sides of my studies were set aside because of it.

> This soul searching is exhausting . . . it is tough to examine yourself all the time. It is easier when the teacher tells you how good you are.

These quotes are taken from students' comments over the three last years and they do not represent one specific class. I have learned that in the future I need to reduce the requirements for the course, to have fewer entries in the portfolio, or to include the action research as part of the portfolio requirements, at the expense of other assignments. I have also found that it was very difficult for the trainees to understand what I wanted from them in the beginning. The instructions need to be very clear, and I have to patiently explain the portfolio again and again. Next year I shall devote some sessions to work on the portfolios, hoping that this might reduce some of the pressure and provide better guidance for those who want it.

Portfolios are time-consuming for a teacher to nurture and then read for assessment purposes, and it is difficult to do this properly in large classes. A group of twenty students is perhaps ideal for me. The next case will illustrate some problems with large courses.

Case 2: Course on Educational Assessment for Novice Teachers
The course on educational assessment for novice teachers is given in the last year of the students' teacher training, when they are already practicing teachers in schools and responsible for their own classes. The trainees are faced with problems of assessing pupils, and they have become familiar with current assessment approaches practiced in schools. The group of trainees in the course is mixed in terms of disciplines—there are novice teachers of mathematics, biology, history, Hebrew language, Bible, and so forth.

The course is a semester-long course of 30 hours—15 meetings of two hours each. However, due to holidays and the occasional strikes, it often happens that the class meets less often than this. The aim of the course is to familiarize the novice teachers with alternative assessment approaches, so they may start applying them in their own teaching practice, moving away from the more traditional psychometric ways of assessing learners which they have experienced themselves and find practiced in schools. The students experience alternative assessment approaches in the course—of which the portfolio is one—as learners, in an intentional attempt to bridge the notorious gap between theory and practice. It is not enough to teach about alternative assessment if the novice teachers do not know how it works in practice—only a personal hands-on experience will really help them realize what alternative assessment means, and what advantages and disadvantages are involved.

The portfolio counts for 100% of the course grade, and is combined of compulsory and optional entries as indicated in Table 2.

Table 2
Portfolio Outline of Topics, 4th-Year Course in Educational Assessment

Compulsory entries: 40 points
Introduction to the portfolio
Summaries of and comments on three articles from the reading list
Educational assessment, what is it?
Why and how do you want to use portfolio in one of your classes?
Reflection on your work with this portfolio

Optional entries: 60 points; choose four assignments
Evaluation of a course you have taken; comparing product to the stated goals
Ways of evaluating teaching and your implementation of it in your own teaching
The story of a test you designed and gave to one of your classes
Explanation and presentation of a table of specification for a test you gave your class
Summaries of and comments on three articles not from the reading list
Psychometric testing versus authentic assessment
Explanation and example of a questionnaire you gave your pupils regarding their feelings about learner assessment
Test-anxiety, how can it be reduced?

A test, designed by the students themselves, taken and self-assessed during the course, is compulsory. The remaining portfolio entries reflect issues dealt with in class. This course is usually a big course with about 50 students, and because it is rather short, I do not get to know each student as well as I do in the course described in Case 1. I understand, accept and regret the feeling expressed by one of the students this last year:

> It is a strange feeling handing in a portfolio, which is so personal, to somebody who doesn't even know my name.

The portfolio is introduced in the course description handed out in the first lesson, and it usually causes great frustration and insecurity among the participants. It is a new concept to almost all of the trainees—they have not seen this in their higher education, nor in earlier schooling.

> When I first heard the word "portfolio" I had no idea what the lecturer wanted from me. It took a long time before I realized what it was all about. I wanted to have a test like in other courses, and that is it. Now I am glad I did not.

Time is spent every course meeting explaining their portfolio assignment, and as part of the course syllabus, at least two lessons are devoted to portfolios as an assessment tool. One of the most problematic issues here is starting the learning dialogue with the students—they are not used to being given repeated opportunities to develop their work, and many of them do not see the importance of it. Some of them hand in the portfolio at the end of the course without having asked me to read it and comment on it during the course.

> It is clear to me that what is missing in my learning process is the lack of dialogue with the teacher. I didn't open such a dialogue by handing her the various entries for comments. The responsibility for this is mine, I chose not to do that. To my defense I can say that the significant learning process in this course took place when I chose the assignments to work on, and wrote the reflections on my own learning. This was the bridge between the assignments and my own teaching, according to my own choice. However, as a teacher in high school, I shall not give up on the importance of having a teaching dialogue with the pupils, and I shall insist on reading all assignments. This is what creates the significant relationship among teacher and pupil. I regret that I missed out on that.

The quality of the assignments is lower without the learning dialogue, and it is obvious that some students compiled the portfolio at the end just to get it done.

> I was very pragmatic choosing the assignments at the end of the course, and I chose those which required little effort on my part.

Those students who did hand in assignments for comments and revision felt that it was worthwhile in terms of their own learning and the relationship they developed with the course teacher.

> I felt that the more times an entry was exchanged between the teacher and me, my learning improved. The relationship between the teacher and me became personal, I knew there was a channel of communication between us; an intellectual dialogue on the topic.

Reflecting on one's own work, seems to be totally strange to most students—this says something about the perception of learning in higher education as only the transmission of information—and it is not a very easy skill to learn.

Reflecting was tough. I had problems taking a distance from my own work. I am too involved.

Examine my own work is one of the hardest things I have done. I don't always think of the reasons for doing things or look at what the gains are. I just do it. I grew with these reflections, not only as a teacher, but also as a person.

The portfolio taught me a lot about my own teaching and how I want to assess my students.

Quite a few of the trainees' portfolios included entries completely without reflection, or with very shallow comments which did not reflect any attempt to develop insight of their own learning.

However, those students—the majority of this class—who became engaged with the portfolio assignment and took the full benefit of me as a tutor for their work, compiled excellent portfolios, and found this a very positive learning experience which they wanted to bring into their own classes.

The main goal of this portfolio was that we had to cope with it. It gave me a possibility to be on the other side of the fence, before I try it with my pupils. It was an interesting an effective way of trying out a new assessment approach. Having experienced it as learners we can better help the pupils.

Portfolio as an assessment tool enables the learners to emphasize the process and not only the product. It is a more humanistic approach aimed at involving the pupils, giving them responsibility and encouraging them to be curious about the subject learned. That is most important. It is formative assessment, but there is also need for summative assessment in education which enables standardization and comparison.

My primary aim in using portfolios in this course is to provide a bridge between the theories of alternative assessment that students discuss in the course and their practical experiences as teachers in their own classes. Based on the comments of the participants, it seems that this aim is achieved. Yet, there are problems in this specific course which are worth mention.

1. *Intensity of the course.* If the course is short, there is no time to develop an ongoing learning dialogue, and the portfolio becomes a file of various assignments the learner merely completed in order to fulfill the course requirements. Even a semester of fifteen weeks does not seem enough, especially when the class meets for only two hours once a week.

2. *The size of the class.* If the class is too large (which for my preference means more than 20 students) it is difficult to develop a personalized channel of communication with each student, and there is a possibility for learners

to "escape" this. Thus, the most important aspect of the portfolio—the support of an ongoing learning process—is lost.

3. *Teacher's authority.* It seems that even with teacher trainees there is sometimes a need for the teacher to be a forceful authority. Demanding that students read various assigments at specific times is necessary in order to ensure the possibility for revision and improvement. It is mostly useless to permit students to do all the assigments at their leisure—most have difficulties taking this responsibility upon themselves, and instead must be continually told to do so.

Keeping these three points in mind, I shall adapt the portfolio work for this course in the future to fit this specific course better. There is still much work to be done, as a student observed:

> My opinion is that the portfolio is a good assessment tool, but as every tool, it does not fit all situations. It was not the best assessment tool in this course.

Case 3. In-Service Course for School Principals

The Israeli Ministry of Education recommends portfolios as part of formative performance assessment for pupils in elementary and secondary schools, and as described in the above cases, teacher trainees at Oranim learn how to apply portfolios as an integrated part of their teaching and assessment approach. One of the problems voiced by teachers has been that while trying to implement some of the new assessment ideas, several have met resistance and often rejection by their school principals. If changes are to take place in schools, they must have the cooperation of—indeed, in some places must even be initiated by—the decision makers, who in most cases are the school principals. This case describes how 35 school principals learned about portfolios by experience—creating a personal portfolio related to their own work at school.

These principals attended a course on educational assessment, where the main course requirement was to present a portfolio at the end of the course. During an entire semester, the principals spent one day a week at Oranim. In addition to the course on educational assessment, they were also given courses in computer assisted learning and management. The course participants held either a BA, a B.Sc. or a B.Ed degree, and they represented a rich variety of Israeli schools, as well as cultures—Arabs, Muslims, Christians Druze, and Jews (kibbutz, circular city, and orthodox yeshiva). Each culture has its own view on education, teaching and learning. 67% of the participants had no background in evaluation and assessment, and of those who did, 18% had taken a previous course with me. Examinations and tests were the only assessment tools used in 85% of their schools, and for 93% of them, the use of portfolios in education was a totally new concept. It was quite a challenge to give a course on educational assessment to this group!

The aim of the course was to change current assessment practices in their schools, and I chose to use an incremental training approach which has been recommended by Tillema (1995), who used it with executives in business. In this approach, the participants must feel that the potential gain from the course content was related to their own work. Thus, I believed it was most important to introduce portfolios through hands-on experience—in essence, to put these principals into practice with their own portfolio.

Also in this course there was great confusion in the group when the course requirements of the portfolio were explained. The majority of these distinguished educators felt at a loss when asked to do something in education they had little or no idea about. The portfolio framework had, as in the other courses discussed here, an obligatory and optional part, and all the assignments were related to their work as school principals—such as evaluation of the school, evaluation of teaching, how to give feedback to teachers, how to introduce changes, what happens during examinations, how educational assessment might be applied in their schools, and so forth (see Table 3).

Reflections asking for self-examination in terms of feelings and learning was a compulsory part of each assignment, and the principals were invited to start working on the assignments at the beginning of the course, and to start an individual learning dialogue with me. It took time before they understood what I meant with that. They were also surprised not to find a number grade on their assignments but instead comments related to specific issues and an invitation (request) for revision. To them, learner assessment had always consisted of handing in one version of one's learning task, receiving a number grade on it, and then moving on—often forgetting both the task and the purpose of it. This was, according to what they told me, the approach practiced in their schools. Little by little, they began to understand that I worked differently in my course—they had as many opportunities to do and re-do each assignment as they deemed necessary, and there would be no grade assigned before the assignment was put in the portfolio at the end.

Table 3

Portfolio Outline of Topics for the In-Service Course for School Principals on Educational Assessment

---

Compulsory entries: 40 points

Introduction; presentation of your school and the assessment approach used in your school before the course

A model of (including instruments) evaluation of your school

Summaries of and comments on three articles from the reading list

A model of (including instruments) learner assessment, based on the principles of this course, to be used in your school

Your reflections on this portfolio project

Optional entries: 60 points, choose four

How to improve teamwork in your school

The responsibilities of the heads of department as you see them

Observation of a teacher and the feedback session. How did you feel? How do you think the teacher felt?

What happens with the teacher and the pupils during a test? Your visit to a class during a test. What did this teach you?

The story of teacher meeting about pupils' marks chaired by you

A model of a pupil's report card, including explanations

A model for teacher evaluation, including explanations

Importance of testing in learner assessment

Ways of assessing learners formatively, and the importance of it

---

I had to spend at least twenty minutes of each lesson on explanations and clarifications, because the anxiety level regarding this new thing—the portfolio—was very high. My first challenge was to reduce this anxiety. The participants also began to realize that the assignments were connected to their own work as principals—at this point, they began to view them as helpful tasks and not only as course requirements. The intrinsic motivation that developed affected their work, which then in turn improved in quality. Some of the principals became quite eager to exploit this learning opportunity as far as possible—they even handed in a revised (and often improved) version each week.

> While compiling this portfolio, I had the opportunity to look at evaluation and assessment in school in a different way. It was a personal experience for me which gave the learner (me) opportunities to show my learning and knowledge in different ways.
>
> The portfolio provides a more in-depth picture of the learner.
>
> There is no doubt that a lot of hard work and thought is put into this portfolio. However, I can also say that I feel that it has all been very worthwhile.

The principals experienced a learning process which will hopefully influence the assessment work performed in their schools in the future. 85% of the course participants said they would introduce portfolios to their staffs and insist that it be tried out. Some began these efforts before the class was even finished:

> I tried to involve the teachers and the staff in what I was learning in the course. I understand that a change must take place, it is only a question of time. The change has to come slowly, if not, it might fail.

The portfolio work in this course caused the participants to question the learner assessment methods used in their schools, and they concluded their own portfolio project with a feeling that this was an experience they had gained from and which they could put into practice in the future. Several of the participants saw the portfolio as evidence of their work as school principals which could be used for presentations to teachers, parents, inspectors, and others. They saw it as documentation of their work.

> Looking back on this portfolio I can see the areas in which it has helped me to develop. First of all, the portfolio has allowed me to view my work in the context of my own setting. Second, it has enabled me to create, with input from the teacher, my own assessment and explore my own concerns by reflecting on different areas in the field of education. Third, it has helped me become articulate—putting my thoughts and feelings into clear speech. Next, during the process of development, the portfolio has allowed me to interact with my colleagues by sharing suggestions and support. Moreover, in the future, this portfolio can hopefully assist me during my job searches, by providing evidence of my competence.
> Before the course I asked myself: "What else can be said about assessment?" I learned it was one of the most important courses I have ever taken.

The problems the participants encountered were mainly focused on the hard work and amount of time the portfolio demanded. They felt it was too much for them alongside their responsibilities in school (this is the learner's voice) and that it would also be too time consuming for the teachers, taking their teaching load into consideration (this is the principal's voice).

I would like to discuss some of the problems that I, as the course teacher, found with the portfolios of this group. I added a meeting to the course the second semester in order to discuss the problems with the course participants.

1. *Framework of the portfolio.* The portfolio as presented in this class was extremely time-consuming for the participants and me, so I agree with their comments. There were too many assignments to work on, and it influenced the depth of the learning on each assignment. In order to have enough time

to work on all the required entries, some of them were done without being read and commented on by me. Because the material was so new to the participants, they needed to be guided in their learning. I was also under pressure to read all the assignments every week and to make sure that helpful comments and guidance were given. So, next time I shall ask for fewer entries to be included in the portfolio. A related point is that teaching time does not reflect only lecture time but also includes working individually with students.

2. *Reflections.* I was surprised that also in this group it was very difficult to promote reflective work, or even to explain what reflection is. For the most part, the principals seemed to understand the theories we discussed on reflective teaching and reflective management, although they had serious difficulty putting the theories into practice. Most did not succeed in engaging a dialogue with themselves—with their colleagues, they could discuss issues of practice, but they could not distance themselves from their own practice in a usefully reflective way.

An example of this was demonstrated by one of the assignments, in which they were asked to observe a teacher and to give feedback to this teacher afterwards. They were asked to analyze how they felt when sitting opposite the teacher, how they felt giving the feedback, and how they thought the teacher felt. I read clear, organized reports on the lesson, and suggestions for improvement, but very few were able to relate to the main issues in the assignment. When I brought this up in class, they said that they had never thought of this aspect of their work, and it was difficult for them to *look at and word their own feelings.* Perhaps reflection is not a skill we are born with—this course seemed to show that in the case of the education profession, it is not a skill we acquire from experience. Serious attention must be devoted to developing this skill among learners, and more importantly, among educators at all levels.

3. *Assessment.* Even though the criteria for assessing the portfolios had been made very clear from the beginning of the course, it was difficult for some of the principals to understand the concept behind the criteria. In all, six of the participants' self-assessment efforts were largely based on the following perspective:

> I did all you told me to do, and I spent a long time on this portfolio.

To these participants the process itself had become more important than the outcome, and they felt they deserved a good grade based on their efforts only. It is important, while working with portfolios—especially with more advanced learners—that the weight given to the final product is not minimized, and that the assessment of the portfolio is based both on the learning process and learning outcome. These six participants were so concerned about their final grade, that I addressed the issue in the extra session with the group. As well, I had their portfolios assessed by a third person, and their final grades were decided between the participants, the third person, and myself.

Based on feedback from the school principals, I can say that they found the course relevant and the portfolio an exciting and worthwhile project to take on.

> It will influence the assessment of both teachers and pupils in my school, and also the assessment of myself as the principal.

> This experience made the whole difference for me. It balanced the fear as opposed to the security and let me sense the change, the effort that should be invested, the benefit that the students can get out of this type of work. Students should be given the chance to leave their mark on their work, to choose what they like to do and to be responsible for it willingly and not by force. I feel that gradually principals, teachers and students will understand that this is not fantasy land, but a great part of reality that should be used by all educators no matter what their specialty is. My fears have been largely reduced this year.

As well, I found the course with the school principals a very rewarding experience for me, as I learned a lot more about the many sides of portfolio work, and I gained knowledge which will influence my future work with this tool.

Each case described in this chapter has been an action research project about portfolios (and human responses to them), and in the last part of this chapter I shall try to draw from my experience a summary of how using portfolios advances the goals of higher education.

USING PORTFOLIOS IN HIGHER EDUCATION

Based on my own experience with portfolios—some of which I have tried to illustrate by the three cases above—I would like to make it quite clear that I strongly believe there is a place for portfolio in all levels of education. The following discussion centers on three aspects of the portfolio—as a learning tool, an assessment tool, and a formative assessment tool. The concepts discussed can be applied generally in classrooms of any educational level.

Learning tool. Portfolios are first of all a learning tool which, if used properly, emphasize the learning process as well as the learning outcome. The idea of learning as a process is legitimized—it is accepted that the product is at the end of a process which differs from learner to learner in terms of length, depth and quality. Teaching in higher education is often conducted in the form of transmitting information to the learners—in terms of lectures and literature—and checked in the form of an examination at the end. In such an environment, the students are largely left alone in terms of their learning process, unguided by the course teacher. By applying the portfolio as the basis for a dialogue between the learner and teacher, the learning environment—and its participants' roles—change dramatically. The teacher is no longer a transmitter of knowledge, but rather one who "triggers" the learner's active participation in acquiring the knowledge. A portfolio is not essential in order to have a dialogue between the learner and the teacher, but it simplifies and organizes the process. This simplicity and organization of the learner-teacher dialogue is what I felt was missing in my own teaching.

Because of the active involvement of the students in their own learning, the motivation changes from an extrinsic, grade oriented learning—which often resulted in shallow learning—to a more *intrinsic, content oriented learning,* resulting in deeper, more serious learning. The students become involved in *choosing* a major part of the issues to be examined in depth (within the framework of the course), and are also given the *responsibility* for deciding how much effort they want to put into the various assigned projects. They are required to *reflect and assess* their work, finding out by themselves who they are as learners and how they learn, as opposed to depending on others to tell them what they can and cannot do.

The portfolio *reflects the coursework* (provided the assignments are related to the course syllabus). The compulsory assignments represent the core of the course, and the optional assignments reflect the many directions for learning that each discipline offers. Thus, within the same course, there is *individual and different learning.*

As a learning tool I see few disadvantages of the portfolio, as long as the teachers and students are given the appropriate conditions for working properly with the tool. Some lecture hours need to be replaced with tutoring hours. Courses cannot be crowded, and they ought to stretch over a longer period of time. Overall, the portfolio can be one of the most effective tools available for accomplishing learning-related objectives—as well as learning about one's own learning processes.

Assessment tool. The use of portfolios as an assessment tool is problematic—especially in higher education, where learner assessment is used for accountability and accreditation purposes. I believe the portfolio has *validity*—mainly content validity, but also the *unitary concept of validity* as described by Messick (1988). Validity has to be examined not only according to the test scores themselves and what they reflect but also in light of what purpose the assessment serves. If the assessment is to serve as an indication of competency—which is used for job application or for placement purposes—the portfolio presents a much wider picture of the learner's abilities than any examination might do. However, if the assessment is meant to compare the achievements of students in memorizing exactly the same knowledge—for example, such factual knowledge as required by the medical profession—the portfolio is not the best tool. The use the assessment is put to becomes important, and the portfolio is not the best assessment tool for every use.

A more serious problem with the use of a portfolio as an assessment tool is the question of *reliability*. There is no one standard format of the portfolio, which makes it difficult to set criteria and standards for assessment. The more unrestricted the criteria are, the more subjective the grading becomes, and the question of reliability thus becomes an increasingly problematic one. The assessment criteria have to be predetermined and made familiar to all the parties involved—the teacher, the learner, and anyone else who may use the portfolio for evaluative purposes. It is also recommended to have more than one evaluator of the portfolio, with the final grade being an average or a negotiated rating produced by the teacher, the learner, and the third party.

Examples of this grading approach can best be taken from sports—for example, gymnastics. The are core and optional elements in a gymnastics exercise, and the various optional parts have different levels of difficulty. In addition, there are standards of performance (if an extra jump or step is made, points are taken off). Each rater gives a mark (subjective) using the predetermined criteria and standards, and the final mark is the calculated average. If there is a great variation in the marks, there is negotiation among the referees.

Learning needs to be assessed in a similar way—enabling the individuality of the learner, but still maintaining the basics, and ensuring that specific standards are required. Learning cannot, in my opinion, be assessed effectively by relying on traditional examination methods. However, a more individualized type of learner assessment is time-intensive and expensive, as it takes more effort and labor, and involves an outside evaluator. Thus, administrative support is crucial to a teacher's successful use of portfolios as an assessment tool.

Formative assessment. For formative assessment purposes—where the emphasis is on giving informative feedback to the learner during the process, to help and guide the learning—the portfolio is an excellent tool. Formative assessment can work well in coordination with the traditional *summative assessment* of the learner. There is, as I see it, a place for portfolio in summative assessment if learning is viewed as individualized, a combination of process and product, and that proper assessment procedures are applied. Indeed, there is no reason why we could not see summative assessment in higher education as a combination of various instruments—the more complete and comprehensive our efforts, the better, as Knight (1996) observes:

> Summative assessment arrangements say a great deal about the qualities of the program. The assessment system is a powerful indicator of how seriously an institution takes its aims, showing whether the aims are an exercise in rhetoric or whether ambitious aims are taken seriously.

There are other advantages of using portfolios in higher education which I would like to mention briefly. The portfolio is evidence for competence and work which might be used by the graduates for job applications and later on for promotion purposes. It is dynamic—the "owner" of a portfolio might remove, add, and change entries according to personal and professional development. It is a dynamic file which professions such as artists, models, architecture, and others have always used. Indeed, throughout life most competencies can be put into a portfolio, especially if we move away from the written evidence of ability, knowledge and skill. Other means for presenting evidence—such as recordings—are acceptable entries in a portfolio. For my teacher trainees, a video recording of them conducting a class session would say more about them as teachers than any written assignments could.

The portfolio can also serve as a link between the various institutions of higher education, providing a more complete profile of a student than any traditional transcript. If I, as the chair of the education department, am to accept and give credit for a course taken by an applicant in another institution, a portfolio would provide much more information about the applicant's knowledge and ability than any number or letter grade does.

CONCLUSIONS

In this chapter, I have tried to explain what a portfolio is and the rationale for using it in higher education—more specifically, in teacher training programs. Three cases have been presented in order to illustrate how I apply the portfolio in my teaching and to document the experiences of my students and my own. I have integrated quotations from the students' portfolios into the text, and I thank my students for allowing me to use their reflections and comments in the paper. Without them I would not have learned as much about portfolios as I did. I have tried to present how I see the portfolio as a learning and as an assessment tool, being fully aware that I am biased, strongly believing in its advantages. I have also made an effort to discuss problems and disadvantages found with the use of portfolios. In summary, I believe I have found through portfolios what I was once missing in my teaching and assessment practices, and I encourage their use as a tool for learning and assessment in higher education.

REFERENCES

Archbald, D.A. (1991). Authentic assessment: Principles, practices and issues. *School Psychology Quarterly,* 6/4, 279-293.

Birenbaum, M. (1994). Alternative assessment; a means to improved teaching and learning. *Hed Hachinuch,* 10, 12-14 (Hebrew).

Dewey, J. (1916). *Essays in experimental logic.* New York, Dover.

Ediger, M. (1993). Approaches to measurement and evaluation. *Studies in Educational Evaluation,* 19/1, 41-49.

Elliott, S.N. (1991). Authentic assessment: an introduction to a neo-behavioural approach to classroom assessment. *School Psychology Quarterly,* 6/4, 273-278.

Gipps, C.V. (1994). *Beyond testing.* London, Falmer Press.

Gottlieb, M. (1995). Nurturing student learning through portfolios. *TESOL Journal,* Autumn, 1995.

Haller, E.P., Child, D.A., & Walberg H.J. (1988). Can comprehension be taught? A quantitative synthesis of metacognitive studies. *Educational Researcher,* 17/9, 5-8.

Harris, M. & McCann, P. (1994). *Assessment,* Oxford, Heinemann.

Knight, O. (1996). Quality in higher education and the assessment of student learning. *EARLI-AE Electronic Conference.*

Koretz, D., Stecher, B., Klein, S., McCaffrey, D., & Deibert, E. (1993). Can portfolios assess student performance and influence instruction? The 1991-92 Vermont Experience, CSE Technical Report 371. National Center for Research on Evaluation, Standards, and Student Testing (CRESST), Graduate School of Education, UCLA.

Messick, S. (1988). Validity. In R.L. Linn (ed.) *Educational measurement.* American Council on Education, New York, Macmillan Pub. Company.

Moss, P.A. (1992). Shifting conceptions of validity in educational measurement: Implications for performance assessment. *Review of Educational Research,* 62, 229-258.

Nevo, D. (1995). *School-based evaluation: A dialogue for school improvement.* New York,

Pergamon.

Rowe, H. (1988). Metacognitive skills; promises and problems. *Australian Journal of Reading,* 11/4, 227-237.

Schön, D.A. (1983). *The reflective practitioner: How professionals think in action.* New York, Basic Books.

Shoamy, E. (1989). Evaluating competence and performance within the foreign language classroom, part 1. *English Teachers Journal,* 9, 20-27.

Smith, K. (1995). Action research on the use of portfolio in the language classroom. Paper presented at the *IATEFL conference.* York University, York.

Smith. K. (1996). School principals' experiential learning about portfolio. Paper presented at the *MOFET International Teacher Training conference.* Wingate Institute for Physical Education, Israel.

Tillema, H. (1995). Changing the professional knowledge and beliefs of teachers: a training study. *Learning and Instruction,* 5, 291-315.

Tomlinson, P. & Saunders, S. (1995). The current possibilities for competence profiling in teacher education. In A. Edwards & P. Knight (eds.) *The assessment of competence in higher education.* London, Kogan Page.

Vygotsky, L. S. (1978). *Mind in society. The development of higher psychological processes.* Harvard University Press, Cambridge, MA.

Wolf, D., Bixby, J., Glenn, J., & Gardner, H. (1991). To use their minds well: Investigating new forms of student assessment. *Review of Research in Education,* 17, 31-74.

CHAPTER 7

Encouraging the Use of Collaborative Learning in Higher Education

Theodore Panitz and Patricia Panitz

Research studies overwhelmingly favor collaborative learning as the most effective form of learning (Johnson, Johnson & Holubec, 1984). Yet, despite all the studies and anecdotal experiences reported by teachers and researchers, the paradigm remains largely unused. This article will explore the nature of collaborative learning in higher education, some obstacles to its successful adoption in academic departments, and what can be done to overcome these obstacles. The paper consists of five sections, each dealing with a different aspect of collaborative learning.

The first section defines collaborative learning in broad philosophical terms and outlines pedagogical models. The definition calls for cooperation and involvement among all people involved in trying to attain educational goals: teachers, students, administrators and parents. The underpinnings provided by the definition form the basis for the remaining parts of the chapter. Part two examines the reasons why more teachers do not use collaborative learning methods. It focuses on reasons why teachers are discouraged from adopting collaborative learning and lays the groundwork for identifying policies and methodologies needed to overcome these blocks. The next three sections deal with different aspects of overcoming difficulties collaborative learning may present: a methodology for starting collaborative learning is suggested; a list of the benefits of collaborative learning is given along with brief explanations; and lastly policies needed to fully implement collaborative learning are presented. While the subject matter of each of the last three sections differs, the content of each is highly intertwined because the methodology is based upon the benefits which lead to the needed policies.

The uniqueness of this paper lies in its analysis of why more teachers do not use collaborative learning and its suggestions for institutional policies which would promote full implementation of collaborative learning teaching techniques at all levels. Several authors have suggested processes for staff development (Cohen, 1992; Cooper, 1992; Joyce, 1992; Schmuck, 1992), but few have analyzed in detail reasons why teachers resist changing from their current lecture methods to collaborative learning techniques.

WHAT IS COLLABORATIVE LEARNING?

Collaborative learning is a personal philosophy, not just a classroom technique. In all situations where people come together in groups, it suggests a way of dealing with people which respects and highlights individual group members' abilities and contributions. The underlying premise of collaborative learning is based upon consensus building through cooperation by group members, in contrast to competition in which individuals best other group members. Collaborative learning practitioners apply this philosophy in the classroom, at committee meetings, with community groups and generally as a way of living and dealing with other people.

As a pedagogy collaborative learning involves the entire spectrum of learning activities in which groups of students work together in or out of class. It can be as simple and informal as pairs working together in a Think-Pair-Share procedure, where students consider a question individually, discuss their ideas with another student to form a consensus answer, and then share their results with the entire class, to the more formally structured process known as cooperative learning which has been defined by researchers (Johnson, Johnson & Holubec, 1990).

The use of pairs can be introduced at any time during a class to address questions or solve problems or to create variety in a class presentation. The Johnsons' approach, which includes pair activities, requires more preparation and structure. They define five elements necessary for a technique to be considered cooperative learning: positive interdependence, face-to-face promotive interaction, individual accountability, interpersonal and small group skills, and group processing. Cooperative learning stresses the social nature of learning and the need to train students how to work collaboratively in order to resolve conflicts, interact appropriately and actively involve all group members.

Many of the elements of cooperative learning are used in collaborative situations. The Jig Saw method (Aronson et al., 1978) is a good example. Students become "experts" on a concept and are responsible for teaching it to the other group members. Groups subdivide a topic and members work together with those from other groups who have the same topic. They then return to their original groups and explain their topic. Ken Brufee (1993) suggests collaborative learning involves giving more mature groups of students control of the learning process, including establishing criteria for grading and group procedures, defining the final product, and presenting the group's results.

This paper uses a definition of collaborative learning in its widest sense, including cooperative learning. Collaborative learning encompasses all elements of group work and learning situations where students cooperate in order to accomplish a specific learning objective.

Why Don't More Teachers Use Collaborative Learning Techniques?
Considering the overwhelming number of benefits created by the use of collaborative learning methods, it is surprising that so few teachers use this paradigm. The cause lies in the current educational system which emphasizes content memorization and individual student performance through competition.

Few teachers or students have had any exposure to the collaborative learning teaching/learning technique. Teachers are not trained during their certification processes in collaborative methods and those that are often receive incomplete training. If teachers are taught by the lecture method while at teachers' college, then it is hardly surprising that this will be the method of choice when their turn arrives to take over the classroom. And the fact that most students have been exposed only to the competitive, individualistic approach used in our school systems today at all levels constitutes a major problem. Students are not likely to change their attitudes from one class to another unless they are trained in collaborative learning techniques. In order to gain a better understanding of the impediments to collaborative learning, we will separate for analysis those areas which affect teachers, administrators, parents and students.

REASONS WHY TEACHERS RESIST COLLABORATIVE LEARNING TECHNIQUES
Loss of Control in the Classroom
Perhaps the biggest impediment to collaborative learning lies in the fact that many teachers feel they give up control of the class if they give more responsibility to the students for their learning. When a teacher lectures she/he gets the feeling that the content is being covered, because it has been presented to the students in an orderly fashion. Many teachers provide lecture notes in an attempt to guarantee student coverage. Collaborative learning techniques encourage students to formulate their own constructs and ways of

understanding the material. The constructivist ideology is foreign to most teachers who have been trained in the didactic method of lecturing.

Lack of Self Confidence by Teachers

It takes a great deal of confidence in one's self and one's students to transfer the responsibility of learning to the student or even to share some of the responsibility. Many teachers lack the self confidence to try methods which may expose them to potentially difficult situations. These may occur when students ask unanticipated questions or act in socially unacceptable ways. Collaborative learning redefines the role of teacher from expert to facilitator. The focus on the student reduces the opportunities teachers have to demonstrate their expertise and might call into question their teaching ability. He/she has to be sure he/she has something to offer, as a person, before a class can be allowed to take some control. Some people cannot face the risk.

There is also a fear of looking stupid. Teachers are defined as being experts in their fields, able to answer any and all questions. In a collaborative learning environment students may ask questions in a manner which is difficult for the teacher to understand. Sometimes it takes another class member to articulate a question or answer a fellow student's question using vocabulary which they can understand. Allowing and encouraging students to answer each other's questions is contrary to the typical teacher centered class. Collaborative learning contradicts the concept that teachers are repositories of subject knowledge, whose role is simply to pour into the open, empty and willing minds of students their vast reservoir of knowledge.

Fear of the Loss of Content Coverage

Teachers fear a loss in content when they use collaborative learning methods because group interactions often take longer than simple lectures. Students need time to accumulate enough information in order to be able to use it within their groups. They need time to work together to reach a consensus and/or formulate minority opinions for presentation to the whole class. A major function of collaborative learning involves teaching students how to work together effectively. Also, teachers superimpose onto collaborative learning their current experiences with the lecture method. For example, many students do not understand the material despite excellent presentations by the teacher and therefore perform poorly on content based tests. Teachers therefore conclude that the situation would be even worse if students work with other students who may be having similar problems. The reality is that when students become involved in their learning their performance rises. Initially groups do work slowly as they learn how to function cooperatively, analyze what works and what doesn't work for their groups, and receive training in conflict resolution. But as students get used to the process, their level of retention and critical thinking increases to the point where they can move through the curriculum faster. If students started using collaborative learning at the elementary levels, less time would be needed for training at the secondary and college levels. Thus many of the concerns college teachers have about keeping up with their schedules would be addressed.

Lack of Prepared Materials for Use in Class

The use of collaborative learning techniques requires teachers to build a set of handouts which create interdependence among students and provides a basis and reason for their working together. Materials of this nature are rare (Irwin et al., 1985). Current textbooks generally offer a set of questions at the end of each chapter which are usually answered by students individually. A few publishers are beginning to tailor their texts to offer one or two questions which can be answered by groups, but supporting materials are not included. Teachers must develop worksheets, project descriptions and other appropriate materials. In addition, few suggestions are provided in the teacher manuals about how to institute group activities. For teachers who are new to collaborative learning, this is a major impediment. Teachers generally adhere to the methods and materials with which they are most familiar, since a major expenditure of effort and time is required to revamp curriculum materials.

Teacher's Egos

Many teachers are wrapped up in their own self-importance and enjoy being the center of attention. The class is their stage and it provides them with an opportunity to show off their knowledge and expertise. Lecturers do not trust students to learn. They think they must tell them what to learn and provide all the structure for the learning to take place. The egotistical side of teaching must be overcome in order for teachers to involve their students actively in the learning process.

Lack of Familiarity with Alternate Assessment Techniques

Assessment is a major concern frequently expressed by teachers who are unfamiliar with collaborative learning. They presume that individual accountability will be lost or that one student will dominate the group or do all the work for the group. They are unfamiliar with how to assess group efforts and assign grades to groups. Often they assume that only one process is appropriate for assessing student performance.

Collaborative learning as defined by Johnson and Johnson (1987) specifically calls for individual accountability as one of its five major components. Another one of the five elements is interdependence, which includes group grading and a reward system for group improvement. The two ideas are complimentary, not contradictory. Because teachers are not trained in alternative assessment techniques they naturally assume the worst, i.e., that the students will not be able to understand and deal with these testing procedures.

Techniques available for assessing groups include: teacher observations during group work; group grading for projects; students grading each other or evaluating the level of contribution made by each member to a team project; extra credit given when groups exceed their previous average or when individuals within a group exceed their previous performance by a specified amount; use of a mastery approach whereby students may retake tests after receiving extra help from their groups or the teacher; and the use of individual quizzes, exams or assignments.

Alternate assessment techniques provide an additional benefit in that teachers can build in reward systems for individual performance and group performance. These reward systems may consist of extra points toward a grade, certificates of achievement, extra time to work on special projects, class recognition for good group efforts or special recognition for work well done.

Concern with Teacher Evaluation and Personal Advancement
The question of teacher evaluation is of great concern to many teachers who consider using collaborative learning techniques. In order for teachers to be properly evaluated the supervisor must understand the nature of this method and accept it as a teaching paradigm. If the department head is a proponent of the lecture method of teaching, then his/her understanding of what he/she observes will be limited (Bliss, 1986). This problem can be overcome by developing a process whereby the teacher and evaluator work closely together to review the class objectives and methods.

Collaborative learning classes often appear to be chaotic since groups work differently than individuals. A noise level exists, even if muted, which is inconsistent with what takes place in a lecture class or with discussion formats (Forest, 1996). It takes a few moments to refocus the class when the teacher wishes to bring everyone together to go over the material or make observations about what is going on in the groups. Groups sometimes digress from the topic at hand and need to be brought back to working on the task. Several students may request the teacher's attention simultaneously. To someone who is untrained in collaborative learning these activities may appear to represent ineffective teaching, which in turn may lead to a poor classroom evaluation.

Students' Resistance to Collaborative Learning Techniques
A cause for concern by teachers starting collaborative learning is the initial student reaction. Students have not been trained to cooperate in an academic environment. The primary approach in our schools is one of competition for grades and recognition. Teachers need to sell the concept of collaborative learning to the students by making clear what the objectives are and what the benefits will be. Until the students become comfortable with this new method, they will express concerns and doubts. Additionally, collaborative learning encourages student input on methodology. Not surprisingly, some of this feedback may be critical. Student criticism may be new to many teachers.

Students feel that the lecture method is "easier" because they are passive during the class while apparently receiving the necessary information. In contrast, interactive classes are very intense. The responsibility for learning is shifted to the student, thus raising the level of critical thinking by each student. This situation is both mentally and physically tiring. The students initially respond by complaining and lobbying for a return to the good old lecture days. For a new collaborative learning practitioner this can be very disconcerting. To the more experienced teacher, this is just part of the process all groups go through as they learn how to use collaborative learning techniques, and begin to see and appreciate its benefits as they move away from the comfortable paradigm of the lecture method.

Also, students may perceive the teacher as not doing his/her job. Collaborative classrooms are student centered whereas in typical classes teacher performance is seen as central to the class. In order to address this concern, teachers need to make clear to the students why they use a particular technique and what the outcomes will be from the activity. Another way for teachers to overcome this perception is to spend time with the groups or with individuals during the class. Teachers may walk around the class to observe groups interacting, make suggestions or ask leading questions in order to help facilitate the groups. The frequent emphasis upon and explanation of their roles in the collaborative learning process is a critical task teachers must do in order for their students to fully understand what they are observing.

Lack of Familiarity with Collaborative Learning Techniques and Class Management

A number of perceived problems are associated with classroom procedures. Teachers are often concerned about the potential dominance by a few students or a few students doing all the work. These questions can be addressed by assigning roles to students and rotating the roles, allowing students to assign performance grades to each other anonymously and specifying what percent of the total assignment was completed by each member, and by the teacher observing each group and making suggestions for more equal participation. Group processing throughout the semester also helps address these issues. Questions about what to do with quicker class members and/or groups who finish a given assignment early can be resolved. Additional activities can be developed or a reward system can be created whereby students are allowed to socialize or work on other materials provided they do not disrupt the students who are still working.

Collaborative learning is difficult to sustain. As in any real life situation, repetition leads to boredom. (This is certainly true if one uses the lecture approach continuously.) A significant advantage to collaborative learning is the variety of classroom activities available to the experienced teacher. When adopting collaborative learning the teacher needs to learn the new techniques, practice them, introduce them into the classroom and work with the students to practice the new methods. Also, it is often necessary to convince the students of the benefits of working together. The fact that the responsibility for learning is being shifted to the students is hard for some students to adjust to.

Other problems: collaborative learning involves trial and error approaches. Not every activity works exactly as planned and constant modification is needed. Some activities work better with some groups than with others and classes react differently to each situation. In some institutions collaborative learning is seen as cheating because the educational pedagogy recognizes and rewards individual effort and competition and discourages cooperation among students. Also, students who are exposed to collaborative learning and have enjoyable experiences in a supportive educational environment have a difficult readjustment back to other classes where collaborative learning is not used.

If the institution has a perspective that says what is going on is material coverage instead of material mastery then the teachers will be less concerned about what students are learning and more concerned about including as much material as they can in a class period. Content versus learning centered classes are the primary focus of modern educational systems. In addition, thinking about learning primarily as a social interaction is a strange idea for most instructors, students and administrators, who expect to see the teacher controlling the class through lectures and/or teacher directed class discussion. Another potential problem arises for students who learn best by the auditory modality and who may be distracted by noise in the class. This problem can be addressed through student social skill development which identifies acceptable ways for students to talk and interact in class.

Lack of Teacher Training in Collaborative Teaching Methods

The current teacher training methodology does not foster collaborative learning. Teachers are not trained to facilitate groups, use brainstorming techniques, facilitate conflict management, or use group dynamics theory. They are trained to be good classroom managers with orderly students quietly listening to their lectures or doing their work individually. Many teachers do not know how or where to start using collaborative learning techniques in their classrooms.

Teachers are not trained to involve their students in the development of class procedures and assessment and are therefore not likely to accept constructive criticism from students. Also, teachers have trouble dealing with dissension in class by students who do not want to use collaborative learning methods. Convincing students that they are learning well or benefiting from this method is not always easy. Therefore, teachers need to be well grounded in the philosophy of collaborative learning and they must have opportunities to practice in a safe environment.

Collaborative learning skills need to be modeled to become effective, yet how many administrators run their schools or departments in a cooperative fashion? Very few meetings are run using collaborative techniques. It takes a great deal of effort to change what one is comfortable doing, especially if the same process has been used for many years. In order to move into collaborative learning teachers must rethink what they are doing in their classes and how they are accomplishing their goals. Most teachers have not seen group work in action so they have very few models to go by when trying to make changes.

Teachers generally reflect the teaching styles of their professors and in turn want their students to emulate themselves. There is a great deal of comfort in propagating the familiar. At the university level the preferred pedagogy is the lecture, thus there are few role models for future teachers who might be interested in using collaborative learning methods. Most professors are more concerned with doing research than with teaching. This situation is reflected in their teaching loads compared to graduate student research supervision. Except within some education departments, very little research goes on in support of good teaching practices. Within institutions there are very few role models to provide mentoring for teachers. In fact, teachers are often criticized by their peers when they do try to institute collaborative learning. Critical comments by teachers about room noise and student activity in the classroom are often used to discourage people from using collaborative learning techniques.

Because teachers receive little training in collaborative learning they are unaccustomed to what takes place in the collaborative learning class. One consequence is that they find it hard to believe that students can be learning the content material while they are socializing in their groups. Social learning is unique to collaborative learning and creates an enjoyable as well as interesting environment. This is not very surprising: human beings are social animals so any situation which encourages and enhances this basic instinct is bound to be deeply satisfying and enjoyable; learning in such instances is magnified, not diminished. Additionally, students' self-esteem builds as they gain confidence in themselves and their peers, leading to additional enjoyment of the learning process. In real life situations people work, learn and socialize all at the same time. If we are to help our students move into social and employment situations, then we need to provide a model for them to follow which includes cooperation and team efforts, as well as individual efforts, in a social environment leading to the accomplishment of their task at hand.

Another consequence of the teacher's lack of familiarity with collaborative learning classes is the feeling of guilt which arises. Teachers do not feel they are teaching if they are not dispensing information. They may appear to be inactive since it is necessary to allow time for the groups to interact without teacher intervention. Even if teachers move around the classroom observing the students or talking to individuals or groups, in their minds they still do not fit the picture of a teacher. Students may comment on the fact that they do not see the teacher "teaching". It takes a high degree of confidence and training to overcome these personal feelings and to resist student pleas to move back to the lecture format.

REASONS WHY ADMINISTRATORS FAIL TO SUPPORT COLLABORATIVE LEARNING TECHNIQUES AND PHILOSOPHY

Lack of Training or Exposure to Collaborative Learning

Many professors start their teaching careers with minimal training in teaching techniques. As they move into administrative positions they advance by starting at the department chair level, then moving up through the division dean position to dean and president. Advanced degrees focus on administrative areas instead of teaching. They do not receive training in collaborative learning as part of their teacher preparation process and do not receive any collaborative learning training in their administrative Masters or Doctoral degree programs. Few administrators seek out information about collaborative learning through seminars or individual courses. Thus they maintain their primary focus on the traditional classroom where the teacher provides students with information via a lecture format and the students listen attentively and quietly. Administrators who lack a well grounded understanding of collaborative learning tend to evaluate teachers who use it negatively and this in turn undermines the teachers' attempts to initiate collaborative learning in their classes.

Lack of Familiarity with Alternate Student Assessment Techniques

As with teachers, administrators have not been trained in the alternative assessment techniques which are vital to collaborative learning. They continue to support the individual, competitive exam systems and discourage techniques which involve group grading. This problem is exacerbated by state assessment tests and the national SAT and Achievement exams which also emphasize individual performance and content mastery instead of process mastery. Grade point averages and class rank are emphasized in order to promote student acceptances into top colleges. Colleges themselves rely heavily on the standardized tests for admissions criteria. College courses are content oriented and competitively graded based upon class curves. Secondary school teachers and administrators attempt to provide classroom environments which model college classes in order to help their students succeed later.

REASONS WHY STUDENTS RESIST COLLABORATIVE LEARNING

Students' Lack of Familiarity with Collaborative Techniques

A major problem in implementing collaborative learning arises because students lack an understanding of the underlying philosophies of collaborative learning. Our current system encourages competition and individual responsibility and discourages student interaction. Understandably, student resentment arises when they are asked to share information and study techniques or to help their peers. The superior students have figured out how to get good grades in a competitive situation and to share that information is a complete anathema. Collaborative learning redefines the role of the student and the teacher and their interrelationships by creating a nurturing environment versus a competitive one.

Fear of Loss of Content and Ability to Achieve High Grades

Students initially do not have a clear way of knowing if the work they are doing is correct. The process of student centered discovery and construction of their own knowledge base is new to most students. It is exactly this process that helps students develop critical thinking skills, but they often resent the fact that group work shifts the burden of learning to themselves. They feel much more comfortable hearing the teacher present the important facts instead of having to sort out what is important. A common fear among students is that all the group members will be wrong, leading to failure.

The collaborative learning process calls for constant review and summary through whole class discussions and presentation of material by individuals and groups. In addition the teacher is continuously observing the groups and making suggestions about how to proceed or where to go to find necessary information. Over time students become more comfortable with the process as they understand that their questions will be answered and that the teacher is an active participant in the process, taking on the role of facilitator or coach instead of expert information presenter.

PARENT REACTIONS TO COLLABORATIVE LEARNING
Lack of Parent Understanding to Collaborative Learning

Our society is not used to collaboration. It is used to authority and direction, particularly in the work place. Management trends such as TQM and CQI with quality teams are slowly being adopted by colleges as well as businesses. Until there is widespread use of teams in businesses and at colleges the parents of students will have little understanding of the collaborative process. Parents are not generally involved at the college level; however, at K-12 parents have a significant impact on the system and here they may impede the implementation of collaborative learning. Parents of upper level students often complain about their children being used as tutors or appearing to carry the load for a group. Students try to enlist their parents in a effort to discourage teachers from using collaborative learning, for all the reasons cited above. Parents rarely visit collaborative learning classes to observe first hand what is taking place, and teachers do not make enough of an effort to invite them into the process. As with teachers and administrators, parents are used to seeing a quiet classroom with the teacher in front lecturing. This is the pedagogy they were exposed to throughout their own education, so they feel comfortable seeing the same approach.

Administrators often react to parent pressure and discourage attempts by teachers to introduce new pedagogies. They give lip service to the concept of active, hands-on learning in groups but in reality do not encourage adoption of these techniques. It will require a significant effort to educate parents as well as students about the benefits and procedures used in collaborative learning classrooms.

GETTING STARTED USING COLLABORATIVE LEARNING TECHNIQUES

Successful implementation of a collaborative learning strategy is much like planning for a journey. The more people you talk to who have been to your destination and the more background research you do, the more successful you will be. As a first step we recommend observing a teacher or teachers who are experienced and proficient in the use of collaborative learning techniques: professors who have excellent reputations among students and teachers for their collaborative learning teaching techniques. Many people profess to use collaborative learning techniques but in reality are not qualified in this area. We recommend several class visits prior to initiating research and reading into collaborative learning techniques, in order to experience first hand the sensations and reactions one has when first observing people placed in groups as the primary instruction paradigm (Kidder, 1989). In an ideal situation the teacher you observe would also serve as mentor and coach. However, if collaborative learning practitioners are not available, then an alternative is to take a course in collaborative learning, being careful to make sure that it is truly an interactive class. The activities provide the personal experiences needed to understand how teachers and students react to collaborative learning.

Once you have decided that collaborative learning is a viable teaching strategy, obtaining training prior to introducing it into your classes is mandatory. We suggest seminars, workshops, and courses which model collaborative learning through interactive activities, and demonstrate specific techniques, warm-up activities and group building exercises. Training should extend over time and not consist of a single seminar or intensive multi-day workshop (Cooper, 1992). Becoming a collaborative learning teacher is an exploratory process which requires practice, analyses, feedback and continual modification. The process is evolutionary and will continue to change throughout one's career (Rolheiser-Bennett & Stevahn, 1992). Continuous self-evaluation and revision of one's techniques, by attending and presenting at collaborative learning seminars and sharing ideas and techniques with colleagues, creates exciting professional development opportunities. Continuously learning new methodologies helps prevent teacher burnout caused by repeating and using the same lecture and class technique every semester.

It is important at this stage to start building a library of books and articles for reference and to provide a philosophical basis for adopting collaborative learning. There are many excellent resources available in the form of edited books (Slavin, 1990; Davidson, 1990; Sharan, 1994), manuals (Johnson, Johnson & Holubec, 1984, 1990,1992; Cooper et al., 1984; Reynolds et al., 1990; Foster, 1993) and magazines (Graves & Graves, 1991) published by collaborative learning practitioners. Of course, the reading you do will be much more meaningful if it is done in the context of initiating collaborative learning.

The best time to start collaborative learning is at the beginning of the semester when students are most receptive to being introduced to new class procedures. It is more difficult, but not impossible if this is the only choice, to switch during the semester after students have become adjusted to particular class procedures. Students need to be sold on the idea of collaborative learning. In our current system collaborative learning is not used by enough teachers to make it familiar to students and thus easily adopted.

Preparation for classes using collaborative learning is the key to success. Explaining in detail why you are using collaborative learning is mandatory, as well as describing the benefits and results. Providing written materials describing collaborative learning, such as journal or newspaper articles, gives students a rationale and philosophical basis for its use. Making clear what process will be used to evaluate students is very important. Possibilities include group grades on projects or tests or individual grades. The criteria for grades must be clear in either case.

When starting collaborative learning, using techniques you feel comfortable with and which have the greatest potential for success is very helpful. Having students work in pairs is the easiest to organize, has the fewest social problems associated with it, and engages the greatest number of students (Schwartz, Black & Strange, 1991). With pairs one person verbalizes while the other listens and responds. This creates an environment where 100% student participation is achievable.

We recommend the use of worksheets, one for each pair, which are handed in at the close of the lesson, and signed by both group members for some form of credit or grade. We suggest using worksheets initially because students and teachers cannot be expected to move from the traditional lecture classroom to collaborative learning techniques like Jigsaw and Structured Controversy overnight. Our experiences have shown that students tend to work independently and need a mechanism to focus their attention on the group effort. Asking students to work on textbook questions does not provide enough incentive to get them to work together (though it's certainly acceptable to use textbook questions in developing worksheets). We think of the use of the worksheet in pairs as a bridging mechanism between the old and the new, as a way of easing or developing a transition into collaborative learning in small steps and measured doses, using materials familiar to both teachers and students, while they acclimate themselves to this new method of learning.

The worksheet in pairs is an excellent method for novice teachers to begin incorporating collaborative learning activities into their classroom. For multiple section classes it might be advisable to try this technique on a single section first in order to evaluate the outcomes and student responses. Try it on your best class. If successful, implementing the technique in all the other sections with a high degree of confidence becomes easier. Changes can be tried prior to effecting a large number of students.

In order to help students begin the process of working collaboratively, it is necessary to provide activities which will foster a cooperative environment and encourage students to get to know each other from different perspectives (Weinstein & Goodman, 1980; Williams, 1993; Johnson & Johnson, 1985a, 1990). This can be accomplished through warm-up and ice-breaking activities. At the beginning of each semester we use a pairs interview technique in which students discuss their interests including career interests, academic majors, hobbies and extracurricular activities, etc. Two specific questions which we want answered are "What is your biggest concern about the course?" and "How to you feel about the subject we are studying?" When we teach math classes the second question elicits many responses which reflect the students' math anxieties, and this provides an opportunity to begin to address them during the first class. Students also learn that they are not alone in their concerns.

When we start using larger groups we use an activity called "Finding Things in Common" in which the group must find, appropriately enough, five things they all have in common which are not related to school, work or family, but are of a personal nature such as favorite musician, food, reading material, or a place they have all visited. This activity helps students get to know each other on a personal level and encourages them to discover commonalties. Another group building activity has each group write on one flip-chart-size paper fears about the course, the semester or being in school generally, and on a second paper their hopes and aspirations or reasons for attending the course or school. The charts are hung around the room and provide a basis for a class discussion about common fears and hopes. What becomes clear is that their fears are often opposite their hopes. This activity gives students a feeling of being interconnected.

A third activity we use is to ask group members to find something in their pocketbook or wallet which will help others in the group get to know them better and to explain why this item reflects their nature or personality. This is an enjoyable activity and helps build a sense of social interaction in an academic setting.

An activity recommended by Nell Warren Associates (Warren, 1995) asks students to draw a picture of themselves on a sheet of paper, write a series of words on a paper, or draw pictures of animals or objects with which they identify themselves. Each participant pins the sheet to his/her clothing and then circulates around the room reading other students' sheets, without talking. Every minute the teacher signals the students to move on to someone new, for a total of ten to fifteen meetings. After the nonverbal activity the group members ask questions of the other participants. At the end of the activity the members briefly discuss their feelings and reactions to this technique. This is a likable activity which in addition to getting students to interact and learn more about themselves, also encourages them to start the process of analyzing group activities and their own reactions to class and group interactions. Other activities include having students make up three statements about themselves, only one of which is true. Then put students into groups and have them guess which statements are true by questioning each other; the questions must be answered honestly. These are just a few of the many activities available to teachers. There are many resources available which describe in detail warm-up and group building activities (Kroehnert, 1991; Scearce, 1992; Weinstein & Goodman, 1980; Williams, 1993).

Using groups of three or more takes more preparation and thought in order to engage all the students in the activity. Role assignment may be needed to insure an equal distribution of effort and training in appropriate group behavior will also be necessary to insure active participation by all members. When introducing a topic the teacher will find it helpful to use a short lecture followed by the collaborative learning activity. It is very comforting to the teacher and student alike to mix lecturing with group work. As the teacher gets more experienced and confident with collaborative learning it becomes possible to start classes with collaborative learning activities and then later use short lectures to highlight concepts or address problems or questions as they arise.

In order to begin using collaborative learning techniques Artzt and Newman (Davis, Maher, & Noddings, 1990) suggest trying them out with homework assignments initially. Students need to be advised that they will be working together during the next class in order to encourage them to do the homework. At the beginning of the class allow ten minutes for each group to compare their homework results and come to an agreement on the best solutions. Then have the group submit one set of solutions. Finally, the teacher leads a discussion on the difficulties the students have encountered. A particular benefit to this process occurs when students have the opportunity to check their homework within the privacy of the group and work out trivial difficulties without needing to involve the entire class. It is also not necessary to discuss all the homework problems with the whole class, thus saving time for additional group work. The teacher has an opportunity during this period to observe each group interacting and to see which students have done the work and at what level of performance.

Another collaborative technique which we find helpful is to assign groups the responsibility for working out one problem or answering one question out of a set of problems, then placing their answer on the board. The teacher may chose one of the group members to go to the board or the group may chose someone, providing they do not chose the same person every time. Several members may work at the board together if they feel more comfortable that way. More accountability accrues when the teacher chooses the presenter because all group members must be informed and ready to do the work on the board. A variation of this technique is to have each student explain his/her approach in a mini lecture and answer other students' questions. This technique is especially useful in mathematics and science classes and has applications in other technical and nontechnical courses as well.

In class, academic games also help build a sense of group cohesion. In Math Olympics, for example, groups of four or five students attempt five problems which are placed on the board. Each group is responsible for answering all the problems. After a set time one member of each group writes their group's answers on a grid on the board. The results are checked for accuracy. The groups are responsible for establishing their own procedures; each member may do one problem or all the problems. They then check with each other to reach an agreement on their solutions. If at any time there appears to be a consensus that the groups are missing a concept, a mini lecture can be given or students may be asked to explain their approaches. While the groups are working, their problem solving activities and interactions may be observed by the professor. At the end of the session a few minutes are allowed to discuss what transpired within their groups and what they can do to improve their working together.

Felder and Bent (1994) recommend the following in-class procedures. Early in a class period, organize the students (or have them organize themselves) into teams of two to four, and randomly assign one student in each group the role of team recorder. Ideally, after no more than 15 minutes of lecturing, give the teams an assignment to do, instructing the recorder to write down the team responses. You may circulate among the teams verifying that they are on task, everyone is participating and that the recorders are doing their job. Stop the teams after a suitable time and randomly call upon students to present their teams' solutions. Suggested topics include: recalling prior material; stage setting by identifying questions under consideration for the day; asking students to think in advance about questions which can effectively motivate them to watch for the answers during the remainder of the class period; responding to questions such as "What procedure could I use here?" or "What would you guess is the next step?"; problem solving—"Turn to page 27 and answer question 5 together"; analytical, evaluative and creative thinking—"List all the assumptions, problems, errors, ethical dilemmas you can find in this case study, scenario, problem solution"; generating questions and summarizing; Jigsaw—each group member is assigned a different part of a question or problem, then they join with members of other groups who have the same section in order to become experts on their topic, and then return to teach the group what they have learned. These are a few of the many activities which may be used to initiate collaborative learning procedures in classes.

Keeping a record of what works and why as you develop collaborative learning techniques is desirable. A teaching journal is very handy for this purpose. Spontaneous changes are sometimes made in techniques based upon student reactions and group results. It is important to make a record of these changes in order to keep track of them and to be able to modify course materials for future use or for sharing with colleagues. It also is helpful to record what doesn't work and the reasons why.

Involvement of students in evaluating the collaborative learning activities and in designing them is important, yet few teachers are trained or encouraged to do this. There are several simple techniques which ask students to write about their reactions to the class or describe what they have learned. The One Minute Paper given at the conclusion of the class (Weaver & Cottrell, 1985; Cross & Angelo, 1993) asks students to describe the most important concept they learned and what question(s) they still have. This helps the teacher determine if the material was indeed understood by the students. We often lecture and presume students understand what we are saying. A variation is the Think-Pair-Share activity, in which students complete the One Minute Paper, share their written comments with a partner, and then with the whole class. Such a technique might be employed at the end of class or at the beginning of the next class to help students verbalize their understanding of particular concepts.

Other noteworthy ideas: asking groups to identify three things they did well and one thing that needs improvement helps focus attention on the groups' social skills. A classroom meeting model can be used to discuss any issue facing a class. To do this sit the students in a circle where they can see each other, and discuss some aspect of the class procedure or content. The teacher may moderate the discussion, or for a more collaborative approach, a ping-pong procedure can be used in which the student speaking recognizes the next speaker and so on. Students can be asked to write about problems they see occurring in class or in their groups, as an individual assignment or part of their regular writing journal.

Collaborative learning is based upon a philosophy of working together. It is necessary for teachers to model this approach by seeking student opinions and suggestions for improvements in the course. In turn students are encouraged to assume an ownership of the class, and very high expectations are set by involving the students with the teacher in designing classes. The class is personalized by the active involvement of the student and teacher in a deliberative process. This is not possible when the lecture method is the only class procedure employed.

When collaborative learning is introduced into a class students need to be trained in group dynamics theory, social skills and conflict resolution. Teachers need to be trained in these areas as well through attendance at workshops, seminars, courses and in-service activities, and mechanisms must be established to determine if groups are functioning properly. To begin, there are several mechanisms available to accomplish the student training. The use of a T-chart specifies what a particular desired activity or behavior should look like and sound like to an outside observer. If equal participation is desired, then the teacher needs to facilitate a class discussion about what student behaviors would be observed during a collaborative learning activity, to insure that this social skill was being accomplished. A collaborative activity might be used prior to the class discussion by involving groups of 2-4 students in identifying and discussing the characteristics first, possibly prioritizing them, and then reporting back to the class as a whole. These characteristics are then placed upon a chart and displayed in a prominent place. For a specified period of time a particular skill is worked on by the class. At the end of each class or activity some time needs to be allotted to review how the groups performed the social skill under study and what might be done to improve their actions and behaviors to facilitate the desired behavior. Another technique is to have group members evaluate each other's performance during an activity as to the amount and quality of the contributions made by each member. Asking students to write about what worked and what didn't is a good way to determine if desired outcomes are being achieved.

Another important mechanism the teacher has to provide feedback to groups comes from the observation of their performance on assignments during class. The teacher generally spends time during each class walking among groups, observing their activities and behaviors, answering questions and socializing with students. This provides teachers with an excellent opportunity to listen to students explain concepts and interact with each other. The teacher may then comment on these observations at the end of class. There are also more formal mechanisms to observe groups, which include activities like tallying how many times each student participates or determining the quality of participation in terms of how many times he/she uses a particular social skill.

Once teachers become comfortable with using groups they may wish to expand their repertoire of activities. Slavin (1990) provides a complete description of more advanced collaborative learning techniques. For the purposes of this paper these techniques will be listed only by name with associated references. Co-op, Co-op (Kagan, 1989); CIRC—Cooperative Integrated Reading and Comparison (Madden, Slavin, & Stevens, 1986); Group Investigation (Sharan & Sharan, 1976); Issues Controversy (Johnson & Johnson, 1987); Jigsaw (Aronson et al., 1978); Jigsaw II (Slavin, 1983): Learning Together (Johnson & Johnson, 1987); TAI—Team Assisted Individualization (Slavin, Leavey & Madden, 1986); TGT—Teams-Games-Tournament (Devries & Slavin, 1978); STAD- Student Teams Achievement Divisions (Slavin, 1978): Structures (Kagan, 1989).

As the collaborative learning process is begun, forming support groups with other teachers in departmental areas or across curricula is desirable. Having a resource group to share ideas and techniques and to discuss new approaches is important. The Johnsons refer to base groups and formalize the process by having them meet regularly to report on specific activities that members have tried. They recommend that teachers sign contracts with the base group to help provide additional motivation for new users of collaborative learning techniques. The formation of support groups is necessary because few teachers use collaborative learning; therefore it is difficult to receive feedback or advice from experienced teachers.

Because collaborative learning is relatively new to many institutions, teachers must work with their supervisors to make sure they are aware of the techniques as well as reasons for using them. Supervisors who are used to seeing orderly, quiet classes with students listening to a lecture need to be informed about the nature of collaborative learning classes, where students talk in groups and socialize while they work on task. A common concern among collaborative learning teachers is that their supervisors will not understand what is taking place in the class and that poor evaluations will result. This problem can be avoided by the institution's providing training for administrators, and by the teachers working closely with their department heads and other supervisory personnel.

BENEFITS OF COLLABORATIVE LEARNING

1. Develops Higher Level Thinking Skills (Webb, 1982a)
Students working together are engaged in the learning process instead of passively listening to the teacher present information. Pairs of students working together represent the most effective form of interaction, followed by threesomes and larger groups (Schwartz, Black, & Strange, 1991). When students work in pairs one person is listening while the other partner is discussing the question under investigation. Both are developing valuable problem-solving skills by formulating their ideas, discussing them, receiving immediate feedback and responding to questions and comments by their partner (Johnson, 1971). The interaction is continuous and both students are engaged during the session. Compare this situation to the lecture class where students may or may not be involved by listening to the teacher or by taking notes (Cooper et al., 1984). In collaborative learning the teacher is able to observe and assess individual student's thinking skills and approach to learning.

2. *Promotes Student-Faculty Interaction and Familiarity*

The collaborative process enables the teacher to move around the class in order to observe students interacting (Cooper et al., 1984). An opportunity is created whereby the teacher can talk to the students directly or in small groups. Teachers may raise questions to help direct students or explain concepts. In addition, a natural tendency to socialize with the students on a professional level is created by approaches to problem solving and about activities and attitudes which influence performance in class. Students often mention offhandedly that they are having difficulties outside of class related to work, family, friends, etc. Openings like this can lead to a discussion of those problems by the teacher and student in a non-threatening way because of the informality of the situation.

3. *Increases Student Retention*

Students who are actively involved in the learning process are much more likely to become interested in learning and make more of an effort to attend school (Astin, 1977). A class where students interact fosters an environment conducive to high student motivation and participation and student attendance (Garibaldi, 1976; Treisman, 1985).

4. *Builds Self-Esteem in Students (Johnson & Johnson, 1989)*

Collaborative efforts among students result in a higher degree of accomplishment by all participants as opposed to individual, competitive systems in which many students are left behind (Slavin, 1978). Competition fosters a win-lose situation where superior students reap all rewards and recognition and mediocre or low-achieving students reap none. In contrast everyone benefits from a collaborative learning environment. Students help each other and in doing so build a supportive community which raises the performance level of each member (Kagan, 1986). This in turn leads to higher self-esteem in all students (Webb, 1982a).

5. *Enhances Student Satisfaction with the Learning Experience*

By their very nature people find satisfaction with activities which value their abilities and include them in the process. Effective teams or groups assume ownership of a process and its results when individuals are encouraged to work together toward a common goal, often defined by the group. This aspect is especially helpful for individuals who have a history of failure (Turnure & Ziegler, 1958) Passive educational experiences where the student is the receptacle for information presented by the expert teacher are inherently dissatisfying.

6. Promotes a Positive Attitude Toward the Subject Matter

Collaborative learning fosters a higher level of performance by students (Bligh, 1972). Their critical thinking skills increase and their retention of information and interest in the subject matter improves (Kulik & Kulik, 1979). When students are successful they view the subject matter with a very positive attitude because their self-esteem is enhanced. This creates a positive cycle of good performance building higher self-esteem, which in turn leads to more interest in the subject and higher performance yet. Students share their success with their groups, thus enhancing both the individual's and the group's self-esteem. Some cooperative learning structures formalize this effect by awarding certificates of achievement or improvement to students, or extra credit to groups for an individual's or group's improvement.

7. Develops Oral Communication Skills (Yager et al., 1985)

When students are working in pairs one partner verbalizes his/her answer while the other listens, asks questions or comments upon what he/she has heard. Clarification and explanation of one's answer is a very important part of the collaborative process and represents a higher order thinking skill (Johnson, Johnson, Roy, & Zaidman, 1985). Students who tutor each other must develop a clear idea of the concept they are presenting and orally communicate it to their partner (Neer, 1987).

8. Develops Social Interaction Skills

A major component of cooperative learning elaborated by Johnson, Johnson and Holubec (1984) includes training students in the social skills needed to work collaboratively. Students do not come by these skills naturally. Quite the contrary, in our society and current educational framework competition is valued over cooperation. By asking group members to identify what behaviors help them work together and by asking individuals to reflect on their contribution to the group's success or failure, students are made aware of the need for healthy, positive, helping interactions when they work in groups (Cohen & Cohen, 1991).

9. Promotes Positive Race Relations (Johnson & Johnson, 1972)

Research into the effect of using cooperative learning with students of varied racial or ethnic backgrounds has shown that many benefits accrue from this method (Slavin, 1980). Because students are actively involved in exploring issues and interacting with each other on a regular basis in a guided fashion, they are able to understand their differences and learn how to resolve social problems which may arise (Johnson & Johnson, 1985b). Training students in conflict resolution is a major component of cooperative learning training (Aronson et al., 1978; Slavin, 1978).

10. Creates an Environment of Active, Involved, and Exploratory Learning (Slavin, 1990)

The entire focus of collaborative learning is to actively involve students in the learning process. Whenever two or more students attempt to solve a problem or answer a question they become involved in the process of exploratory learning. They interact with each other, share ideas and information, seek additional information, make decisions about the results of their deliberations and present their findings to the entire class. They may tutor their peers or receive tutoring. Students have the opportunity to help structure the class experience through suggestions regarding class format and procedures. This is a level of student empowerment which is unattainable with a lecture format or even with a teacher-led whole class discussion.

11. Fosters Team Building and a Team Approach to Problem Solving while Maintaining Individual Accountability (Cooper et al., 1984; Johnson, Johnson, & Holubec, 1984)

A major function of collaborative learning is team building. This is accomplished through a variety of techniques used throughout the duration of the semester. During the first few weeks of a collaborative class, warm-up activities, getting to know class members' names, and practice exercises help acclimate students to cooperative learning. As the semester progresses, group building exercises and group processing are important techniques for helping students understand how they are functioning in their groups and what they can do to improve. Regarding individual accountability, at the end of each content section an exam or paper or other assessment mechanism is used to determine how well individual students have mastered the material (Slavin, 1983b). Group projects or group tests may be given in addition.. Quizzes during the semester may also be given individually, thus maintaining a strong element of accountability by each group member. Numerous grading schemes exist which bring both elements together such as providing bonus points for group members when the group exceeds its previous group average on a test by a specified amount.

12. Encourages Diversity Understanding (Burnstein & McRae, 1962)
Understanding the diversity that exists among students of different learning styles and abilities is a major benefit of collaborative learning. Lower level students benefit by modeling higher level students and they benefit by forming explanations and tutoring other students (Swing & Peterson, 1982; Hooper & Hannafin, 1988). Higher level students benefit by explaining their approaches. Students observe their peers in a learning environment, discuss problem-solving strategies and evaluate the learning approaches of other students. Often behaviors which might appear odd when taken out of context become understandable when the opportunity is presented to students to explain and defend their reasoning. For example, Americans signal agreement by nodding vertically while students from India nod horizontally. Very little opportunity exists for students to explain their behavior in a lecture class, whereas in a collaborative learning environment discussions of this nature occur continuously. Warm-up and group building activities play an important role in helping students understand their differences and learn how to capitalize on them rather than use them as a basis for creating antagonism.

13. Encourages Student Responsibility for Learning (Baird & White, 1984)
Promotive interaction, a foundation principle of cooperative learning, builds students' responsibility for themselves and their group members through a reliance upon each other's talents, and an assessment process which rewards both individuals and groups. Students assist each other and take different roles within their groups (such as reader, recorder, time keeper etc.). An emphasis on student involvement is created in the development of the processes which the group follows. The empowerment of students produces an environment which fosters maturity and responsibility in students for their learning. The teacher becomes a facilitator instead of a director and the student becomes a willing participant instead of a passive follower.

14. Involves Students in Developing Curriculum and Class Procedures (Kort, 1992)
During the collaborative process students are asked to assess themselves, and their groups as well as class procedures. Teachers who are confident in themselves can take advantage of this student input to modify the makeup of groups or class assignments and alter the mix of lecture and group work according to immediate student feedback. The teacher does not have to wait until the results of the section exam are returned to make alterations which will help the students understand the material. Students who participate in

structuring the class assume ownership of the process because they are treated like adults, and their opinions and observations are respected by the authority figure in the class.

15. Students Explore Alternative Problem Solutions in a Safe Environment (Sandberg, 1995)

Many students are hesitant to speak out and offer opinions publicly in a traditional classroom setting for fear of appearing foolish. When students work in groups, solutions come from the group rather than from the individual. In essence, the focus is removed from the individual, thus diffusing the effects of criticism, even constructive criticism, from any one student. Students can propose ideas and theories to their peers prior to formulating a final response, and then rehearse their presentation in an informal setting. If a group response is the end product, then the entire team becomes responsible for the answer. Collaborative learning creates a safe, nurturing environment, where students can express themselves and explore their ideas without the fear of failure or criticism. In a lecture format an individual student responds to a question before the entire class without much time to think about his/her answer; such a situation creates a threatening environment.

16. Stimulates Critical Thinking and Helps Students Clarify Ideas Through Discussion and Debate (Johnson, 1973; 1974)

The level of discussion and debate within groups of three or more and between pairs is substantially greater than when an entire class participates in a teacher led discussion. Students receive immediate feedback or questions about their ideas and formulate responses without having to wait for long intervals to participate in the discussion (Peterson & Swing, 1985). This aspect of collaborative learning does not preclude whole class discussion. In fact whole class discussion is enhanced by having students think out and discuss ideas thoroughly before the entire class discusses an idea or concept. The level of discussion becomes much more sophisticated. In addition, the teacher may temporarily join a group's discussion to question ideas or statements made by group members or to clarify concepts or questions raised by students.

17. Enhances Self-Management Skills (Resnick, 1992)

Collaborative learning inherently calls for self-management by students. In order to function within their groups they need to come prepared with assignments completed, and they must understand the material which they are going to contribute to their group. Students are given training about what their responsibilities are toward the group and how to be an effective group member. They are also given time to process group behaviors, such as checking with each other to make sure homework assignments are not only completed but understood by each group member. These promotive interactions help students learn self-management techniques.

18. Fits in Well with the Constructivist Approach (Davis, Maher, and Noddings, 1990)

Only when students formulate their own constructs and solutions are they truly thinking critically. Collaborative techniques create a constructivist approach when students become actively involved in defining questions in their own language and working out answers together instead of reproducing material presented by the teacher or the textbook (Wooley et al., 1990).

19. Establishes an Atmosphere of Cooperation and Helping Schoolwide (Deutsch, 1975; 1985)

Most schools celebrate individual student performance through athletics, clubs or extracurricular activities even when these accomplishments are the result of team efforts. In contrast, collaborative learning focuses attention on the accomplishments of the group. Students are trained how to interact positively, resolve disputes through compromise and/or mediation and encourage the best performance of each member for the benefit of the group. Teamwork is the modus operandi and inter-group cooperation is encouraged. Even when group competitions are used such as in STAD (Slavin, 1987), the intent is to create a positive helping environment for all participants.

20. Students Develop Responsibility for Each Other

In a traditional competitive classroom students are concerned with their individual grades and where they fit into the grade curve (Stahle, 1986). Emphasis is placed on doing better than everyone else (Bonoma et al., 1974). In the collaborative class the opposite is true. Mechanisms are in place which create interdependence among students and reliance upon others for the group's success. A nurturing atmosphere is created whereby students help each other and take responsibility for their entire group's progress. Group celebration of individual and group performances promote a supportive atmosphere and highlight each student's responsibility to the entire group.

21. Builds More Positive Heterogeneous Relationships

The current educational system rewards students achievement by separating students of differing abilities rather than encouraging students to utilize their abilities to help each other. Collaborative learning fosters student interaction at all levels (Webb, 1980). Research has shown that when students of high ability work with students of lower ability, both benefit. The former benefits by explaining or demonstrating difficult concepts which he/she must understand thoroughly in order to do so, and the latter benefits by seeing a concept modeled by a peer. Both observe each other's approaches to problem solving and begin to appreciate their differences (Johnson & Johnson 1985c).

22. Encourages Alternate Student Assessment Techniques (Rosenshine and Stevens, 1986)

Collaborative learning provides the teacher with many opportunities to observe students interacting, explaining their reasoning, asking questions and discussing their ideas and concepts (Cooper et al., 1984). These are far more inclusive assessment methods than relying on written exams only (Cross & Angelo, 1993). In addition, group projects provide an alternative for those students who are not as proficient in taking written tests based upon content reproduction. Also, group tests give students an alternate way of expressing their knowledge, by first verbalizing their solution to their partner or group prior to formalizing a written response.

23. Fosters and Develops Interpersonal Relationships (Johnson and Johnson, 1987)

The reliance on base groups to help individuals keep track of each other's performance, the interdependence created by self and group assessment and improvement techniques, and the social nature of collaborative learning processes all combine to improve interpersonal relationships among students. Collaborative learning encourages out of class work by the groups, bringing them together in a combined academic and social experience which continues over long periods of time.

24. Modeling Problem-Solving Techniques by Students' Peers (Schunk and Hanson, 1985)

Students often learn more by listening to their peers than they do by listening to an authority figure like a teacher (Levin, Glass & Meister, 1984). Peers often have a better understanding of what other students don't know or causes them difficulty than the teacher does. The focus is on the student, not the teacher. In addition to shifting responsibility for learning onto students, collaborative learning provides an opportunity for students to demonstrate their knowledge by helping their peers (Bargh & Schal, 1980), an especially important advantage over the lecture method or class discussion form of teaching.

25. Students Are Taught How to Criticize Ideas, not People (Johnson, Johnson, and Holubec, 1984)

A function of collaborative learning is to help students resolve differences amicably. They need to be taught how to challenge ideas and advocate for their positions without personalizing their statements. They are also taught conflict resolution methods, which are important for real life situations as well as being useful for academic endeavors.

26. Sets High Expectations for Students and Teachers

Being made responsible for one's learning and for one's peers presumes that each student has that capability. Inherently high expectations are established for students. By setting obtainable goals for groups and by facilitating group interaction, teachers establish high expectations which become self-fulfilling as the students master the collaborative approach, learn how to work well together in teams, and demonstrate their abilities through individual tests and a variety of other methods. Higher self-esteem and higher expectations are the outcomes.

27. Promotes Higher Achievement and Class Attendance (Hagman and Hayes, 1986)

Students who develop personal professional relations with teachers by getting to know them, and who work on projects outside of class, achieve better results and tend to stay in school (Cooper et al., 1984). Teachers who get to know their students and understand their problems can often find ways of dealing with those problems. They have a great advantage in formulating ways of assisting their students. Students are often inspired by the teacher who takes the time to get to know them and encourage them to aspire to better performance (Janke, 1980).

28. Students Stay on Task More and Are Less Disruptive

An enormous hidden benefit of collaborative learning is one most attractive to teachers: it negates many forms of student disruptive behavior. As any teacher knows, it is extremely easy for only one (or more) member(s) of an entire class to disrupt class proceeding when the lecture method is employed. In contrast, when students are working in groups, the stage is removed from those who try to act out (Stahle & VanSickle, 1986). It is very difficult for an individual to gain the entire class's attention when the class is working in many smaller groups. Within groups intense work is being carried on because more students are involved actively in the process. The collaborative learning activities are very focused and often create a high degree of concentration by group members. Thus they will not be distracted by an individual acting out in another group or trying to gain the class's attention.

29. Greater Ability of Students to View Situations from Others' Perspectives (Development of Empathy)

Students using collaborative learning methods are encouraged to question each other, debate issues, and discuss each other's ideas and approaches to answering questions and solving problems. A much deeper understanding of individual differences and cultural differences among students is developed (Yager et al., 1985b). Because students work in a supportive environment where group processing skills are taught, they are much more inclined to accept different approaches than if they work in a competitive, non-interactive system which credits individual effort above team effort (Johnson, 1975a; 1975b). Additionally, students are exposed to many more methodologies with collaborative learning than those presented by the teacher using a lecture.

30. Creates a Stronger Social Support System (Cohen and Willis, 1985)

Collaborative learning uses students' social experiences to encourage their involvement in the learning process. Warm-up exercises and group building activities used throughout the course build a social support. The teacher plays a very active role in facilitating the process and interacting with each student. Administrators, school staff, and parents become integral parts of the collaboration process, thus building into it many possibilities for support for any individual who develops problems, both academic and social (Kessler & McCleod, 1985).

31. Creates a More Positive Attitude Toward Teachers, Principals, and Other School Personnel by Students and Creates a More Positive Attitude by Teachers Toward their Students

The level of involvement of all the participants in a collaborative system is very intense and personal. Students get to know teachers personally. Teachers learn about student behaviors because students have many opportunities to explain themselves to the teacher. Lines of communication are opened and actively encouraged. Teachers have more opportunities to explain why policies are established and the system allows students to have more input into establishing policies and class procedures. The empowerment created by the many interpersonal interactions leads to a very positive attitude by all parties involved.

32. Addresses Learning Style Differences Among Students (Midkiff and Thomasson, 1993)

Students working in collaborative classes utilize each of the three main learning styles: kinesthetic, auditory and visual. For example, material presented by the teacher is both auditory and visual. Students working together use their kinesthetic abilities when working with hands-on activities. Verbal and auditory skills are enhanced as students discuss their answers together. Visual and auditory modalities are employed when students present their results to the whole class. Each of these learning styles are addressed many times throughout a class in contrast to the lecture format which is mainly auditory and occasionally visual.

33. Promotes Innovation in Teaching and Classroom Techniques (Slavin, 1980; 1990)

Collaborative learning processes include class warm-up activities, name recognition games and group building activities, and group processing. Students work in pairs or larger groups depending upon the task at hand. Group work on content takes many forms, including pairs or groups working on individual questions, problem assignments, projects, study activities, group tests, etc. Classes are interesting and enjoyable because of the variety of activities available for use by the teacher. In fact, collaborative learning effectively addresses the "Sesame Street" syndrome in which modern students are used to being exposed to information in short, entertaining sessions. These same students are also used to high tech computer systems which deliver material in a variety of ways including video, text, graphical illustrations, and interactive systems. Collaborative learning effectively matches or exceeds the above approaches to learning by actively involving every student.

34. Classroom Anxiety Is Significantly Reduced (Kessler, Price, and Wortman, 1985)

In a traditional classroom when a teacher calls upon a student, he/she becomes the focus of attention of the entire class. Any mistakes or incorrect answers become subject to scrutiny by the whole class. Such experiences produce embarrassment and anxiety in many students. In contrast, in a collaborative learning situation, when students work in a group, the focus of attention is diffused among the group. When an answer is presented to the class it represents the work of the entire group; therefore no single individual can be held up to criticism. In addition, the group produces a product which its members can review prior to presenting it to the whole class, thus diminishing prospects that mistakes will occur at all (Slavin & Karweit, 1981). When a mistake is made, it becomes a teaching tool instead of a public criticism of an individual student. Coincidentally, the general class attitude is one of cooperation and nurturing, not criticism.

35. Test Anxiety Is Significantly Reduced (Johnson and Johnson, 1989)

Competition increases anxiety and makes people feel less able to perform. Collaborative learning creates the opposite response from students. It provides many opportunities for alternate forms of student assessment as described above. This situation leads to a reduction in test anxiety because the students see that the teacher is able to evaluate how they think as well as what they know. Students are not locked into a testing format which requires memorization and reproduction of basic skills. Through the interactions with students during each class, the teacher gains a better understanding of each student's learning style and how he/she performs. An opportunity is thus afforded to provide extra guidance and counseling for the students or to establish alternate forms of assessment. This type of interaction is completely lacking in a lecture class.

36. Classroom Resembles Real Life Social and Employment Situations

Students socialize with family members and friends and work in situations which require team work and group work. Training in collaborative learning followed by group activities and processes provide an environment in which students can practice building good social skills, process beneficial group behavior, and generally observe each other's actions and reactions to their behaviors (Breen, 1981).

37. Students Practice Modeling Societal and Work Related Roles

In collaborative classes students may be assigned roles in order to build interdependence within the groups. Roles such as reader, recorder, reporter, materials handler, time keeper, skeptic/challenger and others are rotated among group members for each new assignment or project (Johnson, Johnson & Holubec, 1984). Students are thus encouraged to develop and practice the skills which will be needed to function in society and the work world (Houston, 1992). These skills include leadership, information recording, communication of results orally and in writing, challenging ideas in a constructive manner, obtaining and distributing materials and information to group members, encouraging member participation, brainstorming, meeting deadlines, etc. (Sandberg, 1995). Wlodkowski (1985) observes that, "If students realize the direct applicability of classroom small group problem-solving to their own lives, motivation to learn will show a marked increase." Building strong social characteristics within students can be practiced in a risk-free environment with support and training from the teacher.

POLICIES NEEDED FOR THE FULL IMPLEMENTATION OF COLLABORATIVE LEARNING IN CLASSES

1) Support and encouragement must come from the highest policy making and financial boards and from the chief executive at the institution. Boards of trustees and presidents must embrace collaborative learning as a high system priority. They must be willing to provide the resources needed to implement collaborative learning in the form of training opportunities and materials. If possible the CEO should participate in administrative training sessions (see policy #7). The CEO must provide the leadership in order to create an environment supportive of collaborative learning.

2) Teachers must be involved from the start in planning for collaborative learning and throughout the process of implementing collaborative learning in their classes. Even though the initial impetus must come from the top levels of administration, the development work must be done by the teachers and department level administrators to guarantee its effectiveness (Guskey, 1986).

3) Funding must be adequate to provide for training workshops, conferences, teacher presentations at conferences and in-house, release time for initial preparation, on-campus activities, materials for use in class and continuous training.

4) Textbook manufacturers must be involved in the conversion to collaborative learning by providing supplemental materials in the form of worksheets, handouts describing group activities, and faculty training materials. Eventually professors will develop materials unique to their courses; however, this process will take several years and an interim approach is needed. Publisher materials will also help model collaborative learning handouts for teachers who are just beginning to develop their own materials.

5) A support group mechanism must be developed and encouraged to involve teachers in the initial development process and in the initial training activities. Meeting times and facilities must be provided along with mentors to help the new groups function (Maher & Alston, 1990).

6) Teachers need to be encouraged to adopt collaborative learning in a risk-free environment (Forest, 1996). The teacher evaluation process must be modified to take into account the different teaching methods used, and student testing through standardized tests must be re-evaluated. Alternative forms of assessment will have to be introduced and accepted in order to provide an accurate assessment of the outcomes of collaborative learning.

7) Collaborative learning should be modeled in institutional decision making. Meetings should be facilitated in a collaborative learning manner. Few leaders appear willing to delegate the power to teachers which is needed to implement institutional change. If we desire teachers to delegate power to their students and give up the control afforded by lectures, then administrators must be willing to make the same changes. Teachers must be given the opportunity to work in collaborative versus competitive environments in order to reinforce the benefits of collaborative learning.

8) Administrators and supervisors should be trained in collaborative learning and group dynamics (Cohen, 1986, Cohen & DeAvila, 1983) in order to be able to evaluate it and model it for the teachers. This goal can be accomplished through seminars, by observing experienced teachers, by taking courses in collaborative learning and through in-service training (Noddings, 1989).

9) A collaborative learning library should be established within the institution and materials provided by teachers should be archived for use by other teachers. Funding must be provided for training materials, books, video tapes, journals, etc.

10) Students should be involved in the process through a student council, advisory group or committee assignments. The student leaders should receive training in collaborative learning also via workshops and in-school activities.

11) The general student population should receive training in conflict resolution, group dynamics and proper social behavior. This agenda could be accomplished outside of regular class time by bringing in experts and student trainers to work with student leaders and with groups of students. Teachers need to be trained in these techniques also. An institutional philosophy of cooperation and conflict resolution must to be established.

12) Teacher training colleges and universities must emphasize collaborative learning as the primary teaching paradigm and hire professors who can teach using collaborative learning methodology. Teachers will follow the same model they were taught by, which explains why the lecture method is predominant. Collaborative learning must be modeled in every college class in order to establish this method in teachers' minds.

13) Colleges must adopt collaborative learning as the primary learning method in order to encourage secondary and primary teachers to follow suit. Secondary teachers use the lecture format because they feel they must train their students to succeed at the college level.

14) Collaborative learning must be implemented at all education levels simultaneously. College professors bemoan the fact that students weren't trained in collaborative learning at the secondary level, high school teachers criticize junior high teachers, who in turn suggest that primary teachers need to start the process. This situation needs to be rectified by everyone's beginning to use collaborative learning so that eventually students will be trained from the very beginning of their education. We can't wait 12 years for the first class to go through the entire process in order for all students to be versed in collaborative learning when they reach college.

15) Absolute grading instead of grading on a curve must be adopted by the institution and alternate forms of assessment (such as group grades and portfolios) must be encouraged. The bell curve grading system by its very nature fosters competition, restricts collaboration, and leads to anxiety among students (Tseng, 1969). Within this system, if one student helps another, then he/she alters the bell curve and lowers his/her own grade. Absolute grading eliminates this threat. Higher standards are set

in that every student who performs well can receive a top grade.

16) Curriculum planning and instruction must go hand in hand. "When a curricula is created, instruction must be considered, and when instruction is planned, curriculum materials must be appropriate for the mode of instruction." (Noddings, 1989).

17) Facilities must be provided which are conducive to CL. Lecture halls with fixed amphitheater type seating make student interaction difficult at best. Rows of desks neatly lined up are anathema to CL. Moveable chairs and/or tables where students can work together must be provided. Tables large enough to seat 5 people would be ideal. This size table would comfortably seat groups of 4 and provide flexibility for larger groups. Classrooms must be large enough to enable the professor to move easily about the room when interacting with the groups.

18) Teachers who are just beginning to use CL must be placed in an environment which will foster success, remove anxiety-producing environments and encourage a major change in teaching style. In order to accomplish this financing must be provided to maintain small class sizes and thus maximize student interactions and familiarity and increase student-teacher interaction. Class sizes of 20 are manageable. Depending on the subject matter smaller classes may be desirable. In our present economy this appears to fly in the face of reality; however, large classes are a major impediment to CL and must be reduced in order to encourage teacher participation.

CONCLUSIONS

Considering the sheer number of identifiable educational and societal benefits created by professors using collaborative learning techniques one would presume that it is the most widely used paradigm. Quite the contrary, the didactic method of lecturing is the most commonly used teaching approach in colleges and universities. The reasons presented in this chapter help us understand why more teachers have not adopted CL at all levels of education. The barriers appear to be formidable. It will take strong, humanistic leadership to encourage teachers to make the changes needed to begin the process of implementing CL in their classes.

The policies required for the complete implementation of CL are presented above. They provide a philosophy and framework within which administrators and faculty can work to make the transition from the lecture method to collaborative learning. The policies call for an institutional philosophy which encourages and supports collaborative interactions among faculty, administrators and students in all college governance activities as well as in teaching. Support must originate from the highest policy-making bodies and chief executives followed by development of collaborative structures by the faculty at each institution. Financial support in particular will be the primary indicator of institutional dedication to this change. Faculty development, appropriately equipped classrooms, small class sizes, training administrators in appropriate evaluation techniques, all require a higher level of funding than is currently provided. If additional funding is not forthcoming, then CL will wither and die instead of expanding as it should to provide students with the best possible learning environment.

REFERENCES

Aronson, E., Blaney, N., Stephan, C., Sikes, J., & Snapp, M. (1978). *The jigsaw classroom*. Beverly Hills, CA: Sage Publications.

Astin, A.W. (1977). *Four critical years: Effects of college beliefs, attitudes and knowledge.* San Francisco, CA: Jossey-Bass.

Baird, J. & White, R. (1984). Improving learning through enhanced metacognition: A classroom study. Paper presented at the annual meeting of the American Educational Research Association, New Orleans, LA.

Bargh, J. & Schal, Y. (1980). On the cognitive benefits of teaching. *Journal of Educational Psychology* 72, pp. 593-604.

Bligh, D.A. (1972). *What's the use of lectures?* Harmondsworth, England: Penguin.

Bliss, T. (1986). Small group work in high school social studies. Doctoral dissertation, Stanford University, CA.

Bonoma, J., Tedeschi, J., & Helm, B. (1974). Some effects of target cooperation and reciprocated promises on conflict resolution. *Sociometry* 37, p. 251-261.

Breen, P. (1981). 76 Career-related liberal arts skills. *AAHE Bulletin* 34(2).

Brufee, K. (1993). *Collaborative learning: Higher education, interdependence and the authority of knowledge.* Baltimore, MD: Johns Hopkins Press.

Burnstein, E. & McRae, A. (1962). Some effects of shared threat and prejudice in racially mixed groups. *Journal of Abnormal Social Psychology* 64, pp. 257-263.

Cohen, E.G. (1991). Finding out/descrubrimiento: Complex instruction in science. *Cooperative Learning* 1, 30-31.

Cohen, E.G. (1986). *Designing Group Work.* New York: Teachers College Press.

_____. (1992). Staff development for cooperative learning: What do the researchers say? *Cooperative Learning* 12(2), pp. 18-21.

Cohen, B.P., & Cohen, E.G. (1991). From groupwork among children to R & D teams: interdependence, interaction and productivity. in E.J. Lawler (Eds.) *Advances in Group Processes* 8, pp. 205-226 Greenwich, Connecticut: JAI Press.

Cohen, E.G., & DeAvila, E. (1983). Learning to think in math and science: Improving local education for minority children. Final report to the Walter S. Johnson Foundation, Stanford, CA: Stanford University Program for Complex Instruction.

Cohen, S., & Willis, T. (1985). Stress and social support and the buffering hypothesis. *Psychological Bulletin* 98, pp. 310-357.

Cooper, C. (1992) Coming of age. *Cooperative Learning* 12(2), pp. 3-5.

Cooper, J., Prescott, S., Cook, l., Smith, L., Mueck, R., & Cuseo, J. (1984). *Cooperative learning and college instruction- Effective use of student learning teams.* California State University Foundation publication.

Cross, P.K. & Angelo, T. (1988, 1993, 2nd ed.). *Classroom assessment techniques: A handbook for faculty.* San Francisco, CA: Jossey-Bass.

Davidson, N. (Ed.) (1990). *Cooperative learning in Mathematics: A handbook for teachers.* Menlo Park, CA: Addison-Wesley.

Davis, R. B., Maher, C.A., & Noddings, N. (Eds) (1990). Constructivist views on the teaching and learning of mathematics. *Journal for Research in Mathematics Education* National Council of Teachers of Mathematics.

Deutsch, M. (1975). Equity, equality and need: What determines which value will be used as the basis of distributive justice. *Journal of Social Issues,* 31, pp. 137-149.

_____. (1985). *Distributive justice: A social psychological perspective.* New Haven, CT: Yale University Press.

Devries, D.L. & Slavin, R.E. (1978). Teams-Games-Tournament: Review of Ten classroom experiments. *Journal of Research and Development in Education,* 12 (Fall), pp. 28-38.

Felder, R.M. & Bent, R. (1994). Cooperative learning in technical courses: Procedures, pitfalls and payoffs. ERIC document ES 377-038.

Forest, L. (1996). How can we talk to each other about change? *Cooperative Learning* 16(1).

Foster, A. (1993). *Cooperative learning in the Mathematics classroom.* New York, NY: Glencoe, division of Macmillan/McGraw-Hill.

Garibaldi, A. (1976). Cooperation, competition and locus of control in Afro-American students. Doctoral Dissertation, University of Minnesota.

Graves, N. & Graves, T. (Eds.) (1991) *Cooperative learning.* Santa Cruz, CA: International Association for the Study of Cooperation in Education.

Guskey, R.R. (1986). Staff development and the process of change. *Educational Researcher* 15(5), pp. 5-12.

Hagman, J., & Hayes, J. (1986). Cooperative learning: Effects of task, reward, and group size on individual achievement. Technical Report 704, Scientific Coordination Office, US Army Research Institute for the Behavioral Sciences, ERIC document #278720.

Hooper, S., & Hannafin, M.J. (1988). Cooperative CBI: The effects of heterogeneous vs. homogeneous grouping on the learning of progressively complex concepts. *Journal of Educational Computing Research* 4, p. 413-424.

Houston, L.S. (1991). Collaborative learning: Preparing for industry, a no-lecture method of teaching English. *ATEA Journal* (Dec-Jan).

Irwin, S., Freeman, D.J., Alford, L.E., Floden, R.E., Porter, N.C., Schmidt, W.H., & Schwille, J.R., (1985). Grouping practices and opportunity to learn: A study within-classroom variation in a content taught class. Paper presented at the annual meeting of the American Education Research Association, Chicago.

Janke, R. (1980). Computational errors of mentally-retarded students. *Psychology in the Schools* 17, pp. 30-32.

Johnson, D.W. (1971). Effectiveness of role reversal: Actor or listener. *Psychological Reports* 28, pp. 275-282.

_____. (1973). Communication in conflict situations: A critical review of the research. *International Journal of Group Tensions* 3 pp. 46-67.

_____. (1974). Communication and the inducement of cooperative behavior in conflicts: A critical review. *Speech Monographs* 41, pp. 64-78.

_____. (1975a). Cooperativeness and social perspective taking. *Journal of Personality and Social Psychology* 31, pp. 241-244.

_____. (1975b). Affective perspective taking and cooperative predisposition. *Developmental Psychology* 11, pp. 869-870.

Johnson, R.T. & Johnson, D.W. (1972). The effects of others' actions, attitude similarity, and race on attraction toward others. *Human Relations* 25(2).

_____. (1985a, 1990). *Cooperative learning—Warm-ups, group strategies and group activities.* Edina, MN: Interaction Book Co.

_____. (1985b). Relationships between black and white students in inter-group cooperation and competition. *The Journal of Social Psychology* 125(4), pp. 421-428.

_____. (1985c). Mainstreaming hearing impaired students: The effect of efforts in communicating on cooperation. *The Journal of Psychology* 119(1).

_____. (1987). *Learning Together and alone: Cooperative, competitive and individualistic learning.* 2nd ed. Englewood Cliffs, NJ: Prentice Hall.

_____. (1987b). *Creative conflict.* Edina MN: Interaction Book Co.

_____, (1989). *Cooperation and competition theory and research.* Edina, MN: Interaction Book Co.

Johnson, D.W., Johnson, R.T., & Holubec, E.J. (1984). *Cooperation in the classroom.* Edina, MN: Interaction Book Co.

_____. (1984, 1990). *Circles of learning.* Edina, MN: Interaction Book Co.

_____. (1988, 1992). *Advanced cooperative learning—revised.* Edina, MN: Interaction Book Co.

Johnson, D.W., Johnson, R.T., Roy, P., & Zaidman, B. (1985). Oral interaction in cooperative learning groups: Speaking, listening and the nature of statements made by high, medium and low-achieving students. *Journal of Psychology* 119, pp. 303-321.

Joyce, B.R. (1992). Cooperation, learning, and staff development: Teaching the method with the method. *Cooperative Learning* 12(2), pp.10-13.

Kagan, S. (1989). *Cooperative learning resources for teachers.* San Juan Capistrano, CA: Resources for Teachers.

_____. (1986). Cooperative learning and sociological factor in schooling. In *Beyond language: Social and cultural factors in schooling language minority students.* Los Angeles, CA: California State University Evaluation, Dissemination and Assessment Center.

Kessler, R. & McCleod, J. (1985). Social support and mental health in community samples. in Cohen and Syme (Eds.) *Social support and health.* New York, NY: Academic Press.

Kessler, R., Price, R., & Wortman,C. (1985). Social factors in psychopathology: Stress, social support and coping processes. *Annual Review of Psychology* 36, pp. 351-372.

Kidder, T. (1989). *Among school children.* Boston, MA: Houghton Mifflin.

Kort, M.S. (1992). Down from the podium. in *New Directions for Community Colleges* San Francisco, CA: Jossey-Bass.

Kroehnert, G. (1991). *100 Training Games.* McGraw Hill Book Co.

Kulik, J.A. & Kulik, C.L. (1979). College Teaching. in Peterson and Walberg (Eds.) *Research in Teaching: Concepts, findings and implications* Berkeley, CA: McCutcheon Publishing.

Levin, H., Glass,G., & Meister, G. (1984). *Cost-effectiveness of educational interventions.* Stanford, CA: Institute for Research on Educational Finance and Governance.

Madden, N.A., Slavin, R.E., & Stevens, R.J. (1986). *Cooperative integrated reading and comparison: Teachers manual.* Baltimore, MD: Johns Hopkins University, Center for Research in Elementary and Middle Schools.

Maher, C. & Alston, A. (1990). Teacher development in mathematics in a constructivist framework. In Davis, Maher, & Noddings (Eds.) *Journal for Research in Mathematics Education.*

Midkiff, R.B. & Thomasson, R.D. (1993). *A practical approach to using learning styles in Math instruction.* Springfield, IL: Charles Thomas Pub.

Neer, M.R. (1987). The development of an instrument to measure classroom apprehension. *Communication education* 36, pp. 154-166.

Noddings, N. (1989). Theoretical and practical concerns about small groups in mathematics. *The Elementary School Journal* 89(5), pp. 607-623.

Peterson, P. & Swing, S. (1985). Students cognition as mediators of the effectiveness of small-group learning. *Journal of Educational Psychology* 77(3), pp. 299-312.

Resnick, L.B. (1992) *Education and learning to think.* Washington, DC: National Academy Press.

Reynolds, B.E., Hagelgans, N.C., Schwingendorf, K.E., Vidahavic, D., Dubinsky, E., Shahin. M., & Wimbish, G.J. (1990) *A practical guide to cooperative learning in collegiate Mathematics.* The Mathematical Assn. of America, Notes #37.

Rolheiser-Bennett, C. & Stevahn, L. (1992). *Cooperative Learning* 13(1), Fall 1992.

Rosenshine, B. & Stevens, R. (1986). Teaching Functions. in Wittrock (ed.) *Handbook of research on teaching,* (3rd edition). New York, NY: Macmillan Publishing, pp. 376-391.

Sandberg, K.E. (1995). Affective and cognitive features of collaborative learning. in *Review of research and developmental education.* Gene Kierstons (Ed.), 6 (4), Appalachian State University, Boone, NC.

Scearce, C. (1992). *100 ways to build teams.* Palatine, IL: IRI Skylight.

Schmuck, R. (1992). Organization development: Building communities of learners. *Cooperative Learning* 12(2), pp. 14-17.

Schunk, D. & Hanson, A. (1985). Peer models: Influence on children's self-efficacy and achievement. *Journal of Educational Psychology* 77(3), p. 313.

Schwartz, D.L., Black, J.B. & Strange, J., (1991). Dyads have fourfold advantage over individuals inducing abstract rules. Paper presented at the annual meeting of the American Educational Research Association, Chicago, IL.

Sharan, S. (1994). *Handbook of cooperative learning methods.* Westport, CT: Greenwood Press.

Sharan, Y. & Sharan, C. (1976). *Small group teaching.* Englewood Cliffs, NJ: Prentice Hall.

Sharan, S. & Hertz-Lazarowitz, R. (1980). Academic achievement of elementary school children in small group vs. whole class discussion. *Journal of Experimental Education* 489, pp. 125-129.

Slavin, R.E. (1978). Student teams achievement divisions. *Journal of Research and Development in Education* 12 (June) 1978, pp. 39-49.

_____. (1980). Cooperative learning. *Review of Educational Research* 50, pp. 315-342.

_____. (1983a). *Cooperative learning* New York, NY: Longman.

_____. (1983b). When does cooperative learning increase student achievement? *Psychological Bulletin* 94, pp. 429-445.

_____. (1987). *Cooperative learning: Student teams.* 2nd Ed. Washington, DC: National Education Association.

_____. (1990). *Cooperative learning: Theory, research and practice.* Englewood Cliffs, NJ:

Prentice Hall.

Slavin, R.E. & Karweit, N. (1981). Cognitive and affective outcomes of an intensive student team learning experience. *Journal of Experimental Education* 50, pp. 29-35.

Slavin, R.E., Leavey, M.B., & Madden, N.A. (1986). *Team accelerated instruction.* Watertown, MA: Charlesbridge.

Stahle, R.J. (1986). From "academic strangers" to successful members of a cooperative learning group: An inside the learner perspective. In Stahle and VanSickle (Eds.), *Cooperative learning in the Social Studies classroom.* Washington, DC: National Council for the Social Studies.

Stahle, R.J. & VanSickle, R.L. (1986). Cooperative learning as effective social study within the social studies classroom. In Stahle and VanSickle (Eds.), *Cooperative learning in the Social Studies classroom.* Washington, DC: National Council for the Social Studies.

Swing, S., & Peterson, P. (1982). The relationship of student ability and small group interaction to student achievement. *American Educational Research Journal* 19, pp. 259-274.

Treisman, P.U. (1985). A study of mathematics performance of black students at the University of California, Berkeley. Doctoral dissertation, *Dissertation Abstracts* 47, 1641-a.

Tseng, S. (1969). An experimental study of the effect of three types of distribution of reward upon work efficiency and group dynamics. Doctoral dissertation, Columbia University, New York, NY.

Turnure, J. & Ziegler, R. (1958). Outer-directedness in the problem solving or normal and retarded students. *Journal of Abnormal and Social Psychology* 57, pp. 379-388.

Warren, N. (1995). *The warm-ups manual: Tools for working with groups.* Toronto, Canada: Warren Associates Inc.

Weaver, R.L., & Cottrell, H.W. (1985). Mental aerobics: The half-sheet response. *Innovative Higher Education* 10, pp. 23-31.

Webb, N.M. (1980). An analysis of group interaction and mathematical errors in heterogeneous ability groups. *British Journal of Educational Psychology* 50, pp. 266-276.

_____. (1982a). Group composition, group interaction and achievement in small groups. *Journal of Educational Psychology* 74(4), pp. 475-484.

_____. (1982b). Student interaction and learning in small groups. *Review of Educational Research* 52, pp. 421-445.

Weinstein, M. & Goodman, J. (1980). *Everybody's guide to non-competitive play: Play fair.* San Luis Obispo, CA: Impact Publishers.

Williams, B.R. (1993). *More than 50 ways to build team consensus.* Palatine, IL: IRI Skylight Publishing.

Wlodkowski, R.J. (1985). *Enhancing motivation to learn.* San Francisco: Jossey-Bass.

Wooley, S., Switzer, T., Foster, G., Landes, N., & Robertson, W. (1990). BSCS Cooperative learning and science program. *Cooperative Learning* 11(3).

Yager, S., Johnson, D.W., & Johnson, R. (1985). Oral discussion groups-to-individual transfer and achievement in cooperative learning groups. *Journal of Educational Psychology* 77(1), pp. 60-66.

Yager, S., Johnson, R., Johnson, D.W., & Snider, B. (1985). The effect of cooperative and individualistic learning experiences on positive and negative cross-handicap relations. *Contemporary Educational Psychology* 10, pp. 127-138.

CHAPTER 8

How Micronesian Students Learn Skills for Personal Adjustment

Issues of Authority, Self-Disclosure, and Cultural Relevance

Kyle D. Smith, Seyda Türk Smith, and Iain K. B. Twaddle [1]

A large proportion of the literature on personal development carries a decidedly Western orientation, which affects the way in which students learn about personal adjustment skills. For example, a popular text for college-level courses in personal adjustment makes characteristically Western assumptions about students' inclinations to direct themselves toward self-chosen goals.

> This book is designed to acquaint you with a general theory of behavior, to guide you through exercises for developing skills in self-analysis, and to provide you with concrete information on how to achieve the goals you hold for yourself. . . . The vehicle for learning will be your own self-analysis, your own program for implementing your values. (Watson & Tharp, 1993, p. iii)

In contrast, cross-cultural psychologists suggest that for many, personal adjustment means accommodating the demands of others.

> Satisfaction about the self within an interdependent framework may result from the recognition that one is performing well in the cultural tasks of belonging, fitting in . . . [and] promoting others' goals. (Kitayama & Markus, 1994)

> For interdependent selves . . . 'adjustment' signifies a willingness to be responsive to others and to regulate one's own demands and desires so as to maintain the ever-important relationship. (Markus & Kitayama, 1991, p. 250)

A student workbook for a personal adjustment course assumes that students will welcome the chance to self-disclose to their instructors and classmates.

> How you use these personal exploration exercises will depend, in large part, on your instructor. Many instructors will formally assign some of these exercises and then collect them, either for individual scrutiny or class discussion. (Weiten, 1994, p. 1).

Yet, such exercises may place non-Western students in a difficult predicament. As the Guam Department of Education recently observed:

> Palauan parents teach their children to keep their problems to themselves [and] to solve their problems without the help of an adult. Family problems in particular are specifically not to be discussed with anyone outside the family (Guam Department of Education, 1992).

As these quotes suggest, non-Western students may learn in ways poorly accommodated by college courses that require self-direction and a willingness to disclose personal information to the instructor. In this chapter, we develop a specific example, discussing ways in which Micronesian students' motives for and approaches to learning depart from those assumed by Western-oriented courses in personal adjustment. We wish to offer two topics for discussion in this chapter: (a) specific, research-based ideas that may help instructors elsewhere who work with Micronesian students, and (b) a general approach to considering collectivist and status-based issues in learning and to modifying assignments accordingly.

TEACHING PERSONAL ADJUSTMENT AT THE UNIVERSITY OF GUAM

Guam, the largest of the western Pacific's Mariana Islands, is a U.S. territory and home to a population of approximately 140,000. The University of Guam (UOG) is the United States' only accredited four-year institution of higher education in Micronesia. Its roughly 3,500 undergraduate students come from Guam itself, the U.S. mainland, the Far East and from three Micronesian nations: the Republic of Palau, the Federated States of Micronesia (comprised of Yap, Chuuk, Pohnpei, and Kosrae), and the Republic of the Marshall Islands. The Micronesian nations comprise hundreds of islands and atolls (of which fewer than 50 are of significant size), spanning more than 4000 kilometers of the western Pacific. The Micronesian region is home to nine distinct languages and many dialects. Individual islands vary widely in the degree to which they have incorporated Western technology and cultural influences. Micronesian nationals constitute roughly 7 percent of UOG's student population. Many are away from their home islands for the first time. Micronesian students are typically housed in on-campus dormitories;[2] in contrast, most other students commute from off-campus homes.

Like many comparable programs at mainland American universities, UOG's Psychology Program offers an elective course in personal adjustment. This course introduces lower-division students to the psychological literatures on stress, coping, and related topics (e.g., social skills; coping with failure or loss; managing conflicts) and on personal growth. Frequently, students conduct a semester-long project applying behavioral principles (e.g., systematic observation of the antecedents and consequences of target behaviors) to some behavior of their own. Popular choices include studying, weight control, exercise, addictions, bad habits, and shyness. After choosing a target behavior, each student makes written observations (a) of relevant situations in which the student behaves well or poorly; (b) what the student actually does in these situations; and (c) the consequences of these behaviors. Working closely with the instructor, the student next identifies several techniques to modify the target behavior's situational antecedents, the behavior itself, and the consequences of the behavior. For example, a student trying to reduce his or her intake of alcohol might avoid situations in which most peers will be drinking; substitute nonalcoholic beverages for beer or wine; and reward himself or herself with extra spending money for every day he or she does not exceed the target intake of alcohol. For many, this project has proven quite successful in ameliorating stubborn personal problems and in providing a set of skills applicable to future problems.

Such coursework, however, may vary in its appeal across cultures. Western (e.g., North American) students typically look forward to their time in college as a period of self-development. They enter the personal adjustment class having some familiarity with (and some curiosity concerning) psychology as a practice. They are often excited about learning some of the arcane techniques that psychologists use to modify behavior and about applying these techniques to themselves. Many seem eager to discuss personal issues with a trained professional (free therapy!), and come frequently to office hours for that purpose.

Orientation materials for new UOG faculty suggested that Micronesian students might not share these characteristics (Wesley, 1991), and our first experiences in teaching the adjustment course at UOG confirmed this. Many Micronesian enrollees apparently chose our course because it was one of a small number available to foreign students who had not yet completed the University's developmental English program. Although some Micronesian students seemed interested in the course, most showed little excitement or curiosity concerning the techniques we promised to teach them. Micronesian students typically contributed little to class discussions, isolating themselves in ethnically homogenous clusters. Many stopped coming to class altogether. When asked to submit weekly assignments applying behavior modification techniques to problems of interest to themselves, some completed thoughtful projects; however, unusually large percentages of Micronesian students either submitted simple repetitions of examples given in class, or submitted nothing. Micronesian students rarely came to talk with us on their own initiative, and those who did come to our offices showed little inclination to discuss their personal concerns or how they might address them in the course. There were notable exceptions, but as a group Micronesian students were unusually likely to lose interest in the course, and to leave it without accomplishing their goals. They seemed unconvinced that the course had much of value to offer them. As matters stood, they may have been correct.

We realized we would have to rethink our approach to the course. As a first step toward doing so, we asked ourselves three interrelated questions. How might Micronesian students' motives for learning differ from the motives assumed by our course? What differences in their approaches to learning might present barriers to Micronesian students in a personal adjustment course? What changes could we make in the course to produce a better fit with Micronesian motives for and approaches to learning?

Our experiences to date with Micronesian students suggested a variety of possible answers, but some no doubt derived from the idiosyncrasies of the particular students involved. To choose several broadly applicable hypotheses for testing with subsequent classes, we compared our experiences and the available data on our students with the research literature on cross-cultural psychology and on Micronesian studies.

RELEVANT RESEARCH

Theoretical models in cross-cultural psychology reduce complex differences between cultures to several factors that predict differences at the level of individual behavior. Two of these factors seemed relevant to the problem at hand.

Individualism-collectivism. Cultures differ in the degree to which they encourage individuals to pursue their own interests and goals and to limit their compliance with demands made by groups. Individualist cultures (e.g., the 'mainstream' United States and Australia) do encourage this; in contrast, collectivist cultures (e.g., traditional Japan, Hong Kong, Venezuela) subordinate individual goals to those of important groups such as family and co-workers (Hofstede, 1980). Individualism fosters the development of an independent self-image, such that the individual focuses on his or her unique capabilities and seeks to apply these capabilities to his or her personal ambitions. Collectivism emphasizes one's interdependence with others and promotes the goals of fitting in and adjusting one's goals so as to maximize the well-being of the in-group. In collectivist cultures, people remain sensitive to the demands of the particular social situation, and are well aware of shifts in their own behavior to accommodate these demands (Markus & Kitayama, 1991). Collectivism also fosters a strong distinction between members of the in-group and outsiders, such that matters of concern to the in-group are not discussed with others (Kim, 1994). In educational settings, cultural collectivism often manifests itself as a reluctance to stand out in the classroom and a desire to promote the performance of one's peers (Goodman, 1994).

Power distance. Power distance refers to the degree to which a culture accepts the idea that power is distributed unequally. In cultures low in power distance (e.g., Denmark, Israel), hierarchies of status are relatively flexible and informal. It would not be uncommon for subordinates to address bosses or teachers by their first names or to socialize with them. In such cultures, people may react to inordinate exercises of power by disagreeing with or challenging the superior. In cultures high in power distance (e.g., Mexico, Singapore, Turkey), subordinates are often quite sensitive to their roles and statuses within an organization. Subordinates treat their superiors with careful respect and avoid doing anything that might suggest a challenge to the superiors' authority. They are unlikely to treat their superiors as friends or confidants (Hofstede, 1980). In educational settings, high power distance often manifests itself in classrooms filled with students who refrain from asking questions, which might be interpreted as a challenge to the instructor's expertise or authority (Goodman, 1994). Moreover, students may be acutely sensitive to differences of socioeconomic status between themselves and their classmates.

Research on Micronesians
The available research on Micronesians strongly suggests that many traditional Micronesian cultures promote collectivism and high power distance. Micronesian extended families and lineages impose an extensive system of obligations on their members (e.g., see Caughey, 1977; Poyer, 1990). Howard (1990) argues that construction of identity within indigenous Pacific cultures is distinctly interdependent:

> A person's character, and by extension a group's character, is a product of one's specific relational history. Rather than being internally located, one's character is dependent upon an ongoing set of relationships that contribute to its formation (and continual reformation). (p. 266)

Consistent with high power distance, Micronesian chiefs and persons with special knowledge are treated with formalized respect. Rigid caste systems exist in several Micronesian cultures, and families acknowledge their places in elaborate hierarchies of status (Robillard, 1983).

Micronesian students on Guam appear to share many of the characteristics of cultural collectivism, interdependence and high power distance. Public school teachers have noted that Micronesian students work best in groups (Schmitz and Türk Smith, 1996) ; they are uncomfortable with being singled out for attention and with speaking in front of large groups. Micronesian students tend to be very respectful of authority figures. They have been socialized to try to do what elders tell them to do, without asking questions. Micronesian students often do not respond to questions, even if they know the answer; they are adhering to an unwritten but powerful rule that says, "Elders speak, juniors listen." They may find it difficult to express their personal concerns openly. However, Micronesian students are easily motivated if they like the teacher or if they are interested in the subject (Guam Department of Education, 1992).

Our own surveys of Micronesian students also provided evidence for cultural collectivism and high power distance. One survey asked students identified by ethnicity only to rate a series of values in terms of their importance. Some values expressed long-term goals of living (e.g., an exciting life; wisdom); others expressed ways of behaving that would further one or more of these goals (e.g., daring; broad-minded). This survey adapted Rokeach's (1973) methods to sets of values valid for international use; see Schwartz (1994) for a detailed description of the approach. In their responses, Micronesian students attached great importance to respecting their parents and elders, gaining the approval of others, fulfilling their responsibilities to others, accepting their positions in life, promoting the security of their families, and showing respect for tradition. A number of them attached little importance to independence and risk-taking. Similarly, the Twenty Statements Test (completing 20 sentences that begin with, "I am . . ."), used successfully in many cultures to define elements of students' self-concepts (e.g., Cousins, 1989), indicated that Micronesian students were likely to list ties to their home islands and families as important aspects of their self-concepts.

In summary, research and theory suggested that our Micronesian students had goals—and perhaps ways of learning—that differed in important ways from those of their more successful Western classmates. Thus, several of our experiences with Micronesian students seemed part of a broader pattern of conflict between Micronesian cultural assumptions and the culture of the classroom. We proposed the following specific hypotheses concerning the nature of that conflict.

HOW MICRONESIAN STUDENTS LEARN: HYPOTHESES CONCERNING MOTIVES, APPROACHES, AND MENTORING

Motives

<u>Hypothesis 1:</u> *As compared with their Western counterparts, Micronesian students will show stronger preferences for material that helps them (a) to "fit in" to important groups, or (b) to be of service to their peers and families.*

We noticed that Micronesian students typically addressed their projects to improving their English or study skills. These topics would not require much personal disclosure, so perhaps they were simply taking the path of least resistance. Still, research on the culturally inculcated goal characteristic of interdependent persons—fitting into important groups—suggested another explanation: that Micronesian students were highly motivated to use our course (and any other opportunity) to adjust to the new cultural setting in which they found themselves. We began to discuss other topics that might help the Micronesians to fit in. Similarly, we looked for topics of special relevance (a) to the larger community of Micronesian students at UOG (i.e., foci of learning that our students might share with the peers they now relied on for so much), or (b) to their home communities in Micronesia. Presumably, course materials addressing such topics would motivate these students to a greater extent than materials on more typically Western concerns like weight loss or low self-esteem.

Approaches to Learning

<u>Hypothesis 2:</u> *Micronesian students will prefer class exercises that minimize attention to individual performance.*

Although Micronesian students were often reluctant to speak up in class, many lost this reluctance quickly and reliably whenever we singled out a Micronesian classmate for praise. Sarcastic asides and derisive snickers ensued as they hammered down "the nail that sticks out." Micronesian students, like many people from collectivist cultures, received praise with gratitude when it was offered in private but few wished to draw attention to themselves in front of their peers. We considered ways of shifting the potential for in-class achievement from individuals to groups.

<u>Hypothesis 3</u>: *Micronesian students will prefer class exercises that do not force self-disclosure.*

Micronesian students so rarely offered information about themselves in class discussions that question-and-comment sessions on coping, anger, and similar topics frequently fell flat. We began to look for ways of adapting material frequently taught through structured discussions to groupwork that would minimize our students' stage fright: essentially, ways of making discussions of personal adjustment less personal.

<u>Hypothesis 4</u>: *Properly motivated Micronesian students are more comprehensive and accurate in their answers than Western students when asked to identify social pressures that contribute to their problems in familiar situations.*

Cultural collectivism encourages individuals to attend with vigilance to the specific demands of the situations in which they find themselves, and to others' expectations of them in particular. This ensures that individuals do not burden others with whom they are interdependent by neglecting responsibilities. Interdependent persons are quite conscious of altering their behavior in response to situational demands (Markus & Kitayama, 1991). Thus, Micronesian students should be well accustomed to an idea basic to behavioral self-change: that their behaviors depend in important ways on the situations in which they find themselves. Many "self-determining" Westerners resist this idea.

This advantage probably would not surface in unfamiliar situations characteristic of a new cultural milieu. But in situations familiar to Micronesian students—such as being offered alcohol and mildly addictive betelnut by friends or relatives—they should recognize the power of the situation on their behavior.

<u>Hypothesis 5</u>: *Micronesian students are acutely sensitive to a lesser status assigned them by non-Micronesian classmates.*

Indigenous Chamorro students usually do not make efforts to get to know their Micronesian classmates. To explain why requires some recent history. Micronesian nationals gained legal rights to live and work in Guam (and elsewhere in the U.S.) with the passage of 1986's Compact of Free Association between the United States, the Federated States of Micronesia and the Republic of the Marshall Islands. Thousands of Micronesians relocated to Guam in search of better living conditions and wages, often taking unskilled or semi-skilled jobs in construction or in the hotels (Rubinstein & Levin, 1992). Guam's Chamorros, who were already dealing with an inadequate infrastructure (including shortages of affordable housing and of health professionals), varied in the degree of hospitality and status they were willing to accord the immigrants (Türk Smith, 1993). Micronesians on Guam often report being treated with prejudice and outright discrimination (Smith, 1994).

Thus, we considered it no coincidence that our students segregated themselves into ethnically homogenous clusters within the classroom. To learn more, we asked our students anonymously to indicate the degree to which they felt close to or distant from other ethnic groups. We found that the Chamorro students took pains to distinguish themselves from Micronesians and often did not want to associate with them (cf. Brislin & Wilson, 1971). For their part, the Micronesian students' natural shyness combined with a recognition of the low status their "hosts" accorded them to minimize their contributions to class. We needed a means of empowering them.

Relationship with the Instructor

Hypothesis 6: *As compared with their North American and Western European counterparts, Micronesian students will more often require a close personal relationship, built on extensive acquaintance and earned trust, before disclosing intimate facts about themselves.*

As mentioned earlier, people in collectivist cultures are expected to solve many if not most of their problems without burdening others. Further, problems that have surfaced in one's relationships with other members of the ingroup are not to be discussed outside the group (Kim, 1994). For both reasons, persons raised in collectivist cultures do not make a habit of confiding their personal problems to strangers, even if the strangers are professionals. Counseling and therapy may be reserved for severely emotionally or mentally disturbed persons, and may carry considerable stigma (Pedersen, 1994). Micronesian students may treat university professors and other authority figures with respect (as high power distance demands), but they will not readily accept professors as confidants. Encouraging an intimate relationship would not only provide us the knowledge we needed to guide our Micronesian students' progress but would also provide these students with another culturally appropriate motive to learn: pleasing an instructor whom they like as well as respect (cf. Guam Department of Education, 1992).

<u>Hypothesis 7:</u> *Once a close relationship is established, Micronesian students may self-disclose at levels deeper than are typical of Western students.*

At the end of one semester, the first author was surprised to receive a male Chuukese student at office hours. The young man, who had said little during the entire term, confided that he was thinking of killing himself. He was severely depressed and felt as though his parents (also residents of Guam) did not really care about him. He had a few other, more distant relatives on Guam, but no one on whom he could rely or ask to mediate his disagreements with his parents. The young man stated that he would not discuss his problem with anyone other than the first author, whom he felt that he could trust after several months' acquaintance.

This episode, although dramatic, was not unprecedented. On several occasions, Micronesian students had come to talk with us and had confided highly intimate details of their lives but only after months had passed: far too late to put the relationship to work for their projects in personal adjustment. Could we find ways of building this trust earlier in the semester?

ADJUSTMENTS IN THE COURSE

In this section, we discuss several changes that we have made in the personal adjustment course. Each addresses one or more of the hypotheses listed above.

Incorporating Material on "Culture Shock"

Our Micronesian students need more than improved English and study skills to negotiate their transition to life on Guam. Psychological acculturation (popularly called "culture shock") involves having to relearn much of what daily life is about, at the very time that one's communication skills may be reduced to those of a child and one's customary social supports are unavailable (Berry, 1990). Not infrequently, the results are a high level of stress and the accompanying stress-related illnesses. The cures (none of them easy) include learning common sources of well-meaning "clashes" between people of different cultures and avoiding the urge to limit contact with one's cultural hosts (Brislin, Cushner, Cherrie & Yong, 1986). We decided to include material on psychological acculturation and means of coping with it in our adjustment course, and to invite students to address them in their self-modification projects. This change addressed Hypothesis 1a.

Incorporating Micronesia-Specific Material on Substance Abuse and Suicide

Abuse of alcohol and other drugs is very common throughout Micronesia

(Marshall, 1993). So too are suicides, particularly among adolescent males in Chuuk and Pohnpei (Rubinstein, 1992). We had dealt briefly with substance abuse and with suicide prevention in earlier iterations of the course, but we decided to increase our emphasis of these "hot" topics, adding Micronesia-specific material based on the articles listed above and placing this material early in the semester. To say the least, we had their attention. It no longer seemed that the course had little to offer our Micronesian students. This change addressed Hypothesis 1b.

Organizing Workshops in the Dormitories in Cooperation with "Graduates" of the Course
We have decided to try working with resident halls coordinators to convene workshops on culture shock, on substance abuse, and on early detection of potential suicides, putting our Micronesian students and their training from our course to work as facilitators in small-group work. We are aware that we must diligently supervise these workshops and provide highly structured materials for the work groups. Still, the technique promises a practical and prosocial outcome to sections of the course of considerable importance to Micronesian communities, and a natural means of helping our Micronesian students contribute to groups of on-campus peers whose support is all-important. This change addresses Hypothesis 1b.

Using Groupwork in Ethnically Heterogenous "Jigsaw" Class Exercises
Our best successes in getting Micronesians to speak up in class came in sessions that involved learning about Micronesia. We now ask Micronesian students to contribute directly to class sessions devoted to culture shock, by teaching an ethnically heterogenous group of classmates about specific Micronesian cultures and what foreigners typically misunderstand about them. Demonstration materials rely on composite case studies prepared in advance, rather than spontaneous self-disclosures. We ask Micronesian students to comment on and elaborate these cases. For example, a number of Federally funded programs in mental health have failed completely in Micronesia, in part because they ignored differences in status among counselors and potential clients (e.g., training outer-island Yapese to counsel everyone in the district, including higher-caste central Yapese; see Robillard, 1983). We ask Micronesian students to teach several such cases to their classmates and to comment on the aspects of Micronesian cultures implicit in each.

By making grades for that section dependent in part on mastery of the

Micronesian-contributed material, we are applying the "jigsaw" technique proven effective in mainland U.S. classrooms in which differences of attributed status are a problem (cf. Aronson & Bridgeman, 1979). Further, we hope that non-Micronesian participants in these exercises will learn from their Micronesian classmates' attention to situational demands (and the lack of attention evident in Westerners' *faux pas* in Micronesia.) This change addresses Hypotheses 2 through 5.

Organizing Intimacy-Fostering Retreats

The third author invited students in one personal adjustment class to participate in a "personal adjustment retreat." The retreat served as the final assignment in a series of class projects but qualitatively diverged from earlier projects in both its format and focus. For their first project, students were required to identify an aspect of their psychological functioning that they wanted to *know more about,* develop strategies to increase their awareness of that aspect, implement the strategies, and record their progress in behavioral charts and descriptive diaries. For their second project, the students were instructed to choose an aspect of their psychological functioning that they wished to *change,* develop a number of self-change strategies, and as in the first project, implement the strategies while recording their progress in detail. Moving beyond the individualistic emphasis inherent in these self-awareness and self-change projects, the retreat encouraged students to enhance their adjustment skills collectively by learning to share their coping strengths with each other. Working in small groups, the students were required to develop exercises focusing on an important aspect of personal adjustment and lead the class through these exercises in a two hour retreat session. They were free to focus on the emotional, cognitive, behavioral, interpersonal, or spiritual realms of psychological functioning; however, they were strongly encouraged to choose activities which highlighted their personal strengths and the strengths found within their families and cultures.

In contrast to the course's other exercises and projects, which were designed solely by the instructor, the students participated in all stages of retreat planning. After many weeks of deliberation, we agreed to hold the retreat on a weekend, two weeks prior to the end of the semester. We chose Peleliu Abai, an outdoor community center run by the Palauan Community Association of Guam, as our location. The Abai, situated in the "boonies" near the Philippine Sea and well away from main roads, provided an ideal haven for peaceful reflection and cooperative work. On the first day of the retreat, the 21 student participants and their instructor gathered at the Abai at 6:00 a.m. for an hour-long "sunrise meditation." This unstructured commencement session was followed by a series of student-led sessions, each lasting approximately two hours, which continued throughout the day until 7:00 p.m. The class returned to the Abai at 6:00 a.m. the following day for another sunrise "awakening," with additional sessions running until 3:00 p.m., at which time the retreat drew to a close. Session topics were student generated; their choices reflected an interest in multicultural issues and holistic approaches to adjustment and coping. Topics included:

– Meditation, Relaxation, and Self-Awareness
– Exploring our Relationship with Nature
– Developing Trust and Teamwork
– Cultural Identity: Presentations of Cultural Songs, Dances, and Games
– Intercultural Interactions: Dispelling Cultural Stereotypes
– Exploring and Sharing our Self-Concepts
– Coping with Conflicts in Interpersonal Relationships
– Exploring the Role of Spirituality in our Lives
– Building Dreams for the Future
– Assimilating Retreat Experiences into Daily Life

The retreat itself was a triumph, much to the credit of the students who took part. Each of the participants struggled with a variety of deeply personal issues; they shared their struggles with their classmates and the instructor; they openly discussed intimate thoughts and feelings; most importantly, at the end of the retreat, they talked about the close bonds which had developed within the class, and expressed their gratitude to each other for the gains they had made in learning to deal with the many difficulties in their lives. In class, two days after the retreat, many students reported feeling "calm," "peaceful," "rejuvenated," and/or "whole." One student declared "It is like I have been floating ever since the retreat ended."

Most striking, perhaps, was the extent to which the Micronesian students participated. Granted, a couple of them "no-showed" and could not be roused from their slumber by telephone calls to the university dormitory! Nevertheless, those who did attend, did so with vigor and contributed significantly to the retreat's success. For example, a highly athletic, yet exceedingly shy Micronesian man, who rarely uttered a word in class, quickly made friends with the other students through his enthusiastic participation in retreat exercises which emphasized shared physical activities (e.g., synchronized movement exercises, nature walks) rather than verbal exchanges. His infectious smile and playful sense of humor contributed greatly to the warm and cohesive atmosphere which arose among the participants. A further example highlights two Palauan women, who said little during regular class discussions, but were quite outspoken when it came to the retreat, even in the initial planning stages. When searching for a secluded setting, it was these two students who recommended the Abai, which the class quickly approved as our retreat site. When the instructor initially proposed that the retreat commence at 7:00 or 8:00 a.m., the two Palauan students scoffed at his laziness and insisted on a sunrise start. At the retreat itself, they certainly played an active role in all of the session exercises, and much to the delight of the class, also provided some of the most enlightening and enjoyable cross-cultural experiences. The first day's lunch break was spent listening to their renditions of cultural legends associated with the Palauan storyboards painted about the Abai. But not only did the class learn Palauan myths, they also found themselves singing Palauan songs, and the tuneful "Ngungil Tutau" soon became the retreat's theme song!

It was not that the Micronesian students contributed more to the retreat than their classmates, for there were many others who also rose to the occasion, but simply that their level of input dramatically increased from that seen in regular class sessions. Based on their limited classroom participation, one might have assumed that the Micronesian students had little interest in personal adjustment and were neither motivated to learn adjustment strategies from their classmates nor inspired to share successful coping styles of their own.

How wrong the instructor would have been to draw such conclusions! The subtle, yet profound shifts that occurred in the Micronesian students at the retreat were unmistakable. They were evidenced in the words of the verbally timid Micronesian man who, at the retreat closing, painstakingly expressed his appreciation to the class for helping him to speak in front of others. They were captured by the creative work of the two Palauan students, whose guided meditation exercise perhaps best illustrates the hidden talents of these often-silent pupils. The two Palauan students brought their classmates away from the Abai and asked them to lie on the grass with their eyes closed under the shade of a large palm tree. With a soothing "new age" piece playing quietly in the background on a portable cassette player, they read the following meditation, entitled *A War Place*, which they wrote for this retreat exercise:

Imagine that you are entering a very sad place. The grass is dead; the ground is hard and dry. You can see dead plants and animals as you look around you. The air is dusty. You can't breathe. You can hear people's voices carried by the wind as they cry for help. You are feeling sad. You look up in the sky as it tells you the sorrows of this place. The clouds are dark, as if the world is mad. You look around you; you can see houses as they slowly burn down; you can see people running around, kids crying. You can hear the people's sadness. You see a small baby on the side of the road nurtured by an eight year old girl. You turn to the other side of the road; you see old people and small kids as they dig into a trash—can looking for food. Their faces are filled with unhappiness, with sadness. Their skin is dry. Their feet are sore from walking without slippers. You want to open up and help these people, but you can't. You feel like your arms are tied, like you can't do anything. You see people walking around in green uniforms. The look of these people makes you feel scared. They are mean and rude. All around you, you can hear explosive sounds. You feel an unusual cold breeze. The place looks clouded. You can hear the thunder and you can see lightning, which signifies terror in the place. You feel like you have been isolated by the terror of this place and you can't get out. As you walk around looking for a way out, you see a lot of sorrow around you. You are hurting inside. As you turn, you see a person in green uniform. You realize the danger you are in and suddenly you hear a distant crack. Then you feel the pain as your body crumbles to the ground. Everything sounds so quiet. Then suddenly you see a dim light. You are confused as you float towards the light. Suddenly, the light becomes brighter and brighter to the point where you can't see anything. You look away to avoid the brightness; when you look back you see a door. You can hear soft music, people laughing, children playing. You make your way towards the door. As you open it, you see a garden of flowers. You feel free; you feel light. You look around you and you see everything is alive and green. You see animals playing, birds flying. You can smell the freshness of the air. You can see the clear blue skies, you can see the brightness of the sun as it shines the place. You can feel the cool breeze. You can see people are equal; they are free; they are happy. You see smiling faces as you look around you. You can sense the love of these people towards each other and towards you. You see brightness everywhere. As the wind takes you around the place, you notice that ever since you entered this place, you were smiling. You have that feeling of being at ease with yourself. All your sorrows, your guilt, and your problems have faded away. You are in peace in this place. What is it about this atmosphere that makes you feel that you're at peace with yourself? Take three minutes to think . . . now slowly open your eyes!

(Orak and Teliu, 1996)

What is it about the atmosphere of the retreat that made the Micronesian students participate so actively and creatively? What factors lead to this dramatic increase in their level of class involvement?

First, the retreat sessions focused on collectivist themes consistent with Micronesian conceptions of the self as interdependent (e.g., *Exploring our Relationship with Nature, Developing Trust and Teamwork, Coping with Conflicts in Interpersonal Relationships, Cultural Identity,* and *Intercultural Interactions).* Stressing social, cultural, and environmental components of the self may be a critical first step in making personal adjustment relevant to collectivist cultures.

Second, the sessions on *Cultural Identity* and *Intercultural Interactions* directly addressed issues of acculturation. Opportunities to learn about other cultures, and to share aspects of their own, are invaluable for Micronesian immigrants to Guam. Moreover, inviting students to present expressions of their cultures (e.g., songs, dances, legends) gave Micronesian students a chance to demonstrate expertise and develop a sense of competence.

Third, the retreat setting was distinctly Micronesian. The sterile formality of traditional classrooms, with their linear arrangement of desks, constrains interpersonal interactions and thus is not conducive to student bonding and self–disclosure. The less structured, outdoor setting of the Palauan Abai may have provided an atmosphere more congruent with Micronesian interpersonal styles. Moreover, holding the retreat on their "turf" may have increased the Micronesian students' comfort and confidence levels.

Fourth, the retreat's structure paralleled collectivistic community life. The weekend–long format created the atmosphere of family living (e.g., breaks, meals, and transportation to and from the Abai were shared together). Micronesians are perhaps more comfortable disclosing to those with whom they share interdependent daily–life activities.

Fifth, the retreat included a variety of learning models: some verbal, some nonverbal. The nonverbal activities (e.g., use of drawing to express feelings, synchronized movement exercises to enhance interpersonal bonding) provided Micronesian students that were not proficient in English with opportunities to feel confident in their interactions with others.

Finally, the students participated in the planning and development of the retreat, and consequently had an investment in making it a success.

We plan to offer similar retreats at earlier points in the semester, in the hopes of encouraging closer relationships with students while time remains to apply them to the course. This first retreat was exceptional, in part because it took place in a culturally appropriate setting that is no longer available to us. However, we can bring the Abai into the classroom by exploring culturally sensitive alternatives to Western teaching models, alternatives that empower minority students through recognition of their unique cultural identities. The retreats address Hypotheses 6 and 7.

CONCLUSIONS

Our experiences with Micronesian students support Goodman's (1994) argument that college instructors must consider possible discrepancies between the levels of collectivism and power distance implicit in students' approaches to learning, and the levels assumed by their course materials. Perhaps many instructors trained in the West would benefit from asking what sort of relationships their culturally different students expect with professors and classmates, what topics appropriate to the course would address issues of intrinsic interest to these students, and what special advantages these students might bring to the classroom.

Not all of the changes outlined here have met with unqualified success. Even where the indications are positive, it is too early to know how much to attribute to the changes themselves and how much to attribute to the particular Micronesian students who welcomed them. We have much yet to learn about collectivism and power distance in the lives of our students, and about the individual cultures our Micronesian students represent. Still, the research literatures in cross-cultural psychology and Micronesian studies have provided some useful points of departure. We hope that our colleagues working with similar problems will consider them.

NOTES

1. Portions of the material in this chapter were presented at the 102nd Annual Convention of the American Psychological Association, Los Angeles, August 1994.
2. We acknowledge that some Chamorros (indigenous Guamanians) refer to themselves as "Micronesians." However, we use the term here in accordance with common usage on Guam to refer to Micronesian nationals. In this chapter, we use the term *Micronesian* because the Palauan, Yapese, Chuukese, Pohnpeian, Kosraean and Marshallese students at the University of Guam seem to share several characteristics relevant to their success in the course under consideration, and that distinguish them from non-Micronesian nationals in the same course. We intend no challenge to distinctions that Palauan, Yapese, Chuukese, Pohnpeian, Kosraean and Marshallese persons draw between themselves in other contexts.

REFERENCES

Aronson, E., & Bridgeman, D. (1979). Jigsaw groups and the desegregated classroom: In pursuit of common goals. *Personality and Social Psychology Bulletin, 5,* 438-466.
Berry, J.W. (1990). Psychology of acculturation: Understanding individuals moving between cultures. In R. W. Brislin (ed.), *Applied cross-cultural psychology* (pp. 232-253).

Newbury Park, CA: Sage.

Brislin, R.W., Cushner, K., Cherrie, C., & Yong, M. (1986). *Intercultural interactions: A practical guide.* Newbury Park, CA: Sage.

Brislin, R.W., & Wilson, R.W. (1971). Perceptions of similarities and differences among ethnic groups at the University of Guam. *Micronesica, 7,* 19-25.

Caughey, J.L. (1977). *Fa'a'nakkar: Cultural values in a Micronesian society.* Philadelphia, PA: University of Pennsylvania Publications in Anthropology.

Cousins, S.D. (1989). Culture and self-perception in Japan and the United States. *Journal of Personality and Social Psychology, 56,* 124-131.

Goodman, N.R. (1994). Intercultural education at the University level: Teacher-student interaction. In R. W. Brislin and T. Yoshida (eds.), *Improving intercultural interactions: Modules for cross-cultural training programs.* Thousand Oaks, CA: Sage.

Government of Guam Department of Education (1992). *The Pacific student.* Office of Curriculum and Instruction, DOE: Agana, Guam.

Hofstede, G. (1980). *Culture's consequences: International differences in work-related values.* Beverly Hills, CA: Sage.

Howard, A. (1990). Cultural paradigms, history, and the search for identity in Oceania. In J. Linnekin and L. Poyer (eds.), *Cultural identity and ethnicity in the Pacific* (pp. 259-279). Honolulu, HI: University of Hawaii Press.

Kim, U. (1994). Individualism and collectivism: Conceptual clarification and elaboration. In U. Kim, H.C. Triandis, C. Kagitcibasi, S. Choi & G. Yoon (eds.), *Individualism and collectivism: Theory, method and applications* (pp. 19-40). Thousand Oaks, CA: Sage.

Kitayama, S., & Markus, H.R. (1994). Culture and self: How cultures influence the way we view ourselves. In D. Matsumoto, *People: Psychology from a cultural perspective* (pp. 17-37). Pacific Grove, CA: Brooks-Cole.

Markus, H.R., & Kitayama, S. (1991). Culture and the self: Implications for cognition, emotion and motivation. *Psychological Review, 98,* 224-253.

Marshall, M. (1993). A Pacific haze: Alcohol and drugs in Oceania. In V.S. Lockwood, T.G. Harding, & B.J. Wallace (eds.), *Contemporary Pacific societies: Studies in development and change.* Englewood Cliffs, NJ: Prentice-Hall.

Orak, N., and Teliu, S. (1996) A War Place. Presentation at the Personal Adjustment Retreat, University of Guam

Pedersen, P. (1994). A culture-centered approach to counseling. In W. J. Lonner and R. Malpass (eds.), *Psychology and culture.* Boston: Allyn & Bacon.

Poyer, L. (1990). Being Sapwuahfik: Culture and ethnic identity in a Micronesian society. In J. Linnekin and L. Poyer (eds.), *Cultural identity and ethnicity in the Pacific.* Honolulu, HI: University of Hawaii Press.

Robillard, A.B. (1983). *Pacific island mental health counselor training: A final program narrative and evaluation report.* Honolulu, HI: Department of Psychiatry, University of Hawaii.

Rokeach, M. (1973). *The nature of human values.* New York: Free Press.

Rubinstein, D.H. (1992). Suicide in Micronesia and Samoa: A critique of explanations. *Pacific Studies, 15,* 51-75.

Rubinstein. D.H., & Levin, M.J. (1992). Micronesian migration to Guam: Social and economic characteristics. *Asian and Pacific Migration Journal, 1,* 350-385.

Schmitz, S., & Türk Smith, S. (1996). *Teacher perceptions of multicultural pedagogy in Guam Public Schools.* Manuscript submitted for publication.

Schwartz, S.H. (1994). Beyond individualism/collectivism: New cultural dimensions of values. In U. Kim, H. C. Triandis, C. Kagitçibasi, S. Choi & G. Yoon (eds.), *Individualism and collectivism: Theory, method and applications* (pp. 85 - 119). Thousand Oaks, CA: Sage.

Smith, K.D. (1994). *A survey of Micronesian immigrants to Guam: Predictors of coping and access to life essentials.* Micronesian Language Institute, University of Guam: Mangilao, Guam.

Türk Smith, S. (1993). *Attitudes of long-term residents of Guam toward immigrants from the Federated States of Micronesia and the Republic of the Marshall Islands.* Micronesian Language Institute, University of Guam: Mangilao, Guam.

Watson, D.L., & Tharp, R.G. (1993). *Self-directed behavior: self-modification for personal adjustment* (6th Edition). Pacific Grove, CA: Brooks-Cole.

Weiten, W. (1994). *Personal explorations workbook for Weiten and Lloyd's* Psychology applied to modern life: Adjustment in the 90s. Pacific Grove, CA: Brooks-Cole.

Wesley, H. (August, 1991). *Micronesian students: The "Island Way" and the "Western Way."* Presentation in orientation program for first-year faculty, University of Guam.

Training and Development of University Teachers

CHAPTER 9

The Preparation of University Teachers
A Cross-National Perspective
Graham Gibbs

BACKGROUND

The core sources for this chapter are unpublished papers presented at the 1996 conference of the International Consortium for Educational Development (ICED), held at Vasa, Finland, entitled Preparing University Teachers.[1] The papers for the conference were of a number of distinct types:

• *Summaries of national practices:*
E.g., Bouhuijs & Keesen (1996) describe developments in The Netherlands and Lewis (1996) gives an overview of faculty development in the U.S.A;

• *Bi-national comparisons:*
E.g., D'Andrea (1996) contrasts the North American emphasis on Teaching Assistant training with the U.K. emphasis on training new permanent full-time teachers;

• *Reports of studies of the effectiveness and impact of preparation programs:*
E.g., Nasr et al. (1996) report the differences between student feedback ratings for Australian lecturers who have undertaken a full Certificate or Diploma-level preparation program with those who have not, and Giertz (1996) reports qualitative data from interviews with those who have taken a compulsory program in Norway;

• *Explorations of key issues and themes:*
E.g., Johnston (1996) emphasizes the need, in the current context of dramatically fast changes in universities, for preparation to produce teachers who can transform teaching and learning practice rather than simply reproduce conventional practice, a theme which emerged as a central concern worldwide. Brew and Boud (1996) identify a second

overarching theme, that of setting the development of teachers as teachers in the context of their wider research, advisory, and administrative roles in universities and the need for programs to prepare academics for all their roles.

Descriptions of particular programs and their underlying rationales: This was the largest single category of papers and examples of contrasting practices from different European countries include Fuglem (1996), Kolmos (1996), and Lonka (1996).

This chapter will present a selection of overarching themes from the conference—those issues, contrasts, and similarities which were highlighted again and again in debate—and identify directions of change in the preparation of university teachers around the globe.

DISTINCTIVE PATTERNS

Some countries have national policy frameworks which shape the provision of training for university teaching. For example, in Norway the government has mandated compulsory initial training for all university teachers, lasting six weeks (Fuglem, 1996). The Swedish government is following suit. In the Netherlands there is a "binary" higher education system with extended compulsory initial training in the non-research sector and very uneven provision in the research universities. This varies from no provision to compulsory provision for all new academics up to and including new full professors.

In many countries there is considerable diversity in the provision of teacher training, and it is difficult to characterize the overall pattern. For example, in the U.K. programs vary in length from about 40 hours to about 500 hours, sometimes leading to a postgraduate qualification such as a Certificate in Teaching in Higher Education. The Staff and Educational Development Association (SEDA) has developed an accreditation scheme for programs, with participants in such accredited programs becoming accredited teachers as described later in this essay. Provision of proper classroom instruction skills for graduate students who teach is patchy, and for part-time and short-contract teachers extremely poor—an issue highlighted by the Higher Education Quality Council in its audits of institutions' quality assurance systems (HEQC, 1994). Responsibility for teacher preparation is held by central human resource development offices in some universities and by educational development units in others, and the location of responsibility is reflected in the content and style of their respective programs. Some of these HRD outfits "outsource" the preparation of their university teachers to commercial providers. The Oxford Center for Staff Development at Oxford Brookes University, for example, has run programs for a wide range of institutions including the University of Warwick and the London School of Economics.

In many countries there are distinctive approaches to the preparation of university teachers which are unique to particular universities but which are not followed elsewhere. For example, at Aalborg University in Denmark there is a very distinctive project orientation and the preparation of teachers is therefore oriented very closely to project supervision as opposed to other kinds of teaching practice (Kolmos, 1996). At the University of Utrecht in The Netherlands the problem-based approach used in medicine and in other subjects again influences the nature of the preparation of university teachers.

In some countries there is very little current provision of teacher preparation programs, and what does exist is often so small scale and informal that it is difficult to identify and characterize. Even where isolated examples of well developed programs exist at one institution (e.g. Garcia, 1996) this reveals little about the extent or nature of provision nationally.

DURATION

In the U.K., the standard qualification for school teachers is the completion of a B.Ed. program, which lasts for approximately 5,000 hours. A Postgraduate Certificate of Education which qualifies those who already have a first degree—and which focuses on process rather than subject knowledge and is therefore more comparable to a program for university teachers who already possess subject matter expertise—lasts for approximately 1,500 hours. The longest programs for new university teachers in the U.K. and The Netherlands are about 500 hours—about a third of the minimum approved length of that for school teachers. In contrast one program for university teachers in the U.S.A. described at the ICED conference lasted for three hours. There is clearly an issue here about how long a program is appropriate. There is a growing consensus in higher education in Europe and Australasia that in the current political and economic climate about 200-250 hours is a reasonable allocation for initial training leading to a qualification. However there is also a strongly held view that programs should ideally not be specified in terms of duration but outcomes or competencies. Several programs already operate in this way and the SEDA accreditation scheme (described below) does not specify inputs or duration but only outcomes. Nevertheless most undergraduate and postgraduate courses worldwide are defined by their length rather than their outcomes, and length will continue to be a policy short-hand until a (much more difficult) consensus can be reached on desired or required outcomes.

COMPREHENSIVENESS

The first issue concerning comprehensiveness is which categories or types of teacher ought to be included. Early in the development of a university's provision for preparing teachers it is common for only one category of teach-ers to be catered for—in the U.S., it tends to be Teaching Assistants, while in the U.K., it tends to be new lecturers. It is still not common for all cat-egories of teachers to be accommodated within a comprehensive support program. Increasingly, however, universities are developing "nested" programs starting with brief courses for Teaching Assistants and part-time teachers with a limited range of responsibilities and developing through induction for full-time teachers, extended certificate programs once induction is complete, and followed by project- and research-based Diploma, Masters or even Ph.D. programs for experienced teachers. In the School of Business at Oxford Brookes University new teachers, of all categories, are gradually introduced to a widening range of teaching responsibilities through a structured men-tor program (Rogers, 1996). Some provision also targets professionals who contribute to teaching (as is common in health science programs).

Comprehensiveness also involves addressing all aspects of a teacher's re-sponsibilities as an academic, not just classroom teaching. Increasingly pro-grams are including management (Neumann & Lindsay, 1996) and other new academic roles (Brew & Boud, 1996). In the U.S., initiatives such as the "Preparing Future Faculty" program are starting to prepare Teaching Assistants for the kinds of academic roles they will be likely to fulfill in col-leges rather than research universities (Lewis, 1996).

Finally, the issue of comprehensiveness involves the debate between com-pulsory versus voluntary programs, and whether preparation which does not include the reluctant—or in particular those who simply do not value teach-ing—can be considered adequate. One solution to this dilemma is to make probation, tenure and, particularly, promotion decisions, take teaching suf-ficiently into account that it would be very risky for new teachers to avoid teaching preparation programs. The changes taking place world-wide in mechanisms to promote and reward excellence in teaching therefore provides a backdrop to developments in preparation. Some programs for new teach-ers culminate in the preparation of a teaching portfolio which may be used at a later stage in promotion, so that new teachers see their preparation as the start of a career-long process which is in their personal interest to take seriously.

OUTCOMES AND THRESHOLD STANDARDS

There is more consensus about the "content" of preparation programs than about the standards they should achieve. Most want to produce competent teachers but few have a definition of competence that others could agree upon. The SEDA accreditation program comes closest to achieving a consensus and there is currently a debate about the possibility of national or international standards of the kind SEDA has specified (Baume & Baume, 1996).

With the notable exception of the U.S., an increasing proportion of university teaching preparation involves formal postgraduate courses leading to specific qualifications, and these normally have to be approved through conventional university course approval processes. As well, in the U.K. and Australia, these are subject to the normal use of external examiners and other robust quality assurance procedures. Formal award-bearing programs are also in operation in Norway, Sweden, and The Netherlands. Here the standards are those of normal academic peer review, and this may bias preparation towards theory and the study of education rather than towards the practice of education.

RATIONALES

There are marked differences between the rationales of university teaching preparation programs. The six main rationales in evidence are:

Classroom Practice
Probably the majority of small scale programs focus on what happens within the classroom and have an orientation to a relatively narrow technical notion of skill and competence, characterized by video feedback on trial teaching sessions.

Educational Theory
This may mean educational and cognitive psychology and communication theory but may also involve understanding the university as an educational system. In the U.K. and Australia the deep/surface approach distinction is a cornerstone of many programs. Some programs have as their goal that teachers have changed their conception of the teaching and learning process, in phenomenographic terms. A

concentration on theory may be characterized by reading, discussion and small scale research projects.

Reflective Practice

An increasing number of programs are informed by Schon's (1983) notion of the reflective practitioner and have an orientation to personal experimentation and reflection in teaching. They tend to be characterized by the use of reflective journals and action learning. A goal of such programs might be that the teacher is more aware of what is going on and can reflect on what has happened, rather than that any particular skills are acquired or that established theories are used in the reflection.

Personal Growth

Becoming a teacher can be stressful and a time of rapid personal development. Some programs have an orientation to personal support and the creation of a safe emotional climate characterized by peer learning communities, mentoring, a lack of formal assessment and the careful management of job demands.

Competence in the Job

This may involve a concentration on the nature of the job of being a teacher and its everyday demands and an orientation to the full range of academic roles and tasks. Such programs may be characterized by pragmatic free-standing training workshops in topics such as time and task management, supervising research students, and attending committees, rather than concentrating on teaching.

Contextual Relevance

This is where that which new teachers need to learn is individually negotiated to suit the context and the teacher. Assessment of the achievement of individual targets or goals may also be negotiated. This may be characterized by the use of portfolios.

Some teacher preparation programs include aspects of all these rationales, by design or accident, while some are designed within a specific paradigm, occasionally aggressively espoused. Sometimes a program operates within one rationale, but the teachers involved would prefer that it operated within another. For example, Isaacs (1996) describes a short initial program at the University of Queensland, Australia, which was concerned with developing reflective practitioners, but where the lecturers involved in the program wanted basic tips to deal with immediate practical problems in their teaching. Until these basics had been dealt with they were unlikely to be ready for open-minded reflection.

DOING IT BETTER VERSUS DOING IT DIFFERENTLY

A shared characteristic of most university contexts is the rapid change experienced in teaching, learning, and assessment methods brought about by such levers as declining resources, increasing class sizes and a shift in university missions towards the employability of students and away from traditional scholarly pursuits. In this context, some programs stress the role of the preparation of teachers in coping with and creating change, and in transforming practice (Roche, 1996), while others appear to assume that preparation is for contexts that have remained unchanged for decades and are unlikely to change. This difference between a focus on fine-tuning conventional practice or transforming it—between tackling yesterday's problems or solving tomorrow's—is one of considerable debate at present, and often highlights the differences of purpose between traditional research universities and new universities with more socially and economically responsive missions. Many of the most firmly-established programs are clearly oriented towards maintenance of the status quo, albeit slightly more effectively practiced than in the past. The form of initial preparation shapes teachers' attitudes towards innovation and change, and towards lifelong learning. Candy (1996) has argued that learning organizations and lifelong learning for academics requires a new form of educational development. There is a danger that traditional forms of preparation for university teachers will make them accepting of traditional teaching paradigms—and merely reactive to problems within this paradigm—rather than what Candy terms "anticipatory."

CONTRASTING NATIONAL PATTERNS OF PREPARATION

To attempt to make generalizations about one country's provision in comparison with another is to oversimplify, and also to take a huge risk. No sooner have you made a generalization than exceptions spring to mind or are brought to your attention. Nevertheless, the contrast between what one might expect to find in, for example, a research university in the U.S. versus one in Australia, helps to clarify the way the issues presented above can lead to very different forms of preparation. In the U.S., preparation tends to be pre-service, in the sense that it takes place while a teacher is still a graduate teaching assistant, before being appointed as faculty. In Australia most provision is in-service, for new lecturers, while they are in their first full-time teaching position and with a full teaching load to manage. In the U.S., teaching assistant programs tend to be very short—perhaps 5–20 hours. In Australia, they would tend to be 60–200 hours. In the U.S., the programs can be huge—over 1,000 teaching assistants at a time at Syracuse or Washington universities—where in Australia, over 50 at a time would be considered large. In the U.S., the focus would be on classroom practice—teaching assistants have limited scope for innovation and limited responsibility for course design or assessment, and preparation programs reflect this. In Australia, even new lecturers might have complete responsibility for a course, and so preparation would be concerned with course and curriculum design, assessment, evaluation and so on, with probably less emphasis on details of teaching technique.

In the U.S., a teaching assistant program might be underpinned by communication theory and cognitive psychology, where in Australia the extensive research evidence cited in McKeachie's Teaching Tips might not be mentioned at all, but Swedish phenomenological work might. Teaching Tips, the most commonly used course text for programs in the U.S., has a 60-page bibliography, but cites almost no practice, evidence or theory from outside the U.S. These marked differences in conceptual underpinnings, sometimes colored by cultural imperialism or ethnocentrism, are quite striking.

A U.S. program might contain advice and feedback on a video of a short practice presentation, emphasizing micro-level skills in simulated contexts. The Australian program might involve reflective self-review following an actual lecture, emphasizing generic features and contextual variables.

Teachers' experience of such contrasting preparation must inevitably be profoundly different, with profoundly different consequences for teaching later in their careers. In particular, teachers in Australasia may lack some of the detailed classroom techniques of their U.S. counterparts, and most academics in the U.S. will have received no training whatsoever in course design.

There are Australian programs which do not look like that described above, and U.S. approaches to preparation which do not resemble standard teaching assistant programs, but this contrast nevertheless has some validity. The source of these contrasts lies not just in traditions—and in national isolation from international developments—but also in different employment practices, quality assurance pressures, and attitudes to academic freedom. In the U.S., many universities rely on an army of teaching assistants, where this is not the case to the same extent in Australia. Australian universities are subject (or were until recently) to robust external quality checks of a kind which would encourage adequate initial training of teachers, where

U.S. universities are largely free of such pressure. And managerialism and industrial approaches to human resource development are much more common in Australia than in U.S. research universities. The kinds of legalistic approaches to employment and government policy initiatives which are prevalent in, say, The Netherlands, are quite outside the experience of most U.S. universities.

CHANGING PATTERNS OF PREPARATION

A number of relatively clear trends can be identified in teacher preparation practices, and international collaboration and sharing of practices is making these trends more coherent and stronger. Programs are much longer than they used to be, much better funded and better supported with, for example, policy on the release of teachers from duties to allow attendance. At some institutions (e.g., Oxford Brookes University in the U.K.), departments are compensated with funds for replacement teaching hours, and lecturers are not allowed to be given teaching, research or administrative duties at the times the program is operating. These supporting policies can cost more than the mounting of the program, but may be crucial to its success. This change in attitude and practical support has come about partly in response to external quality assurance pressures—of a kind largely missing in the U.S. where such expansion and commitment is less marked—and the need for teaching to be much more cost-effective in the face of devastating resource problems.

Universities are taking preparation more seriously. Voluntary "drop-in" programs are being replaced by compulsory programs. In some cases, such as in Sweden and Australia, substantial progress has been made in the duration, sophistication and reputation of programs without the need for compulsory attendance. In Sweden, the government is imposing new requirements and in Australia there is a lively debate about the trade-offs between reaching teachers whom voluntary programs cannot reach, and about potentially damaging the style and feel of existing voluntary programs.

In many contexts, initial training is being linked to personnel decisions: to probation, tenure or the achievement of particular academic positions. At the University of Utrecht, as at the Swedish University of Agricultural Sciences at Uppsala, Sweden, teaching qualifications are now required for Associate Professor status (Bouhuijs & Keesen, 1996; Beckman, 1996). It is interesting to speculate what impact it would have on the quality of teaching in the U.S. if a postgraduate qualification in teaching were a prerequisite for tenure! Currently, policymakers, scholars, and professional organizations—such as the American Association for Higher Education's "Roles and Rewards" movement—are beginning to tackle this kind of issue.

Programs which previously focused purely on formative observation of teaching are starting to have to make what are in effect competent/incompetent or pass/fail decisions with severe career consequences. At present there is great reluctance to do this. However, in the U.K., four-year school teacher training has generally included a school-based "teaching practice" period in the very first term, which students can fail—and if they fail they are forced to choose a different career. Medicine, law and other professions also have cut-off points to prevent those without the appropriate vocation or aptitude from entering the profession. It is unclear why teaching in higher education should be different, however tough the decision making may be. During the transition from amateur to professional attitudes toward teaching, those making these decisions may be unpopular, but soon these decisions will become part of an accepted process of entry into the profession, and the status of teaching competence will become much more highly valued as a result.

There is an increasing differentiation of the changing needs of university teachers at different stages of their career. American work has recently taken into account the evolving focus of attention of very new teaching assistants—for example from anxieties about self-perception to concerns about basic skills to an orientation towards effectiveness and improvement—and attempted to design programs in stages to accommodate this changing focus. In the U.K., programs may involve a short initial "nuts and bolts" training course, and do not move into a "reflective practice" stage until initial anxieties have settled down. There are also an increasing number of "nested" programs with Postgraduate Certificate courses leading on to Diploma, Masters and even Ph.D. programs. The SEDA accreditation scheme in the U.K. is developing an initial stage for part-time teachers and teaching assistants, short of a full teacher accreditation.

There is a growing trend towards widening the focus of preparation to include aspects of an academic's job other than teaching. A number of programs emphasize management skills training and even allow teachers to branch into management or teaching specializations within Certificate programs (e.g., Neumann & Lindsay, 1996). Other programs address entrepreneurial activities, marketing of courses, preparing business plans and other skills required in a modern competitive university (c.f. Brew & Boud, 1996).

There is a strong move towards accreditation, certification, and formal recognition of the learning outcomes of preparation programs. This may take legalistic forms. In the U.K., there is currently pressure from the main unions to professionalize as a way of protecting full-time academics from cheaper part-time staff. Some universities are introducing initial training as a legal protection, following cases where lecturers not gaining tenure successfully argued in court that they were not adequately trained for their job.

The most conspicuous instance of this trend is the Staff and Educational Development Association (SEDA) Teacher Accreditation Scheme in the U.K. (Baume & Baume, 1996). SEDA offers to accredit institutions whose programs meet certain requirements (which specify outcomes rather than processes or inputs) and embody certain values. As it specifies outcomes it can accommodate the accreditation of prior learning of experienced teachers who did not have any preparation when they first entered universities. University teachers who successfully complete such programs become accredited teachers. By the start of 1997, 30 institutions will have voluntarily applied for and achieved accreditation, paying for the privilege of being reviewed against SEDA standards, and 40 more will be at some stage of accreditation—together, a total of about 40% of the entire higher education sector in the U.K.. Institutions in Australia and Singapore are also seeking accreditation, and at the ICED conference a number of countries expressed interest in the possibility of a European-wide accreditation system which could accommodate regional variations.

In the U.K., the effect of this entirely voluntary scheme on the length and sophistication of programs has been dramatic. Existing programs now have a standard against which to calibrate themselves, and universities which do not take preparation of their teachers seriously have a very clear benchmark against which to judge their own provision. External quality judgments are now much easier. Only five years ago such an accreditation system would have been unthinkable, as it still is in some countries, and provision would not have been adequate to meet the requirements of a worthwhile accreditation system. Now even the top research universities and the ancient institutions in the U.K. are seeking accreditation for their teacher preparation programs.

The ICED conference was established to improve international collaboration, but it was clear that the internationalization of practice for the preparation of university teachers was already well advanced in some countries. Weeks et al. (1996) describe an international "benchmarking" process, through which the provision for the preparation of university teachers at the Queensland University of Technology was systematically compared with universities at Alverno, Berkeley, Madison-Wisconsin, and Texas at Austin in the U.S.A., Brighton and the SEDA Accreditation process in the U.K., among others. The use of portfolios, originally developed by the Canadian Association of University Teachers (CAUT) in the late 1970's—as well as by Seldin in North America, and by Gibbs and others in the U.K. and Australia in the early 1980's—was recently found to be embedded in programs for the preparation of university teachers in The Netherlands (Wubbels, 1996) and Finland (Tenhula, 1996). The use of mentoring as an integral part of preparation practices is also evident in a number of countries, being developed in parallel with formal teacher preparation programs (Blackwell & McLean, 1996).

CONCLUSION

Practices for the preparation of university teachers in Europe and Australasia are developing rapidly in scale and sophistication, supported by formal policy and increasing professionalization. Clear trends are emerging in the forms this development is taking and international collaboration is accelerating development and creating more coherent trends with considerable benefits to those involved. At present, the U.S. is largely uninvolved in this development and its preparation practices comparatively limited in scale, sophistication, and organizational support in comparison.

In Europe there is considerable momentum behind the development of policies and practices which increase worker mobility between member states of the European Union through 'harmonization' of training standards and qualification frameworks. There is growing collaboration between voluntary national educational development organizations in devising common frameworks for accreditation for university teachers and the sharing of course materials—including distance learning programs—and an increasing willingness by governments to impose legal frameworks requiring compliance. There is European Union funding available to support such convergence of practice. The extent of current collaboration or uniformity of practice should not be exaggerated, but the direction of movement is clear enough. This is a very different environment than experienced currently in the U.S., where government intervention in specifying minimum professional training standards is less culturally acceptable even for public school teachers, let alone for teachers in private universities. The differences in these cultural contexts are likely to widen the divide between the U.S. and Europe in terms of policy.

The challenge for those involved in educational development will be to continue to share practices, materials which support preparation programs, and research evidence of the effectiveness of different preparation practices, regardless of the formal differences. The involvement of U.S. organizations in the activities of international organizations such as ICED will help. The awareness of U.S. university presidents and administrators of the potential economic and academic challenges posed by a fully-trained academic work force in Europe would probably help, too.

NOTES

1. Abstracts of these ICED conference papers can be found on the world wide web at http://www.lgu.ac.uk.deliberations and papers can be obtained directly from the authors.

REFERENCES

Baume, C. & Baume, D. (1996). A national scheme to accredit university teachers. International Consortium for Educational Development in Higher Education Conference. Vasa: Finland.

Blackwell, R. & McLean, M. (1996). Preparing new academic staff: The role of the mentor. 21st International Improving University Teaching Conference. Nottingham.

Bouhuijs, P. & Keesen, F. (1996) Preparing University Teachers in The Netherlands: Issues and Trends. International Consortium for Educational Development in Higher Education Conference. Vasa: Finland.

Brew, A. & Boud, D. (1996). Preparing for new academic roles: A holistic approach to development." International Consortium for Educational Development in Higher Education Conference. Vasa: Finland.

Candy. P.C. (1996). Promoting lifelong learning: Academic development and the university as a learning organization. *International Journal of Academic Development* 1:1, pp7-19.

D'Andrea, V. (1996). Graduate teaching assistants: Preparation programs in the U.S. and the U.K.: The best of both worlds. International Consortium for Educational Development in Higher Education Conference. Vasa: Finland.

Eckman, B. (1996). Compulsory pedagogical training as a requirement for an associate professorship. International Consortium for Educational Development in Higher Education Conference. Vasa: Finland.

Fuglem, M. (1996) Preparing university teachers in Engineering and Architecture at the Norwegian university of science and technology. International Consortium for Educational Development in Higher Education Conference. Vasa: Finland.

Garcia, J.C. (1996). University teacher training in Spain. International Consortium for Educational Development in Higher Education Conference. Vasa: Finland.

Giertz, B. (1996). Long-term effects of a program for teacher training. International Consortium for Educational Development in Higher Education Conference. Vasa: Finland.

Higher Education Quality Council (1994). *Learning from audit.* London.

Johnston S. (1996). Addressing the "big picture": Teacher preparation as part of induction into academic life and work. International Consortium for Educational Development in Higher Education Conference. Vasa: Finland.

Kolmos, A. (1996). Training project provision. International Consortium for Educational

Development in Higher Education Conference. Vasa: Finland.

Kristensen, E. (1996). Faculty development program assessment by visiting committee. International Consortium for Educational Development in Higher Education Conference. Vasa: Finland.

Lewis, K. (1996). A brief history and overview of faculty development in the United States. Training project provision. International Consortium for Educational Development in Higher Education Conference. Vasa: Finland.

Lonka, K. (1996). Activating instruction: How to foster study and thinking skills. International Consortium for Educational Development in Higher Education Conference. Vasa: Finland.

McKeachie, W. (1996). Critical elements in training university teachers. International Consortium for Educational Development in Higher Education Conference. Vasa: Finland.

Naidoo, K. (1996). Self-evaluation: A strategy for preparing university teachers. International Consortium for Educational Development in Higher Education Conference. Vasa: Finland.

Nasr et al. (1996). The relationship between performance between university lecturers' qualifications in teaching and student ratings of their teaching performance. International Consortium for Educational Development in Higher Education Conference. Vasa: Finland.

Neumann, R. & Lindsay, A. (1996). Developing an integrated course in university teaching, management and administration. International Consortium for Educational Development in Higher Education Conference. Vasa: Finland.

Roche, V. (1996). Learning from action and action from learning: Emerging paradigms for development in a constantly changing world. International Consortium for Educational Development in Higher Education Conference. Vasa: Finland.

Rogers, A. (1996). A staff induction and support system. International Consortium for Educational Development in Higher Education Conference. Vasa: Finland.

Schon, D.A. (1983). *The reflective practitioner.* New York: Basic Books

Tenhula, T. (1996). Improving academic teaching practices by using teaching portfolios: The Finnish way to do it. International Consortium for Educational Development in Higher Education Conference. Vasa: Finland.

Weeks et al. (1996). Preparing university teachers in Australia: Benchmarking best practice. International Consortium for Educational Development in Higher Education Conference. Vasa: Finland.

Wubbels T. (1996). Portfolios in a faculty training program and assessment procedure. International Consortium for Educational Development in Higher Education Conference. Vasa: Finland.

NOTE: All references from the ICED Preparing University Teachers Symposium, Vasa, Finland, can be found on the world wide web at: http://www.lgu.ac.uk.deliberations and obtained by email from the authors.

CHAPTER 10

Academic Staff Development in Southern Africa
The Botswana Model

Michael J. Herrick

INTRODUCTION

"To teach is to learn twice" said philosopher Joseph Joubert in Pensées (1842). When we teach something, we re-examine it well enough to know it in its complexity and ramifications. Thus we learn it twice: as we have studied it in the past and as we study it now. As well, we learn twice when we begin to talk about what we have only read. Reading someone's words is one way of knowing, but being able to discuss those words and concepts in words of our own is another way of knowing: interpreting, analyzing, extending, and applying. So when we teach, when we engage in the scholarship of teaching, we learn twice.

However, Joubert may have had another thought in mind when he made his statement: not only do we learn what we are teaching, we learn how we are teaching. How often do lecturers walk away from a lecture thinking: "There's the lecture I planned to give, there's the lecture I gave, and there's the lecture I wish I had given?" We learn twice by reflecting on the practice of teaching. A staff development program which focuses on university teaching can assist lecturers in learning and improving how they teach, and can encourage them to focus not only on the practice of teaching but also on the idea of enhancing student learning (Barr & Tagg, 1995).

Regardless of its setting—herein the setting will be a university of approximately 5,000 students and 500 academic staff in Southern Africa—a staff development program must have a presence in the university, offer attractive programs, persuade individuals to participate, and have the support of university policy if university teachers throughout the institution are to learn about and improve their teaching.

FORMS OF SCHOLARSHIP

Research

Faculty in Botswana are not unlike faculty elsewhere in the world: research and teaching are two primary responsibilities of their profession. These activities each pose their own sets of problems and rewards. Many academics in Botswana engage in the first three of Boyer's (1990) four kinds of scholarship: discovery which is "the commitment to knowledge for its own sake," integration which "seeks to interpret, draw together, and bring new insight to bear on original research," and application which relates "theory to practice and service . . . to bridge the gap between discovering knowledge as an end in itself and serving the needs of the larger world." A typical university's research mission can be described as follows:

> Higher education institutions have the main responsibility for training a country's professional personnel, including managers, scientists, engineers, and technicians who participate in the development, adaptation, and diffusion of innovations in the economy. Such institutions should create new knowledge through research and advanced training and serve as a conduit for its transfer, adaptation, and dissemination (Salmi et al., 1993:1).

As lecturers progress toward obtaining tenure and becoming professors, they experiment with these kinds of scholarship until a match is found, that is, a propensity toward one rather than another. The preference may come from the kind of training engaged in at the master's or doctoral level: for example, having studied under the supervision of a like-minded, established scholar in a research university where there are resources, time, and incentive to engage in scholarship.

Other academics do not take the research route; they obtain a master's degree through course work alone, earn a post-graduate degree that focused on reading and experimental research, or simply have only baccalaureate degrees. Many universities in developing countries have appointed faculty who do not hold graduate degrees, as highly-educated teachers are difficult to find. As a result, there is a large segment of academics in Botswana who are not accustomed to doing research or do not possess the training required for quality research. As well, there are academics who have settled comfortably into a routine, or perhaps in administration, or—quite often in developing countries—they find themselves in universities that have few resources to keep their libraries current with the knowledge explosion occurring in each field of study.

Teaching

As Boyer observed, the scholarship of teaching makes the work of the academic "consequential only as it is understood by others . . . . It means not only transmitting knowledge but transforming and extending it, communicating knowledge so that it is shared with students whose ability to understand, inquire into and appreciate it are being developed." However, as many have observed, academic responsibilities and rewards are more often tied to research than to teaching. At many colleges and universities, there is likely to be a reward system associated with research, that is, getting published, which does not ordinarily favor teaching. In developing countries, the lack or reward for teaching is compounded by the general problem of low pay for academic jobs, which pushes academic staff into second jobs or careers, and which in turn seriously affects their teaching.

Additionally, whether young lecturers or senior academics like to teach or not, it is nevertheless a responsibility facing them every day for nine months of the many years of their careers. Propensity and preparation for teaching has, heretofore, been an individual concern. And while academics are expected to teach, there is very little emphasis in any higher degree program or graduate training on teaching. The need for staff development programs is as widespread as the need for graduate training. In a new or developing university, teaching staff are often mostly junior lecturers who will need training in course design, delivery, and evaluation skills, while more established universities may have a number of senior staff who could benefit from career reconceptualization (Wheeler and Schuster, 1990) or a 're-fresher' course on teaching practices. Thus, both academics and institutional administrators face a dilemma surrounding a focus on one form of scholarship over another.

STAFF DEVELOPMENT PROBLEMS AND APPROACHES

A University Dilemma

Problems related to different forms of scholarship can be found at most any university in Botswana or elsewhere. The university may have academics who are (1) unfamiliar with research methodology, (2) too narrowly focused or inflexible in their preferred methods of teaching, (3) unprepared to teach, (4) feeling unrewarded (or underpaid) for teaching, (5) many years past their early post-graduate training and in need of review courses, both of content knowledge and research methodology, or (6) unmotivated and in need of career enhancement. In developing countries, scholars have noted the additional problems that lead to "a decline in the quality of teaching and learning," such as "overcrowding of lecture rooms, inadequate staffing, deteriorating physical facilities, poor library resources, insufficient scientific equipment, poor quality staff at all levels, lack of properly conducted research, low staff morale, inadequate salary and other rewards for staff . . . ." (Mukherjee and Singh, 1993:1) So many problems may exist in these institutions that staff development seems destined for defeat before even commencing the difficult task of helping fewer teachers do more with less.

However, the university has no choice but to at least attempt to ensure that its academic personnel are prepared and their knowledge current. It must therefore develop training programs for research and teaching. In developing nations, these are often mostly in-service training programs, usually because of the enormous expense of sending personnel outside the region or overseas. For example, in 1995, Botswana spent approximately P100000 (US$30,000) per person for faculty involved in foreign exchange. In institutions where much of the staff have only bachelor's degrees, the need for academic staff development is critical. However, looking globally, the need for staff development is just as real in the Northern hemisphere as in the South.

A Developed World Example
In Canada, for example, there has been much public criticism of the university professoriate in the last five years. Echoing Boyer's (1990) observations, a national commission (1991:63) reported that "teaching is seriously undervalued at Canadian universities and nothing less than a total re-commitment to it is required." In response, the University of Manitoba assembled a commission to investigate the province's primary higher education resource: a university system with 20,000 full-time and 16,000 part-time students and 4,000 teaching staff (Roblin et al., 1993). What they found initially was "that, by and large, university performance is not well understood by the public." They questioned the value of research, the quality of teaching, and the effectiveness of university and community service and found each wanting. They concluded that their three institutions must give teaching a high priority. Thus they recommended that the small University Teaching Service, which had existed since 1972, be expanded and used as a system-wide resource. The University Teaching Service currently offers workshops that focus on teaching and research, publishes a newsletter, conducts a peer-consultation program, sponsors action research in teaching, stocks a library of printed materials, and provides confidential consultations to individuals seeking to improve their teaching.

Southern African Examples

There are many other examples of staff development programs in the developed world. But what about Africa? Activities related to the improvement of university teaching and learning received special impetus from various seminars and workshops held in Eastern and Southern African countries under the auspices of the German Foundation for International Development (Deutsche Stiftung für internationale Entwicklung) from 1986 through 1991, culminating in collections of proceedings and a textbook titled *Teach Your Best: A Handbook for University Lecturers* (second edition in 1995). This initiative influenced the establishment of University Teaching and Learning Centers at institutions in Dar Es Salaam, Zambia, and Zimbabwe; the development of Senate committees for University Teaching and Learning at Maseno University College (Kenya) and the University of Malawi; and led to the Harare Recommendation, which encouraged:

> the establishment of staff development centers (SDCs) where none exist, and the appointment of coordinators for professional staff development [to] facilitate and coordinate activities aimed at professional staff development and enhance the competency of the university academic staff in specific areas of teaching and learning; research and publication; university management and administration; guidance and counseling; and community service (Mukherjee & Singh, 1993:26).

Moreover, a network of like-minded individuals resulted in the distribution of an occasional newsletter, dedicated to University Staff Development in Eastern and Southern Africa (USDESA). Funding for these initiatives does not always come locally. For example, at the Universidade Eduardo Mondlane, in Maputo, Mozambique, the Staff Development Project (STADEP) is funded by Rijksuniversiteit Groningen. For the rest of sub-Saharan Africa, in November 1994, the Association of African Universities held a special Consultative Meeting on Staff Development in Higher Education for all principal staff development officers, exclusive of South Africa. In South Africa, there are a number of notable programs in existence, for example, at Witswatersrand and at Stellenbosh; in other institutions of higher learning there are numerous academic development programs for staff and students to compensate for the differences in skill levels of students disadvantaged by apartheid (see Mehl, 1992). In July, 1996, the University of Kassel was proposing to offer a major staff development workshop for the Southern African Development Community at the University of Botswana, funded by the German Foundation for International Development.

A BOTSWANA PROBLEM

The government of Botswana has adopted a policy of staffing positions within the national economy exclusively by citizens of Botswana. This policy is referred to as localization and is directed at reducing the reliance on expatriate staff for teaching and administration. Through its Staff Development Fellowship (SDF) Program the University of Botswana hopes to achieve this national policy of localization. Thus, the university has a policy of pre-service training and academic progression which involves sending citizen staff abroad for specializations not offered at the University of Botswana. In 1994-5 there were as many as 41 staff abroad for Ph.D. training; 33 for master's degrees; 30 Staff Development Fellows; and 5 in administration. In all, there were approximately 300 person-years of paid training opportunities. The impetus behind this influx of support for training is obvious: the university expects to see a doubling in size by the end of the decade. Though the number of staff training opportunities will decrease in the future and the number of expatriate staff will decrease to a smaller—yet constant—portion of faculty, there will still be a large number of staff in training abroad (especially for Ph.Ds). This aspect of external training is handled by an assistant registrar who reports to the Deputy Vice Chancellor of Academic Affairs.

Additionally, heads of department have certain training and development responsibilities. Besides helping administer the university and encouraging research, they are responsible for their teaching programs: specifically, (a) to ensure that the teaching program is being satisfactorily carried out, (b) to supervise SDFs in the performance of their teaching and/or research, (c) to assist junior staff to develop teaching skills, (d) to advise on appointments, contract renewals, promotions and salary adjustments, and to assist in the recruitment process, and (e) to monitor and report on staff performance in the annual staff review. This aspect of in-house training is assisted by the Higher Education Development Unit.

A BOTSWANA SOLUTION

In Botswana the idea that university lecturers can improve their teaching and other academic work through relevant training was accepted by the University of Botswana as early as 1986 when Dr. N. Boreham of the University of Manchester was commissioned to study staff development and university teaching methods. His report proposed the establishment of a University Teaching Methods Unit in the Faculty of Education to carry out a program involving training of Staff Development Fellows (SDFs), activities for experienced lecturers, and management development for heads of department.

The University of Botswana hosted a workshop in 1986, to discuss the idea and feasibility of offering in-service staff training. This resulted in the establishment of the Higher Education Development Unit (HEDU) by the Senate in May 1988, providing a structured framework and institutionalized setting for tertiary teaching and learning activities. Until 1992 when the first coordinator of the unit was appointed, Dean Frank Youngman and Dr. Sid Pandey of the Faculty of Education kept the idea alive with several university workshops, SDF inductions, and the publication of a bulletin. HEDU's establishment preceded the Botswana government's 1994 restructuring of the education system. The White Paper which resulted from the restructuring initiatives recommended that: "All tertiary education institutions should take immediate steps to ensure that lecturers acquire an appreciation of basic pedagogical skills and competencies. To facilitate this, institutions should make a conscious effort to set up units for the purpose." (Republic, 1994:71) The evolution of the Higher Education Development Unit certainly reflected the perspectives toward teaching that the government's leaders sought to promote.

THE HIGHER EDUCATION DEVELOPMENT UNIT

The Higher Education Development Unit at the University of Botswana attempts to promote more than a minimum "appreciation of basic pedagogical skills and competencies." HEDU has become successful, but not without the difficulties which typically face every newly-established academic staff development center, as will be observed later in this chapter. First, however, one must understand the scope of activity which the HEDU developers sought to achieve. An examination of HEDU's terms of reference shows the intended range of its services in promoting the professional development of academic and senior administrative and library staff in the institutions of higher education in Botswana, thereby improving the effectiveness and efficiency of these institutions.

(i)   To provide an induction and training program for staff development fellows.

(ii)   To provide opportunities for experienced staff to improve their knowledge and competencies in the areas of teaching and research.

(iii)   To assist heads of departments and others in developing their management ability, and to provide advice and information on procedures and methods for departmental reviews, staff performance appraisal and course evaluation.

(iv)   To administer the student assessments of staff performance (SAS) at the end of each term and process results for distribution to teaching staff.

(v)   To identify research needs in the area of higher education policy and practice in Botswana.

(vi)   To assist the university library in developing an appropriate collection of books, journals and other resources relating to higher education.

(vii)   To produce a regular bulletin on items of interest from the current literature and elsewhere.

(viii)   To act as liaison with similar units or programs in other universities to mutual benefit.

The terms (i-iv) give HEDU the mandate to train for improved teaching and management at all levels, to assist in and conduct research in higher education (v-vi), to keep staff informed (vii), and to coordinate with other staff development units.

AREAS OF RESPONSIBILITY

Once the university accepts the notion of staff development, whose responsibility does it become? According to Smith (1992), there are a number of loci of control. (1) Is it management's responsibility? That is, should the chief administrative officer (Vice Chancellor, Rector) send out a directive that there will be training and empower and require that his deans and heads of department see to it, or institute a staff development unit (SDU) to do it? This gives staff development the weight of authority and policy. Immediate supervisors of academic staff, that is, department heads, could appraise staff and direct their attention to areas of improvement. (2) Is it the responsibility of the academic staff themselves? Academic staff are constantly aware of their successes and failures as teachers and researchers. They should initiate activities through the help of their department heads and request the SDU to carry it out. (3) Is it the mandate of a central staff development unit to devote itself to improving the quality of teaching and research on campus? This SDU would have the expertise to carry out this function. (4) Should there be a Teaching and Learning Committee (Pendaeli, 1990) made up of various representatives who funnel training requests from staff and heads to SDU's? Finally, (5) should there be a "decentralized partnership model" which works within the specific discipline and attempts to match specific training to specific teaching tasks?

HEDU AS A CENTRALIZED UNIT

The Higher Education Development Unit follows the third model in that it is a separate unit designated to implement staff development. It initially serviced four faculties and the library for a total of about 500 personnel. HEDU also took responsibility for a fifth faculty (agriculture) and responded to the needs of affiliated colleges of education before a sixth faculty (engineering) was added in 1996. Thus the staffing ratio for the one coordinator became 1:800. The coordinator, appointed in 1992, was an associate professor on leave from a Canadian university, selected through the assistance of a CIDA-funded link. He stayed for four years from 1992-1996. His combination of prior experience and skills, MBA and Ph.D., propensity for writing and editing, and action-oriented personality provided a vital energy for the development and operation of the unit. Of the staff development styles described by Brew (1995), this coordinator personally ranked doing first, thinking about it second, and getting someone else to do it third. Despite the huge ratio, he was able to count on a number of enthusiastic colleagues at the grassroots who supported a gradual move toward the decentralized partnership model of staff development—a model which focused on serving specific departmental needs.

HEDU is located in the Faculty of Education as a department and was initially in the education building as an office. Its activities were initially coordinated by the Head of the Educational Resources Center under the supervision of the Dean of Education. In 1996, with a tiny recurrent budget (about US$5000) HEDU had its own coordinator who was still under the supervision of the dean with an initial appointment within the Faculty of Education as an associate professor. However, the coordinator was able to have the HEDU office relocated in an area conceptually central (and politically neutral) to the university, so that teaching, library, and administrative staff would have open or confidential access to it.

A university task force on restructuring has proposed a larger, future role for HEDU within a Center for Academic Development. Here a director would monitor the quality of all university programs, related staff development, and student academic development. The HEDU coordinator would become a Senior Academic Staff Development Officer with similar responsibilities as the current ones. This officer would then report through the director of the center to the newly created position of Deputy Vice Chancellor of Academic Affairs. Thus HEDU would be removed from the Faculty of Education and made a university-wide facility.

THE PROBLEM WITH LOCATION

There is a problem with the inclusion of a university-wide personnel service within a Faculty of Education. Though done of necessity when HEDU was first conceptualized and established, this location has meant that the coordinator and the unit have been seen as belonging to the Faculty of Education. The Faculty of Education, with only 19.4% of the university's total staff, has provided slightly more than one-third (38%) of the participants of HEDU activities over the four years. The Faculty of Social Sciences, with 31% of all university staff, had significantly less participation (31%), and the Faculty of Sciences even less (28%). In essence, the Faculty of Education used this university-wide service nearly twice as much other—and much larger—university Faculties.

There are a number of reasons for this higher level of participation by the Faculty of Education. First, HEDU is seen as one of the departments of the Faculty of Education by many academics throughout the institution. Second, advertising for the various HEDU activities is done first in the Faculty of Education because of the location of HEDU's secretarial support. Third, most HEDU activities are held in the spare classrooms or committee room of the Faculty of Education. Fourth, the Coordinator of HEDU is an Associate Professor in the Faculty of Education. Fifth, members of this Faculty may be more concerned about the value of professional development in teaching. After all, education is their discipline, and they may be interested in learning more about techniques which they in turn might teach their own students. Sixth, other Faculties and departments may be reluctant to take "training" from a sister Faculty—a reflection of academic cultural norms throughout many disciplines and in all parts of the world.

To counter this problem of location, an advisory committee for the unit had been established with the function of advising on the policies and programs of the unit and of reviewing its activities. Such a committee is crucial to a program, especially in a growing university, because it can foster a sense of ownership and involvement for the other faculties. (Wheeler & Schuster, 1990:281) The committee consists of representatives from each faculty, the library, the registrar's office, the National Institute for Research and Development, and the Staff Development Fellowship program. It is chaired by the Deputy Vice Chancellor of Academic Affairs. The committee is scheduled to meet twice a year (in October and March) and report to the Senate through the Academic Planning Committee. Unfortunately, the committee has not met regularly nor has it become a serviceable committee like the University Teaching and Learning Committee at Dar es Salaam.

Finally, HEDU's first impact on teaching staff outside of the Faculty of Education came from the solution to a fortunate problem. For the first six months of the HEDU's existence, there was no secretary nor computer, and the coordinator had to use the central computer center for typing correspondence, seminar notes, and much of the first HEDU bulletin. At the six terminals in this center, various teaching staff were puzzling over the uses of their word processing software, and frequently consulted the coordinator for his assistance. The camaraderie which was established during these small helping sessions remained throughout the next four years and convinced these first contacts of the benefits of informal, and later formal, training.

TARGET GROUPS

All teaching, library, and administrative staff of the University were invited to participate in the services of HEDU as outlined in the terms of reference. This said, offering to help professionals improve their skills is a delicate proposition, requiring the best application of adult learning psychology. Lecturers are employed to teach and research: thus once lecturers are appointed, they often express the opinion that their ability to teach is taken for granted. Staff development programs are then sought voluntarily—if at all—by these individuals. Yet all professional work can be seen as a continuum of expertise, from apprenticeship to mastery. A good staff development program should be able to assist at various stages in an academic's career.

The Staff Development Fellows receive specific orientation to teaching in the university by attending a three- or five-day induction workshop. The workshop is usually followed up by monthly workshops on relevant methodology. In addition each SDF is encouraged to confer once a term on his/her progress in university teaching. Beginning lecturers are invited to the initial and monthly SDF workshops as space permits, and some volunteer to learn about specific methodology and issues in university teaching. Senior lecturers and professors are invited from time to time to special issues or methods workshops which are open to all university staff on a first-come registration basis (modified so that as many faculties as possible can be represented). Department heads and deans are invited to specialized workshops on administrative or academic issues as identified from time to time.

GENERAL COURSE OFFERINGS

The workshops, short courses, and seminars conducted by the HEDU indicate the capacity it developed to answer the needs of lecturers as identified in consultation with lecturers and heads of department and as determined by an analysis of the results of the Student Assessment of Staff. Workshop topics also reflect the current teaching issues discussed by the USA Conference on Improving University Teaching, Canada's Society for Teaching and Learning in Higher Education, and the United Kingdom's CVCP's Universities' Staff Development and Training Unit. However, program planning is still a weak area, due in part to the absence of regular meetings of the advisory committee.

The primary emphasis of HEDU in the years 1992-1996 has been to develop the capacity to offer teaching workshops often enough to serve the large number of staff. These workshops regularly reflect the expertise of the coordinator who has often been the primary instructor. As well, the coordinator has solicited others to participate as unpaid facilitators. All workshop offerings were listed in a semester calendar of events. One necessary activity has been the constant promotion of offerings by mailing and posting of information. Initially workshops attracted 1% of university teaching staff; however, following a growing history of successful workshops, approximately 4% of all university staff (20 of 500, on average) attend each workshop. There are other kinds of workshops or seminars which only departments could conduct (and HEDU could facilitate). These are the content-oriented, departmental seminars which enable young and experienced lecturers and professors to keep up with the knowledge explosion in their disciplines.

Short seminars for two or four hours with a tea or lunch break have proven to be most popular. Refreshments were provided inexpensively by the local catering service, and informal discussions during the breaks gave lecturers an opportunity to expand upon the message of their seminars and make cross-disciplinary contacts.

The following examples of short seminar topics demonstrate that these could be offered for longer periods of time or in smaller modules for departmental meetings:

- Introduction to Teaching workshops for 1 to 5 days;
- Critical Incidents in Teaching, based on the University of Victoria (Canada) video vignettes and conducted as lunch-and-learn or brownbag sessions;
- teaching skill modules like Effective Lecturing and Standardizing Marking;
- student learning seminars like Teaching/Examining for Cognitive Development, Promoting Active Learning, Writing as a Tool for Learning;
- scholarship and research workshops on Productivity and Publishing, Us-

ing the Library as Teaching and Research Resource, Updating Survey Research Skills, Writing Workshop (twice a week for two months);
- for department heads: Information Needs Workshop and Teaching and Its Assessment/Staff Appraisal;
- and finally, other topics as requested, such as, Confidentiality in Counseling, Gender Equity in the Classroom, Developing a Promotable Teaching Portfolio, and Computer Awareness.

In four years, there were 68 various and repeated activities involving 1,223 participants for 5,744 hours of training. Approximately 230 different individual names were registered, with eighty of those individuals (one-third of citizen staff) accumulating twenty or more hours of participation.

SHORT COURSES

To utilize the time during the academic year when there were two short study breaks in October and February and to incorporate the SDF induction program, a "Short-Break Short-Course" was developed, which was attended in full by twenty UB staff. An additional ten teaching staff dropped in at various times during the week to fill in gaps in their professional development. The short course was based on the 1995 DSE handbook *Teach Your Best,* and covered the following topics:

The Role of the University Lecturer	Promoting Active Learning
The Learning Process	Using Instructional Media
Course Design	Devising Test Questions
Giving the Perfect Lecture	Assessing Students
Handling the Tutorial	Action Research and Publication

Throughout the week, emphasis was placed on the paradigm shift from teaching to student learning. Handbooks and certificates were given to participants.

A similar short course on updating research skills was offered for twenty-five UB staff and conducted through the university's National Institute for Research and Development. Topics included research culture, research design, questionnaire development, review of statistical procedures, writing and publishing. Training and updating in research is an on-going activity, especially as libraries expand and enhance services with electronic media.

PERSUASION—GETTING STAFF TO SIGN UP FOR COURSES

As a newly-conceived, centralized unit in which all participation was voluntary, HEDU faced an enormous task of creating a need for training. Not only was formal training not in existence, it was almost unknown in the eyes of lecturers who believed teaching to be something done in primary and secondary schools. Notices on bulletin boards and copies to mail boxes were not sufficient media to provide the information necessary for staff to learn about training or be convinced of its value. Indeed, "one of the most challenging tasks is the cultivation and fostering of an institutional climate that accepts in-house training as part of a lecturer's professional development." (Griffiths, 1993:256) Moreover, the African context demanded the personal approach. Through personal contact it was possible to reach a number of staff but not all 500 in the first four years of operation. Personal contact, for instance, enabled the coordinator to discover what content was being taught in various classrooms; thus, relevant articles on how to teach such content could be copied and distributed. The coordinator surmised that constantly putting information in teachers' and administrators' hands and on their desks would keep the training effort on their minds.

STAFF BULLETIN

The coordinator used a bulletin to actively encourage teaching staff of the University of Botswana to share their reflective experiences and practices.[1] The pages of the *HEDU Bulletin* were used to publish personal experiences (successful and otherwise), or reflections which lecturers wanted to share with their colleagues or make the subject of action research. This invitation was based on the idea of valuing teachers' experiences as the subject of research. Writing and publishing about one's teaching greatly increases the attention one pays to his or her own teaching. This is a basic tenet behind the notion of reflective teaching.

To facilitate the development of staff writing about university teaching, a writing workshop in 1994 was followed by a publishing workshop in 1995. Problems of structuring academic discourse, writing in a second language, developing, and supporting and referencing ideas were tackled in the writing workshop. Chief among these were the research skills needed so that junior staff could position their developing ideas within a tradition of scholarship in their particular fields. One of the features of the publishing workshop was a vigorous review of academic theses previously written by the participants, in an effort to develop their writing to levels suitable for publishing in an academic journal of their field. Participants also learned which journals might be likely to publish their work. Articles promising enough to be developed into longer research pieces were guided toward refereed journals. Short articles submitted to the bulletin sometimes seemed to be too focused on a particular course, and were revised to be of interest to more university staff. Very promising articles were expanded to address a larger international audience such as the readership of *College Teaching*.

In four years, the *HEDU Bulletin* published 40 articles written by University of Botswana staff, with ten more contributed by international scholars, and an additional ten written by the editor. Staff began to look forward to its regular publication, some even agreeing that the *HEDU Bulletin* was "an informative and entertaining read" and "a useful periodical for all those involved in teaching and management at university level." (Lomer, 1995)

The coordinator used the bulletin as a staff development tool in a number of ways. First, by persuading individuals within departments to openly discuss their observations and experiences, it was hoped that others would be influenced to reflect on their teaching and that individuals would enter into dialogue with each other about teaching.

Second, materials and articles, relevant to Botswana, produced by HEDU participants could be (and were) used in subsequent workshops. Third, other articles, written by professionals engaged in similar situations, permitted local staff to see similarities between African teaching concerns and those of academics throughout the world. Fourth, the bulletin was put in the mailboxes of all teaching staff. As the issues accumulated (160 pages in four years), they became a collection of articles about teaching at UB—articles that showed mini-action research concerns of UB teaching staff, articles that demonstrated reflection, articles which were a constant reminder that HEDU existed, was doing something and could do something for them.

Finally, contributions to the *HEDU Bulletin* were considered useful as indicators of scholarly research and publication. This was of particular importance for faculty seeking tenure or promotion, or even contract renewal. As a matter of policy, according to the Revised Guidelines for Appointments, Promotions and Review of Staff, staff at the University of Botswana could include these articles in their CVs.

STUDENT ASSESSMENT OF STAFF

To determine students' evaluations of the courses they attend, HEDU conducts the Student Assessment of Staff (SAS) at the end of each academic year. HEDU revises as necessary, distributes, collects, processes and returns questionnaires to department heads for distribution to their staff. HEDU assists in the interpretation of results for heads or individual staff as requested—in full confidentiality. This procedure had been experimental for three years and, after a considerable amount of debate, was approved as university policy by the Senate in 1994 that all courses be assessed at end of term. Though the Academic Staff Development Center at Witswatersrand, South Africa, has found conflict in the role of conducting student assessments while simultaneously promoting teaching, HEDU welcomed the dual functions. Since the data from student assessments assist HEDU's efforts, HEDU has tried to dispel the "threat" of evaluation through the explanations in the bulletin and departmental seminars.

The SAS instrument has been found, through research at UB, to be a valid and reliable procedure for evaluating teaching which elicits fair responses from the students (Tharakan & Herrick, 1994). The SAS consists of questionnaires given out to students at the end of each course, which allow students to comment on twenty or so specific and four open-ended questions describing various teaching behaviors. The twenty questions are structured around eight components of effective teaching:

Course organization: teaching staff could participate in workshops on how students learn, curriculum development, course design and delivery to improve this area.

Rapport with students: teaching staff could be counseled to make themselves more available to students after class, more open to student responses, and more observant of the student as an active learner. Workshops could include development of questioning skills, listening skills, communication skills.

Skill in teaching: teaching staff could participate in training sessions on lecturing, presentation skills, voice improvement, audio-visual aids.

Course work load: teaching staff could look at this component and wonder if they are being personally difficult in their relations with students, making the course difficult to understand, making the workload too heavy for the level, being unnecessarily hard to maintain "standards," or teaching a course which is misplaced in the program.

Course grading/examination: workshops dealing with cognitive development, setting examination questions, constructing tests, marking course work, marking essays, supervising projects would help teaching staff improve here.

Impact on students: teaching staff could be advised to make relevant applications and place the course in professional context or at the appropriate level in the curriculum. Readings and seminars on student learning and cognitive development might be useful to improve student perceptions of the value of the course.

Teacher enthusiasm: career counseling and peer consultations would be helpful in this area as would content-specific conferences to update course content.

Over-all effectiveness: it would be useful for teaching staff to see themselves in relation to the same course taught in the department, to the department average, other courses on the same level taught in the faculty, and to the faculty average as a whole. Large discrepancies would then be subjected to closer analysis, discussion, and soul-searching.

From the responses to the SAS instrument, the lecturer can then see where he or she stands in relation to any and all of eight teaching behaviors. At the end of the Spring term in April 1996, the SAS collected a total of 16,317 student responses to 730 courses.

HEDU conducted departmental seminars to demonstrate how the data on the computerized rating sheets could be interpreted and used to improve an individual's teaching. Information resulting from the assessments enabled the coordinator, the head of department, and the lecturer to work together on specific workshops, seminars, consultations, and visitations to improve specific skills. Therefore an individually-tailored program could be worked out for the benefit of each teacher. This gave considerable substance and valuable follow-up to teaching appraisal and development.

THE IMPORTANCE OF UNIVERSITY POLICY

A university must assist in supporting in-house training by developing and maintaining a policy statement.[2] The statement should guarantee that staff development has stature, procedure, and value. Unless there is a policy which promotes staff development, developers may eventually run out of means of persuasion, and staff may run out of enthusiasm, leaving a large number of academics unaffected. For instance, a 1994 survey of UB lecturers' attitudes toward training revealed that only 40 percent thought that improvement in teaching would significantly contribute to their career progression. Forty-two percent did not know if it would, and 18 percent responded that it would not. In order to make all staff focus more on their teaching, two policy decisions definitely gave greater emphasis to in-house, in-service staff development. Both of these decisions are reflected in the University's (1996) "Revised Guidelines for Appointments, Promotions and Review of Staff": the development and support of the HEDU and its activities, and mandatory attendance for beginning lecturers at a staff development program.

INDUCTION PROGRAM

In 1996, the university also approved a policy stating that attendance at a Staff Induction Program is necessary for beginning lecturers to be confirmed. Additionally, all teaching staff can cite attendance at or involvement in staff development or activities as assessable areas or sources of information leading to contract renewal, promotion, etc. This policy led to the HEDU Induction Program.

The HEDU Induction Program is a twenty-hour workshop or short-course orientation to university teaching which results in the award of a HEDU Induction Certificate of participation. As well, teaching staff who had participated in HEDU activities were invited to qualify for a HEDU Induction Certificate once they had accumulated twenty hours of attendance at various HEDU activities. In addition, any teaching staff who had participated in similar (but non-HEDU) professional development activities for at least twenty hours were also invited to apply in writing for a HEDU Induction Certificate (unless they had already received similar recognition). In April 1996, a reception was held at which eighty members of the UB teaching staff were awarded HEDU Induction Certificates for participation within the four years of September 1992, through April, 1996. While this may seem rather a small token, it is symbolic of the institution's recognition of the importance of developing its staff's teaching skills.

POSSIBILITIES

Faculty careers are developmental (Wheeler & Schuster, 1990), but teaching can plateau if staff are unaware of various growth points in their teaching, especially if they want to become mentors of students as independent learners (Kugel, 1993). Thus, staff development is more than persuading lecturers to improve "basic pedagogical skills." To meet all the needs of all staff may be impossible, but HEDU's program of providing information and training, counseling, and evaluation has become a strong enough base to support a number of potential additional activities which are being considered in many universities worldwide.

Action Research

Schön (1995:27) advocates the establishment of a "new scholarship . . . a kind of action research with norms of its own," while Kember and Gow (1992:299) support "action research for the purpose of improving the quality of student learning." One possible new activity of HEDU is in training staff to engage in action research in their classrooms. The cycles of planning, acting, observing, and reflecting can lead to a greater understanding of problems facing the lecturer, to an approach to solving them, and to collaboration with others who might be able to make structural changes to prevent them in the future. Furthermore, writing about experiences and drawing conclusions from them leads to theory constructed from practice. One staff development program in Hong Kong led teachers into action research with positive results (Kember and Gow, 1992). In Austria, lecturers undertook action research "to offer deeper insights into the participants' own practical 'theories' of what they intend to accomplish in the classroom and how they want to achieve these goals." (Scratz, 1992:81) The purpose of the Austrian program was to overcome the short term effects of most staff development activities and involve lecturers in a lengthier process of working on their teaching.

Department-Specific Initiatives

General pedagogical and curricular principles often are useful to disciplines in different ways; for example, an approach which works well in a biology classroom may not work so well in a course on Shakespearean plays. Thus HEDU, as does any academic development unit anywhere, faces the challenge of meeting specific departmental needs, which sometimes can present advantages in that the number of colleagues in the seminar are smaller and share a mutual disciplinary affiliation. To do this effectively, the "decentralized partnership model" (Smith, 1992) needs to be revisited. The decentralized partnership model has a number of advantages, especially for a large university with huge departments.[3] But even in a smaller university, the centralized coordinator, with the help of a departmental liaison, could work from within the department or faculty to service the needs of the immediate staff, much like many of the Academic Development Units of South African universities. As an insider, the liaison, with similar knowledge yet perhaps without special skills to assist in training to accomplish specific tasks, would work with the department head and the centralized coordinator to bring in outsiders as necessary to enhance staff development. The central academic development coordinator could be called upon to meet the needs identified by the liaison. However, there is sometimes a tendency among academics to reject educational activities offered from within an institution, while accepting advice from experts from the outside (Smith, 1992:40).

Teaching Portfolios

Another possible activity of HEDU includes showing how to develop a teaching portfolio or dossier (Wright, 1996), which collects specific materials as examples of multiple areas of teaching. These materials can be categorized, summarized, and peer-reviewed to present a description of the effectiveness of a person's teaching. Areas of strength can be observed, and weaknesses or missing areas targeted for development. A portfolio is a useful way of enabling academics to track teaching performance or involvement in professional growth activities (Bland & Schmitz, 1990), and to present the information to department heads or promotion committees for appraisal.

CONCLUSION

Scholarship is the business of the University of Botswana. The business of the Higher Education Development Unit is the enhancement of that scholarship by promoting staff development. The model described here is one in which a single, central coordinating staff developer minds the store, keeps the meat red, the potatoes new, the mealies white, has fast-food items on the shelf, and smiles at the customers. This approach builds so much goodwill that staff development becomes invaluable. Though practically impossible to evaluate, the effect of staff development surely adds value to the teaching and learning activities of a university.

Like consumers, academics do what is in their best interest. It is in their best interest to realize their full potential. It is in their best interest to be competent in what they are doing, even if solely for the purposes of recognition and promotion. It is in their best interest to be confident in front of students and peers so they are seen as knowing what they are doing. Competence and confidence in all four kinds of scholarship (Boyer, 1990) can lead to self-esteem, job satisfaction, and enhanced reputation, both for the teacher and the university. But most importantly, achieving higher levels of competence in teaching, through whatever means available, can enhance student learning.

NOTES

1. The following articles appeared in the March 1996, bulletin (* indicates UB-staff-written): The Teaching Dossier in Higher Education, University Teacher as Academic Guide, *English Language Output of UB Students, To Teach is To Learn Twice, *Facilitating Learning at UB Through Reading, *Partners: Librarians and Lecturers at UB, *Successful University Teaching, Course Development as an Act of Scholarship, *CD-ROM Countdown, HEDU Induction Certificate.
2. Such guidelines can be found in Guildford (1990) and Griffiths (1993).
3. For a successful model see DeZure, 1996

REFERENCES

Barr, R.B. & Tagg, J. (1995). From teaching to learning: A new paradigm for undergraduate education. *Change,* 27 (6), 12-25.

Bland, C.J. & Schmitz, C.C. (1990). An overview of research on faculty and institutional vitality. In Schuster, J. H. et al. (Eds.), *Enhancing faculty careers: Strategies for development and renewal.* San Francisco: Jossey-Bass, pp. 41-61.

Boyer, E.L. (1990). *Scholarship reconsidered: Priorities of the professoriate.* Princeton: Princeton University Press.

Brew, A. (Ed.) (1995). *Directions in staff development.* Buckingham: Open University Press.

Commission of Inquiry on Canadian University Education (1991). *Report.* Ottawa, Ontario: Association of Universities and Colleges of Canada.

DeZure, D. (1996). Closer to the disciplines: A model for improving teaching within departments. *AAHE Bulletin,* 48 (February), 9-12.

Griffiths, S. (1993). Staff development and quality assurance. In Ellis, R. (Ed.) *Quality assurance for university teaching* Buckingham: Open University Press, pp. 248-269.

Guildford, P. (1990). *Staff development in universities of the United Kingdom.* Sheffield: CVCP Universities' Staff Development and Training Unit.

Kember, D. & Gow, L. (1992). Action research as a form of staff development in higher dducation. *Higher Education,* 23, 297-310.

Kugel, P. (1993). How professors develop as teachers. *Studies in Higher Education,* 18 (3), 315-328.

Lomer, Cécile (1995). *The African Book Publishing Record,* XXI (3) 203,

McCaughey, R. (1993). But can they teach? In praise of college professors who publish. *Teachers' College Record,* 95 (Winter), 242-257.

Matiru, B. & Mwangi, A. (Eds.) (1995). *Teach your best: a handbook for university lecturers.* (2nd ed.) Bonn: Deutsche Stiftung für internationale Entwicklung.

Mehl, M.C. (1992). Meeting the academic challenge of development productively. In *The Proceedings of the 7th Conference of the South African Association for Academic Development* (pp. 1-17). Port Elizabeth Technikon, December 3-5.

Mukherjee, H. & Singh, J.S. (1993). *Staff development approaches in higher education: Learning from experience.* London: Commonwealth Secretariat.

Pendaeli, J. (1990). Reflections on ten years of university teaching and learning improvement (UTLIP) at the University of Dar es Salaam. *Papers in Education and Development,* 14, 1-12.

Republic of Botswana (1994). *Revised national policy on education.* Gaborone: The Government Printer.

Roblin, D. et al. (1993). *Post-secondary education in Manitoba: Doing things differently.* Winnipeg: University of Manitoba.

Salmi, J. et al. (1993). *Higher Education: The lessons of experience.* Washington, DC: The World Bank.

Schön, D.A. (1995). The new scholarship requires a new epistemology. *Change,* 27 (November/December), 27-34.

Scratz, M. (1992). Researching while teaching: an action research approach in higher education. *Studies in Higher Education,* 17, 81-95.

Smith, G. (1992). Responsibility for staff development. *Studies in Higher Education,* 17 (1), 27-41.

Tharakan, C.T. & Herrick, M.J. (1994). Reliability and validity of instrument items for the student evaluation of university teaching (the Botswana experience). *Improving University Teaching: Proceedings of the 19th annual conference,* University of Maryland (July 1994), 209-218.

Wheeler, D.W. & Schuster, J.H. (1990). Building comprehensive programs to enhance faculty development. In Schuster, J.H. et al. *Enhancing faculty careers: Strategies for development and renewal.* San Francisco: Jossey-Bass, pp. 275-297.

Wright, A. (1996). The teaching dossier in higher education. *The HEDU Bulletin,* 14 (March), 2-5.

CHAPTER 11

A University Teaching Practicum
Unpacking the Model
John Dwyer

INTRODUCTION

This century has seen tremendous change in the composition of a typical university's faculty. Years ago, it was not uncommon to find a university teacher who had not received their doctorate or some form of terminal graduate degree. Today, such a find is truly rare, as years of graduate study have become necessary for entry into the academic profession. Another significant change in the professoriate has been the widespread adoption of research as coin of the realm in academic reward structures. Pressures on faculty to do research have in turn led to a considerable increase—most notably at research institutions—of graduate students becoming the front-line teachers of first-year undergraduate students.

As graduate training has thus grown in its relative importance to the academy, one might assume that training for being a university or college professor would involve a fair amount of attention to pedagogical theory and methods. However, this is not the case—providing graduate students with significant preparation for classroom instruction is relatively unheard of in Australia or the UK, is fairly sophisticated in some parts of the U.S., and is in its infancy in Canada. This chapter describes the development and early successes of a teaching preparation program for graduate students at a Canadian university.

A BRIEF HISTORY

The "University Teaching Practicum" at York University was originally conceived by Professor Pat Rogers, the academic director of the university's Center for the Support of Teaching from May 1989 until June 1994. The Center is supported by administrative funds for the purpose of providing instructional development, and the Center's academic director is a tenured faculty member. The Center sponsors several programs and services—such as workshop series, focus group discussions, conferences, and guest lectures, and helps facilitate several departmental teaching development programs, notably in Administrative Studies and Mathematics. These activities provided a foundation upon which the practicum's efforts were built—indeed, the practicum was designed to provide a flexible structure bringing together a variety of programs and services that were already in place.

The university teaching practicum admitted its first candidates in January 1994, and by the end of the same year over 150 graduate students from 20 graduate programs were registered. By May 1996, 299 students were enrolled in the practicum. Students are encouraged to complete the practicum over a period of *at least two years* in order to allow ample time for teaching practice, experimentation and reflection.

Several institutions throughout the world have designed instructional programs which focus on the nuts and bolts of classroom interaction and assessment, although alternative forms of assessment are not often considered.[1] The York practicum was designed to provide graduate students with a means for documenting and gaining recognition for their teaching development activities. Additionally, the practicum leaders chose to emphasize a gradual and reflective developmental process. Practicum participants are encouraged to take the time necessary to develop a personal philosophy of teaching, with an understanding that this philosophy will change over time.

ELEMENTS OF THE PRACTICUM
Workshops
Workshops are provided that encourage candidates to engage in all facets of course development and design. Practicum participants are asked to create their own evaluative instruments and to provide evidence that not only have they used these evaluations but have also made changes to their teaching as a result of the feedback received. They are also encouraged to provide opportunities for informal evaluation and more immediate forms of feedback. As proponents of the reflective practitioner approach to teaching will agree, everyday experience needs to be enriched by contemplation over an extended period of time.

The practicum offers a rich variety of workshops that change from year to year. These workshops for teaching assistants range from the practical (e.g., how to deal with conflict in the classroom) to the theoretical (e.g., the challenge of diversity). The practicum also offers an annual series of workshops and focus group discussions entitled *Teaching Assistants Re-thinking the Classroom*. Participants in these workshops are required to read and be prepared to discuss topics like the growth of personality, the politics of teaching and learning, and working with learning differences. Unlike other practicum workshops—where workshop leaders could either be faculty members or more experienced teaching assistants—these highly interactive sessions are organized by the participants themselves. They allow teaching assistants to explore issues of relevance to them, and encourage them to explore progressive educational ideas.

To graduate from the practicum, participants are required to complete 25 hours of workshops, of which at least five must be discipline-specific. When the practicum was instituted, only 6 departments had developed fledgling programs of disciplinary teaching development, so participants were permitted to substitute reports or analyses on the literature about teaching within their disciplines. In a short amount of time, teaching assistants began to develop discipline-based workshops within their own departments, and several of York's departments now have institutionalized these activities. One department—Mathematics and Statistics—even compensates their graduate students for the time spent learning about teaching within the discipline. The increase in departmental programs is the direct result of a new program established in 1996 by the Dean of Graduate Studies. Under this program, the Dean has provided funding to 16 interested departments, to be used in hiring two Graduate Assistants to work together to develop disciplinary-based teaching development activities for graduate students. The practicum's workshop intiatives have benefitted more than graduate students, as several have generated interest and attendance among faculty members.

Voluntarism

Participation in the university teaching practicum is purely voluntary, which is an important point to consider in any program such as this. In their article, "Developing Teaching Skills During Graduate Education," Robert Diamond and Franklin Wilbur (1990) describe the ways that institutions can make use of existing resources and academic constituencies in order to establish practica. Many of their comments are extremely valuable—particularly their emphasis on gradually building upon the teaching culture that already exists rather than attempting drastic administrative change—with the possible exception of their claim that a teaching program should "be required of all teaching assistants." It is this author's conviction that the voluntary principle is essential to the integrity of the York University teaching practicum and contributes significantly towards the enthusiasm of the program's participants.

Collaboration and Consultation

Practicum participants are required to collaborate with their colleagues, partciularly in the area of feedback. If university teaching is to be a truly developmental and continuous process, it seems essential that colleagues talk to one another and share their experiences as classroom facilitators, mentors, and teachers in the deepest sense. One of the mandatory components of our practicum, therefore, is that participants provide evidence that they have engaged, on at least two occasions, in the sharing of feedback on a colleague's teaching.

It is also important to create a social environment in which consulting was not merely required behavior but part of a real teaching and consulting culture. The Center created a *Consulting Manual* for teaching assistants in order to help them perform consulting roles more effectively. The *Manual* includes a section on constructive feedback that emphasizes specificity, sharing, good timing, clear communication and attention to the consequences of feedback.[2]

An additional avenue for collaboration and consultation is provided in York's Teaching Assistant Assistance Forum. The forum consists of experienced teaching assistants who can act as consultants for one another as well as for novice university instructors. Over a short period of time, the forum adopted a new name—the Teaching Assistant Resource Group (TARG)—and began to expand the scope of their activities. TARG continues the consulting function of the original forum and holds regular drop-in-sessions where teaching assistants can talk about their teaching experiences "in an atmosphere of peer consultation and discussion." TARG also views its role as an advocate for teaching assistant issues and continues to help Center staff organize specific events such as Teaching Assistant Day.

Autonomy for Teaching Assistants

One of the organizational characteristics of the teaching assistant culture at York is robust independence. During the early 1990s, the Center's academic director actively sought to provide more autonomy and ownership for teaching assistants of their own professional development. A reflection of this concern was in the establishment of the position of Graduate Teaching Associate (GTA), a position which carries the responsibility for assessing and meeting teaching assistant development needs. The first GTA was appointed by the Center's academic director in May 1992. By the time the Practicum admitted its first candidates in January 1994, two successive GTAs had established a variety of programs and organized activities for teaching assistants.

Sometimes, members of the university administration are taken to task by TARG, either for not doing enough for teaching assistants or for ignoring issues that are of importance to them. But the relationship between this graduate student organization and the Center, on the whole, is respectful and symbiotic, with TARG acting as key recruiters for the practicum and as a pool of workshop leaders, and with the Center attempting to ensure that teaching assistants' pedagogical interests are met.

TARG has also made a commitment to helping the York University community in general. For example, workshops on equity and diversity had been offered at York for many years prior to this period and by many groups and organizations including the Center. However, in the last 2-3 years, there has been much less activity by the Center, and definitely no leadership, in the area of equity and diversity. TARG participants have responded by developing workshops on equity and diversity issues at York to fill a need left by this void. The interest, support and even the criticisms of TARG are the best evidence that the practicum is a vibrant and progressive pedagogical process.

Videotapes

Participants in the practicum have their teaching videotaped, and they are encouraged to develop ideas for improvement of their teaching based upon this experience. In some instances, students are videotaped in groups, and an experienced teaching assistant or skilled teacher connected with the Center often does the filming and leads the discussion in a critical yet supportive manner. In this approach, each student gives a 15 minute presentation and then the practicum leader and the participants sit as a group in order to engage in collegial discussion. Everyone is asked to discover the positive attributes in the teaching of the other but also to provide concrete suggestions for future improvement. These sessions usually turn out to be extremely valuable and participants often describe them as the single most valuable component of the practicum. In fact, participants' expectations from these sessions are extremely high and they invariably come well prepared. Some use the sessions to obtain practice in more formal lecturing, while others demonstrate and discuss tutorial or seminar techniques.

The Teaching Dossier

Another significant component of the practicum is the *teaching dossier.* Teaching dossiers in Canadian universities are similar to teaching portfolios in the United States and other countries. (For more on portfolios and their uses, please see Kari Smith's chapter in this volume). At some universities in Canada, the documentation of teaching has been encouraged since the 1980s (Vanderford, Eison, and Olive, 1996), so it was only natural to have our students generate formative dossiers as evidence of their development throughout the practicum.

The objective of the dossier assignment was not to evaluate but rather to provide a means for documenting growth and the attainment of program requirements, and to introduce students to an effective means of engaging in continual reflection on their teaching. Thus, participants were required only to complete their dossier and be able to demonstrate within them the completion of all practicum tasks, including the construction of a philosophy of teaching. However, in some instances at the student's request, a dossier may be read with care, and the readers may discuss their observations with the author and provide feedback.

Because practicum participants know that their dossiers may be read by respected teaching professionals—and that their efforts, initiatives and insights can be discussed at length—they usually put a great deal of work into these products. Their dossiers often contain thoughtful essays on teaching within their discipline. Several students have appended their teaching dossiers to their applications for teaching positions, to excellent effect. The use of dossiers has set a standard for all future practicum participants—the submitted dossiers are increasing in number and their quality has always been very high.

Overall, the York practicum is multi-dimensional and offers graduate students a rich learning experience in teaching methods and theories. Participants and graduates have provided both constructive criticism and supportive feedback of the practicum. However, as indicated in the following discussion, there is still much work to be done.

DISCUSSION

Establishing a university teaching practicum as a truly integral part of graduate student professionalization can be a difficult task, although at York it was welcomed and supported with open arms. While many university administrations and faculties are busily debating issues relating to the professional responsibility of tenure-track professors towards their students and their accountability to the community, they may often forget to pay close attention to mentoring the professoriate of the future. Instead, support for developing teaching skills among graduate students may stem from departmental fears that teaching assistants are not prepared to cope effectively with new and diverse student populations and may pose problems for departments in the form of complaints, grievances, and students being 'turned-off' from the discipline. Support from central university administrators can also be equally utilitarian, particularly when graduate teaching practica are seen as useful for attracting a higher quality of graduate student to one's institution. A common result of these utilitarian approaches is a perspective towards a teaching practicum that may lose sight of the experience and needs of the graduate students who will enroll in them.

An ideal university teaching practicum should provide its graduates with the knowledge and skills and that will allow them to take responsibility for their teaching and for their ongoing development as university teachers. It should be flexible enough to respond to both individual and disciplinary needs without being held captive to either. And it should encourage the pooling of information and the active collaboration that can only advance university teaching.

Mentoring and Morale

An increasing number of scholars in the U.S., Canada, and elsewhere are concerned with how to move graduate training away from the traditional emphasis on research skills. Boyer (1990) recommends that graduate programs must encompass teaching preparation seminars and programs in order for a new generation of "intellectually vibrant" scholars to emerge. From the perspective of organizational socialization, it is clear that mentoring and role models can also provide a critical tool for achieving this goal. Graduate students routinely describe collaboration with peers as useful (Baxter-Magolda, 1996), but they are more satisfied when they can find experienced mentors from their own discipline. Moreover, a large number of successful university teachers ascribe their success to having had such a mentor early on in their career (Meyers, 1995). Indeed, research conclusively demonstrates that one of the most pressing anxieties of graduate students is to find such a mentor (Avery and Gray, 1995).

The students who really thrive in the York practicum are quite often the ones who have found a willing mentor from among respected members within their own department. Other students benefit from the mentoring and consulting which they provide each other. Supportive role models help to build up a student's confidence and thereby encourages them to experiment and take risks as teachers. While faculty should encourage their graduate students to develop skills that enable them to publish articles and manuscripts, departments should encourage faculty—particularly those who are most respected for their teaching skills—to mentor the university teachers of the future.

The Future of a University Teaching Practicum

Relevance, subtlety, and prestige are valuable commodities in the increasingly intense market for graduate students. It is not surprising, therefore, that York's Faculty of Graduate Studies, which provides partial funding for the practicum and officially recognizes its graduates, is currently developing a new program based on this initiative. The Center was approached by the Dean to develop an alternate, more intensive, and evaluated program of teaching preparation—a Graduate Diploma in University Teaching and Learning. This is currently being designed by a collaborative group involving the Center, teaching assistants, and faculty, and will be built around a course on University Teaching and Learning which has been offered every year from 1989 to the present. In other words, the Diploma will provide an alternative route for extending the experience for those teaching assistants who wish to delve deeper into the topic and are willing to take the time to do so.

Additionally, the university teaching practicum has forged ties with units throughout the university, gaining trust and respect from departmental chairs and committees, which helps to further the Center's goals. For example, the author was recently invited to join a meeting of 17 Chemistry and Computer Science students who sought to explore the uses of the department's practicum in developing their skills as laboratory instructors and graders. The interest is clearly there for all parties to create something that better fits the experience of science teaching assistants.

As well, several departments have made significant strides towards appreciating the teaching efforts of their teaching assistants. For example, a number of department representatives recently met with practicum coordinators to help develop a series of guidelines for creating teaching awards for their teaching assistants.[3]

The perceptive reader will recognize that relationships of this kind take enormous amounts of time and tremendous effort to build. They may not get the same kind of publicity that is reflected in our more glossy newsletters, impressive workshop schedules, or highly publicized teaching and learning events. But just like the extra attention given to videotaping teaching assistants' teaching and the care with which their teaching dossiers are read, these efforts have enormous pay-offs.

CONCLUSIONS AND SUGGESTIONS FOR FOSTERING A TEACHING CULTURE
This essay has argued that the success of any teaching development program for teaching assistants depends upon attracting individuals who have a genuine concern for teaching and promoting collegial discussion and mentoring relationships. The author has advocated the notion that a university teaching practicum should focus on student interests and needs rather than institutional objectives, and joins the call throughout higher education for a renewed commitment towards the development and recognition of good teaching. It is observed that while many faculty who are currently involved in the mentoring of teaching assistants were once mentored by senior professors in their academic departments, such mentors have been in increasingly short supply over the last twenty-five to thirty years.

The intensification of research and its sharp differentiation from university teaching is largely an institutional response to the externalization of "power, prestige and reputation" throughout the academy. The measurement of scholarship has shifted quite dramatically from within particular institutions to an external scholarly community. In the process, scholarly reputations and credentials have become divorced, not merely from the particular institution, but also from university classrooms (Kameen, 1995).

For a practicum to really have its desired effect, it is important that we as faculty members begin to rekindle the teaching culture in our departments. At the very least, this means that those who work in the field of teaching assistant development must attempt to cultivate relationships with individual university units. These relationships have to be based on respect and collaboration. Departments are not inclined to listen to those who preach, but they will consult on areas of mutual interest. Given the importance of one's discipline in the lives of most faculty worldwide (Boyer, Altbach & Whitelaw, 1994), research and programs that encourage teaching development within the disciplines are more likely to achieve significant results. As well, faculty across disciplines share similar concerns about classroom instruction. The practicum at York found considerable interest and support among senior faculty members for programs in areas that include: learning how to deal with large classes, using instructional technology, coping with learning differences and student diversity, and dealing more effectively with conflict in the classroom. In the pure and applied sciences, practicum leaders worked closely with committees that seek to improve science students' creative, critical and collaborative skills.

One lesson to be learned from creating and nurturing the York University Teaching Practicum is that the teaching development of teaching assistants is not something that can or should be pursued separate from other teaching and learning initiatives. It is, however, one of the central axis points for pedagogical change at York and the crucible where university teachers of tomorrow are formed. As such, it merits not only our attention and concern but our dedication.

NOTES

1. See, for example, "Challenges and Strategies for Helping GTAs Develop Teaching Portfolios," *The Journal of Graduate Teaching Assistant Development*, 3(2), 1996, p. 61-68.
2. See especially William H. Berquist & Steven Phillips (1975), *A Handbook for Faculty Development, Vol. I* (Dansville, NY), p. 224-225.
3. These guidelines were reprinted in the *York University Gazette* and are attached to this article in the form of an appendix.

REFERENCES

Avery, P.B. & Gray, P.L. (1995). "Mentoring graduate teaching assistants: Creating an effective mentor/mentee relationship," *The Journal of Graduate Teaching Assistant Development*, Vol. 3, No. 1, pp. 9-19.

Baxter-Magolda, M.B. (1996). Epistemological development in graduate and professional education. *The Review of Higher Education*, Vol. 19, No. 3, p. 298.

Boyer, E.L., Altbach, P.G. & Whitelaw, M.J. (1994). *The academic profession: An international perspective*. Princeton, NJ: Carnegie Foundation for the Advancement of Teaching.

Boyer, E.L. (1990). *Scholarship reconsidered: Priorities of the professoriate*. Princeton, NJ: Carnegie Foundation for the Advancement of Teaching.

Diamond, R.M. & Wilbur, F.P. (1990). Developing teaching skills during graduate education. *To Improve the Academy*, Vol. 9, pp. 199-216.

Kameen, P. (1995). Studying professionally: Pedagogical relationships at the graduate level. *College English*, Vol. 57, No. 4, pp. 448-460.

Meyers, S.A. (1995). Mentor selection and use by first-semester graduate teaching assistants. *The Journal of Graduate Teaching Assistant Development*, Vol. 3, No. 1, p. 27f.

Vanderford, M.L., Eison, J. & Olive, T. (1996). Challenges and strategies for helping GTAs develop teaching portfolios. *The Journal of Graduate Teaching Assistant Development*, Vol. 3, No. 2, p. 61.

Weimer, M.E. (1991). *Improving college teaching*. San Francisco, Ca: Jossey-Bass.

Some Thoughts on Creating Teaching Awards for Teaching Assistants

Many of York's departments are currently establishing teaching awards for their teaching assistants. These awards are extremely important because they encourage teaching assistants to become the best teachers that they can be and because they establish pedagogical ideals that can only improve university teaching in the future. Creating teaching awards for teaching assistants also addresses an issue that is of paramount importance to graduate students who are teaching many of our front-line courses. At the Center for the Support of Teaching, students consistently expressed their concern that they find it difficult to get the encouragement and respect that they feel they earn when striving for excellence in both teaching and research. They are anxious to be reassured that their own department recognizes that developing teaching skills is honorable and worthwhile. And they are looking for incentives to develop critical pedagogies and innovative techniques and technologies.

If your department is thinking of establishing a teaching award for your teaching assistants, you might want to think about making the following recommendations explicit in the way that you frame the preamble and criteria for the award. But please remember that these recommendations are designed to be encouragement to teaching excellence rather than a checklist that must be met by all candidates:

- The best teachers are those who respond to student feedback and whose teaching evolves as a response to that feedback. Encourage your teaching assistants to develop and use evaluations that are relevant to their teaching situations.

- An ability to motivate and enthuse students is a clear indication of teaching excellence, but it is just as important to look for the teacher who is able to show students how to improve their work and develop their critical skills.

- Good teaching is inclusive teaching. That means that teaching awards should emphasize an ability to deal effectively with different learning styles and diversity in the classroom.

- Many graduate students want to experiment with new teaching strategies, techniques and technologies, but their vulnerable status occasionally gives rise to concern about making mistakes or organizing teaching activities that fail. Teaching awards that encourage risk-taking and experimentation could do much to offset these fears.

- Departmental awards probably need to distinguish themselves from university-wide awards and to put the teaching emphasis within a context where it truly belongs—inside the discipline. Departmental candidates for teaching awards should be encouraged to explore publications and examples of *disciplinary teaching*.

- Teaching excellence serves a valuable but limited purpose when it is confined to a single classroom. Departmental teaching awards should put a premium on collegiality and shared knowledge. In that way, examples of good teaching and the teaching experiments that work can permeate through the department's teaching assistant community.

- Closely related to the above, departments might want to give special consideration for those teaching assistants who organize or conduct teaching workshops for their colleagues.

- Departments might also want to consider the added value that their teaching assistants can provide if they are members of the national or international teaching community. It is relatively easy, for example, for teaching assistants to join the Society for Teaching and Learning in Higher Education (STLHE) or to subscribe to one of the many listservs devoted to college and university teaching.

- In the Center, we are finding that a significant number of the students working through the University Teaching Practicum are engaged in research projects that dovetail disciplinary and pedagogical concerns. Departments might wish to encourage their students to conduct scholarly research in areas related to university teaching, and to make that a professional consideration when choosing award winners.

The best way to establish teaching assistant teaching awards that really count is to ensure that their terms of reference are integrated with departmental concerns. Just how that might work certainly will vary from department to department and will reflect particular research and teaching cultures. What is of utmost importance, however, is that these awards have genuine status, reflect teaching excellence, and remain as free as possible from any of the political or personal divisions that characterize even the best departments. I would suggest in closing, therefore, that the committees who compose the terms of reference for teaching awards, and who select the teaching assistants who will receive them, be composed of members of the department who are recognized for exemplary teaching themselves.

Introduction to *The University Teaching Practicum Handbook*

This *Handbook* provides detailed information on the *University Teaching Practicum*, a program of professional development in university teaching and learning for students enrolled in a graduate program at York. The *University Teaching Practicum* admitted its first candidates in January 1994, and currently over 300 graduate students from 20 graduate programs are registered. In December of 1994, the first graduate of the practicum was officially recognized by York's Faculty of Graduate Studies.

The primary goal of the practicum is to provide opportunities for candidates to develop the knowledge and engage in the practices required for effective university teaching in their own (or a related) discipline. Candidates are encouraged to enrich their understanding of the philosophy and goals of higher education and to increase their awareness of the ethical and equity issues that relate to university teaching. In addition, candidates are required to develop an understanding of the following areas:

- theories of pedagogy, individual learning and human development
- teaching strategies, techniques, and technologies
- critical, collaborative, and teamwork skills development
- lesson and course design, including the preparation of learning objectives
- instruments for assessing student and teaching performance
- a range of self- and peer-assessment techniques and strategies

Another goal of the practicum is to provide graduate students with an instrument for reflecting upon their development as university teachers and with an effective vehicle—the teaching dossier—for documenting that development. The practicum teaching dossier may also prove useful for future university employment and promotion purposes.

Upon completion of the practicum, candidates present their teaching dossier to the Center for the Support of Teaching (CST). All dossiers are authenticated by the CST and those dossiers that fulfill the practicum requirements are forwarded to the Faculty of Graduate Studies for formal recognition. Successful candidates will receive a letter confirming that they have completed the practicum from the Dean of Graduate Studies.

Although the main purpose of the practicum is to ensure that York's graduates are prepared to perform as effective university teachers, those planning to

---

The University Teaching Practicum Handbook was developed for York University by Pat Rogers and John Dwyer. Pat Rogers was the first Academic Director of York's Center for the Support of Teaching. An inspirational teacher, Professor Rogers established the University Teaching Practicum and attracted its first participants.

pursue a career in other professions may wish to enroll in the program in order to develop and improve their communication, collaborative, and mentoring skills.

Admission Requirements

Any student enrolled in a graduate program at York is eligible to enroll in the practicum. Students in either a masters or doctoral program of study may enroll in the practicum. Since learning to teach effectively is a developmental process, candidates are strongly encouraged to complete the practicum requirements over a period of *at least two years*. Students who are currently in the final year of a graduate program must seek special permission from a representative of the CST to enroll in the practicum.

Practicum Requirements

Candidates develop their teaching through a combination of independent study and participation in a variety of workshops, seminars, conferences, courses, focus group discussions, and teaching-related activities. While they are completing the practicum, candidates are responsible for compiling evidence of their participation in program components and must document their activities by preparing a teaching dossier.

The following minimum requirements for accreditation are listed with estimations, where possible, of the time required to complete practicum components. Since the program is designed to meet individual needs, and since teaching at the postsecondary level involves knowledge of teaching, student learning, disciplinary content, and teaching methods specific to one's own or related disciplines, the time required to complete the practicum may vary considerably.

i) **General principles of pedagogy.** A variety of general areas of pedagogy are examined through independent study, workshops, seminars, conferences and courses. A minimum of 25 hours of participation in workshops and seminars (or CST approved individual studies) is required. At least 5 hours of the 25 must be devoted to teaching methods appropriate to one's own discipline. For the purpose of the practicum:

- *independent study* means research on teaching is conceived, initiated, and conducted by the student in order to master areas required by the practicum.
- *workshops* are group meeting to discuss university teaching issues or to participate in experimental projects related to teaching.
- *seminars* are discussion groups on advanced pedagogic subjects that are typically directed by a tutor or specialist.
- *conferences* are meetings that are organized by postsecondary institutions for the discussion of interrelated teaching and learning issues.
- *courses* are organized classes that are usually offered for credit by postsecondary institutions.

ii) **Practice and analysis of teaching.** All candidates are required to have some teaching experience (i.e., one full T.A. or 20 hours of *Apprenticeship* to an experienced faculty member) and to engage in ongoing, systematic evaluation of their teaching practice and performance (i.e., a total of approximately 15 hours of self-evaluation, student evaluation, and colleague evaluation).

iii) **Teaching documentation.** On completion of the practicum, candidates are required to submit a teaching dossier documenting their teaching accomplishments and their participation in the program. Candidates are advised to begin working on their dossiers at an early stage of the practicum and to maintain their dossiers on an on-going basis. Candidates should expect to spend between 15 and 25 hours constructing their teaching dossiers.

Images of Policy, Structure, and Organization

CHAPTER 12

Benchmarking Teaching Performance in Universities
Issues of Control, Policy, Theory, and "Best Practice"

Margaret Robertson

THE CONTEXT

Many of my more experienced colleagues see university teaching in the post-modern context amid an array of paradoxical dilemmas which lead them to bouts of melancholy and whimsical musings on ways to survive. Their crystal ball gazing does not readily reveal opportunities, as the ground rules move quickly from goal to goal. In fact, in the widest context there is the temptation to describe universities in the late 1990's as gloomy places where despair is taking over from hope for the longer term future.

These feelings reflect a climate of change where leadership appears to have taken on new meanings. For instance, in the United Kingdom, and more recently in Australia, the politics of universities have become embattled in public debate and governmental decision making. The quiet, dignified and scholarly disputation behind cloistered bricks and mortar have been replaced with public rallies, raised voices, and front page media reporting. This marks a new era in the life of universities, one that departs from the long tradition of an autonomous, mostly unquestioned base of power. Arguably, these same tensions are felt around the globe. It is fair to say that university contexts in Europe, North America, and Australia have all experienced the horrors associated with cost-cutting measures that lead to large class sizes, fewer resources, and changed working conditions (Stanley & Reynolds, 1995).

Part of the turmoil comes from external calls for accountability measures that have credibility in the wider community. Shrinking economies in what are mostly Western cultural settings have led to pressures on universities to provide evidence of budget effectiveness. Measures can be varied, but in the final summation they need to be in terms that 'open the fiscal books' to public scrutiny. These demands have seen universities scrambling to find ways of providing the required data, with solutions from the world of business as an obvious source for models. Needless to say, the business paradigm—with its emphasis on productivity—does not sit well with many academics. While academics generally agree on what constitutes research productivity, and thus how to measure it, few agree on a common definition of effective teaching. A reasonable conclusion is that the negative reaction towards an emphasis on productivity in academe is not so much related to intrusiveness but rather the underlying lack of valid and reliable measures of teaching and program effectiveness.

In this chapter, the notion of measuring teaching performance is explored through an analysis of a few of the complex variables involved in the debate, including the teaching and learning process, changing cultures, and their impact on teaching staff. Finally, a strategy is examined for a way forward that may satisfy the needs of external decision makers and policy leaders of universities. Examples are drawn primarily from the Australian context, yet they illustrate both international and intranational tensions in universities and the ways in which they gain expression in unique geographic, socio-cultural, and political contexts.

BENCHMARKING: WHAT IS IT AND HOW DOES IT HELP?

One of the models taken from business that has widespread application in post-modern universities is 'benchmarking'. Popularized by Robert Camp (1989), benchmarking draws its strengths from Eastern philosophies that emphasize superiority and the importance of knowing your competitors. In Camp's view this also involves knowing your operation and a willingness to incorporate into your practices the best that is available. Continuous measurement of performance against competitors is implicit as is the search for reference points against which valid judgements are to be made. Simply defined, benchmarking is the establishment of these reference points by which one compares performance over any given length of time.

As a philosophy it is difficult to argue with the intent of benchmarking within the university context of the late 1990's. It seems reasonable to ask that university teachers keep their practices current, dynamic, and competitive. Indeed, this notion is no stranger to their environments. In the research culture of typical modern universities the practice of assessing one's familiarity with current issues in their field has long been present within a system of refereed articles and research grants. As well, these processes have well-established routes for measuring "quality," usually through external indices or other judgements of performance. However, university teaching has a different history. Here the traditions are embedded in scholarly reputations of academics which include their expert discipline knowledge and communication techniques as well as their pedagogical knowledge of what some call the art (and others call the science) of teaching. In fact, the teaching context of universities highlights the wisdom of another observation on benchmarking—there is no one way to do it (McNair & Lebfried, 1992). Nevertheless, there is some general agreement that benchmarking is about continuous improvement. Reflective practice is widely recognized as a way to improve teaching. However, while there are seemingly clear reference points against which university researchers can measure their performance, they seem much less clear for university teachers.

In brief, if you take the view that benchmarking is about improving outcomes, with very specific recommendations regarding processes to be implemented in order to achieve the desired endpoints, there are major questions to be resolved before global standards in university teaching are likely to appear. Some of these will relate to who sets the agenda or whether the leadership comes from external or internal forces, manager or educator.

So Who Makes the Decisions?
The stimulation for global standards or competencies in university teaching appears linked to management searches for examples of "best practice" (Robson, 1995). Terms borrowed from business such as "Benchmarking" (Riley & Nuttall, 1993) and "Total Quality Management" (Lewis & Smith, 1994) have been introduced which, whether liked or abhorred, are widely practised and available models for universities to follow. Indeed, where international travel has not served to filter the constructs of these paradigms, Internet access has undoubtedly helped the debate spread to various corners of the globe. In fact, one could argue that in the competitive climate for students faced by universities everywhere, there are forces so strongly at work towards globalizing practices that they may lead to a homogenizing effect on university teaching. Fortunately, geography, and unique interactions of people and places should guarantee limitations to this process.

Who makes the decisions? Universities traditionally have relied on external funding agencies. Hence politicians, business entrepreneurs, or decision makers who allocate funds have a large stake in the outcomes of universities to provide the expertise for their future enterprises. Obvious questions to be asked are: How are teaching and learning defined? Who decides what happens with teaching programs—external moderators or internal processes? How are the Vice Chancellors and senior administrators handling the pressures of diminished resources? What kinds of evidence are they demanding as proof of performance? What leadership can academic staff take in any decision making about changing teaching practices? How much say do and should students have?

Who decides—and what can be decided—might seem to be simple questions. However, it would be a foolish observer indeed who viewed university settings with such a regulated and simplistic view. In pragmatic terms, the implementation of any change to teaching practices in universities depends on the co-operation of university teachers, students, and administrators. As well, their collective views are crucial for any informed debate on the impact of external attacks on the institution's operational autonomy (Fullan, 1991).

The method one chooses for analyzing these complex questions undoubtedly depends on personal contexts. Coming from a long career in teaching, my approach is to examine the issues from the perspective of an educator and thus challenge the inadequacy of decision-making that relies disproportionately on the mood of statisticians and bureaucrats. To do this requires a search for knowledge about what we mean by teaching and learning, or as Camp (1989) might say, knowing your operation. This, then, can become the starting point for developing measures for comparative analysis. Hence, what follows is a conceptual framework on university teaching. This is used for providing the reference for a critique of policies and programs of accountability for university teaching, including the directions taken in the Australian case study described later in this chapter.

UNIVERSITY TEACHING: AN INDIVIDUAL VIEW
Knowing what educational theorists use as determinants of expert teaching practice involves a theory of teaching and learning along with an understanding of the desirable learning outcomes (Dunkin, 1995).

A Theory of Teaching and Learning
In the past, educational theorists have generally referred to teaching and learning as inseparable terms. Amazingly, only recently has this marriage of terms entered the rhetoric of universities. Thus, it is worthy of reflecting on what we mean by 'teaching' and 'learning'.

A simple model is useful for this purpose. Using the metaphor of a bridge in architectural terms (see Figure 1) it is possible to imagine a construction taking place that is continually growing towards completion of the project, provided appropriate effort is contributed by the relevant participants. On the one side of the bridge is the learner or, in class terms, the aggregate of students. Each student as a learner has a profile of needs and expectations

Figure 1
Elements of a Model for Teaching and Learning

Students	<...............Bridge...............>	Aims
Prior learning		Curriculum guidelines
Preferred learning styles		Assessment criteria
Motivation		Professional bodies
Expectations		Government accreditation
Perceptions		Industry needs
Personal resources		Resources
Other contextual influences		Other higher education bodies

that are far ranging and complex. The accumulated prior knowledge and experience of individuals will bring to the teaching and learning context as many world views as there are students. This vast and rich resource, if utilized constructively, can generate a synergy in the group where higher order thinking processes are nurtured and flourish. At the same time, university students as adult learners are likely to have preferred learning styles that can result in mismatches with teaching approaches and cause a great deal of distress. Research indicates this phenomenon is most apparent when "east" meets "west" or when students from Confucian backgrounds, where didactic approaches are common, are confronted with the highly interactive student-centered approaches or processes more common in the 'west' (Biggs, 1994). Motivation is crucial in overcoming the obstacles that can arise through personal views. Except, perhaps, when belief systems are widely disparate, strong motivation can generally assist the process of conflict resolution. The desire to learn may exist for many different reasons including: qualifications, personal satisfaction, employer prerequisites, and retraining. But 'good' teachers are able to provide for diverse needs and personal goals (Ramsden, 1992). A constructivist approach such as that proposed by the bridge metaphor recognizes the value of responsive and reflective teaching which meets the needs of individual learners.

On the other side of the bridge are the aims, goals, outcomes, and competencies or standards that set the program of teaching. In university teaching this generally means looking carefully at the fine print of rather weighty formal documents that have been subjected to a whole feast of accreditation procedures—often external as well as internal to the university. Such documents generally reflect the influence of related professions, discipline specific wisdom, and increasingly, the needs of industry and commerce. In Australia, this is illustrated by the strong drive of governments and industry to introduce the principles of competency based standards (Burns, 1995; Collins, 1993) into courses so that they will dovetail with vocational and technical higher education programs. Inevitably, given the nature of federal government funding to Australian universities, this strong outside influence is and will continue to be felt by university curriculum decision makers. Increasing accountability measures are an expression of these pressures as well as fiscal problems in the wider social spectrum of publicly funded institutions. So the need to articulate learning outcomes and evaluate the effectiveness of programs in meeting these targets is becoming part of the culture of university teaching in Australia, as indeed it seems in other international settings.

To return to the bridge metaphor, the role of the teacher can be explained as that of 'bridging the gap' between learner and teaching aims. Thinking architecturally, bridge construction requires 'pillaring' from both ends for the construction to be sound and herein lies the analogy with university teachers. In order to promote learning there must be flexibility in the program for the teaching to translate the content in ways that will build on students' existing understandings and enhance their prior knowledge and skills. A measurement of good teaching ought to be how well the students progress from the starting point along the path to the set targets. Good teaching can enhance the opportunities for students to succeed. Research shows that good teachers or 'expert' teachers (Berliner, 1994; Dunkin, 1995) have skills at explaining and bridge building that are superior to 'novice' or beginning lecturers. They are cognizant of the diverse needs of students, including style and prior knowledge. They recognize that the content of what is to be taught needs structuring in ways that promote learning for meaning and understanding (Ramsden, 1992). Furthermore, if the teaching aim of the university is to promote higher order thinking skills, then teaching techniques need to be developed that promote enquiry and go beyond rote learning and memorization or direct transmission of information. Perhaps here lies the first benchmarking dilemma. That is, how do you measure the presence of reflective practice and then equate this to student achievement?

In brief, the bridge metaphor reminds us that university teaching is inextricably bound to a theory of learning. The process is dynamic, interactive and contextually bound to personalities, skills and experience, physical as well as social environments, and the expertise of the lecturer. Often linked with grand theatrical performances, a good lecture experience is not an end in itself. Rather than expert orators, 'good' university teachers describe their roles in terms of facilitating learning. As many scholars have observed, in the end it is the learners who will reflect the quality of university teaching with their actions and successes.

Deep versus Surface Learning

Implicit in this discussion on the relationship between teaching and learning is a belief regarding the quality of learning outcomes. The history of universities has been synonymous with scholarly pursuits such as the dialectic of dialogue, debate and argument or hypothesizing, research and analysis. Such endeavors rely on critical thinking and higher order thinking skills. Yet, it is only in recent times that the teaching of scholars or lecturers has been subjected to close observation, in order to assess what strategies are likely to lead to these desired skills.

Research shows that much of the teaching in undergraduate programs is designed to promote 'surface' outcomes with an emphasis on information transmission, memorization, and recall (Schmeck, 1988). This can lead to conflict, especially where expectations are inclined towards seeking evidence of problem solving, enquiry based skills and deductive reasoning. Educators maintain that 'deep' learning, or the kinds of learning for meaning and understanding that are the hallmarks of higher order reasoning, requires teaching strategies that match the objective. Open-ended questioning techniques, problem solving approaches, co-operative learning, and an emphasis on Socratic dialogue or interactive discussion are a few of the strategies that have been linked to deep learning outcomes. If this is not fully understood in the design of measures of learning outcome, then the risk is superficial learning rather than the more desirable learning for life.

The Role of Research in Teaching Best Practice

One of the great anomalies that has come to pervade university culture is the belief that research is a domain separate from teaching. Sadly, in many contexts, this has led to the diminution of teaching to a secondary role with clear evidence of the status of research activities in promotions and staff appointments. And yet, ironically, universities came into being as places where scholars could concentrate their endeavors on the pursuit of knowledge and engage or tutor young scholars. While not wishing to enter into a debate on the meaning of research, it seems important to remind ourselves that good teachers have always been researchers (Dunkin, 1994). The quality of the content of what is taught is reliant on the vigilance of the lecturer as a scholar. Arguably, university teaching is meant to be at the forefront of change, and promotion of critical thinking on existing ideas is the way in which change can be guided.

To this end, in what can be seen as a healthy element within Australian universities, we have recently witnessed an increasingly widespread use of "action research" (Kemmis & McTaggart, 1988; Zuber-Skerritt, 1992) as a technique for providing feedback on teaching and evaluating new approaches. Usually reliant on group activity, the action research model is based on four stages of reflecting, planning, implementing the plan, and evaluating progress in a spiral approach that is ongoing and targeted toward a series of related goals (see Figure 2).

Figure 2
Action Research Spiral

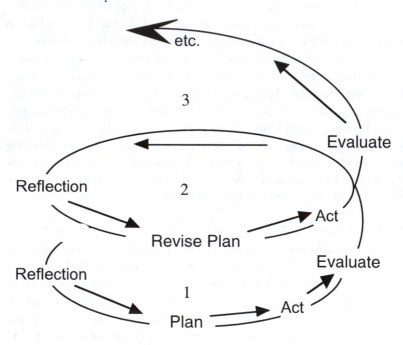

The action research process, however, works equally well with individuals wishing to examine their own teaching, perhaps with the outside advice of a colleague as a peer adviser or critical friend. In fact, in many of the graduate programs in the field of tertiary teaching, action research forms an integral part of the teaching approach. The notion of being a participant observer sits well with academics who recognize the value of being able to measure change. Furthermore, in purely pragmatic terms action research has convincing strengths as an accountability measure. The requirement to make explicit one's teaching skills and achievements means that lecturers who can demonstrate their care and concern for self-improvement are at an advantage during annual reviews.

Most Australian universities in the late 1990's have elaborate appraisal or evaluation procedures for tertiary teaching and staff performance. Data from action research activities are constructive for these purposes and signal personal interest in the evaluation of teaching that is likely to lead to enhanced productivity. The separate agendas of academics and administrators are thus satisfied. University academics can shape their teaching goals in these processes and presumably justify claims to the superiority of performance as the benchmark.

Summary of Conceptual Observations on Teaching and Learning
Discussion about university teaching in the late 1990's requires careful analysis of current realities. In truth, the amount of change, and numbers of agencies who lay claim to legitimate voices regarding the change, are somewhat overwhelming. Observers who strive for a coherent understanding of what is happening in the global arena of university teaching need some structural framework to interpret and respond to the forces of change. In this regard it is important to recall some fundamentals of good teaching—good teachers promote learning and universities are places of learning. Any debate about teaching must be concerned with the impact of change on the realities of learners and their learning. Accommodating the needs of learners then must be the challenge for university, government, professional, and wider community agendas. Sadly, the strength of this conviction is certainly under threat as the following overview of tensions and dilemmas indicates.

DILEMMAS FOR UNIVERSITY TEACHING

For whom does the university exist? In the past this may have been a simple question to answer. Moving towards the twenty-first century the question becomes different according to personal perspective. Governments, administrators, academics, students, and the community all have views and are not always in harmony. Governments, it seems, fluctuate between further cost-cutting to education—which affects the general skill level of the population—or maintaining high levels of spending on education. In Australia, the recent 1996 federal budget introduced further increases in entry fees for university courses at the same time as a decrease in real funding support. The issue of students fees or HECS (Higher Education Contribution System) is not new in Australia, although other countries, particularly in the European Union, seem to have so far avoided shifting much of the burden of paying for higher education onto their students.

However, there is little doubt that policy decisions which adopt a 'user pays' approach have significant effects on universities and their student populations. First, access is affected—as the personal cost for university tuition is raised, the social ramifications of who is prepared to pay generally impacts most on lower income families (Chapman, 1996; Winefield et al., 1993). In fact, recent figures in Australia suggest a decline in interest in university education, with fewer applicants for placement. Second, this trend of declining applicants often gives governments justification for restructuring funding levels. In turn, this has an impact on staffing levels, class sizes, and teaching arrangements. Thus, university administrators find themselves caught between external policy decisions and internal arrangements that lead to pressures for doing more with less, while striving to appease the obvious concerns of academics, students, and the broader community. Maintaining core programs for major government agencies such as teacher education and nursing has to be weighed against entrepreneurial research and teaching activities as well as issues of social justice, community, civic and cultural needs.

So the dilemmas are many and largely intertwined. As a means of understanding more about how these relate to the accountability issues of teaching in universities some purpose is served in looking more closely at a few of the tensions. They are: traditional perspectives amid current realities, vocational trends versus academic approaches to policy decisions, the impact of 'home shopping' via the Internet, and managerialism in decision making. Following this, a case study related to university teaching is presented, in order to illustrate how many of these tensions play out in one Australian mid-size (total enrollment approximately 12,000) university.

Tradition versus Current Realities
As university employers seek ways to respond to government calls for accountability on spending, university academics find themselves being required to spend more and more time filling in forms for audits of research and teaching. It is no longer sufficient to appear successful—near and far you now have to 'prove' this. For the highly self-motivated teaching and researching academic there is often the cry that such requests are a waste of time, an intrusion into one's time which could otherwise be spent on more productive tasks that could bring honor and funds to the university. Herein

lies the dilemma in current realities. Traditionally academics have been blessed with a great deal of freedom and could be regarded in many ways as being self-employed. They have been largely 'free' to choose the content and mode of delivery of their courses as well as the assessment tools. Research programs have been self-generated or collaborative ventures with colleagues and research students and most often involve external funding or competitive grants. In addition, academics have been free to comment on social policy and involve themselves in community activities related to personal interest and expertise. Within this structure teaching has had a relatively low profile when compared with research, and academics have not been required to undergo any teacher training prior to taking up their academic appointments (Gibbs, 1996; Ramsden et al., 1995).

In general, universities have been largely self-governing, protected institutions with autonomous structures that have enabled the community of scholars to make their own decisions (Treunen, 1996). Now they, like all publicly funded institutions, have to compete for their share of the public purse and that means providing evidence to support a genuine case for maintenance of funding levels. For academics protected under old traditions of academic freedom, this has led to legal debates over what constitutes intellectual property, contract employment rather then tenured placement, and enterprise bargaining amid new industrial/employer relationships (Spearritt & Thomas, 1996).

As a direct result of the changes to the funding rules Australian universities have introduced a series of evaluation instruments to assess the quality of teaching and service delivery. These vary markedly from campus to campus. Some combine qualitative and quantitative instruments while others rely almost exclusively on quantitative data. For example at the University of South Australia, with over 30,000 students, a well-documented statement on the evaluation of teaching and learning (Center for University Teaching and Learning, University of South Australia, 1994) supports the need for both kinds of data. It is heartening that this document emphasizes the need to value teaching as well as to evaluate teaching. As stated, "Evaluation of teaching entails a great deal more than conducting and analyzing student evaluation questionnaires" (p. 57). The trend of many Australian universities towards the use of (usually five-point) Likert-type scales for summative ratings is argued as placing too much faith in the 'efficacy' (p. 73) of such ratings and denying the complexity of student cohorts. The need to be reductionist in order to provide figures for bureaucrats can be very costly in human terms and fail in the endeavor to reach better standards. Such criticisms recognize the importance of building into questionnaires and other forms of feedback a genuine commitment to diagnostic or formative assessment, with the specific purpose of assisting the improvement of teaching rather than making judgements for an external and often excessively threatening audience. Among the many problems associated with standardized questionnaires are their validity across a range of teaching areas as well as the ways in which they are interpreted. For instance, there is significant criticism among academics regarding the tendency to treat all items equally regardless of discipline. The pattern is for all items to be scored then the summative award given, thus ignoring any possible internal imbalance of items.

Ironically, it is the reliability and validity of these questionnaires that raise much skepticism among academics, including those whose discipline encourages positivist empiricism. As the case study described later in the chapter shows, this can have its positive side and can lead to constructive learning within an academic community, albeit at a cost.

In addition to the requirement of supplying data regarding the effectiveness of university teaching, another dimension to these accountability pressures is the inevitable need to curb expenditure on academic salaries. Most Australian universities have experienced a shift in employment conditions towards contracts and away from tenured positions. Despite the lifting of the compulsory retirement age, many 'aging' and senior academics have felt pressure to take retirement packages. A more ruthless approach has been to make positions redundant. The trend is towards the appointment of junior academics for contracts, usually of three to five years. Thus, as the working conditions of teaching staff change, learning environments and teaching programs are changed. Many observers argue that it is a good thing for students to be introduced to the 'fresh' approaches of early career academics. Others see difficulties, especially related to levels of experience and confidence to express opinions in a system where personal futures are rather uncertain and a great deal of energy needs to be invested in building a curriculum vitae and applying for the next contract.

Another approach taken by academic departments, themselves squeezed for funds, is to appoint increasing numbers of part-time, casual staff. This strategy has the advantages of significant cost savings as well as releasing full-time senior academics to pursue entrepreneurial activities and research commitments. However, again there are grave concerns expressed regarding the quality of learning and the continuity and coherence of programs. Where students experience a proclivity toward 'outsiders' as teachers there is little opportunity for the pastoral care and counseling dimensions which have traditionally been seen as part of the role of teachers.

In brief, the certainties of the teaching and learning environments that enabled lecturers in the past to develop their personal following and culture are gone. Changed employment conditions and moves towards employing casual, short term contract staff create new tensions and seem to place emphasis on outcomes rather than the pleasure of the journey within a community of scholars.

Vocational versus Academic Teaching

One of the first moves towards rationalization of higher education in the United Kingdom and Australia was to amalgamate institutions. Both countries have chosen to include former institutes of technology in their higher education policy plans, such as the polytechnics in the United Kingdom and the Colleges of Advanced Education in Australia. A similar process is currently taking place in New Zealand. For traditional universities this has been viewed as a further erosion of the fabric of academe, where emphasis on scholarly pursuits, with time to 'read' in your chosen discipline, is competing with vocational programs that have explicit links to industry and training. However, taking a more detached view, there is some evidence to suggest that the move has enabled the best of both educational environments to flow between the various institutions. The move brings a flexibility to recognized teaching that has not existed previously. Wider opportunities exist for students with the imprimatur of university status of what was previously accessible generally only to elite scholars. And, for teaching staff in polytechnics there have been incentive programs to upgrade qualifications and broaden their responsibilities within the research arena. In the latter, a common result has been a flow of rather lucrative grants from industry as the obvious partner in many of the traditional teaching programs associated with vocational education. Hence, for students and staff there have been benefits from better relations with the world of work.

Part of the history of vocational teaching is set in a political framework aimed at rationalization and economies of scale within the higher education sector—and particularly with adult education (Burns, 1995). In the United Kingdom, the United States, Australia and New Zealand, especially in training programs, recognition of prior learning has become an important issue, with pressure from governments to see the rules articulated with general education in schools and other centers of higher education, including universities. In these countries pressure from employers has led to legislation in favor of standardizing teaching and learning outcomes in the form of competency based standards. These standards contain similar statements (Borthwick, 1993) as illustrated by the following list of "Key Competencies" adopted in Australia and described in the Mayer Committee Report (1992):

- Collecting, analyzing and organizing information
- Communicating ideas and information
- Planning and organizing activities
- Working with others and in teams
- Using mathematical ideas and techniques
- Solving problems
- Using technology

The Key Competencies have become the basis for curriculum reforms in vocational education. This policy seeks to ensure the easy passage from one program to another through a process of credit transfer (National Board of Employment, Education and Training, 1994). Where lifelong learning is the espoused belief of policy makers, such recognition of prior learning is integral to a well-structured set of options in the education agenda of the country. The political agenda behind this policy is clearly related to a drive for more accountability in higher education.

The integration of the vocational system with a traditional educational environment is not so simple. For example, Australian universities are experiencing strong pressure from outside sources to adopt a similar competency based approach to teaching and thus provide easy access for movement between universities and colleges of technical and further education. But the price in adopting this vocationalism in universities is high. Polytechnics exist primarily for training purposes and thus their programs have explicit learning outcomes that are standardized throughout the country. A regulated environment of standardization causes tensions in research universities which, quite apart from their separate identities, are communities that traditionally emphasize individualism in programs and learning outcomes. The argument being used against similar moves for universities is that an academic education was never meant to be articulated in terms of performance criteria as implied in statements of outcomes or standards. Knowledge is not easily defined in scholarly terms and the relationship to deeper levels of understanding is beyond our ability to anticipate. As well, the notion that a curriculum could be standardized across institutions and within similar academic programs seems contrary to all beliefs regarding the content of teaching in universities. Many academics shudder at the prospect of externally driven standards for their courses, arguing that the country needs more 'clever' people. Arguably, clever people do not emerge easily from teaching environments where there is little room for individual freedom of expression, and outcomes are predetermined. Here lies the dilemma. Society needs creative, innovative theorists who can generate new ways of viewing issues and develop the prototypes for our global future. But so does society need practitioners who can guarantee skills and competencies in a highly complex technologically focused world.

Despite these concerns the polytechnics have exported some of the thinking regarding standards to universities, and professional programs like nursing have sought to adopt performance-linked courses. They illustrate the diversity of universities in the late 1990's, and, far from threatening the traditions, can be viewed as complementing the options available. The fact that there are now several kinds of universities is a reality that should not be threatening. Universities with vocational and professional orientations seem to have a place in juxtaposition with academic programs. That being the case, there is need to explore further the relationship between the various programs and seek ways to provide for movement of student enrolments.

So, while the relationship of vocational and academic education is in its infancy, with many unresolved dilemmas related to standards or benchmarks for external comparisons, there are opportunities for innovative thinking and teaching. Perhaps this relationship is the basis of a new paradigm for university teaching in the twenty-first century.

'Home Shopping' versus Traditional Delivery

The implosion of knowledge that has led students to particular centers of learning since medieval times is now viewed by many as an anachronistic and a luxurious way of learning which few can sustain or afford in the postmodern era. While prestigious addresses with historically significant bricks and mortar are likely to maintain their attraction for learning, there is no doubt that accessibility to courses—particularly via the Internet and World Wide Web sites—has helped to internationalize even the most traditional institutions. Boundaries and cloistered walls that enshrine learning are outmoded, and frontiers are possible wherever networks exist for students, staff, and places of learning to link together. In the late 1990's the implosion that led to cities of past social structures (Mumford, 1961) is being replaced by the explosion of knowledge availability that leads to the virtual city or landscape of cyberspace. In fact, in spatial terms, the delivery of teaching has become multi-dimensional, with traditional lecture theatres and tutorial rooms alongside distance packaging, video-conferencing, on-line library catalogues, electronic publications and e-mail networks all presenting new options for learners. The 'place' of learning can be almost anywhere, and particularly where it is convenient for the student. A home computer, modem, fax machine and telephone line can be sufficient means of access to comprehensive university teaching programs. The world of work has entered a different paradigm where communication skills rely on software programs and on-line information. Face-to-face contact is not so important as step by step decision-making via well-documented support with online materials.

This option is attractive for many learners who have found it is not so easy to attend lectures at particular times in particular places. Clashes with the demands of much needed part-time and full-time employment as well as child care responsibilities can be eased when learning access is flexible for the learner. Furthermore, the provision of networked learning means that learners can choose from a wider smorgasbord of offerings and from universities physically located near and far. In post-graduate programs especially, it is not uncommon to have a 'class' of students scattered all over the world.

Critics of this approach generally raise the question of interpersonal relationships and the importance for learners to have face-to-face contact with each other and their teacher. But the reality seems to be that fewer people in a physical setting can produce more discussion of better quality and achieve goals more efficiently. For managers, not surprisingly, this provides an easy and attractive solution for building more efficient systems. So what is the absolute or optimum learning environment? Can we judge the advantages and disadvantages of approaches before monitoring the processes over time? As an educator and observer of teaching practices in a variety of teaching and learning settings in schools and higher education in several countries it has often seemed to me that classrooms or lecture theatres can assume a life of their own that isolates the learning from the real world. In Socratic dialogue the quality of the dialectic is all important for the learning process between teacher and learner. No reference exists to buildings or designer spaces for this process. The 'place' could be anywhere, as Dewey (1916) reminds us when emphasizing the importance of acknowledging the quality of experiential learning from everyday contexts not associated with formal learning. 'To experience' in the formal sense is not necessarily 'to know', for as T.S. Eliot stated, it may be a case of "we had the experience but not the meaning." Classrooms in the traditional forms are but one option for teaching and learning to take place. Perhaps, ironically, the end of the twentieth century seems to be bringing us back to a review of fundamentals of what it is that is at the core of effective teaching and learning relationships. The quality of the exchanges should not be dependent on place.

Early research suggests that the power of the Internet is such that it is aiding the motivation of learners. Of course, one can question what it is that people are attracted to when 'surfing the net', and maybe it is not necessarily the kind of information that is prescribed in program curricula. But there is an attraction to this new medium that has the potential to match or exceed any prior invention including the advent of the press and mass communication by radio, telephone and television.

The interactivity of the medium has implicit interpersonal protocols and skills which if dealt with intelligently could surpass the traditional modes of learning in a number of ways with much wider access to ideas. For this development of a technological society, the old paradigms are inadequate (Laurillard, 1993). A new mindset needs to be fostered so that teachers and learners can collaborate in pursuing the benefits of the technologies. In Australia, close to one in two households have personal computers (1996 estimates). Home accessibility to networks means that the shopping process is already part of the emerging online community culture. And, as market researchers confirm, all smart shoppers look around before buying. Thus, universities have another benchmark to reach. That is, the approval rating of potential clients or students who perhaps for the first time have diversified choices regarding who will provide their education. This is a challenge that university teaching can hardly avoid. In times of fiscal constraints, any decrease in public funds means that enrollments need to be pursued from all possible sources. Building a reputation as a home learning provider is one way to find new revenue sources in what is a highly competitive market. However, within this arena a new benchmark is developing for measuring successful university teaching.

Managerialism versus Collegiality in Australian Universities
Universities are often described as closed social systems. As a community of scholars who have largely managed their own affairs with the benign benevolence of funding sources, universities have long enjoyed privileges and been protected from the hurly-burly of the commercial world of big business. The culture within has respected the equal rights of academics, with the provision of democratic processes that have enabled them to have a voice in policy decisions of the university—until recently. Today's institutions have turned away from this approach, as larger universities adopt increased managerial infrastructures that include human resources and elaborate data systems.

The inevitable shift in direct access to funds within universities away from the academics themselves has led to a division of power that brings disquiet and concern for academic staff as teachers and researchers. Academic staff feel disenfranchised by what they view as a transfer of decision making to managerial staff who are removed from their worlds and deal in rationalities that do not fit often with the complexities of academic life. Managerial or 'top-down' decision making has the advantage of satisfying the immediate needs of bureaucracies and supplying the necessary data for accountability purposes. However, such managerial practices conflict with the culture of collegial decision making that characterizes the traditional value systems of universities (Moses, 1995). The traditional lines of decision making in universities are based on structures that do not adjust easily to the new style.

Part of the existing problem within Australian universities, as Ingrid Moses (1995) sees it, is the neglect of administrators and managers to explain the value system of manageralism and to reconcile differences with the traditional system of collegiality. She states: "As such there is no shared discourse, the very legitimate attempts to make academic staff more accountable towards their students, towards each other, the institutions, and the public are discredited" (p.13). What has happened is a tendency for the agenda set by the government to be "slavishly and literally" (p.15) followed with little regard to the tensions and trends within the higher education system. Her view is that where this trend is permitted to flow without checks and balances, a "public servant mentality" is likely to evolve which may lead to "reactive curricula which prepare students for immediate employment but not for taking up leadership positions in society or showing the flexibility they need in a fast changing environment" (p.14).

This paints a somewhat depressing picture, but one balanced by the view that amid all these changes university academics retain confidence that their environment allows freedom to determine course content and that opportunities exist to apply for competitive funds to pursue personal goals in teaching and research. Hence, lost power in one sense encourages the creative mind of the academic to seek personal satisfaction where doors remain open. As Moses states: "Even though academic staff feel alienated from their institutions' administration, they do not feel disenfranchised in their academic work" (1995: 14). And, given the gathering of intelligent minds within the system, it can be assumed that academics will continue to take lateral thinking approaches to maintain the integrity of their positions and their personal power to determine their own futures.

Herein lies the opportunity for change within the university system.

Those who have studied university decision making maintain that when facing change academics like to accommodate the pressures in their own ways (Robertson & Gaite, 1996). Consequently, a logical response to external agendas is to translate the needs to an acceptable internal agenda or one which has ownership by both academics and managers (Fullan, 1991). Where there remains confidence within the system and the top-down effects have avoided robotic responses there is hope of bottom-up solutions that reflect the culture and values of the institution. Such outcomes require new dialogues where initiatives of academic staff and administrative staff can be seen to be and indeed do operate as complementary.

One advantage that Australian universities have is a system where the vice-chancellor or outside voice for the institution is the most senior academic on each campus. The collective group of vice-chancellors have their own national committee and can (and largely do) provide a powerful lobby group for the system—one that is generally listened to by governments and ministers in charge. And, while the role is one of negotiation on behalf of their respective universities with government and policy makers, there is a feeling by academics that some control of the changes can be maintained while the appointment exists under the present terms. Accepting that the role also carries with it responsibility for implementing external demands the vice chancellor is seen by the optimists as a sympathetic voice for their concerns. In fact, as reflected in the case study described below, there is evidence of the power that vice chancellors can have to implement a vision that reflects the needs of a university striving to compete in the post modern era.

The case study shows that there are a range of strategies to deal with current and projected realities that have come from the 'bottom' and gathered momentum with the recognition of their value and assistance to the wider agendas. While the driving force behind these responses can be traced to collegial support groups there have been co-operative responses from senior administrators contributing to a balanced integration of external agendas with internal decision-making based on collaboration through formal committees and informal networks.

A CASE STUDY OF CHANGE IN AN AUSTRALIAN UNIVERSITY
Evaluation of Teaching and Learning

In 1992, faced with the government's decision to audit Australian universities and link funding to ranked outcomes, the response of one mid-size university was to introduce a 'quick fix' solution to an apparent lack of data on teaching. A standardized evaluation of teaching and learning instrument known as SETL was introduced and academics were encouraged to use this with their undergraduate teaching. Staff were told that the instrument was to provide 'formative' assessment of their teaching. It was meant to be non-threatening. However, academic staff did feel threatened, and history will show that they were justified, as the results of the SETL instrument have evolved as a key benchmark of teaching for tenure and promotions procedures and the allocation of competitive grant moneys for teaching. Far from formative assessment for the development of teaching and learning, the reality of SETL has been summative assessment, as comparative data are provided for ranking and cross-department tables.

In a large university this management decision may have been catastrophic for academics. Fortunately, in a small university the channels of communication enable faster responses. While the instrument provided quick quantifiable data on teaching, it failed to recognize diversity and the complexities of teaching and learning environments. It was, in fact, a contradiction in policy to the reality of the teaching and learning culture. On the one hand, the government was demanding (and still is) to see structures and evidence from these. On the other, academics were (and still are) striving to meet the changing needs of learners, to be responsive to the technological age with flexible delivery, and valuing diversity rather than uniformity. Fortunately for this university all academics regardless of seniority were affected, from heads of department to untenured junior staff. The agenda of the Academic Senate, the powerful decision making body on academic matters, soon became a forum for debate on the topic, and the resultant formation of the Teaching Committee has lead to a gradual shift from full-scale top-down managerial decisions on teaching to a process embedded in dialogue between colleagues. For instance, there has been the gradual acceptance of the value of some forms of qualitative data as legitimate for the evaluation of teaching. Hence, as a catalyst, the turbulence created by the introduction of the SETL instrument has had on balance a number of positive outcomes. There is now a forum for discussing issues related to teaching with agendas that can be processed from diverse sources, including academic staff and senior administrators.

The Role of the Teaching Committee
Since its beginnings in 1994, the expanding role of the Teaching Committee has reflected a cultural change among academic staff towards valuing teaching. With this renewed interest a growing acceptance has evolved that teaching as well as research can be improved, and that what constitutes qual-

ity in teaching should not be exclusively a private agenda. There is in fact a place for peer review. Partly, the Teaching Committee fulfills that role. As a sub-committee of Academic Senate, with appointed and elected members of academic staff and students, the Teaching Committee is responsible for decisions regarding a number of awards. All are based on criteria developed by the Teaching Committee and approved by Academic Senate. The highest level of these awards are Teaching Excellence Awards with essential criteria including:

- high level of interest and enthusiasm in undertaking teaching and promoting student learning.
- responsiveness to assess student learning and to provide students with worthwhile feedback.
- ability to stimulate curiosity and independent learning in all students and creative work in advanced students.
- evidence of leadership and innovation in teaching, including the enhancement of teaching quality in colleagues.

This prestigious award is widely accepted as an automatic benchmark for promotion. To a lesser extent this also applies to the Teaching Merit Awards which rely heavily on student and peer nomination. In a way, these awards have stimulated reflection on teaching and provided guidelines to staff about accepted 'best practice' in teaching based on current literature and research. For all faculty these award programs offer a source of constructive advice about teaching that can be used in appraisal processes and annual reviews. And for those who receive the awards there is the strong possibility of positive career path development. Overall, the awards have acted as a stimulant for rejuvenated thinking on teaching and learning.

In 1996 the Teaching Committee received a greater level of support with its elevation to the same status (in financial terms) as the university's Research Committee. With its own funding now guaranteed from the central pool of university funds, it has the resources to create changes and follow these through. The vision for this increased role comes from the Vice Chancellor's belief that a small university needs to focus its energies on quality in teaching outcomes and consolidate its position as a center of teaching and learning excellence. To this end a great deal of energy has been spent on encouraging dialogue between academics and the Vice Chancellor with the aim of clarifying needs and building partnerships in the restructuring processes that have a viable base for the future. Thus, the leadership shown in the university studied has enabled the 'bottom-up' responses of committed academics to have a legitimate place or forum to deliver requests for change.

The Role of Staff Development

Coincidentally, as the university studied sought ways to benchmark teaching outcomes to supply data to external funding sources, academic staff were given an opportunity to engage in teaching and learning professional development workshops. A proposal put forward by academic staff in the Faculty of Education to offer graduate course content in the areas of Adult Learning and Tertiary Teaching to colleagues in other departments was timely and encouraged. This proposal had several positive attributes including:

- It met the needs of senior administrators, including heads of departments, to provide advice on how to improve existing teaching practices, which in turn would contribute to better results in the standardized evaluation. Thus, the university's central funding, planning and policy committee was prepared to risk money to support the project.
- Working academic staff were the proposers of the suggested workshops. Unlike staff development officers they could legitimately claim to understand the problems facing teaching academics. They too faced the challenge of the standardized instrument and knew from day to day working experience what it was like to experience funding cuts that result in larger class sizes and fewer support staff. More than act as facilitators, the workshop leaders could genuinely empathise with staff problems. Colleagues were working with colleagues. This was and has continued to be a powerful factor in the ongoing success of this program.
- Cross-department exchange could focus thinking on teaching and learning rather than discipline-specific content. As the program has proceeded there has been a widening acceptance that what constitutes good teaching is transferable across cognate areas. The contexts change but the principles related to the learner regarding motivation, building bridges to understanding, learning styles and assessment and evaluation have validity regardless of specific knowledge and skills base. Many staff located in a diverse range of departments across the university were already of this opinion but were often lone voices. The workshops provided the opportunity for reflection on their teaching practices in a supportive environment away from other agendas.

Hence, goodwill for the proposal existed from diverse quarters. It was an acceptable response to a perceived dilemma and one that was owned by academic staff. It was not imposed.

The First Group—1994: An Important Beginning
All academic staff were invited to participate in planned workshops timed to coincide with the mid-semester break. Two groups of staff were identified and eight-day programs spread over two weeks were arranged. In hindsight this was too long, but from another perspective the time was invaluable for the ongoing friendships and networks that have resulted.

Forty-five academic staff participated, including four heads of department, and with experiences ranging from twenty years plus in university teaching environments to beginning teachers. They represented departments as diverse as agriculture, mathematics, nursing, psychology, law, zoology, computing, education, aquaculture, chemistry and medicine.

The program provided a skeletal structure, with content on a range of teaching and learning issues. However, the strong focus was on enabling participants to share experiences regardless of background and position. The process was important for generating a group dynamic that has continued to flourish in a number of strengthening ways. In essence the workshops promoted a camaraderie and re-affirmed the importance of collegial decision making. Outcomes have included:
- e-mail networks for continuing the exchanges of ideas.
- follow-up meetings to re-affirm support, celebrate successes and act as a forum to reflect, evaluate and plan new strategies.
- department-based activities including discussion groups, support for grant applications and staff development activities.
- peer support for colleagues through clinical supervision and review of existing practices.
- mentoring of early career staff.
- a voice to channel concerns from the 'bottom' to the 'top'.
- an avenue to gain accredited qualifications in approved postgraduate courses on teaching. (Four academic staff have pursued this for formal accreditation.)

In general the initial 'groups' were regarded as an outstanding success. The positive feedback to senior administrators was ample justification for the expenditure. The program met the needs of staff and provided tangible evidence of the university's support for staff development and its commitment to improvements in the quality of teaching and learning outcomes. All agendas appeared to be met from this initiative primarily because it developed within the existing value systems. In support of Moses' view (1995) the culture accommodated the process.

Continuing Success since 1994

Similar programs were run in 1995 and 1996 with parallel courses in special interest areas. Apart from the extended workshops, now pruned to four days with a one day follow-up, the most popular other courses have focused on the use of the internet for teaching purposes. At the time of this writing approximately 200 staff have participated in these activities and the 1997 program is in the planning stages.

Faculty of Education academic teaching staff remain as the organizers, thus adhering to the view that practicing teachers who are themselves experiencing the demands of new accountability measures have the highest credibility among colleagues in other departments. There is genuine empathy for the stress that is felt, which is tempered by knowing and understanding the teaching and learning processes and being able to translate this knowledge to colleagues. As well as assisting in this unscrambling of external demands, the building of networks and supporting personal endeavors is central in the program design. Careful attention is given to maintain relevancy in content so that it reflects changing contexts and, where possible, anticipates new trends and directions. In the 1995 and 1996 programs emphasis has been given to providing skills with the application of the World Wide Web to teaching and learning environments. This comes from recognizing that the Internet is a potent educational tool for the future, and there is urgency to place much more emphasis on building curriculum frameworks that accommodate rapidly changing knowledge bases and flexible delivery programs.

Senior Administrators' Views

From *ad hoc* funding arrangements in 1994-95, the tertiary teaching workshops have gradually received formal status and are now part of the annual budget. Any doubts that may have existed initially have been outweighed by the widening body of support. In essence, the culture within the academic community has been translated into policy. The policy implementation serves as an apt conclusion for this bottom-up initiative for change. It sits in harmony with the Teaching Committee's objectives and contributes to official rhetoric on teaching and learning. What is also appealing about this policy is that it supports content that has a theoretical foundation in educational principles of constructivism in teaching and learning. The bridge metaphor presented in Figure 1 is being translated into practice.

Participants' Views

Late in 1995 the workshop leaders surveyed forty-five previous workshop participants for their views on personal experiences and advice for future directions. The open-ended questionnaire was distributed by electronic mail prior to Christmas at a time when staff have holidays. Nevertheless, twenty responses were received, all of which were positive reflections on the impact of the workshops they attended. As one respondent noted "the tertiary teaching workshop is a vital tool in transforming teaching in this university. It invigorates the tired and disillusioned and it helps those who want to start the journey towards quality teaching."

In brief, the workshops continue to provide the stimulus for staff to focus on common concerns regarding teaching. They enable teaching academics to seek answers beyond the discipline specific context of their everyday working environments in a supportive and collaborative setting of mutual respect and interest. Perhaps some find affirmation for existing practices, but for many the insights gained from the extended workshop time with colleagues has provided a new and challenging purpose for their work. And, given the diversity of skills and creative thinking of individuals it is not surprising that the group dynamics have generated continuing activity beyond the initial workshops.

Beyond the Workshops

At the instigation of four 'graduates' of the 1995 workshops a series of 'brown bag' meetings were commenced early in 1996. 'Brown bag' meetings are informal lunch gatherings where it is common practice to bring your own lunch thus not breaking into the formal time of other commitments. The four academic staff involved in organizing these meetings represent disciplines in law, philosophy, nursing and zoology. All are very experienced lecturers who have felt rejuvenated, as one describes the feeling, and excited about the prospect of working to implement new practices in teaching and learning in their departments. At the same time interest was triggered by personal contexts. For example, when a lecturer with a Ph.D. in Zoology was asked to reflect on the value of the workshops she remarked that for the first time she was provoked to think about learning in the context of teaching. Together this small group have become advocates of reflective teaching practice. Through e-mail networks they have quickly broadened their membership to approximately twelve 'regulars' with a further ten or so staff who attend when other commitments permit. Their meetings are held irregularly but usually bi-monthly in different departments around the campus. Participants welcome the opportunity of meeting in new locations and finding out about colleagues' environments in their university. An agenda is set and interested staff are asked to do two things for each meeting. First, contribute to the theme for the meeting either with resources, personal experience, or supportive discussion. Second, they are asked to bring to the group's attention a problem they are facing in their teaching. The latter is meant to encourage support for sharing amid a non-threatening and trusted group of colleagues.

The view by participants in this support group for university teaching is that is fulfills their expectations. It is encouraging that the group is becoming known as a reference group for administrators to consult with over teaching issues. On its agenda for future activities is the establishment of a formal identity with a Web page and forum for exchange of ideas with colleagues in other universities. The use of electronic publication is also a goal. The group has adopted the pragmatic view that to succeed, roles of research and teaching need to be rationalized. One way of achieving both needs is to publish papers on teaching activities. The group is acting as a peer support mechanism for achieving this end.

DISCUSSION

The staff development workshops conducted in this Australian university and the support group for university teaching staff are powerful examples of 'bottom-up' responses to external agendas. It is clear that staff who participate enjoy the interaction and are not so daunted by the 'top-down' decisions described earlier, perhaps because of the mutual support they find. They model well the principles of co-operative learning. Their pursuits also model the way in which leadership by the educational decision makers of course planning—the teachers themselves—can be restored in the debate. In the context of current realities including the growing vocationalsim, interactive media and global learning environments change is inevitable and inappropriate solutions are likely. However, as the case study has shown, the impact can be eased where academic staff play an active role and are prepared to speak with a collective voice. The quest for benchmarked performance in universities needs collaborative decision making with the views of all interested parties considered.

SUMMARY

At the beginning of this chapter questions were raised regarding who has (and who should have) control of practices in university teaching. The broadening need for accountability from governments—and more directly from university administrators—is noted along with their focus on outcomes and performance linked indicators. Most have their origins in notions from industry, including Benchmarking, Best Practice, and Total Quality Management. These paradigms do not sit well with traditional university teaching activities and are cause for a great deal of angst in the systems. In fact, in 1996, this resulted in Australian university communities combining to express their frustrations with a series of rolling strikes around the country. Attending these strikes were students, academic staff, and top administrators, including the committee of vice chancellors. Part of the frustration has been the apparent loss of franchise in the political decision-making that has always been part of the collegial culture of universities.

Amid this political struggle for a share of the public purse there is the reality of the forces towards globalization in teaching. With their access to the information super-highway, students are no longer dependent on the content supplied by their teachers and libraries. They can shop around to find which university offers the course they are looking for to best meet their needs. For universities this is a further reality of the essential need for new approaches to teaching and learning. Whatever is devised will need to rely on processes that complement rather than compete with the new technologies. Old habits need reviewing, and colleagues and administrators need support to take risks, try new approaches, and work collaboratively to make decisions.

As observers note, what is required is some translation of the external needs to internal cultures of universities. Preparing university students for the new century relies on decisions built from partnerships. The struggle to achieve this in Australian universities comes at a time of competing agendas, where too often top-down decisions dominate work practices and teaching environments. The solution lies in taking control of these external agendas and ensuring that the benchmarks used for the accountability procedures are valid, reliable, and a genuine reflection of current realities of students' learning environments. Translating external agendas into the internal structures both informal and formal, is the challenge we face. Where bottom-up decisions evolve, there is every likelihood of ongoing commitment regardless of the scope of external demands of benchmarking performance or any other quality control mechanisms. In fact, I have no doubt that many academics would welcome opportunities to share their expertise. Collegiality provides the energy to cope with rapid change and ensure the ongoing vitality of universities rather than a "withering on the vine."

REFERENCES

Berliner, D.C. (1994). Expertise: The wonder of exemplary performances. In J.N. Mangieri and C. Collins Block (Eds.). *Creating powerful thinking teachers and students: Diverse perspectives.* New York: Harcourt Brace, pp. 161-186.

Biggs, J. (1994). What are effective schools? Lessons from East and West. *The Australian Educational Researcher,* 21(1), 19-44.

Borthwick, A. (1993). Key competencies—uncovering the bridge between general and vocational. In C. Collins (Ed.), *Competencies: The competencies debate in Australian education and training.* Canberra: The Australian College of Education, pp. 21-34.

Burns, R. (1995). *The adult learner at work.* Sydney: Business and Professional Publishing.

Camp, R.C. (1989). *Benchmarking: The search for industry best practices that lead to superior performance.* Milwaukee: ASQC Quality Press.

Centre for University Teaching and Learning University of South Australia. (1994). *Guide to valuing and evaluating teaching in the University of South Australia.* Adelaide: The University of South Australia.

Chapman, B. (1996). The rationale for the Higher Education Scheme. *Australian Universities' Review,* 39(1), 43-50.

Collins, C. (Ed.). (1993). *Competencies: The competencies debate in Australian education and training.* Canberra: The Australian College of Education.

Dewey, J. (1916). *Democracy and education.* New York: The Macmillan Company.

Dunkin, M. (1994). Award winning university teachers' beliefs about teaching. *Higher Education Research and Development,* 13(1), 85-92.

Dunkin, M. (1995). Concepts of teaching and teaching excellence in higher education. *Higher Education Research and Development,* 14(1), 21-33.

Fullan, M.G. (1991). (2n Edn.). *The new meaning of educational change.* New York: Teachers' College Press.

Gibbs, G. (1996). Preparing university teachers: An international overview of practice and issues. Paper presented at the Twenty-first Improving University Teaching International Conference, Nottingham.

Kemmis, S. & McTaggart, R. (Eds.). (1988). *The action research planner.* Deakin University Press.

Lewis, R.G. & Smith, D.H. (1994). *Total quality in higher education.* Florida: St.Lucie Press.

Laurillard, D. (1993). *Rethinking university teaching.* London: Routledge.

Mayer, E. (1992). *Putting general education to work: The Key Competencies report.* Report to the Australian Education Council and Ministers for Vocational Education, Employment and Training, Melbourne.

McNair, C.J. & Lebfried, H.J. (1992). *Benchmarking: A tool for continuous improvement.* Essex Junction: Oliver Wright Publications, Inc.

Moses, I. (1995). Tensions and tendencies in the management of quality and autonomy in Australian higher Education. *The Australian Universities' Review,* 38(1), 16-20.

Mumford, L. (1961). *The city in history.* London: Penguin Books Limited.

National Board of Employment, Education and Training. (1994). *Credit transfer and the recognition of prior learning.* Canberra: Australian Government Publishing Service.

Ramsden, P. (1992). *Learning to teach in higher education.* London: Routledge.

Ramsden, P., Margetson, D., Martin, E. & Clarke, S. (1995). *Recognising and rewarding good teaching in Australian higher education.* Canberra: Australian Government Publishing Service.

Riley, K. & Nuttall, D. (Eds.). (1993). *Measuring quality: Educational indicators—United Kingdom and international perspectives.* London: The Falmer Press.

Robertson, M. & Gaite, J. (1996). Bottom-up responses to top-down decisions: Developing a teaching and learning culture. Paper presented at the Twenty-first Improving University Teaching International Conference, Nottingham.

Robson, R. (1995). Achieving world class performance through workplace change and best practice. *Unicorn,* 21(2), 13-23.

Schmeck, R.R. (Ed.). (1988). *Learning strategies and teaching styles.* New York: Plenum Press.

Spearritt, P. & Thomas, J. (1996). Academic intellectual property in a new technological and industrial context. *Australian Universities' Review,* 39(1), 29-33.

Stanley, G. & Reynolds, P. (1995). Performance indicators and quality review in Australian universities. *Higher Education Research and Development.* 14(2), 245-254.

Treunen, G. (1996). The changing state-university relationship: State involvement in academic industrial relations since the Murray Report. *Australian Universities' Review,* 39(1), 51-58.

Zuber-Skerritt, O. (1992). *Action research in higher education.* London: Kogan Page Limited.

Winefield, A., Tiggeman, M., Winefield, H.R. & Goldney, R.D. (1993). *Growing up with unemployment.* New York: Routledge.

CHAPTER 13

Work-Based Experience and Higher Professional Learning in British Universities

Terry Hyland

INTRODUCTION

This chapter seeks to explore issues related to the drive for competence-based education and professional training promoted by the National Council for Vocational Qualifications (NCVQ) in Britain. It is argued that while it is appropriate for higher education institutions to be concerned with vocational matters, current policy directions belie a dangerously shallow view of university education as merely job training. The intellectual and ideological vacuum created by the "industrialization of higher education" (Hyland, 1996a) leaves universities vulnerable to attack from all political sides. Higher education leaders must push for the widespread adoption of a conception of learning that incorporates both the needs of the labor market and economic regeneration as well as the need for moral and political responsibility.

BACKGROUND

The expansion of higher education in Britain and Europe over the last decade or so has entailed movement from an elite to a mass system of access to higher education (though, invariably institutions are being asked to fund increased access with minimal or zero increases in funding and resources (Titmus, Knoll & Wittpoth, 1993). This movement has been accompanied by a range of philosophical, organizational, curricular and pedagogic changes and developments (Barnett, 1990, 1994). Chief among such change factors has been the increasingly centralized role of state involvement in the determination of more and more aspects of education and general social life (Jenkins, 1995) both in Britain (Whitty, 1990) and across Western Europe (Moon, 1990). The evolution of the 'corporate state' (Ranson, 1994) and the transformation of public service culture—bringing with it growing governmental interference in pedagogy and curricula from school to university—

poses particular challenges and problems for professional teachers committed to the ideals of experiential learning (Griffin, 1992) and to a normative conception of education as the development of knowledge, skills and understanding (Peters, 1966).

Alongside the growth of centralized control of education, there has been a 'vocationalization' (Hyland, 1991) of the curriculum at all levels in line with the "growing clamor from industry for the graduates it employs to have more work-related skills" (Barnett, 1990, p. 158). Neave (1992) has noted the "strengthening of the vocational element in the higher education systems of Western Europe" (p. 23) resulting in a tension between "training in the mastery of techniques specifically geared to one precise occupation" and "general study and the acquisition of understanding" (pp. 5-6). Broadly similar trends towards a "more vocationally or professionally oriented conception of advanced learning" in the German education system have been discussed by Gellert & Rau (1992) and echoed in observations on higher education in France (Lamoure & Rontopoulou, 1992) and in Norway (Berg, 1992). Indeed, as Esland (1996) has observed, this 'globalization' of vocational trends can be seen to match the globalization of capital and industry in the current world economic climate.

HIGHER EDUCATION IN TRANSITION

All of these developments need to be placed within a context defined by what has been referred to as the 'identity crisis' (Avirim, 1992) of the modern university which, externally, "stems from growing pressures on the university to prove its pragmatic utility" and, internally, "from a lack of firm and shared belief within the university concerning the nature of its educational mission" (p. 183). Barnett (1990) sums this up in his account of the current "undermining of the value background of higher education" (p. 8). The idea is that contemporary higher education is being undermined epistemologically, through relativistic theories of knowledge and, sociologically, through the loss of academic freedom and autonomy as a result of the increasing influence of the state, industry and other agencies over what goes on in higher education institutions.

The vulnerability of universities in such an intellectual and ideological vacuum leaves higher education open to attack from all sides, perhaps especially from the "professional training lobby" working towards the "industrialization of higher education" (Hyland, 1996a) by means of competence-based education and training (CBET) strategies popularized through the work of the increasingly powerful National Council for Vocational Qualifications (NCVQ) in Britain. As Barnett (1990) correctly points out, there is the twofold danger that such developments "are likely to lead to the curriculum being dominated by technique" and that the "techniques in question are imported from the outside world and are imposed arbitrarily upon, and unconnected with, the curriculum" (p. 159). The preferred answer to this challenge is offered in the form of a reconstituted and 'emancipatory' concept of liberal education which—incorporating such features as critical perspectives, interdisciplinarity, open and self-directed learning—would seek to "neutralize the effects" (ibid., p. 203) of the forces currently threatening higher education.

The reality of such alleged threats and the nature and role of universities in modern (or post-modern) societies are, of course, highly contentious topics within the contemporary debate about the contested nature of higher education, and commentators such as Bloom (1988) and MacIntrye (1990) have offered highly original and perceptive diagnoses of the current malaise. Mendus (1992) has observed that an element common to all such accounts is some version of the 'myth of the fall'—the suggestion that there has been a "loss of integration in modern society" which is contrasted unfavorably with some prior era "when wholeness and coherence were the order of the day" (p. 177). In the process of challenging such a perspective Mendus observes that, although the new visions of higher education derive from a variety of different philosophical and political traditions (from neo-conservative to post-modernist), a unifying element is the general belief in the importance of fostering criticism and self-reflection. Prescribing a centrist position between Bloom's suggested return to the "great tradition" and MacIntyre's idea of a diversity of higher education institutions to mirror the contemporary plurality of values, Mendus argues (in an account of critical higher education practice similar to that offered by Barnett, 1994) that students should become "critical creators as well as critical discoverers" (ibid., p.182).

Such sentiments take us to the heart of the experiential tradition (Mezirow, 1990) and connect well with Kolb's (1993) conception of experientialism. This conception is centrally concerned with the activity of learning and with the need for "active experimentation at one extreme and reflective observation at the other," so that the learner "moves in varying degrees from actor to observer, and from specific involvement to general analytic detachment" (ibid., p.148). Such an account is also broadly similar to those offered by contemporary adult educators seeking to prescribe new visions for learning and development in what they regard as deeply troubled times. Collins (1991), for instance, has criticized the "technicist obsession" which characterizes much current adult education activity and recommends a return to an "emancipatory critical practice" and a "transformative pedagogy" which would allow teachers to "envisage themselves as intellectual-practitioners rather than technicians" (p.188). In a similar vein, Usher (1992) outlines a post-modern perspective on adult education which, remembering "its history as an oppositional discourse," can help us to "open ourselves, through critical dialogue, to the humanistic tradition" (pp. 212-13).

As a way of illustrating how the current challenges to higher education may be met through strategies drawn from this broad experiential tradition, I propose to examine developments within the field of higher professional education and development, particularly within the teacher education and health sectors.

THE VICISSITUDES OF PROFESSIONAL LIFE

Recent policy developments in the public sector have led to allegations of widespread "de-professionalization" (Chitty & Simon, 1993; Barton, et al., 1994) in teaching, health services, and related occupations as a result of centralized commitments to the ideologies of market forces and input/output efficiency and accountability. Russell (1994) is of the opinion that relations between the professions and central government are at their lowest ebb since the seventeenth century under Oliver Cromwell's rule, and Stronach (1995) observed recently that "professional life in Britain has developed a new vocabulary—innovation fatigue, early retirement, stress, overload and breaking point." Given all the recent 'policy hysteria' in the public sector, it is little wonder that large numbers of professionals now feel "overstretched and under-valued" (p. 9).

There are a number of ways in which professional studies and practice have been affected by recent policy developments. Firstly, the culture of public service professions in fields such as health, education and social work has been transformed through the gradual evolution, from the 1970s onwards, of the 'corporate state' characterized by pragmatism and technical rationality through which "production replaces consumption as the important preoccupation . . . while efficiency becomes the overriding priority above the previous social democratic goals of equality and social justice" (Ranson, 1994, p. 43). As Rustin (1994) has argued in relation to this transformation of the public service ethic:

> To manage a budget and to achieve the public service equivalent of profit has become the central concern of a whole stratum who previously thought of themselves as committed mainly to providing a public ser-

vice. Seducing and cajoling the public sector middle class into the embrace of the market has been a key objective of public service reforms (pp. 76-77).

Secondly, stemming from these radical shifts within the public sector, professional studies and education and training generally have been forced to change in order to accommodate what Elliott (1993) calls the 'social market' model according to which the "outcomes of professional learning are construed as quantifiable products which can be pre-specified in tangible and concrete form" (pp.16-17). A major vehicle for such change has been the competence-based education and training (CBET) strategy popularized through the work of the National Council for Vocational Qualifications (NCVQ) and now officially endorsed by and enshrined in Britain in Department for Education and Employment policy through national targets and funding regulations (Burke, 1995).

Although originally introduced with the limited purpose of accrediting work-based vocational skills, CBET has extended its remit well beyond this domain and now influences developments at all levels of education and training, including professional studies and higher education (Hyland, 1994a; Barnett, 1994). The NCVQ model of CBET is, in fact, highly suitable for effecting the de-professionalizing and marketizing changes referred to above. Its basic principle is that of "behaviorism with its implication that the significance of theoretical knowledge in training is a purely technical or instrumental one" (Elliott, 1993, p.17). CBET strategies offer a "production technology for commodifying professional learning for consumption" and also operate as an "ideological device for eliminating value issues from the domains of professional practice and thereby subordinating them to political forms of control" (ibid. p. 23,68). All such developments in bureaucratic rationality involve the key elements of efficiency, calculability, predictability, and control which have played a large part in the "McDonaldization of higher education" (Hartley, 1995) in Britain within the wider framework of the continuing rationalization of modern Western societies (Ritzer, 1993) in conjunction with, what Lyotard (1984) has called, the "mercantilization of knowledge" (p. 51).

Since, as I will be suggesting, it is precisely the epistemological and especially the ethical dimensions of professional theory and practice which are most distinctive of and indispensable to the continuous renewal and rational development of professionalism in education and other public service sectors, the impact of 'McDonaldization' and related de-professionalizing forces needs to be resisted vigorously by practitioners and educators working in these domains. Accompanying these recent changes has been the "return of the mentor" (Caldwell & Carter, 1993)—a renewed emphasis on the workplace as a principal site of professional learning—and it may be that the new models of work-based learning provide the most effective means of renewing professional values and commitment in the public services. I intend to explore the potential of work-based learning strategies for promoting a conception of "extended professionalism" which is "rooted in a certain ethically conditioned appreciation and sensitivity to the needs . . . of clients together with the informed wisdom and integrity to respond adequately to those needs" (Carr, 1994, p. 47).

COMPETENCE AND PROFESSIONAL PRACTICE

Apart from the shortcomings of CBET in terms of its conceptual and epistemological incoherence and reliance on discredited behaviorist learning theory (Hyland, 1994b), a number of critical studies have noted its reductionist approach to knowledge and values and its tendency to de-skill occupational roles (Callender, 1992; McHugh, Fuller & Lobley, 1993; Ashworth, 1992). Such weaknesses and limitations take on even greater significance when applied to higher level vocational and professional studies (Hodkinson & Issitt, 1995).

In spite of recent attempts to extend CBET way beyond its original remit to incorporate so-called "higher level skills" (Barnett, 1994; Hyland 1996b; Employment Department, 1995), there is a fundamental and glaring counter-intuitive aspect of an enterprise which seeks to upgrade vocational and professional studies by means of a CBET system of NVQs which its chief proponents claim "has nothing whatsoever to do with training or learning programs" (Fletcher, 1991, p. 26). If National Vocational Qualifications (NVQs) really are "independent of any specific course, program or mode of learning" (NCVQ, 1988, p.v) and "firmly rooted in the functions of employment . . . without imposing an educational model of how people learn or behave" (Jessup, 1991, p. 39), how can such a strategy contribute at all to the enhancement of any specifically educational endeavor or to the promotion of a learning society?

This puzzling feature of CBET may be dispelled by examining the vast gulf which exists between rhetoric and reality in this sphere. Whatever may be claimed about the independence of competence outcomes from learning programs, the actual implementation of CBET across a wide range of occupational sectors has resulted in a reduced curriculum (Raggatt, 1994), a loss of significant theoretical content (Smithers, 1993), a restriction of student-teacher interaction (Hyland, 1994c), and a de-skilling of work roles (Callender, 1992). All the evidence indicates that it is simply not feasible to try to separate means and ends, learning and assessment (Wolf, 1995) in such an arbitrary manner. Moreover, how can a behaviorist-inspired CBET system which is concerned almost exclusively with products possibly service the needs of professional studies characterized by an emphasis on processes, growth, and development?

Programs of professional development in further education (Kerry & Tollitt-Evans, 1992), higher education (Barnett, 1994), and the caring professions (Hodkinson & Issitt, 1995)—though employing a wide range of conceptual schemes and methodologies—tend to display a common distaste for technicist and behavioral models, preferring instead to found practice on ideas developed in the cognitive/humanistic tradition (Eraut, 1994). Although this experiential tradition is eclectic—drawing on the ideas of Dewey and Piaget as well as the critical theory of Habermas and Freire—it shares a set of common assumptions about learning summarized by Kolb (1993) as a "process whereby knowledge is created by the transformation of experience" (p.155). There is an overt and radical mismatch between such preferred modes of learning and behaviorist-inspired CBET approaches (Hyland, 1994c) captured perfectly in Kolb's observation that, "from the perspective of experiential learning, the tendency to define learning in terms of outcomes can become a definition of non-learning" and hence is "maladaptive" (op. cit., p.144). In a similar vein, Ashworth (1992) has argued that the mainstream "model of competence provides solutions to the specification of learning outcomes which are normally inappropriate to the description of human action or to the facilitation of the training of human beings" (p.16).

Mainstream CBET practices are, in fact, structurally incapable of furthering professional development beyond the level of collecting evidence to satisfy performance criteria (Ramsay, 1993). The main problem is that CBET systems really only value the achievement or rather the accreditation of competence, not its development and growth over time. As Chown & Last (1993) note in their critique of the applications of CBET models to post-school teacher education, the "model cannot acknowledge the growth of competence. It does not admit a change in competence which is not allied to a change in organizational function" (p. 21).

Although the concept of professionalism is bound to be something of a contested concept, certain key epistemological and ethical dimensions of practice are stressed in all the philosophical and psychological accounts of professionalism (Larson, 1977; Langford, 1978; Eraut, 1994). What is clear is that these distinctive features of professional work are seriously under valued if not overlooked completely in behaviorist CBET systems (Hyland, 1994a). In such approaches, knowledge belongs to "the realm of inputs rather than outputs" and "its introduction can only be justified if it is a necessary condition for generating the desired behavioral outcomes of learning" (Elliott, 1993, p.17). Similarly, the inter- and intra-relationships between professionals, their colleagues, and clients demand a high level of ethical and moral understanding that tends to be ignored in CBET systems, which either serve to neutralize practice or reduce values to mechanistic competencies. The obsession with collecting evidence to satisfy competence criteria is intensely individualistic and not able to accommodate the important aspects of teamwork and collegial collaboration in professional work (Ashworth, 1992, Chown & Last, 1993).

Moreover, such technicist approaches to education and training do not acknowledge the extent to which professional knowledge, skills, and values are a product of joint social action developed through engagement in a complex set of interwoven social transactions (Wertsch, 1991). As Carr's analysis vividly demonstrates, most problems in professional spheres such as teaching call for a "moral rather than a technical response," and practice needs to be characterized in terms of "virtues rather than skills." He explains that:

> To speak of a bad plumber, for example, is by and large to identify someone who does a technically poor repair job rather than (say) overcharges, whereas talk of an unsatisfactory lawyer or general practitioner is for the most part of someone who does not take proper time to understand his or her clients' needs in a proper spirit of care and concern . . . . Where concerns are professional, then, the emphasis is upon the ethically principled or moral quality of the response to the clients' needs (1994, pp. 47-48).

NEO-FORDISM, LEARNING AND COMPETENCE

Jessup (1991) claimed that the new model of teaching and learning based on competence outcomes is the only one capable of bringing about the "skills revolution" and "learning society" (pp. 95,98) required to increase economic competitiveness in the new post-industrial—or 'post-Fordist'—era. There is now widespread acceptance of this official line that employees of the future will require a range of "flexible" or "transferable skills" (Sieminski, 1993, Esland, 1996). Alternatively, following the critique of Finegold & Soskice (1988), recommendations cite the need for the improvement of "core skills" and the advantage of "multi-skilling" if Britain is to develop a "high-skills, high-value-added industrial and commercial strategy" (Bennett, Glennerster & Nevison, 1992, p. 4). All these objectives are now inextricably linked with the standard model of CBET and enshrined in the new national target for education and training in Britain (NACETT, 1995).

This official line has, however, been subjected to a more searching and critical analysis by a number of commentators. Edwards (1993), for example, has argued that the so-called flexibility and openness of employer-defined competence approaches actually mask a reality in which "discourses about open learning" come to be "strategically ranged to normalize a view of the future of work—based in structural unemployment and underemploy-ment—as not only inevitable but also preferable" (p.185). CBET strategies which are apparently accessible to all—seemingly open as to means yet closed on ends defined by employers' needs—are ideal vehicles for ensuring that "persons will be disciplined into certain forms of behavior and more readily managed within a social formation of structural inequality" (ibid.). As Sieminski (1993) suggests, only a minority of core workers in the new flex-ible labor force of the future will require high-level skills. NVQs will pro-vide an essentially low-level training for "those who will occupy an uncertain future being assigned to the periphery of the labor market" (p. 99).

Rather than the application of post-Fordism to education and training, Field (1993) argues that:

> Competency based assessment threatens to become the new Fordism of the education system. The proliferation of competency specifications and the increasing precision with which competencies are stated parallels the 'parcellization' of the work-force and labor process. As competencies are differentiated more finely, so it becomes more and more possible to nar-row the scope of initiative and field of responsibility of each individual in her work . . . (p. 48).

There is thus a logical link between the de-skilling and de-professionalizing forces mentioned earlier and the development of a so-called 'flexible' and marketized approaches to education and training under a corporate state.

The apparent contradiction between post-Fordist demands for high-level skills and the narrow low-level occupationalism which actually characterizes present trends may be explained by considering contemporary approaches as neither post-Fordist nor Fordist but as instances of 'neo-Fordism.' Brown & Lauder (1995) remind us that the organizational re-structuring, applica-tions of new technologies and moves to "flexible accumulation" commonly identified with post-Fordist enterprises do not "necessarily lead to changes in the nature of skills and involvement which are required in order to compete in 'high value' production" (p. 20). Many economies, including Britain, have really opted for 'neo-Fordist' solutions which "can be characterized in terms of a shift to flexible accumulation based on the creation of a flexible workforce engaged in low-skill, low-wage temporary and often part-time employment" (ibid.). The fact that most of the vocational initiatives of the last decade or so have been almost exclusively concerned with lower level and narrowly focused, occupationally-specific skills is logically connected with such developments (Field, 1995).

PROFESSIONALISM, SHARED LEARNING, AND THE WORKPLACE

By combining the neo-Fordist and de-professionalizing forces referred to above, it is possible to explain a number of recent trends in vocational and professional studies. The labyrinthine "occupational mapping" exercise currently being carried out in the further education sector (Further Education Unit, 1994) and the "job competence analysis" conducted in British universities by the Universities Competencies Consortium (UCC, 1995), become less mysterious when linked with the requirements for control and cost-efficiency in a marketized system. In a similar way, the introduction of Training and Development Lead Body (TDLB) standards into further education and professional studies (Chown & Last, 1993) and the casualization of the education labor force through massive redundancies (Santinelli, 1995) combined with the creation of a pool of cheap labor in the form of the Education Lecturing Services agency (Dore, 1995) are fully in line with these general 'McDonaldizing' policies.

The location of vocational/professional learning in the workplace has been a feature of recent developments in education and industry, though it is important to note the wide range of interpretations of work-based learning currently operating in different sectors. Certainly in an industrial context, job-based training has often been linked to the neo-Fordist low-cost, low-level activity associated with developments in Britain over the last decade or so (Marsden & Ryan, 1995). In teacher education, the recent attempts to locate training in schools and colleges rather than in higher education programs (Barton et al., 1994) can be interpreted within the de-skilling and de-professionalizing paradigm and, as Smith (1995) observed, the transfer of professional education generally from universities to the workplace through the NCVQ competence system may be "designed to render professionals redundant and their professional institutes obsolete" (p.12).

However, though the threats to professional standards and practice implied by such moves are indeed serious, there are also possibilities within the new work-based models of learning which can enable practitioners and educators to not only counter any such threats but also to enhance and foster the 'extended professionalism' referred to earlier. The new emphasis on the workplace as the principal site of professional learning can be seen as an affirmation of the research surrounding the efficacy of the 'reflective practitioner' model which has been fully elaborated by Elliott in what he calls the 'practical science' approach to teacher education. The foundation of this strategy—which makes use of the "knowledge-in use" and "theories-in-action" concepts first developed by Argyris & Schon (1974)—is that "professional judgments and decisions are ethical and not just technical in character," that "professional knowledge consists in repertoires of experienced cases," and that "systematic reflection by practitioners in their practical situations plays a central role in improving professional judgments" (Elliott, 1993, pp.67-8).

Applying these ideas to the initial education and training, induction, and ongoing development of practitioners, such an approach has influenced 'coaching' schemes in industry (Slipais, 1993), the 'preceptor' programs in the health occupations (Kitchin, 1993) and the various 'mentor' schemes in teacher education (Turner, 1995). However, though such approaches are inspired to some degree by a commitment to the value of experiential and work-based learning, there are significant differences in terms of organization, culture, and professional orientation—elements which are of vital importance in relation to the fundamental ethical dimensions of professional practice referred to earlier. There have been a number of creative attempts to counter the more restrictive and technicist elements of the competence challenge in the fields of health, education, and social work (Hodkinson & Issitt, 1995), and what is happening in mentorship and school-based teacher education schemes provides a useful example of the nature and site of current professional struggles.

There have been two main responses to the British government policy of seeking to locate initial teacher education predominantly within schools. The 'corporate' model (Bridges, 1995, p. 69)—based on the training schemes of large organizations such as ICI and Sony—interprets the social market literally and makes the individual school the central unit of the delivery of education and training. This model is fully in line with the logic of opted-out, grant-maintained schools which, having lost links with local education authorities in Britain, now have to purchase all services, including training and staff development, from external agencies (Fitz, Halpin & Power, 1993).

The weaknesses of this model have become evident in recent years: concentration on one institution tends towards a parochialism of interests, a narrow institution-specific conception of theory and practice, and a loss of connection with broader professional concerns (Barton, et al., 1994).

Recognizing these dangers, a number of schools and teacher education institutions have developed a more 'collaborative' (Bridges, 1995, pp. 70-72) model which stresses the importance of maintaining close relationships between higher education institutions and clusters of schools. Using this system it is possible to offer trainees a much wider range of experience across schools and also to reinforce the central importance of the epistemological underpinnings of practice and the need to maintain an alertness to changes and developments within the field. The need for independent thought and critical consciousness on the part of public service professionals takes on increasing importance at a time when the standard policy-making process is essentially top-down, non-consultative and "impoverished" (Gipps, 1993, p. 36).

SHARED LEARNING AND HIGHER PROFESSIONAL EDUCATION

Teachers working in opted-out schools, nurses employed in newly-independent 'trust' hospitals and, since April 1993, further education lecturers in the new corporate colleges can easily become isolated from collegial and professional values and thus vulnerable to the managerialist policies of market-oriented, individualistic and increasingly insular institutions. Alienated in this way there is far less likelihood that critical professional debate and alternative perspectives will serve to temper the top-down policy-making of an increasingly centralized bureaucracy dominated by technicist and instrumentalist ideological commitments.

Similarly, the individualistic values associated with the social market model of public service provision will be magnified when combined with a CBET strategy for workplace learning which—reinforced by performance indicators, league tables and competition between institutions—celebrates corporate self-interest at the expense of teamwork, strategic collaboration and community service. This would be disastrous for both professionals and their clients since it marginalizes and perhaps even obscures the basic conception of professional practice as a social activity concerned with issues which require "collective, rather than merely individual, action" (Barton et al., 1994, p. 540).

The new models of professionalism in education, health and social work are essentially client-centered (Hodkinson & Issitt, 1995) and thus require a response from professionals which increasingly depends on concerted team efforts. As Senge (1990) has amply shown, "teams, not individuals, are the fundamental learning unit in modern organizations" (p. 10) and, particularly in the reaction of British health professionals to new challenges, the 'shared learning' strategies (Dechant, Marsick & Kasl, 1993) have proved their worth in terms of the enhancement of inter- and intra-professional activity to the benefit of both clients and professionals. Such emergent models of team learning become "increasingly more generative of new thinking as members challenge one another's thinking, reframe their perspectives, and build on integrated perspectives to create new knowledge" (ibid., p. 13).

This basic message is essentially the same when applied to more general spheres of activity in contemporary universities. It is quite proper for higher education institutions to be concerned with vocational matters, providing that 'vocational' is interpreted broadly as commitment to "an internal set of demands and standards in the career being followed" rather than in the narrowly utilitarian language of 'vocationalism', which "stands for temporariness and a shallowness of commitment" (Barnett, 1994, p. 68). This is exactly the message contained in Arendt's distinction between 'work' which "must have a point which the workman (sic) can endorse, a purpose with which he can associate himself" (Herbst, 1973, p. 61) and 'labor'—the "price we pay for whatever advantages the rewards of labor will buy" (ibid., p. 59). Similarly, when contemporary commentators on vocational education highlight the confusion between vocational studies as preparation for work and programs concerned exclusively with job training for employment (Skilbeck et al., 1994), they are doing no more than re-affirming Dewey's message issued 80 years ago which challenged the "antithesis of vocational and cultural education" based on the false oppositions of "labor and leisure, theory and practice, body and mind" (Dewey, 1966, p. 301).

If Dewey's conception of vocational education as an activity which "stresses the full intellectual and social meaning of a vocation" (ibid., p. 316) is taken seriously by university educators, then the important instrumental function of preparing people for adult and working life—and the contentious issue of the relationship between universities, industry, and the state—will be placed in a proper perspective. Higher education institutions should concentrate on what they do best: the development of research and critical practice through engagement with the "processes of learning" (Wyatt, 1990, p. 127) and which pays due attention to the role of higher education as a "process of human development orientated towards some conception of human being" (Barnett, 1994, p. 189). This will call for a renewed conception of scholarship which celebrates the inter-relationships between teaching and research and supports an "approach to teaching which emphasizes its interactive nature and applies to it the critical orientation of research" (Rowland, 1996, p. 16). In addition, in the interests of the new models of public service professsionalism outlined above, university teachers must come to "see the significance of students' perceptions of the subject matter and of their learning . . . thereby enhancing their learning and keeping the subject matter open to continual critique" (ibid., p. 18).

It is in the sphere of policymaking in the public services that the ethical dimensions of professional practice need to be constantly renewed and reinforced. In spite of the impact of the market model, the emergence of the 'learning organization' has served to re-emphasize the importance of teamwork and collaboration at all levels in industry and the public services. Markets, after all, can be fundamentally irrational (Smith, 1996) and, therefore, do not offer an ideal basis on which to plan public service provision in fluid socio-economic circumstances. As Caldwell & Carter (1993) note, recent trends represent a "drive for a stronger culture of service in the public sector" (p. 208), and the emergence of the work-based mentorship and preceptorship schemes can be regarded as a reflection of this.

Certainly, the most successful and genuinely flexible post-Fordist industries have been those which have interpreted the new conditions as calling for "relations of equality" in organizations which can "encourage a synthesis of members' interests" so that the "flow of value-adding knowledge helps legitimate the organization as a learning community" (Zuboff, 1988, p. 394). The idea of the learning community—whether this is in education or industry, the public or the private sector—is dependent upon "collective intelligence" (Brown & Lauder, 1995, p. 28) and action derived from consensual understanding, and it is precisely such an approach which has enabled the 'social partnership' models of education and training provision to produce such enviable education and training systems in Europe (Green, 1995).

As Ranson (1994) observes, the values of learning—whether this is work-based, vocational, academic, or professional learning—are actually moral values based upon civic virtue, caring, and responsibility. In the midst of the often vacuous rhetoric surrounding the 'learning society' project in contemporary British education and the patent failure of 'McDonaldized' and 'market forces' approaches to education and training (Evans, 1992; EPI, 1995; Hodkinson & Sparkes, 1995), we are reminded by Ranson et al. (1996) that:

if society is seriously to address the problems facing education then the solution requires more than a quantitative expansion or more adaptation of existing systems. Rather it will need a reform of the organizing principles of learning: from an instrumental purpose—supporting the needs of the labor market and economic regeneration—to the moral and political purpose of cultural renewal; from learning for economic interest to learning for citizenship (p. 25).

As intellectual debate on the nature, scope and future of British higher education is heightened during the government-sponsored national inquiry into higher education due to report in Autumn 1997 (Hodges, 1996), the chairman of the inquiry committee, Sir Ron Dearing, could do worse than consider placing such a conception of learning at the heart of his committee's deliberations.

REFERENCES

Argyris, C. & Schon, D. (1974). *Theory in practice: Increasing professional effectiveness.* San Francisco: Jossey-Bass.

Ashworth, P. (1992). Being competent and having 'competencies'. *Journal of Further & Higher Education,* 16 (3), 8-17.

Avirim, A. (1992). The nature of university education reconsidered. *Journal of Philosophy of Education,* 26 (2), 183-200.

Barnett, R. (1990). *The idea of higher education.* Buckingham: Open University Press.

Barnett, R. (1994). *The limits of competence.* Buckingham: Open University Press.

Barton, L., et al. (1994). Teacher education and professionalism in England: some emerging issues. *British Journal of Sociology of Education,* 15 (4), 402-407.

Bash, L. & Green, A. (eds.) (1995). *Youth, education and work.* London: Kogan Page.

Bennett, R., Glennerster, H. & Nevison, D. (1992). *Learning should pay.* London School of Economics/ BP Education.

Berg, L. (1992). Vocationalism in Norwegian higher education: rhetoric or reality? *European Journal of Education,* 28 (1/2), 79-88.

Bloom, A. (1988). *The closing of the American mind.* London: Penguin.

Bridges, D. (1995). School-based teacher education. In Kerry, T. & Shelton-Mayes, A. (eds.) *Issues in mentoring.* London: Routledge/Open University.

Brown, P. & Lauder, H. (1995). Post-Fordist possibilities: Education, training and national development. In Bash L. & Green A. (eds.) *Youth, education and work.* London: Kogan Page.

Burke, J.W. (ed.) (1995). *Outcomes, learning and the curriculum.* London: Falmer.

Caldwell, B.J. & Carter, M.E.A. (eds.) (1993). *The return of the mentor: Strategies for workplace learning.* London: Falmer.

Callender, C. (1992). *Will NVQs work? Evidence from the construction industry.* University of Sussex: Institute of Manpower Studies.

Carr, D. (1994). Educational enquiry and professional knowledge: Towards a Copernican revolution. *Educational Studies,* 20 (1), 33-52.

Chitty, C. & Simon, B. (eds.) (1993). *Education answers back.* London: Lawrence &

Wishart.

Chown, A. (1992). TDLB standards in FE. *Journal of Further & Higher Education*, 16 (3), 52-9.

Chown, A. & Last, J. (1993). Can the NCVQ model be used for teacher training? *Journal of Further & Higher Education*,17 (2), 15-26.

Collins, M. (1991). *Adult education as vocation*. London: Routledge.

Dechant, K., Marsick, V. & Kasl, E. (1993). Towards a model of team learning. *Studies in Continuing Education*, 15 (1), 1-14.

Dewey, J. (1966). *Democracy and Education*. New York: Free Press.

Dore, A. (1995). Sales talk from lecturers' agency. *Times Educational Supplement*, 19.5.95

Edwards, R. (1993). The inevitable future? Post-Fordism in work and learning. In Edwards, R.,Sieminski, A. & Zeldin, D. (eds.) *Adult learners, education and training*. London: Routledge/Open University.

Elliott, J. (1991). A model of professsionalism and its implications for teacher education. *British Educational Research Journal,* 17 (4), 309-318.

Elliott, J. (Ed) (1993). *Reconstructing teacher education*. London: Falmer.

Employment Department (1995). *A vision for higher level vocational qualifications*. Sheffield: Employment Department.

Employment Policy Institute (1995). *The skills mirage*. London: Employment Policy Institute.

Eraut, M. (1994). *Developing professional knowledge and competence*. London: Falmer.

Esland, G. (1996). Knowledge and nationhood: The new right, education and the global market. In Avis, J., et al. (eds.), *Knowledge and nationhood: Education, politics and work*. London: Cassell.

Evans, B. (1992). *The politics of the training market*. London: Routledge.

FEU (1994). *Occupational and functional mapping of the further education sector*. London: Further Education Unit.

Field, J. (1993). Competency and the pedagogy of labour. In Thorpe, M, Edwards, R. & Hanson, A. (eds.) *Culture and processes of adult learning*. London: Routledge/ Open University.

Field, J. (1995). Reality testing in the workplace: Are NVQs employment led? In Hodkinson, P. & Issitt, M. (eds.), *The challenge of competence: Professionalism through vocational education and training*. London: Cassell.

Finegold, D. & Soskice, D. (1988). The failure of training in Britain: Analysis and prescription. *Oxford Review of Economic Policy,* 4 (3), 21-53.

Fitz, J.,Halpin, D.& Power, S. (1993). *Grant-maintained schools: education in the market place*. London: Kogan Page.

Fletcher, S. (1991). *NVQs., standards and competence*. London: Kogan Page.

Gellert, C. & Rau, E. (1992). Diversification and integration: the vocationalization of the German higher education system. *European Journal of Education,*28(1/2), 89-100.

Gipps, C. (1993). Policy-Making and the Use and Misuse of Evidence. In Chitty, C. & Simon, B. (eds.) op.cit.

Green, A. (1995). The role of the state and the social partners in VET systems. In Bash, L. & Green, A. (eds.) op.cit.

Griffin, C. (1992). Absorbing experiential learning. In Mulligan, J. & Griffin, C.(Eds): *Empowerment through experiential Learning*. London: Kogan Page.

Hartley, D. (1995). The McDonaldization of higher education: Food for thought? *Oxford Review of Education*, 21 (4), pp. 409-423.

Herbst, P. (1973). Work. Labour and university education. In Peters, R.S. (ed) *The philosophy of education*. London: Routledge & Kegan Paul.

Hodges, L. (1996). Mr. Fix-it to put work first. *Times Higher Education Supplement*, 8.3.96

Hodkinson, P. & Issitt, M. (eds.) (1995). *The challenge of competence: Professionalism through vocational education and training*. London: Cassell.

Hodkinson, P. & Sparkes, A. (1995). Markets and vouchers: the inadequacy of individualist policies for vocational education and training in England and Wales. *Journal of Education Policy*, 10 (2), pp. 189-207.

Hyland, T. (1991). Taking care of business: Vocationalism, competence and the enterprise culture. *Educational Studies*, 17 (1), 77-87.

Hyland, T. (1994a). Experiential learning, competence and critical practice in higher education. *Studies in Higher Education*, 19 (3), 327-339.

Hyland, T. (1994b). *Competence, education and NVQs: Dissenting perspectives*. London: Cassell.

Hyland, T. (1996a). The industrialization of higher education: A critique of NCVQ and DfEE policy. *Educational Change & Development*, 17 (1), 29-36.

Hyland, T. (1996b). Through a glass darkly: A critique of the NCVQ visions of higher level vocational qualifications. *Oxford Review of Education;* 22 (3), 357-362.

Hyland, T. (1996c). Professionalism, ethics and work-based learning. *British Journal of Educational Studies*, 44 (2), 168-180.

Jenkins, S. (1995). *Accountable to none: The Tory nationalization of Britain*. London: Hamish Hamilton.

Jessup, G. (1991). *Outcomes: NVQs and the emerging model of education and training*. London: Falmer.

Kerry, T. & Tollitt-Evans, J. (1992). *Teaching in further education*. Oxford: Blackwell.

Kitchin, S. (1993). Preceptorship in hospitals. In Caldwell, B.J. & Carter, M.E.A. (eds.) op.cit.

Kolb, D. (1993). The process of experiential learning. In Thorpe, M., Edwards, R. & Hanson, A. (eds.) op.cit.

Lamoure, J. & Rontopoulou, J.L. (1992). The vocationalization of higher education in France. *European Journal of Education*, 28 (1/2), 45-56.

Langford, G. (1978). *Teaching as a profession*. Manchester University Press.

Larson, M.S. (1977). *The rise of professionalism: A sociological analysis*. Berkeley: University of California Press.

Lyotard, J.F. (1984). *The postmodern condition: A report on knowledge*. Minneapolis: University of Minnesota Press.

MacIntrye, A. (1990). *Three rival versions of moral enquiry*. London: Duckworth.

Marsden, D. & Ryan, P. (1995). Work, labour and vocational preparation: Anglo-German comparisons of training in intermediate skills. In Bash, L. & Green, A. (eds.) op.cit.

McHugh, G., Fuller, A. & Lobley, D. (1993). *Why take NVQs?* Lancaster University: Centre for the Study of Training and Education.

Mendus, S. (1992). All the King's horses and all the King's men: Justifying higher education. *Journal of Philosophy of Education*, 26 (2), 173-182.

Mezirow, J. (1990). A critical theory of adult learning and teaching. In Tight, M. (ed.) *Adult learning and teaching*. London: Routledge.

Moon, B. (1990). Patterns of reform: School control in Western Europe. In Moon, B. (ed.) *New curriculum—national curriculum.* London: Hodder & Stoughton.

NACETT (1995). *Review of the national targets for education and training.* London: National Advisory Council for Education and Training Targets.

NCVQ (1988). *Initial criteria and guidelines for staff development.* London: National Council for Vocational Qualifications.

Neave, G. (1992). On instantly consumable knowledge and snake oil. *European Journal of Education,* 28 (1/2), 5-28.

Peters, R.S. (1966). *Ethics and education.* London: Allen & Unwin.

Raggatt, P. (1994). Implementing NVQs in colleges: progress, perceptions and issues. *Journal of Further & Higher Education,* 18 (1), 59-74.

Ramsay, J. (1993). The hybrid course: Competences and behaviourism in higher education. *Journal of Further & Higher Education,*17 (3), 70-89.

Ranson, S. (1994). *Towards the learning society.* London: Cassell.

Ranson, S., et al. (1996). Towards a theory of learning. *British Journal of Educational Studies,* 44 (1), 9-26.

Ritzer, G. (1993). *The McDonaldization of society.* London: Pine Forge Press.

Rowland, S. (1996). Relationships between teaching and research. *Teaching in Higher Education,* 1 (1), 7-20.

Russell, C. (1994). Professions in the firing line. *Times Higher Education Supplement,* 20.5.94

Rustin, M. (1994). Unfinished business—from Thatcherite modernization to incomplete modernity. In Perryman, M. (ed.): *Altered states, postmodernism, politics, culture.* London: Lawrence & Wishart.

Santinelli, P. (1995). Part-timers lose most jobs. *Times Higher Ed ucation Supplement,* 26.5.95

Senge, P. (1990). *The fifth discipline: The art & practice of the learning organization.* New York: Doubleday.

Sieminski, S. (1993). The 'flexible' solution to economic decline. *Journal of Further & Higher Education,* 17 (1), 92-100.

Skilbeck, M., et. al. (1994). *The vocational quest.* London: Routledge.

Slipais, S. (1993). Coaching in a competency-based training system. in Caldwell, B.J. & Carter, M.E.A. (eds.), op.cit.

Smith, D. (1996). Do markets work? *Social Sciences.* Economic and Social Research Council), Issue 30, p.8.

Smith, P. (1995). NVQ peril for professions. *Times Higher Education Supplement,* 24.2.95

Smithers, A.(1993). *All our futures: Britain's education revolution.* London: Channel 4 Television 'Dispatches' Report on Education.

Stronach, I. (1995). Policy hysteria. *Forum,* 37 (1), 9-10.

Titmus, C.,Knoll, J. H. & Wittpoth, J. (1993). *Continuing education in higher education: Academic self-concept and public policy in three European countries.* University of Leeds: Leeds Studies in Continuing Education.

Turner, M. (1995). The role of mentors and teacher tutors in school-based teacher education and induction. in Kerry, T. & Shelton-Mayes, A. (eds.) op.cit.

UCC (1995). *Job analysis feasibility study.* London: Universities Competences Consortium.

Usher R. (1992). Experience in adult education: A post-modern critique. *Journal of Philosophy of Education,* 26 (2), 201-214.

Wertsch, J. (1991). *Voices of the mind*. London: Harvester Wheatsheaf.

Whitty, G. (1990). The new right and the national curriculum: State control or market forces? In Moon, B. (ed.) op.cit.

Wolf, A. (1995). *Competence-Based Assessment*. Buckingham: Open University Press.

Wyatt, J. (ed.) (1990). *Commitment to higher education*. Buckingham: Open University Press.

Zuboff, S. (1988). *In the age of the smart machine: The future of work and power*. New York: Basic Books.

CHAPTER 14

Quality versus Quantity Objectives
Effects of the Danish University 1990 Bachelor Degree Ordinance on Students' Educational Experience

Tronie Rifkin

Virtually all higher education systems face the challenge of preparing their nation's youth for survival and success in a complex, knowledge-based, post-industrial society. The rapid expansion and growth experienced by many higher education systems in Western Europe over the last 50 years has exacerbated this challenge. Higher education systems have been struggling with the often conflicting public demands to accommodate larger and larger numbers of students while simultaneously providing them with a quality education (Neave, 1985; Perkin, 1977; Teichler, 1977).

Due to social, political, and economic pressures in Western Europe throughout the 1980's and 1990's, these demands have become a central focus of public conversation about higher education. In response, governments have formulated and implemented national policies that simultaneously attempt to maintain access to higher education and to provide a quality education to students. Many of these policies mandate changes in the structure and content of the curriculum, governance, and finance of higher education institutions and require that these institutions show program improvement, present quantifiable measures of student performance, and demonstrate greater efficiency and more effective use of resources (Gordon and Partington, 1995). The underlying intention of these policies is to influence the quality of the education delivered by higher education institutions and experienced by students, although the means of assessing educational achievement is often defined in terms of quantifiable outcomes such as productivity and efficiency. Thus, moving from an educational system accustomed to accommodating few (an elite system) to one accommodating many (a mass system) has resulted in an inherent conflict between quality and quantity objectives (Warner, 1977) that is likely to have an impact on higher education depending upon which of these objectives is given greater weight.

Picturing universities and how they function in terms of quantity objectives is by no means new. Quantitative outcomes are measured in terms of the number of students who enroll, pass exams, or graduate, and in terms of the productive and efficient use of resources. Such measures are useful to determine appropriate class size, number of courses that should be offered in any given field, and faculty and staff needed to meet curricular goals. Such measures also help determine labor market trends and provide an accounting of the costs of educating students. Today, the general public is becoming increasingly concerned over this latter point—costs incurred in educating students. As Trow has stated, "The more higher education grows, the more money is needed for it, the more interest there is in it among larger parts of the populations, [and] the greater demand there is for tight control over its shape and costs" (1973, p. 50). Accountability mechanisms—loosely defined as the imposition of quantitative targets and objectives on the educational system and holding it accountable for meeting those objectives—are seen by many as the most straightforward means of controlling costs and monitoring use of resources. In the formulation of higher education policy, quantitative objectives are more easily understood by the public than measures of quality objectives—for example, improving the quality of teaching and learning.

Quality objectives in higher education are certainly much more difficult to conceptualize. However, Bowen (1980) offers a helpful perspective—a university produces qualitative outcomes by performing principal, well-defined functions such as education, research, and public service. In performing the function of education, higher education is engaged in the production of learning. As Bowen observed,

> Learning, in this sense means knowing and interpreting the known (scholarship and criticism), discovering the new (research and related activities), and bringing about desired change in the cognitive and affective traits and characteristics of human beings (education) (p. 8).

Learning can—and perhaps should—be considered the chief product of higher education. It consists primarily of changes in people—changes in their knowledge, their characteristics, and their behavior. Outcomes in higher education, then, are not only the transformation of resources into tangible products—rather, they are the transformation of resources into desired intangible qualities of human beings. The quantity *and* quality of the learning produced is largely determined by the amounts and kinds of resources used and by the ways in which they are used. Through the major function of instruction, the institution hopes to influence students, faculty, and members of the public to help set students on a course of continuing and desirable activity and, subsequently, to achieve broad social and cultural advancement of the entire society. Yet, sometimes nations and their higher education systems lose sight of this ideal when trying to accommodate growth with limited resources; and consequently, educational opportunity becomes a struggle between quantity and quality objectives rather than a harmonious objective between the two.

DANISH HIGHER EDUCATION—A CASE IN POINT

The Danish higher education system is one example of a Western European country that has undergone dramatic expansion and change over the last 30 years. It has expanded from a system serving an elite portion of Danish society to one approaching the scale of mass higher education. Like other Western European countries, the Danish higher education system has been struggling to manage continuing growth in its student population, while seeking to provide a quality education. In response to this struggle, the Danish University—under the direction of the Danish Ministry—implemented a new degree structure in 1990—The Bachelor of Arts Degree Ordinance (BA). The BA was designed to accommodate continued growth in the number of students seeking higher education by moving students through the system in the most efficient and productive manner possible. Attaining the kind of efficient and productive course of study these leaders envisioned required sweeping changes in the form, structure, and content of the undergraduate curriculum. In addition, several accountability mechanisms were developed as part of the BA policy, to quantitatively measure its success in terms of desired levels of productivity and the efficient use of resources. This chapter explores the development and effects of the Danish University's BA initiative, as an illustration of the inherent conflict between quantity and quality objectives which many higher education policies worldwide have encountered.

THE ROAD TO THE BA: A BRIEF DISCUSSION OF DANISH HIGHER EDUCATION

Origins

The Danish higher education system began in 1479 with the founding of the University of Copenhagen. Although other institutions—namely the Royal Academy of Arts, the Royal Veterinary and Agricultural University, and the Technical University—were founded, it was not until the 1920's that

Denmark's second university (the University of Århus) was established. The remaining three universities—Odense (founded in 1964), Roskilde (founded in 1972), and Aalborg (founded in 1974)—were founded in the second half of the twentieth century in an attempt to meet the educational demand of the ever-growing student population. The population of students wishing to enter Danish universities expanded rapidly, thereby taxing both the institutional climate and culture, as well as the already limited budgets of the universities.

Means of Accommodating Student Population Growth

For the Danish University, the rise in the number of matriculating students led to dramatic change. In 1958, 4,700 students were admitted to the Danish University; by the 1970's, the number of students had approached 26,000 (Stybe, 1979). Even with the establishment of three new universities (Odense, Roskilde, and Aalborg) to accommodate the growth in student numbers, the Danish higher education system was experiencing input overload. In order to control this state of disequilibrium, the formerly open admissions policy supported by the Danish Parliament and the Ministry of Education in the 1960's—which guaranteed a university education to all who graduated from the gymnasium[1]—became, in 1977, a restricted admissions policy whereby admission was limited to students with the highest Upper Secondary School Exam scores, or the equivalent[2] (Laursen, 1993). Even with such restrictive measures, throughout the 1980's the number of students who graduated from the gymnasium, passed the Upper Secondary School Examination, qualified for university admission, and were admitted to the university steadily increased to reach a new peak at 34,700 in 1990 (Conrad, 1990).

At the same time this growth in student population occurred, the university was experiencing another problem—low graduation rates. By Ministry of Education standards, students were expected to complete the university *Candidatus Degree* (equivalent to the Master's Degree in the United States) within four to five years. By 1987 only 25% of students who matriculated in 1980 had completed their degree (Conrad, 1990). It became clear that as long as the numbers of students interested in a university education grew, and the numbers of graduates remained low, it would be difficult for the system to catch up and reach a desired state of equilibrium, even with a restricted admissions policy.

To solve this problem, the Ministry of Education ratified a new degree structure—the Bachelor of Arts Degree—that would matriculate and graduate students in three years instead of allowing them to continue until they obtain the *Candidatus Degree*. One of the main purposes of the BA was to make a series of gradual readjustments to the form, structure, and content of the education provided by the university, with the aim of "rationalizing studies" (Conrad, 1990). The new degree structure demanded the following: flexibility, ability to transfer coursework to other areas of study within the university, emphasis on short-cycle studies, and development of applicable workplace skills. Also, the BA required institutions to develop highly specified plans for study content and detailed examination criteria. In the past, the characteristic form of instruction was the seminar, marked, on the whole, by a personal relationship between student and teacher. Under the new degree structure the emphasis is on the transmission of skill and knowledge, and increasingly formal instruction is carried on through large lectures supplemented by seminars often taught by teaching assistants. The implication of these changes is a shift in the function of higher education from one of shaping the character of students to one of preparing large numbers of individuals for careers in an advanced industrial society.

Means of Accountability

In the economic sphere, the Danish national debt registered as one of the highest among the Organization of European Cooperation and Development (OECD) countries in the 1980's. Because the Danish University is publicly financed, the severe economic problems of the country were felt in the educational sector. The larger the Danish higher education system grew, the more critical and intertwined became the relations of the state to higher education. By the 1980's, partly due to the nation's overall economic situation, government policy focused on the economics of higher education by cutting back and placing tighter controls over the level of public funds allocated to the universities. This process of understanding the value of higher education in economic terms has, in recent years, reached its full expression. Today, control over shape and costs has become the principal objective of higher education administration. Government policies toward Danish higher education focus on the efficient use of resources—in other words, *quantifiable* outcomes. Some of the best examples of this come from three accountability mechanisms introduced by Danish government to accompany the new degree structure: 1) limiting student financial aid to three years only *(Statens Uddannelsestøtte)*; 2) implementing an accounting system—the taxi-meter system *(studietrinstilvægster)*—that funds higher education by financially rewarding institutions for successfully passed student exams; and 3) using a first-year qualifying exam to determine whether students are "academically suited" to continue their education *(stopprøver)* (Mortensen and Gregersen, 1993).

Student Financial Support (Statens Uddannelsestøtte/SU). Until the 1980's all students admitted to the university received some form of financial support. However, as the number of graduates declined and the number of matriculating students rose, total government expenditure for student financial support sky-rocketed (Ellerhøj and Grane, 1986). The implementation of the three-year BA degree provided the perfect opportunity to modify the existing financial aid system. The system no longer provides financial support without question. Students receive initial support but must periodically validate their status in the university by submitting evidence of having sat for exams equivalent to a certain amount of coursework per support period. Aid discontinues after three years regardless of how close students are to completing their degree. Extensions are granted to those students who have been ill or to women who have given birth.

The Taxi-Meter System (Studietrinstilvægster). Another component of educational financing, this system controls the financial well-being of institutions and individual departments and divisions. In the past, institutions were financed by the number of student places available; the new policy allocates funding to the institution contingent upon individual student success on course final examinations. Students who pass course exams are considered "effective" students. According to Conrad (1990), a university professor and division chair, this means that "students who abandon their studies or who are not actively engaged in their studies are not 'effective' or resource-productive" (p. 215).

From the state's perspective, the advantages of such a system are twofold: 1) it accounts for funds provided by society—the funds received by the university are in essence a reward for successfully passed student exams; and 2) it pressures disciplines with low production rates to improve their success rates and their financial status.

First-Year Qualifying Exam (Stopprøver). A strategy that is administered internally rather than externally, this exam tests students in their subject area after the first year of coursework in order to determine whether they are "academically suited" to continue their university education (Mortensen and Gregersen, 1993). In order to take the exam, students must pass coursework equivalent to 3/4 of a year, at minimum. If they fail the exam three times, they are dismissed from the university.

Implications

Such accountability mechanisms raise questions about the purpose and quality of the education provided by the university. What had once been a system that had been willing to teach just about anyone was becoming a system that would only cater to the best students, in a way that would ensure that quantitative criteria for educational success—especially the success of the *system* (rather than the success of the students)—would be met. The Danish University BA policy and its concomitant accountability mechanisms reflect current discussions in higher education which are dominated by questions of quantitative development—of university enrollment capacity, graduation rates, and the productive and efficient use of resources—while other themes, such as quality of the educational experience for students, are being forced into the background.

A STUDY OF DANISH STUDENT AND FACULTY RESPONSES TO THE BA POLICY

This study seeks to discover from student and faculty academic advisors whether or not the BA policy has affected teaching, learning, and students' educational experiences, and if so, how. Specifically, this study is interested in researching two areas in which the BA has an impact on education. First, what impact have changes in curriculum content and format had on teaching and learning? Second, what impact has the emphasis on quantitative outcomes such as productivity and efficiency had on students' educational experience?

Method

This study was conducted between September 1993 and June 1994 at Copenhagen University, Denmark and used a qualitative methodological approach—the interview. A group of student and faculty academic advisors were interviewed. Conducting interviews of student and faculty academic advisors was considered to be the most direct and efficient method of gathering data and one that would provide the most depth and insight into sensitive issues.

Participants

Two sets of participants from the Department of Humanities at the University of Copenhagen were used in this study. The first set comprised twenty of thirty students who held positions as student academic advisors; 12 female subjects and 8 male subjects. The second set comprised ten faculty academic advisors; all male participants.

Interview Questions

Four interview questions were constructed in order to elicit findings regarding the impact changes in the content and format of the curriculum have had on teaching and learning and the impact of accountability mechanisms on students' educational experience. All participants were asked to respond to the following four questions concerning the impact of the Danish University 1990 Bachelor of Arts Degree Ordinance (BA):

1) What are the positive and/or negative effects of the BA on your educational experience?

2) What role does productivity and efficiency play?

3) Has the student-professor relationship changed since the implementation of the BA?

4) Has the quality of instruction changed?

Procedures

Appointments were made to interview participants. All interviews began with a brief introduction as to the purpose of the study and a general overview of the questions that would be asked. The interview procedure followed a format that is consistent with interview methodology found in qualitative research (Tesch, 1990; Strauss, 1987). The interview session took place in the student or faculty academic advisor's office and lasted approximately 30 minutes to an hour depending on interviewee interest in elaborating on responses. The participants were advised that all responses were confidential but that they had the right to not answer any questions they felt uncomfortable answering and could stop the interview at any time during the session.

Results

Question 1: Positive and/or Negative Effects of the BA

Student Academic Advisor Responses. Student academic advisors voiced the benefits of a short-cycle degree. "Students can leave the university with a BA after three years instead of getting stuck at the *Candidatus* (Masters) level. At least, now students have an option to finish their studies sooner than under the previous degree structure and to enter the work force without a *Candidatus* Degree, if that is what they want to do." Another benefit of the BA is the evolution of a more streamlined program of study. One student academic advisor said, "Now you know what courses are necessary to acquire general knowledge in your subject area."

On the negative side, a number of student academic advisors expressed views that contradict the benefits of a streamlined program. They indicated that students express severe frustration with the lack of flexibility in the BA course structure. Examples of this frustration include: "the model is tight;" and "I feel as if I'm in a factory." Some responses pin-pointed specific elements in the system. Examples include: "there is too much structure in the course content"; "teachers direct too much"; "it is a continuation of the gymnasium (high school)"; "there is a loss of freedom"; "students are not independent or cultivated"; "we are taught to be generalists rather than specialists"; and "the inelasticity ruins the student milieu."

Faculty Academic Advisor Responses. Faculty advisors also discussed student satisfaction with the opportunity, if desired, to leave the university after three years with a viable certificate in hand. Faculty advisor responses also concurred with student academic advisors on the advantages of an organized and structured course of study. However, they also described the primary negative attribute of the BA using the exact same words as the student advisors—"The model is too tight." Despite faculty academic advisors' concurrence on many elements, their focus was different from that of the student advisors. They viewed the BA as forcing courses and instruction to become "modularized and compartmentalized." From their experience in the classroom and from their discussions with students seeking academic counseling, they felt that students "compartmentalize knowledge." One faculty advisor said, "Students acquire knowledge in one part of a subject but are unable to make connections to the broader view." Another faculty academic advisor was very concerned about the inelasticity of the BA. His focus, though, was not as much on the compartmentalization of knowledge, although he indicated it contributed to his overall concerns, but on the difficulties the BA presents to students with creative talent. "Over the last three years, I have seen students who are creative rather than disciplined get lost in the system or drop out. Also, if you miss a step, a procedure, or aren't sure about the subject you want to pursue, it is difficult to survive."

Question 2: Role of Productivity and Efficiency
The responses to this question revolve around the three critical accountability mechanisms introduced by the state to advance the success of the BA degree structure—student financial support (*Statens Uddannelsestøtte/SU*), the taxi-meter system *(studietrinstilvægster)*, and the first year qualifying exam *(stopprøver)*. As mentioned earlier, these initiatives were introduced in response to a shift in Danish higher education policy towards a stronger focus on the efficient use of resources.

Student Academic Advisor Responses. Student academic advisors pointed out that the single most pressing concern students bring to them is their student financial support: "They come for advice and are extremely anxious about the possibility of failing exams and potentially losing their financial support." As a consequence, students are under extreme time pressure and regret that they have "no time to do anything but read and study the text and lecture notes . . . there isn't even time to explore an area of interest beyond the text." Of greater concern, however, is the fact that "the time pressure forces students to focus on the material that will be on the exams instead of taking an interest to learn about the subject matter." Along a similar vein, students often come to counseling and complain that "the pressure of exams interferes with my thoughts about the subject." To summarize the effects of SU under the new BA degree, as one student academic advisor observed, "Students are more conscious about the economics of their studies than their studies."

The taxi-meter system *(studietrinstilvægster)* is another accountability mechanism viewed by student advisors as a way to promote productivity and efficiency in the educational system. This system rewards the university financially for each student that passes a course exam. Students are well aware of the pressures on faculty to produce students who will pass exams, and they sense that faculty are viewed as better teachers if students are able to pass the exams. One student stated, "Measuring the quality of education by the number of students who pass exams is a means of controlling and molding students and what they learn . . . [this] has adverse effects on the students and their education." Others indicated that the pressure to pass exams is so great that students neglect to become involved in political or extra-curricular activities. Worse, students regret the lack of time to view the material critically and feel they are not developing critical thinking skills.

Concerning the first year qualifying exam, student academic advisors strongly emphasized three points. The exams 1) serve no functional purpose, 2) are costly in terms of time and money spent on their administration, and 3) have a negative effect on students' educational experience. Qualifying the lack of functional purpose of the exam, one student advisor summarized student concerns with the following comment, "It is hard enough to get into the university these days, so it is not fair to throw students out after one year. Students are motivated ahead of time. They don't need a threat to motivate them. It's just one more thing to think about to get it all to fit together." Student advisors noted the development of intense competition between students that never existed before as an insidious, yet pervasive, effect of the exams. Additionally, as one student advisor commented, "It also affects the social and political life of the university and creates a very insecure atmosphere."

Faculty Academic Advisor Responses. Responses from faculty advisors were very similar to the responses from student advisors for all three accountability mechanisms. Faculty academic advisors faulted the stringent financial support system for many of the students' woes. They indicated concerns about financial aid and its effect on coursework as a predominant reason students seek out the faculty advisor. They also noticed that students spend a lot of time and energy worrying about their financial support and agreed with student advisors that this time could be better spent worrying about coursework.

One faculty advisor clarified the purpose of the taxi-meter system in one sentence. He said, "The structure of the BA reform needed a way to justify the education the university was providing." Faculty advisors also viewed the taxi-meter system negatively. Their concerns focused on the restraints the system puts on classroom instruction. "There is no time to answer tangential questions or to stray from the course outline. Students must master the material required to pass the exams." Faculty limitations in the classroom have consequences for student learning. As one faculty advisor put it, "The professors at the university remark that students are less socially dependent on the system, but at the expense of learning to be independent thinkers."

Faculty advisors also pointed out another very harmful yet subversive effect of the taxi-meter system. Initiated as a measure of productivity offering financial rewards, it is also inadvertently being used as a means of measuring the quality of instruction and student learning. Those departments and institutes that are more successful in preparing students for exams and passing them are viewed as better. "There is a subtle notion surfacing. The professor whose students take and pass the exam must somehow be better or more efficient. This professor makes the division look good, too, so he receives greater recognition for his classroom instruction."

Faculty academic advisors remarked on the purpose of the first year qualifying exams by stating, "There already exist de facto exams in the institutes. Students have 1,000 qualifying exams during their course of study—professors try and stop them (the students) the day they enter the system." All the faculty advisors made clear the time efforts and costs involved in implementation and administration. They added that nervousness and increased competitiveness are results of the first-year qualifying exam and negatively impact students.

Question 3: Changes in the Student-Professor Relationship

Student Academic Advisor Responses. "The university student-professor relationship has become a continuation of the gymnasium (high school) student-teacher relationship," was a widely held opinion among student advisors. What this statement conveys is that the relationship between student and professor has not developed to the next level of maturity. An example of the gymnasium (high school) student-teacher relationship is summarized by one student: "The students take less responsibility for their education while the service minded teachers nurse their students." The explanation given for this change in relationship is student nervousness and insecurity, and "because the students act like high school students professors treat them accordingly."

The student-professor relationship has changed, and the pressure on faculty to prepare students to succeed on exams has also resulted in a change in instructional orientation. One student academic advisor relayed her own experience as well as that of her fellow students. "Professors view and treat students as if they are gymnasium students who need to master the material in order to pass the exam. They do not treat us as university students who are here to grow and develop intellectually and psychologically."

Another identified area of concern is the lack of student-professor contact. This is largely due to the growing replacement of professors with teaching assistants, the lack of time to discuss material beyond the syllabus, and the lack of understanding professors have for students' position and circumstances. As one student advisor commented, "It has not occurred to teachers that society's demands on students are different from teachers demands on students."

Faculty Academic Advisor Responses. Faculty advisors supported student advisor responses concerning changes in the student-professor relationship. Faculty advisors admitted that they and their colleagues see students as young, insecure, and dependent on faculty for guidance. Faculty advisors were also concerned about the lack of contact between faculty and students. They mentioned three trends in this area since the implementation of the BA: 1) it is becoming more and more difficult to follow the academic path of students; 2) independent study projects which require close contact with a project advisor are no longer of interest to students and near extinction; and 3) the number of students assigned to a limited pool of faculty is increasing.

Question 4: Change in the Quality of Instruction

Student Academic Advisor Responses. Students were more forthcoming on this question than faculty advisors. The implementation of the BA degree forced the development of a new academic format which students consider a positive outcome of the reforms. Students feel "more teaching and more classes has been a plus for the quality of instruction. Instruction has improved because the professors have to teach the subject." Half of the students interviewed also recognized that the new academic format has been experiencing a three-year trial period; some of the present courses never existed before in their present form, and, as a result some of the courses and their contents have required some readjustment. To this half of the student academic advisors the glitches in restructuring are viewed as a positive step toward improving the quality of instruction. "The courses and content are continually being rearranged and adjusted to fit the needs of students and the BA structure better."

However, since the implementation of a more streamlined academic structure, many of the courses normally taught by the full-time professors are now taught by teaching assistants. Students feel the quality of instruction has suffered because of the waning influence of traditional scientific and theoretical research as an integral element in university instruction. Student advisors reported that the theoretical foundation in their degree has moved to the higher degree levels. "University assistants are simply teachers and not researchers." Student advisors indicated that students are introduced to many theoretical tools but never have an opportunity to experience or exercise them—"Too little of the teacher's research enters the classroom." Also, students expressed concern over the growing number of students being admitted into the university. "The university admits more students than it can handle. The result is too many students per teacher, not to mention per academic advisor. The more students in the classroom, the less time the professor has to answer questions, go off on tangents, and provide critique and feedback on written work."

Faculty Academic Advisor Responses. Faculty advisors unanimously felt that a lot of effort and hard work went into establishing a new academic format and pointed out that "if the new academic format has affected the quality of instruction it has improved it." One faculty advisor stated, "Students who finish today are technically better due to better teaching."

Faculty advisor, like student advisors, were concerned about the overuse of teaching assistants, but they did not think there was any solution to the problem. They admitted teaching assistants offer them a reprieve from their already taxing obligations and responsibilities. One faculty advisor commented sadly, "the traditional professor is becoming a 'diminishing tribe'."

DISCUSSION

This study sought to discover what effects the implementation of the BA policy has had on teaching, learning, and students' educational experience. Specifically, the goals were to determine 1) what impact the changes in content and format of the curriculum have had on teaching and learning, and 2) what impact the emphasis on quantitative outcomes has had on students' educational experience.

The impact of changes in the content and format of the curriculum emerged in responses to the question concerning the positive and negative effects of the BA. Overall, student and faculty academic advisors consider the new academic format a positive change. Described by many as streamlined, it offers students a wide array of new and existing courses to choose from, outlines of course content, comprehensive and cohesive programs within disciplines, and the opportunity to graduate after three years with a viable degree.

Despite the enthusiasm over the efficient organization of the curriculum, the changes may be at the expense of flexibility. Students are frustrated by rigidity in the system and see their courses as too structured and modularized. A system that is rigid to the point where it is able to accommodate only those individuals who are able to comply with the format raises concerns.

As one academic advisor stated, "Over the last three years, I have seen students who are creative rather than disciplined get lost in the system or drop out."

The new degree structure has considerably altered the university classroom atmosphere as well. Delivery of course material and the type of faculty-student interaction are more similar to what takes place in a high school classroom than what is expected to take place in a classroom that is designed to foster individual development. As many of the study's participants observed, this approach to teaching often results in passive learners who lack curiosity, critical development, and political initiative. These students master material and move through the system at the expense of learning to be independent thinkers and at the expense of developing their knowledge, character, and behavior. Reinforcement of the passive student role runs the risk of stifling creativity and imagination. As Warnock (1973) noted, "a good education must, above all things, be directed toward the strengthening of the faculty of imagination" (p. 112). In addition, the increased use of university assistants and the consequent inclination toward eventual standardization of courses and their content runs the risk of removing any opportunity for scientific and theoretical transfer back to the students.

The responses of both faculty and student academic advisors suggest that the structure imposed on the curriculum and the classroom by the BA has neglected, or lost sight of, the importance of deep processing in both student learning and faculty teaching. Essentially, the point is that we need to get students to think about their learning and teachers to think about their teaching. Learning is more likely to be remembered and used if it is meaningful. "Students do not use deep processing when examinations require only memorization of facts" (Wright, 1995).

Faculty and student academic advisor responses to the question concerning the role of productivity and efficiency in the BA policy raise little doubt about the emphasis on quantity objectives. Each of the three accountability mechanisms—student financial aid, the taxi-meter system, and the first-year qualifying exam—illustrates some of the issues that arise when concerns about accommodation and cost-effectiveness override concerns about educational quality.

The effect the emphasis on quantity objectives has had on students' educational experience is evident. Student and faculty advisor responses suggest that an increasing level of concern over student financial aid in its current form is consuming students' time and energy, and distracting them from learning. The stringent rules, which threaten discontinuation of financial support if the student is unable to progress through the coursework without difficulty, make no allowances for special situations or circumstances—there is no flexibility in the system to accommodate anything beyond the prescriptive and calculated allotment of financial aid. As a result, students are nervous about losing financial aid, and thus concentrate their efforts on studying the material required to pass their exams. Because student progress through the curriculum—including passage of course sequences and intermediate examinations, and ultimately, completion of the course of study—is considered a positive effect of strict financial aid, it is viewed as an important indicator of program quality. However, the type of student emerging from this program may lack motivation, initiative, and the ability to think independently.

Whereas student financial support controls the student, the taxi-meter system controls the faculty. This system can be likened to a cost-benefit analysis approach often used in business where an economic value is assigned to the benefits of production. The problem that arises here is that a monetary value is placed on passed exams as a reward for faculty performance within institutions. In such an environment, the financial reward, and not learning, can easily become the goal of teaching. In other words, teaching is not viewed as a means to improve the quality of the students' education (Wright and O'Neil, 1995)—the university's preoccupation is with getting the teaching done, not with doing it well. Signs that this is already occurring are apparent in the changed instructional orientation of the faculty toward the students. Faculty do not have time to answer students' questions, and students sense that faculty—albeit, most likely without conscious effort or intent—attempt to control and mold students and what they learn more than they would if the taxi-meter system did not exist.

The purpose of the first-year qualifying exam is to weed out students who are not "academically suited" for a university education, in order to replace those students with new enrollees. Unfortunately, the exams have come to be viewed quite differently by members of the university. "These exams do not really limit the advancement of those who are less intelligent . . . rather, they limit the advancement of those who have a family, a job, or personal idiosyncrasies that do not fit into the existing structure." Students feel threatened by these exams, and faculty view them as an expensive and administrative hassle.

All three accountability mechanisms limit the criteria of success to quantitative outcomes and provide no information about qualitative effects. Pressures on students to succeed in order to retain financial support or continue their studies, and pressures on faculty to produce "effective students" (Conrad, 1990) send a message that productivity and efficiency of the system are more important than the quality of the product produced. "When higher education institutions are viewed and comprehended in terms of a business or factory production model, then society runs the risk that the products and processes of higher education institutions are only judged in terms of institutional profits and efficiency. If this happens, then some of the fundamental values and characteristics of higher education disappear into the background" (Van Vught, 1994, p. 12).

Studies of teaching and learning have shown that teaching does indeed have marked effects on study approaches and learning quality and that, in addition to what is taught, "there are marked influences from the general 'learning ambiance' in a department, including workload, teaching methods, choice of assessment tasks, opportunity for faculty-student interaction, and similar components of the academic environment" (Knapper, 1995). Other study findings also suggest that students who conceive of learning as a quantitative increase in knowledge, or as memorizing, are unlikely to adapt a deep approach to learning (Trigwell, 1995). Conversely, students who conceive of learning as the abstraction of meaning, or as an interpretive process aimed at understanding reality, are more likely to adopt a deep approach to learning the topic. Thus, there is evidence to suggest that the changes in curriculum content and format accompanied by accountability measures required by the Danish University 1990 BA Ordinance have created a pedagogical atmosphere that negatively affects students' educational experience.

CONCLUSION

In a study of the West German higher education system, Teichler (1977) observed that relationships between expansion and quality are directly addressed in proposals to limit most courses of study to three years or else greatly expand short-cycle higher education. "Here the creation of capacities becomes the dominant goal . . . for which the educational quality may be sacrificed to a certain degree" (Teichler, 1977, p.85). As this study shows, Teichler's observation can be used to describe the impact of the BA policy in Danish higher education.

External entities want a productive and efficient university system, but they also want the university to provide a quality education. The Danish University 1990 Bachelor Degree is a policy that is driven by quantity objectives. As such it has aggravated tensions between elitist traditions and mass higher education as well as raised issues concerning academic standards and the quality of students' educational experience. This does not mean such a policy has been completely detrimental to the Danish higher education system. In some respects, the policy has been beneficial—students are pleased with the restructured form and content of the curriculum. On the other hand, students expressed strong feelings about the lack of flexibility in the system and its effects on their educational experience. As has been illustrated by the effects of the BA on Danish higher education, accountability systems can be costly to the most crucial goals of teaching and learning. It has been argued (Lewin, 1952) that emphasis on quantity objectives alone do not effect change in the long term but must be complemented by investment in enhancement initiatives. Such enhancement programs seek to engage faculty in the development of projects which will motivate their colleagues to explore and apply innovative approaches in the various aspects of their work. Using this case study showing the effects of one policy on one nation's higher education system as an example, institutions should consider how much quantity or productivity and efficiency are allowed to govern the policies the system adopts. If the chief product of a quality university education—learning, in all its manifestations—consists primarily of changes in people—changes in their knowledge, their characteristics, and their behavior—it is important to tackle the aspects of an educational structure that may be negatively affecting the quality of teaching and learning that is taking place.

NOTES

1. Gymnasium is a three-year course leading to the Upper Secondary School Exam which qualifies the student for admission to the university and other higher education institutions.
2. The Upper Secondary School Exam is a written examination in Danish and other subjects administered after the third year. The higher preparatory examination (H Exam) is an alternative and equivalent to the Upper Secondary School Exam. It was introduced at the end of the 1960's for those young people and adults who at some point had left the educational system but wished to return to it.

REFERENCES

Bowen, H.R. (1980). *Investment in learning*. San Francisco, CA: Jossey-Bass Publishers.
Conrad, J. (1990). Prospects for the 1990s: Necessary renewal or alarming change in the Danish higher education system? *European Journal of Education,* 25(2), 203-218.
Ellerhøj, S. & Grane, L. (Eds.). (1986). *Københavns universitet 1479-1979*. Copenhagen, Denmark: GEC Gads Forlag.
Gordon, G. & Partington, P.A. (1995). The Impact of national developments on the

quality of university teaching. In Wright, Alan (Ed.) *Teaching improvement practices. Successful strategies for higher education* (pp. 369-392). Bolton, MA: Anker Publishing Company, Inc.

Knapper, C.K. (1995). Understanding student learning: Implications for instructional practice. In Wright, Alan (Ed.) *Teaching improvement practices. Successful strategies for higher education* (pp. 58-75). Bolton, MA: Anker Publishing Company, Inc.

Laugesen, J. (1993, September 2). Universitetsvirksomhed. *Humanist,* p. 4-5.

Laursen, P.F. (1993). Students' choice and social selection. *Scandinavian Journal of Education Research,* 37(4), 279-291.

Lewin, K. (1952). *Field theory in social science.* London, UK: Tavistock.

Mortensen, K.P., and Gregersen, Frans (1993). BA og tilvalg: En historisk føljeton. *Det Humanistiske Fakultets Tutorseminar,* Copenhagen, Denmark: Copenhagen University.

Neave, Guy R. (1985). Elite and mass higher education in Britain: A regressive model? *Comparative Education Review,* 29(3), 347-361.

Perkin, H. (1977). Mass higher education and the elitist tradition: The English experience. *Western European Education,* 8(1-2), 11-35.

Strauss, A.L. (1987). *Qualitative analysis for social scientists.* Cambridge, MA: Cambridge University Press.

Stybe, S.E. (1979). *Copenhagen university: 500 years of science and scholarship.* Copenhagen, Denmark: G.E.C. Gad Publishers.

Teichler, U. (1977). Problems of West German universities on the way to mass higher education. *Western European Education,* 8 (1-2), 81-120.

Tesch, R. (1990). *Qualitative research. Analysis types and software tools.* New York, NY: The Falmer Press.

Trigwell, K. (1995). Increasing faculty understanding of teaching. In Wright, Alan (Ed.), *Teaching improvement practices. Successful strategies for higher education* (pp. 76-100). Bolton, MA: Anker Publishing Company, Inc.

Trow, M. (1973). Problems in the transition from elite to mass higher education. Princeton, NJ: Carnegie Commission Report on Higher Education.

Van Vught, F. (1994, June 9-10). The new context for academic quality. Paper presented for the Symposium "University and Society" Wirtschaftsuniversit, Vienna.

Warner, R. (1977). Mass higher education and the elitist tradition. *Western European Education,* 8(1-2), 3-4.

Warnock, M. (1973). Towards a definition of quality in education. In Peters, R.S. (Ed.), *The philosophy of education* (pp. 112-122). Oxford, England: Oxford University Press.

Wright, W.A. (1995). Introduction. In Wright, Alan (Ed.) *Teaching improvement practices. Successful strategies for higher education* (pp. ix-xii). Bolton, MA: Anker Publishing Company, Inc.

Wright, W.A. & O'Neil, M.C. (1995). Teaching improvement practices: International perspectives. In Wright, Alan (Ed.) *Teaching improvement practices. Successful strategies for higher education* (pp. 1-57). Bolton, MA: Anker Publishing Company, Inc.

CHAPTER 15

From Experiment to Enterprise
Distance Teaching at the University of the West Indies
Howard A. Fergus

INTRODUCTION

The term "bimodal" is being increasingly employed to describe the thrust in distance teaching and learning in addition to conventional face-to-face lecturing at the University of the West Indies (UWI) (Perraton, 1995). Both activities are not, however, mutually exclusive. Distance teaching as it exists today and as projected is the result of a gestation and evolution over almost two decades. In distance teaching, the typical transaction among teacher, learner and learning materials—whether printed materials or audio and video tapes—takes place, but it is possible for teacher and learner to never meet face to face. On the other hand, there can be various degrees of contact between the two, whether personally or through various telecommunications media.

This chapter outlines and analyses the origin and development of distance teaching at the UWI and the changes in teaching methodology that are associated with it. The first section examines the origin of the concept, the second deals with its acceptance and institutionalization and the third with its current privileged status. In the fourth and final section I draw certain conclusions with emphasis on the dominant knowledge delivery mechanism and the potential impact of distance teaching on the general teaching culture at the UWI.

THE EXPERIMENT

Pioneered by Dr. Fred Nunes and colleagues in the Faculty of Social Sciences at the Jamaica campus in 1977, what is now referred to as distance teaching was called the Challenge program precisely because it was a peripheral activity for persons outside the walls of the University; they were given the opportunity to challenge the system and accumulate credits without any tuition from University faculty on the campus. Strictly speaking it was not at the outset distance teaching at all but an outreach program which offered certain educational opportunities to the far-flung constituents of a regional university which serves a straggling archipelago of islands stretching from the Bahamas in the north to Trinidad in the south (a distance of 1,800 miles) with outposts as far west as Belize and as far east as Barbados.

This project was in fact designated Challenge Examinations, for it actually allowed enterprising students to write the first-year examinations in a degree program provided that they satisfied normal matriculation requirements and had registered as bona fide students of the University, albeit in a second rate sense. It was not dissimilar to the opportunity given by London University for external overseas students to acquire degrees without leaving their country. In both cases the students sought and obtained tuition elsewhere possibly on their initiative. This is part of the challenge which lay further in the fact that the non-campus student must take the same examination as the campus counterpart who is a student by occupation, is in contact with professional and assumedly competent lecturers who are at the advancing frontiers of knowledge, and has access to adequate learning resources including proper libraries. These resources are not usually available to the student-adventurer who typically has a full-time job. Consequently, the course demands a high level of motivation, commitment and discipline (Fergus, 1981). Even so, it takes the student two years to complete a first-year course.

The only teaching-related move made by the UWI faculty was to approve the names of persons selected locally to provide tuition in some courses and to provide syllabi or course outlines. The Challenge prototype of distance teaching would not have been possible without Resident (Extra-Mural) Tutors—UWI outreach representatives in the various territorial outposts. They too embraced the challenge. Drawing on their experience in mobilizing learning resources and organizing courses for adults, they provided such learning support for the students as they could including engaging local tutors. Nunes recognized their critical role when he said in a 1977 letter to resident tutors: "What happens to the notion of Challenge examinations is now very much in your hands and the candidates performance." Thus the idea of distance teaching being driven by team work and collaborative effort was established from the very beginning. The quote from Nunes also underscores the essentially laissez-faire position of the teaching staff at the central campus in Jamaica as far as the actual delivery of learning to these enterprising students was concerned. Even at a relatively short distance, they were not really UWI students.

It was the resident tutor who saw to it that teaching was provided, thereby expanding the local academic program which was hitherto confined largely to secondary level work. Where their own subject specialty allowed, they themselves taught, and they scouted their territories for subject teachers. The usual screening and meticulous selection process was abandoned because these tutors were not UWI staff, and the catchment from which to draw them was in most cases minuscule; some were themselves graduates of the UWI and some had been educated elsewhere. For example, some accounting teachers were drawn from among the practicing accountants of city firms—most of whom were not UWI graduates. A few tutors had formal teacher training skills, but most did not. In any case such training was, in the majority of cases, geared to primary and secondary school teaching and not to the teaching of adults. The delivery of learning at the initiation of distance teaching was characterized by a marked miscellaneity, and a lack of relevant training apart from the general orientation to the program which resident tutors provided for the local tutors.

It is worth observing that this situation did not differ significantly from what is found on the campus. The UWI has always had a Faculty of Education or its equivalent, but its focus is primary and secondary education. (Some training initiatives for adult educators have been made by the Department of Extra-Mural Studies (now School of Continuing Studies), but I know of no University lecturer who has ever been a student of these courses). So the situation as far as lecturer training is concerned was very much the same at the center and the periphery, except that at the center there were professional lecturers with experience in teaching at a postsecondary level.

Without training, persons tend to teach in much the same manner in which they were themselves taught. In fact, in an unpublished study at the University of Nottingham, B. Leighton (1975) found (albeit with some qualification) that in the majority of cases the influence of teachers early education is stronger than the influence of teacher training on their own teaching. The situation could be worse where there is no training at all. Many of the early Challenge tutors were neither lecturers nor teachers by profession. It should not be surprising therefore that the dominant teaching mode adopted by the these tutors was primarily a didactic or recitative one—the kind of approach to teaching that Paulo Freire criticized as the "banking concept of education" (Freire, 1972, p. 46). With both lecturers and students operating part-time, the customary pressure to cover syllabi was even greater than usual. The temptation for one to make deposits of knowledge on the other as recipient with scant room for inquiry or exchange of ideas was more likely. Certainly, there were exceptional tutors and exceptional classes, but we are describing the generality.

This mode of teaching, combined with various problems in quantity and quality of support materials, contributed to high drop-out rates. Table 1 presents the drop-out rates for St. Lucia and other relevant data for the first years of the program in that country. The completion rate improved somewhat over time but with little change in the subjects passed.

Table 1

Drop-out Rates for First Years of Distance Education in St. Lucia

Year	Registered	Drop-Outs	Subjects Offered	Passed	Drop-out Rate
1977/78	10	8	Accounting I Politics Statistics	2	75%
1978/79	13	10	Accounting I Economics Sociology	3	77%
1979/80	14	7	Economics Sociology Politics	7	50%
1980/81	14	5	Politics Sociology Economics History	9	36%

Source: Challenge Data, University Center, St. Lucia

Generally, by the third and fourth year, the Challenge program was realizing moderate success. In Antigua, which had a reasonably well organized library, 75% of the students who enrolled in Challenge courses ultimately completed the 1978 examinations—of them, 56% passed in one subject, and 50% passed in more than one (Bird, 1978). In 1981, 23 individuals completed exams in 38 subjects, achieving 17 passing grades, 11 re-takes, and 10 outright failures (Bird, 1981). Other territories showed similar progress. In St. Kitts of 18 students who registered in 1978-79, 12 completed examinations, with 6 obtaining passing grades. In the following year of 30 who registered, 26 completed examination papers, 11 earned passing grades, and 4 were allowed to re-take their exams (Richardson, 1980).

By the end of its first two years—that is, the initial experimental period—

the Challenge scheme was extended for a further two years presumably because of the promise it held for accelerating training at the tertiary level. The public service sector in particular benefited, as the Certificate in Public Administration—which could now be completed in its entirety off campus—was introduced. During its third and fourth years, the program began to attract significant financial support. A subsidy from the St. Lucian Government enabled the resident tutor to mount a four-day workshop in 1981, using lecturers from the Trinidad campus of the University of the West Indies. Private grants also allowed Antigua to bring lecturers to that state for weekend teach-ins and tutorials. This strategy of students meeting together with lecturers in workshops occasionally (though these were too few and far between), was and remains vital to the distance teaching mode. It is somewhat analogous to the regional tutorials which are regarded as critical to the success of the British Open University model.

After four years of experimentation, distance teaching began to gain some acceptance with the UWI. Some governments recognized its value and gave financial and moral support—in some territories this took the form of half or full-day releases to facilitate private or group study. The originator described the results as "very encouraging". Recognition came from the central administration of the University, but it was grudging and guarded; it warned that the number of courses has to be limited lest Challenge examinations become an undue burden on the University's resources. Whatever the teaching mode, official recognition and resources are not irrelevant to a discussion on pedagogy. If distance learning were to succeed, it needed a certain level of material support—and support is contingent upon central recognition.

Up to this point distance teaching at UWI was a marginal activity with the Mona Faculty of Social Sciences and the Resident Tutor and their students as the key players. It should not be surprising that the courses taught and degree programs offered—Bachelor of Social Sciences Part I and the Certificates in Public and Business Administration—all emanated from the Faculty of Social Sciences. In the next developmental phase, other Faculties would be involved and the Challenge approach would begin to assume some elements of an instructional system owned by the UWI.

LIMITED ACCEPTANCE

Central to this phase was the establishment and operation of an interactive teleconferencing system and a modest production of instructional materials. By 1983 the system was operational and consisted of a combination of technology as this excerpt from a 1986 Report indicates. From the Mona (Jamaica) campus—the nerve center—the process worked as follows:

> the signal travels by a four-wire telephone line to the Kingston offices of the Jamaica International Telecommunications Company and thence by microwave circuit to their satellite ground station . . . . It is relayed via the INTELSAT flight 4 satellite . . . to Trinidad and by microwave link, to the Cable and Wireless office in St. Lucia which is the hub of the system. From there it goes out to the international gateways in Dominica, Antigua and Trinidad by microwave circuits and to Barbados by tropospheric scatter. The final link to all the University sites is by four-wire telephone lines. (Lalor & Marrett, 1986, p.16)

This education by teleconferencing was an experiment funded by the United States Agency for International Development. As only three of the non-campus territories were involved, the first three years, 1983-86, could be considered as the period of the pilot study. This was appropriately called the University of the West Indies Distance Teaching Experiment (UWIDITE). That the leading personality behind the experiment—indeed the director of the project—was of Pro-Vice Chancellor rank, was of great significance.

Teaching through teleconferencing facilitated expansion of the scope of distance teaching. It expanded from the Faculty of Social Science to include Law—which offered the LLB Part One and a Certificate in Introductory Legal Studies—and the Faculty of Arts and General Studies, which offered First Year courses in the Bachelor of Arts program. In addition, a variety of non-credential professional courses were offered in such areas as health and nutrition, agriculture and science technology.

Fortunately, some attention was eventually given to the quality of instruction. The need for teaching materials beyond the course outlines was recognized. In the words of an official document, this would be "something longer and more detailed than good lecture notes which would direct the student very closely to the course offerings, indicate possible problems areas and provide, as necessary a guide to additional reading and study." (Lalor & Marrett, 1986, p. 25) Printed booklets and audio and video cassettes were intended, although the latter would be very long in coming. Such materials were certainly needed to help improve an environment in which adult learners struggled to succeed, not only without the benefit of well-equipped libraries—and in some cases, there was no library at all—but often without even an adequate supply of text books. This meant that tutors and students often relied on a judicious combination of in-text guidance and independent study.

Acceptance of this need for materials—and their accompanying uses—was far from unanimous, and the provision of print material to students even in the form of lesson notes was by no means universal. The 'banking' concept was still dominant, and the learning transaction was typically between the voice and a person—and in many cases, the potential for interaction was scarcely considered.

There are other problems which are not of a pedagogical nature bearing on the entire instructional system. Once printed materials were put in the public domain, the issue of who would own the copyright had to be settled. In cases where UWIDITE funded production, it was agreed that the organization would jointly own the copyright with the author, who could also sell the material.

What was important at this stage was that there was at least limited acceptance of the principle that distance learning and teaching requires a well organized instructional system that would involve a team of persons with shared goals. In addition to the UWIDITE management and technical staff—which are inherently critical to the system—presenters, researchers, consultants, and even graphic artists were part of such a team.

Since commitment to teaching materials from the center and indeed funding for the materials were limited, local tutors continued to play a pivotal role in the scheme. The University recognized their importance and the need to provide them with some orientation. Consequently a number of local tutors from various islands were assembled at the Barbados campus for discussion on the various courses with the campus tutors of those courses. This happened just once or twice, but it reinforced the recognition of the need for training as well as for meaningful articulation among those who designed, taught and evaluated the courses taken at a distance.

Presenters at the Mona center were not all entirely void of training. The Washington-based Academy for Educational Development which was associated with the implementation of the project included training in its portfolio. Training sessions were mounted both for the technical staff and the curriculum and instructions staff. The involvement of the UWI Faculty of Education in these programs, albeit limited, was a welcome move. Some of the print material produced for these sessions reveal a decided methodological orientation. Examples include the "UWIDITE Course Development Manual" by Zellyne Jennings and Christine Marrett, "Distance Teaching with Video Productions" by C. Marrett, and "Managing a Distance Teaching Session" by V. McClenan. Marrett and McClenan belonged to the UWIDITE staff, but Jennings was a reputable Faculty of Education scholar. Her involvement augured well for distance teaching. In a new sense, then, many seeds for creative development were sown in this period. The figures in Appendix A (again using St. Lucia) illustrate the changing scope of distance teaching.

THE ENTERPRISE (PRIVILEGED STATUS)

The ideal distance learning system as envisaged at the UWI is still in the process of evolving, but the chances of attainment of the ideal are propitious because of the official status that it has been granted in the University. In its Development Plan 1990-2000 AD, the UWI projected an enrollment target of 18,500 of which 2,200 would be distance education students. Distance learning is therefore seriously perceived as a critical mechanism for rapid human resource development in the community served by the University. As an indication of UWI's commitment to this new endeavor, a three-man team headed by Dr. William Renwick of the Commonwealth of Learning (Vancouver, Canada) was appointed to advise on the direction forward. Several topics addressed in their Report—institutional support, pedagogical modalities, and training and evaluation—frame the discussion for the remainder of this chapter.

INSTITUTIONAL SUPPORT

The establishment of a Distance Education Center headed by a Director was a major development, and its five primary functions are instructive:

(a) To work with and guide academic staff as they develop and edit distance-education materials.
(b) To set up, supervise and monitor student tutorial and support services in cooperation with campus and non-campus academic staff.
(c) To act as the first point of reference for distance-education students, ensuring that any student difficulties are resolved as rapidly as possible by academic or administrative staff as appropriate.
(d) To have responsibility for the quality of all University distance-education activities.
(e) To undertake formative evaluation on distance-education activities. (UWI, April 1995 p.1)

At this administrative level, attention is to be paid to pedagogy, and judging from the rhetoric, the governance of distance teaching is intended to be not only student-friendly, but student-centered. The reference to formative evaluation seems innocent enough, but it signals a serious intention to systematically and progressively develop an instructional system, making adjustments as prudence and sound course preparation and pedagogical principles dictate.

In addition to the Center, there is an Advisory Board on distance education comprising senior decision makers of the University, chaired by the Pro-Vice Chancellor for Academic-Affairs and with representation from the Resident Tutors, the on-the-ground managers of the system. This structure should ensure central administrative attention, as well as a reasonable allocation of resources—both of which are necessary if the endeavor is to succeed. With this kind of administrative arrangement, faculty members are more likely to see distance teaching as integral to their work—indeed, perhaps even as having prestige. With proper central funding, it would be easier to cross the conceptual border from 'challenge experiment' to distance teaching as a thriving enterprise. Equally important, UWI has agreed that funding must be more easily made available for training—a confirmation of the observation earlier that training is indispensable to the success of distance teaching as a mode of knowledge delivery. The reasonable assumption here is that all of this administrative machinery has important implications for the quality of teaching at a distance. Indeed, these are vital aspects of teaching support in general.

In the same vein, it is worth mention that with the support of participating governments, the University has been able to secure a major loan from the Caribbean Development Bank, with the primary aim of upgrading and extending the telecommunications aspect of the project. However, even in negotiating this loan, concerns about the system and quality of instruction were prominent. A total of US$1,500,000 is earmarked for expenditure on curriculum development and the production of teaching materials.

The following excerpt from a circular letter from the University Director of Administration/Registrar to the resident tutors underscores the changing administrative climate which underpins distance education in this region:

> You will be pleased to know also, that in order to address the concerns and frequent complaints about administrative delays relating to student matters such as admissions, registrations, and examinations, a Deputy University Registrar has been appointed, not only to service the meetings of the new Boards, but to ensure that there is efficient and timely administration of student affairs for Non-campus countries and Distance Education students.

PEDAGOGICAL TECHNIQUES

Currently the dominant approach is for the course lecturer or presenter to lecture over the telecommunications system in a fairly conventional way. The student purchases a supplemental course book to accompany these lectures. A model is currently in development, in which the course material that is placed in the hand of the student is inherently self-instructional. This technique, incidentally, is not entirely new to the Caribbean—the Commonwealth Youth Program (CYP), headquartered in Guyana, has been experimenting with training youth workers in the region in a Diploma Course using this identical mode for its handbooks. The difference here, is that where the CYP used local tutors for tutorial sessions, the UWI will use a faculty member—who may or may not be the author of the course materials—to conduct the tutorials by teleconferencing. This is seen as a more dynamic, creative, and economical way of using the technology.

Basic information which can be read from a handout will not be presented on the UWIDITE system. The teleconferencing periods will be fewer, and will be reserved for cognitive encounters. Ideally, the course materials will be based on sound pedagogical principles and will be written in a manner to aid and induce an active sense of engagement and learning. The persona of the instructor becomes evident in the learning material, just as the planning and writing of courses are infused and informed by pedagogical styles and principles.

An article in the *New Distance Education Newsletter* provides six useful elements to describe the entire distance learning and teaching system.

(a) A study guide: the student reads a study guide, which carries the main burden of teaching and takes the place of on-campus lecturers.

(b) Assignments: students will do written assignments included in the study guide and send them on to a tutor for marking.

(c) Readings: in most courses students will receive a volume of readings to supplement the teaching in the guide.

(d) UWIDITE: tutorials and seminars to back up the printed materials will be arranged on the UWIDITE telecommunications system.

(e) Other media: wherever possible students will get audio cassettes as well as study guides. Video-cassettes and the use of computer conferencing may follow.

(f) Face-to-face sessions: there will be opportunities for students to come together either for a local tutorial within their own territory or at a session in the vacation on one of the campuses.

(UWI, 1995, pp. 2-3)

This is in reality a mix or continuum of teaching strategies which ranges from reading the text through interactive teleconferencing to close-up tutorials inter-changes. Some of it is still futuristic, but it has the potential to transform not just the present teleconferencing mode but the whole attitude towards pedagogy in the UWI.

The new system incorporates a role change for the local tutor—the lynchpin of the former approach to distance education in the region. His role will change from being the chief dispenser of information to one of tutor or counselor (Perraton, 1995, p. 8). Resident tutors Bellott and Steele have suggested a 13-point workplan for the local tutor, which includes regular tutorial sessions with students, assisting them with planning weekly schedules, giving first marks and immediate feedback, exposing students 'to good study habits,' keeping records of their attendance and progress, and ensuring that the site has copies of recommended books and readings in sufficient quantities (Steele and Bellott, 1995). Such an agenda may prove too wide, duplicative, and even expensive, but it illustrates the perceived importance of the local tutor in this instructional scheme as well as the multi-faceted nature of the support needed in distance education.

There may be a variety of views toward the role of the local tutor, but there is general agreement on the need for counseling as a supplement to course delivery. Scholars have observed the need for advice on course and program choice, on study and essay writing skills, and on approaches to writing examinations (Renwick et al. 1992). Resident tutors have always assisted with some of these tasks on an ad hoc basis, but the present intention is to institutionalize counseling as an aspect of the new instructional environment.

The perceived role of the local tutor underscores the continuing need for face-to-face contact in the evolving dispensation. And as we have observed before, the best practice in open or distance learning suggests that there is no substitute for students meeting together and with facilitators at one level or another. We have to be careful, however, that even though the nature of the contact is different from the conventional situation, we do not end up with so much contact that one of the crucial advantages of distance teaching technology—the economy of scale realized by teaching large numbers—is not counterbalanced and nullified by the number of functionaries we feel obliged to utilize in the new process.

TRAINING

Good training invariably enhances teaching, and given all the new capabilities required for these new pedagogical approaches, it should not be surprising that a regime of training is contemplated. The range of persons requiring
training will include course writers, resident tutors, local tutors, and faculty
members—both as course writers and as presenters or instructors. As evidence of the importance attached to training, a professional with the title
of Training Specialist has been engaged at the Distance Education Center.

Discussions on training are already being held with the UWI Faculty of
Education as a potential ally—if not a primary supplier—of training. While
the Faculty has trained persons for tertiary education, they have not had a
tradition of training university staff in pedagogical skills. Indeed, many of
the university's faculty have relatively little formal training in pedagogy, adult
learning, or student development. Depending on their previous career path,
a few have had professional training, and a smaller few have taken the UWI
Diploma course in education, but these are the exceptions.

If distance teaching highlights the need for teacher training of university staff generally, it will have served a dual purpose and at a propitious time.
Although ability to teach has been long accepted as one of the criteria for
professional advancement, the actual emphasis has been almost exclusively
on publications. An effort has been made more recently to provide more
emphasis on the teaching criterion. Moreover, a program instituted by the
Vice Chancellor to award faculty excellence includes teaching as one of the
categories of service which attracts recognition. It seems reasonable that if
teaching ability is to be a premium in an institution whose business is about
education, it must provide its own staff with the capability to educate—a
capability which includes not only knowing what to teach, but knowing how.

Distance teaching is poised to move towards a new level of prominence
and support in the region. Training has already been provided for course writers, and course instructors will be next. Less pretentious than many
on-campus faculty members, resident tutors recognize their need for training and are enthusiastic about attending their first workshop in student support services, scheduled for January 1997. They are also keen to have the
local tutor, a vital link in the delivery chain, trained in the distance education instructional mold. Resident tutors Steele and Bellott envisage training for local tutors as facilitators of face-to-face learning as well as
correspondence "teachers." Their rationale is that:

It is likely that local tutors will experience some difficulty in adapting their accustomed teaching style from conventional to a distant mode, the latter implying greater emphasis on interaction in which the tutor acts as facilitator. Additionally, students who are themselves not familiar with the technologies of studying at a distance, may exert pressure to have the tutor revert to a more didactic teaching style (Steele and Bellott, 1995, p. 5)

If, as they also suggest, the course instructor is to ensure that teleconference seminars are used "to instruct the local tutors of their role in the pedagogy," the training of the course tutors themselves cannot be left to chance. It is evident that the training of a range of enablers and facilitators has to be part and parcel of the technology of distance learning and teaching.

EVALUATION

No discussion of an instructional system is complete without reference to evaluation. Renwick et al. (1992) lamented the absence of comprehensive data on the distance teaching experiment including information on the academic progress of students. This will be remedied in the new system, but evaluation will hopefully go even further in the future to inform instructional styles. If Renwick's advice is heeded, distance education should be approached in a context of evaluation, research, and development. "And those who are writing, developing and teaching courses for distance study should have regular access to feedback information from their students on the effectiveness of the study packages, tutorials, and other forms of support intended to facilitate their learning" (Renwick et al., 1992 p. 50). Some of the research may have to be carried out by the Faculty of Education—who should be included at every stage—but much of the evaluative feedback can come from resident tutors, local tutors, and students through the co-ordination of the Distance Education Center—which, depending on its resources, can also engage in action research directly connected with the methodologies of distance teaching.

CONCLUSION

Distance teaching is the brave new enterprise at the UWI—it has moved from stage of articulation to stage of action. The momentum behind this initiative is driven in part by needs demonstrated among the distant communities served by the University and in part by the University's own acute awareness of the need to accelerate the process of human resource development throughout the region. The challenge is to meet these needs in a cost-effective and sustainable manner. The drop-out rate on distance learning is not just a reflection of its demand for uncommon commitment but is also often a function of the quality of the teaching and support services available. Any evaluation of the UWI experiment will show that these have been far from adequate.

It is encouraging that the UWI has taken a comprehensive view of the new enterprise and sees the nature and quality of instruction as an important part of a complex of interrelated services—consideration of teaching cannot be isolated from discussions on management and resources. The systemic changes that have been introduced have served to raise the image of distance teaching in the University. Having its own directorate with a Board headed by a Pro-Vice Chancellor and representatives of key players should guarantee not only prestige but also resources. The endorsement of the regional development bank is of both material and symbolic significance.

Distance education is a wave of the future. It is therefore no longer the peripheral or marginal activity that it was in 1978. One has to hope however that the day when distance education students will attain anything resembling parity of treatment and esteem on the part of faculty is not very far away. Training and orientation programs for instructors and even registrar's office staff should take into account these attitudinal problems. Of course the esteem must also be demonstrated in the quality of support services as argued here and elsewhere.

If the development of distance teaching proceeds along the lines envisaged in this chapter, the pedagogical skills of lecturers in general throughout UWI could improve. A new culture of teaching could develop, in which a transition from the concept of lecturer as a dispenser of information can change to that of university teacher where the emphasis is on facilitation and the strategic arrangement of the several units that are necessary for productive cognitive and affective engagement. In an article critical of the University dictum of "publish or perish," *The Economist* observed that "only a handful of universities properly train their teachers to teach" (August 1996, p.14). If distance teaching points the UWI in the direction of 'training teachers to teach,' the outcomes will surely be revolutionary.

REFERENCES

Bird, E. (1978). *Annual Report 1977-1978.* Antigua, Department of Extra-Mural Studies.

Bird, E. (1981). *Annual Report 1980-1981.* Antigua, Department of Extra-Mural Studies.

Fergus, H. (1981). Challenge examinations in the lesser developed countries of the English-speaking Caribbean. *Bulletin of Eastern Caribbean Affairs* Vol. 7, No. 4. Institute of Social and Economic Research UWI, Barbados.

Freire, P. (1972). *The pedagogy of the oppressed.* Middlesex, Penguin Education.

Lalor, G. & Marrett, C. (1986). *Report on the University of the West Indies distance teaching experiment.* Kingston, Jamaica: University of the West Indies.

Leighton, B. (1975). The relation between teaching behaviour of adult education language tutors and their previous education and training. (Unpublished M. Phil Dissertation) University of Nottingham.

Perraton, H. (1995). Developing distance learning at the University of the West Indies. (Unpublished Paper) UWI, Barbados.

Renwick, W., Shale, D. & Rao, C. (1992). *Appraisal of distance education at the University of the West Indies: Draft report for comment.* Commonwealth of Learning, Vancouver.

Richardson, C. (1979). *Annual Report 1978-1979.* St. Kitts, Department of Extra-Mural Studies.

Richardson, C. (1980). *Annual Report 1979-1980.* St. Kitts, Department of Extra-Mural Studies.

Steele, B. & Bellott, E. (1995). The local tutor: Function and duties in the pedagogy of distance education: A position paper for discussion. (Unpublished) UWI, Barbados.

The Economist (1996). Teaching Spires. (August 24th).

The University of the West Indies (1995). Courses being planned and developed. *Distance Education Newsletter* (Barbados) No. 1, April 1995.

Registration/Examination Results 1995/96, St. Lucia

Semester I

Course	Number Registered			Number Sitting			Number Passing			Percentage Pass Rate
	M	F	T	M	F	T	M	F	T	
SY 13G	10	29	39	7	22	29	3	10	13	45%
EC 16A	15	36	51	14	31	45	9	8	17	38
MS 15A	15	65	80	15	56	71	7	27	34	48
GT 11A	12	46	58	13	43	56	11	44	55	96
UC 10A	5	4	9	4	2	6	4	0	4	67
E 10B	3	2	5	3	1	4	2	1	3	75
LA 11A	4	3	7	1	1	2	1	1	2	100
H 17C	4	2	6	3	1	4	1	1	2	50
H 16A	0	2	2	0	1	1	0	0	0	-
E 10A	2	1	3	2	0	2	2	0	2	100
LA 10A	3	2	5	1	2	3	1	2	3	100
LA 13A	2	3	5	2	0	2	2	0	2	100
EC 10C	12	41	53	10	40	50	7	7	14	28

Semester II

Course	Number Registered			Number Sitting			Number Passing			Percentage Pass Rate
	M	F	T	M	F	T	M	F	T	
GT 11B	1	10	11	1	8	9	1	8	9	100%
LA 10B	2	3	5	1	0	1	1	0	1	100
LA 11B	3	3	6	2	0	2	2	0	2	100
MS 15B	13	52	65	11	41	52	7	35	42	81
MS 18A	10	48	58	10	37	47	10	33	43	91
MS 12A	11	15	26	9	12	21	7	10	17	81
E 10C	4	2	6	4	1	5	2	0	2	40
EC 14D	15	55	70	11	49	60	5	24	29	48
EC 14B	0	1	1	0	1	1	0	1	1	100
EC 10E	15	40	55	15	32	47	6	13	19	40
H 10D	0	5	5	0	5	5	0	5	5	100
H 16B	4	3	7	4	1	5	4	1	5	100
LA 12B	2	3	5	2	2	4	2	2	4	100
UC 10B	4	4	8	4	1	5	3	0	3	60

Full Year

Course	Number Registered			Number Sitting			Number Passing			Percentage Pass Rate
	M	F	T	M	F	T	M	F	T	
GT 423	3	16	19	1	14	15	0	12	12	87%
GT 424	3	12	15	1	10	11	1	10	11	100
MS 436	15	28	53	11	26	37	7	19	26	70
MS 488	15	44	59	11	33	44	10	26	36	82

Source: University Center, St. Lucia

CHAPTER 16

Integrating Writing Skills into the Curriculum of the Disciplines
A Social Constructionist Approach

Sheila Vance and Glenda Crosling

INTRODUCTION

One of the more common complaints heard about today's college and university education is that its graduates do not have the level of writing skills needed by employers. However, few university teachers consider this to be within the scope of their classroom responsibilities. In higher education, writing development is often seen as an additional and subsidiary component which must compete for space in an already crowded syllabus. Moreover, while academics may believe in the importance of enhancing students' writing ability, they perceive their primary responsibility to rest with subject content and often do not consider themselves to have sufficient expertise in teaching writing. In the light of this conundrum, this chapter explains how academics in all disciplines can integrate writing into their curricula, in collaboration with language specialists. The nature of this collaboration, its theoretical underpinnings and particular teaching strategies are outlined, together with other elements impinging on integrated programs, such as the multicultural student cohort and the increasing use of technology. The theoretical approach is then illustrated through two case studies involving teachers and students in computing and commercial law courses.

WRITING IN AUSTRALIAN UNIVERSITIES

The writing programs described in the following pages must first be understood within the context of the Australian tertiary system. Most often the task of teaching students to write is devolved to writing specialists placed outside, both physically and academically, the disciplinary context. Teaching students to write, that is, how to communicate their disciplinary knowledge, is not normally considered to be within the domain of the subject specialist, who is concerned principally with content knowledge. In Australia, most undergraduate degrees are of three years duration, without a general "freshman" year. English departments teach literary analysis to English literature students only; composition is not taught as part of the degree nor as a compulsory subject for all university students. Hence, those students who receive writing instruction do so through the voluntary programs run by Language and Learning Units. Many such units were originally instituted in response to changes in the student population, with increasing numbers of non-traditional students (i.e. students from non-English speaking backgrounds (NESBs), disadvantaged students, mature-age students, and so on). Many have operated independently of other academic departments, offering generic courses in academic skills. However, for some time there has been a movement toward more context-specific instruction and toward integrated programs run in collaboration with discipline specialists, to the benefit of the entire student cohort. This is the approach the authors have taken in their programs at Monash University.

THEORETICAL FRAMEWORK FOR INTEGRATED WRITING INSTRUCTION

Most writing handbooks or style guides foster the notion that there are two distinct stages of writing: composition, where the writer simply transcribes thought already formed; and editing, where the writing is "fixed up" according to the received wisdom of the style guides. The tendency is thus to view writing as the application of grammatical rules, a mechanical process which can be isolated from the subject content, incorporating a fixed body of "skills" which can be fully mastered (Foster, 1983). This view belies the complex relationship between thought and language and is not supported by studies which have shown that generic writing and study "skills" do not appear to be transferable across contexts, and that de-contextualized courses foster a surface approach to writing and learning (Biggs & Moore, 1993; Martin & Ramsden, 1986; Ramsden, Beswick, & Bowden, 1986). Even 'basic' skills may be influenced by the writing context, with grammatical error often being linked to the constitution of meaning rather than a failure to understand or apply grammatical rules (Taylor & Nightingale, 1990). Hence written expression cannot be viewed in isolation from content. Moreover, a piece of writing may be error-free, but nevertheless ineffective in terms of its rhetorical[1] purpose (Foster, 1983).

As the language and rhetorical structures used will vary with the writing context, our writing programs take a discourse level approach, emphasizing the way meaning is made in the overall text. That is, the focus is on the way that the organization of the ideas and the sentences achieve the writer's purpose and this is derived from an evaluation of the context, including its salient values and expectations. In turn, this influences the sentence level gram-mar and the lexical choice.[2]

Written texts are viewed as acts of communication between writers and readers within social settings (Nystrand, 1986), which in the tertiary envi-ronment are the disciplinary contexts. Spoken and written texts are social acts through which meanings are exchanged, and the social reality created and maintained (Halliday, 1978). Thus, the focus is on the functional role of language and the way that it is used to achieve particular purposes in par-ticular settings (Backhouse, Dudley-Evans, & Henderson, 1993; Love, 1996). In other words, language is not simply a transparent window on the content but the avenue through which meaning is created in a social con-text. For example, a scientific article is often viewed as an "objective" fac-tual report, or simple recount of what was done. Further examination, however, reveals a very complex rhetorical argument in which the author tries to persuade his or her audience of the value of the work, marshaling evidence to mark its place within the established literature, anticipating and rebut-ting potential criticism. Rarely does the linear written *description* of the ex-perimental process match the *actual* research process; rather events are reconstructed in a manner designed to serve the author's purposes (Myers, 1991; Swales, 1987; Lewins, 1992).

This approach accords with the social constructionist view of literacy which stresses that across disciplinary contexts, the structure of knowledge is not universal, but rather a "consensus arrived at for the time being by com-munities of knowledgeable peers" (Bruffee, 1986, p. 776). That is, the way ideas are put together to form concepts and the processes by which these concepts are combined varies across disciplines: they have, for example, their own methods of evaluation, argumentation and use of evidence, which im-pact on the language and structure of the discourse (Becher, 1981; Chanock, 1994; Parry, 1990; Taylor et al. 1988; Toulmin, Reike & Janik, 1984). The resulting shared expectations regulate the world view of members and thus the interpretation made of experience (Bizzell, 1992).

In learning to think, read and write within these disciplinary communi-ties, students need to develop a sense of objectivity akin to an ethnographic approach, examining the discipline's "implicit knowledge and everyday prac-tices" (Clifford & Marcus, 1986, p. 3). Such an approach enables students to appreciate the world view and values of the discourse, and the influence of these values on styles of thought and writing. It also enables them to de-code and recode the discourse, to discern the elements of audience and pur-pose, and understand why the discourses take their particular forms. If they can develop such an approach, they can adapt their language use and writing to appropriate forms as the situation requires (Berkenkotter, Huckin & Ackerman, 1991).

One way to orient students to disciplinary expectations is to make them explicit. Students need to be aware of the expectations of their audiences, which consist of established members of the disciplinary discourse communities who hold implicit assumptions of the shape that the writing should take. Such explication is helpful for all students, but especially so for NESB students who may operate with different expectations concerning discourse conventions.

WRITING IN A MULTICULTURAL CONTEXT

As well as learning to make meaning in disciplinary contexts, students from language and cultural backgrounds other than English need to make other adjustments. Martin (1985) speaks of these students as disadvantaged "outsiders" because they may not appreciate the cultural conventions encoded in the English language and so in their writing may apply discoursal and cultural conventions from their first language and educational culture. By deviating from established academic conventions, students may violate English or Western reader expectations (Purves, 1988). Thus, while their writing may be relatively correct grammatically, it may be received as strange or not quite right (Ostler, 1987; Leki, 1992).

In written discourse, intercultural differences can be manifested in issues such as what is considered relevant and logical, how it is organized, who may construct an argument and what constitutes proof, and what are the rights and responsibilities of writers (Leki, 1992; Kaplan, 1966; Hinds, 1987). At the organizational level in academic writing, students may apply "indigenous discourse patterns" (Fry, 1996, p. 13) and these may be inappropriate. While the Western preference is perceived as linear with pieces of information flowing logically one from another, the Asian preference is said to be one of indirection with the topic viewed from different perspectives (Kaplan, 1987). Another example is Arabic discourse which characteristically includes parallel constructions and repetition of main points leading to an overall sense of balance (Ostler, 1987; Farquharson, 1988). A reader with Western discoursal expectations could experience frustration with such writing, perceiving the former as circular and unfocussed and the latter as repetitive.

Argumentation, that is, the provision of evidence in support of assertions, may also vary interculturally (Leki, 1992). In some cultures, conventions such as drawing analogies and appealing to intuition are considered appropriate but if used in Western discourse may conflict with the reader's expectation of how a point should be argued. Another element of variation concerns critical comment. Individuality is a strong theme in Western academic philosophy, characterized by ". . . creative, critical and responsible" minds (Kadar-Fulop, 1988, p. 37). However, it seems to be a less emphasized educational value in some Asian cultures with implications for the way students deal with dissenting opinions in their reading and writing (Kadar-Fulop, 1988; Osterloh, 1986). Willingness to write critically may also be affected by cultural factors—for example, the sanctity of the written word in the Qu'oran may be transferred to other written material and impinge on students' critical commentary. Moreover, "it would be unusual for a Middle Easterner to write down a critical judgment of anyone"—the expectation is to be polite consistently, even to people disliked (Parker, 1986, p. 95).

Non-native student writing may also be affected by the position such students adopt in relation to their readers. Their writing may reflect a subordinate student and dominant teacher relationship so that the style is "circumlocutory, repetitive and formalized," avoiding the topic because it is impolite for young people to question the views of those in authority or to be direct and raise objections (Ballard & Clanchy, 1991, p. 47). There are also differences in the ways students perceive the responsibilities of writers in relation to their readers. In some languages—such as English—the writer is responsible for making clear to the reader the link between ideas, whereas in other languages—such as Japanese—it is up to the reader to draw the links (Hinds, 1987). The effect is that, in English, the writer gives direction to the reader—transition and discourse markers guide the reader as to the cohesion of the piece and the logic underpinning assertions and conclusions. In contrast, it seems that Japanese writers like to give dark hints and to leave behind nuances, with transition markers being more subtle and requiring a more active role for the reader (Suzuki, cited in Hinds, 1987).

The social constructionist approach is thus of benefit to all students, regardless of background, as it seeks to explicate the discoursal context, providing insight into the underlying disciplinary cultural conventions as well as elucidating the values informing Western academic discourse. Further contextual elements to be considered are the processes involved in researching, reading, and writing and the impact of reading and writing media on these processes.

WRITING AND READING PROCESSES

We have suggested that writing and its instruction ought not be viewed as isolated activities but as activities reflective of the social context. A further consideration is that exclusive attention to final written products may suggest a linear approach to writing, which belies its recursive nature and interdependency with reading processes. Writing is rarely a formulaic exercise of plan-outline-write-edit but rather is an exploratory, generative, and recursive process—planning, drafting, and revising are "heavily interwoven" activities (Hayes & Flower, 1986). Teaching should thus aim to facilitate the development of a range of composing strategies for students to draw on as they face different writing problems. In terms of its relationship to reading, academic writing in particular is heavily dependent on and interwoven with the writings of other authors, requiring the student writer to synthesize and integrate information from other texts. Reading forms the genesis of the critical comment to be incorporated into students' writing. Therefore, the reading of disciplinary texts and articles provides implicit knowledge about methods of argumentation and organization within the discipline (Connor, 1996). Teaching reading strategies for different types of texts and reading purposes complements this tacit knowledge of discourse structures.

As computers are a dominant writing medium in Western universities, we will need to bear in mind the impact they have on reading and writing practices and the construction of knowledge, adjusting our teaching of these processes accordingly.[3] Composing with a word processor may encourage a deep level, recursive approach to writing, as it facilitates experimentation with organization, paragraph structure, and phrasing. However, some studies have found that word processing may encourage recurrent surface level revising, thus interrupting writing flow. According to Pennington (1993), these variations may be accounted for by the students' level of experience and their conceptions of both the writing process and computer use. Novice learners typically begin with a disjointed, non-integrated model of the particular area of learning, focusing on individual features rather than on holistic or global aspects. For example, in first using a computer, learners may treat it as a typewriter or notepad, while at a later stage they will understand it to be a writing environment for the generation of text. Similarly, novices' early conceptions of the writing process may focus on surface level revision rather than global revision. Thus, in seeking to develop students' composing strategies, their models of computer use and of the writing process must be addressed. A second variable to be considered is the type of task: comparison and argumentative tasks may require more frequent high-level revisions than do reporting and structuring tasks. Furthermore, the current state of a writers' knowledge may determine the amount of problem-solving activity and hence the amount of deep level revision (Eklundh, 1994).

Electronic networks can also be used to facilitate writing development, enabling communication with peers in the writing process and in the reshaping of text. As a supplement to and not a replacement for oral discussion (Lewis, 1994; van der Geest & Remmers, 1994), e-mail can facilitate group projects, where all students receive a grade for the same piece of work, and collaborative writing, where a student receives feedback from peers (Lewis, 1994). In their critiques of others' work, students are encouraged to focus first on global elements of organization, use of evidence, audience and purpose, and then on surface errors of spelling and grammar in later drafts. One of the advantages of using e-mail is that potentially marginalized students, such as NESB students who may be loathe to speak out in a group discussion, can have an equal voice. Use of networked collaboration may better prepare students for a workplace environment which incorporates multi-authoring of documents and the use of e-mail as a dominant mode of discourse (Lewis, 1994; van der Geest & Remmers, 1994). As Lewis (1994) points out, such peer collaboration is supported by the social constructionist view that writing is a social, collaborative act of communication between writer and audience and that the knowledge communicated is a construct of language and social context.

As computers are increasingly used as text sources, we also need to consider their impact on reading strategies. In comparing printed and screen texts in terms of reading speed and comprehension, screen texts appear not to inhibit detailed reading but significantly affect the ability to skim and browse (Foertsch, 1995). The screen has the effect of compartmentalizing text, preventing a holistic view, with implications for students' understanding and retention of information obtained on-line. Mental constructs of a particular knowledge area require a sense of the whole, a structure within which details may be placed. Moreover, as the location of information on the page is often used as a retrieval cue, without a visual context the screen reader may have difficulty recalling items because the same retrieval cue is linked with too many pieces of information (Foertsch, 1995). Foertsch (1995) suggests that, as screen texts are less differentiating, we will need to develop new information processing skills.

The development of the hypertext environment may also impact on reading and composing texts. With non-linear, modular, and associative hypertext documents, print reading strategies do not translate well; there may be navigational problems, disorientation and cognitive overload, caused by an overwhelming amount of loosely connected and unstructured information (Palumbo & Prater, 1993). Hypertext thus requires the development of new reading skills, navigational methods and approaches to researching and synthesizing, in accessing vast repositories of knowledge. In teaching researching and reading strategies, we need to remain conscious of this changing learning environment, as "novel problem solving based on access to information will become a necessary job skill" (Palumbo & Prater, 1993, p. 69).

As screen-based texts may encourage a focus on discrete items of information rather than the larger picture, writing instruction should aim to compensate for this by helping students gain a global view of the subject and its discoursal structures. Also, where practicable, aspects of the researching and writing process itself should be modeled to assist students to reflect on their own practices and develop a repertoire of effective composing strategies. As expert writers within the discipline, the subject lecturers may attempt to verbalize their own problem solving and writing processes, including the false starts, blind alleys, and recursive elements of their work. The students themselves are also encouraged to verbalize their approaches, thus making them more conscious of the process involved and providing opportunities to learn from others.

EXPLICATING DISCIPLINARY GENRES
Just as the context of a writing situation shifts, so do the language features and rhetorical strategies of a disciplinary genre change (Freedman & Medway, 1994a).[4] Hence, when introducing disciplinary genres to students, certain principles are followed. Firstly, a descriptive rather than prescriptive approach is taken. Numerous studies of genres have shown that while it may be possible to identify trends or features which commonly appear, equally as often there are innovative variations within the genre which cannot be accounted for by an idealized model (Bazerman, 1988; Freedman, 1993). Hence, rigid models are avoided as they often do not reflect the variation in practice; instead students are encouraged to consider possible structures and the particular demands of the writing context in making their own choices for their texts (Vance, 1995). Secondly, several examples of the genres are used as a means of enhancing student understanding of the writing task. Concrete examples have a greater impact on understanding than abstract models alone; for example, discussing more or less successful examples of an executive summary for a report makes the abstract instruction, "summarize the contents of the report in the executive summary," more tangible.

While professional examples of disciplinary discourse (for example, journal articles) provide valuable discoursal knowledge, student texts also play a significant role in exploring why some texts are more or less successful. Moreover, they truly represent the genre within which the students are operating, as they will not be producing academic journal papers but novice research papers. Also, papers which are annotated by the lecturer provide valuable insight into what is required. Saying "there should be more analysis" is insufficient if the student does not know what analysis in the subject means; through comparing previous student work containing more and less analysis, the students can "see" what is meant.

Clearly, the subject lecturer has a major role to play in explicating the features of the relevant genres; however, we need to go beyond simple transmission of information to a passive audience (for example, simply stating, "note the following features of the introduction"). To encourage active learning, students participate in group discussion of the sample texts and of their own writing and reading processes. They learn from each other through hearing other students' critiques of the samples and by reading what their peers have written and in this process also clarify their understanding of subject content. Tutorial work also includes practice assignments, as many genre theorists would argue that simple explication of the genre is insufficient without performance: "full genre knowledge only becomes available as a result of having written" (Freedman, in Freedman & Medway, 1994a, p. 206). These assignments give students the opportunity to learn by doing and improve on their performance prior to grading.

Another important principle in teaching disciplinary genres is the use of authentic writing tasks (Freedman, 1993). Care must be taken to ensure that writing tasks arise naturally from the subject tasks and are not simply "tacked on" to existing course content. Each writing component should be integrated fully with the aims and objectives of the subjects. As mentioned previously, an obvious way to facilitate the students' transition to the disciplinary context is to make our expectations and evaluative criteria explicit; to provide objectives and rationale for each teaching exercise; and to give criteria for marking.

Having outlined the theoretical underpinning and general teaching strategies of the integrated language programs, the following sections address the relationship between subject and language specialists and describe two approaches to setting up programs.

COLLABORATION BETWEEN SUBJECT AND LANGUAGE SPECIALISTS

The conception of writing fostered by style guides described earlier is one of the reasons subject lecturers often feel "unqualified" to provide instruction on writing within their disciplines, for they "equate advice about writing with advice about grammar", knowledge beyond their own area of expertise (Radloff & Samson, 1993). However, as we have seen, content and the means of its expression are not easily separable; hence, writing instruction should focus on meaning-making rather than on the mechanics or formulaic models of essay writing. This is best effected within the disciplines themselves, for each discipline has its own meaning-making structures and criteria.

Subject specialists who subscribe to the traditionalist conception of writing described above negate their own extensive knowledge about writing within their disciplines. Through publishing, setting and marking assignments, applying for grants, they have intimate, if tacit, knowledge of the rhetorical structures employed. Because they have internalized these structures, often they are no longer conscious of the strategies employed, and so they too need to become ethnographers (Bazerman, 1988). Close collaboration with the language specialist increases their *explicit* understanding of the knowledge they possess *implicitly* and therefore increases their confidence in teaching writing to their students. The language specialist, on the other hand, learns a great deal from the subject specialist about the ways in which knowledge is constructed within the discipline, its central concepts, ways of structuring information, and so on, thus facilitating the improvement of their own teaching practice.

This approach may be usefully described as transdisciplinary, to borrow a model of collaboration from special education. Like the interdisciplinary model, the transdisciplinary model incorporates the sharing of expertise and decision-making; however it also allows for "role transition or role release." That is, team members teach one another to "a high level of understanding and skill that allows them to release to one another professional interventions that previously were guarded and protected by each discipline" (Garner, 1995, p. 5).

PROGRAMS INTEGRATING WRITING IN DISCIPLINARY CONTEXTS

The are two ways to go about integrating writing with discipline content: (a) the subject specialist incorporates writing pedagogy into his or her subjects; or (b) the language specialist is initiated into the discourse and provides instruction.[5] In the former situation, the language and subject specialists collaborate on the development of teaching materials and share teaching methods. The actual instruction may also be shared, either through team teaching or through occasional "guest" lectures by the language specialist. An adjunct program, on the other hand, runs parallel to the main curriculum. Collaboration and team teaching are also integral to this approach, although usually the language specialist is primarily responsible for teaching. These adjunct programs are closely tied to the curriculum, using the content of the subject "as the point of departure" (Brinton, Snow & Wesche, 1989, p. 2), thus providing a useful forum for students' literacy instruction and development.

A major advantage of such programs concerns student motivation. At a time when students are pressured to keep up to date with their studies, often there is limited time or energy to devote to literacy enhancement, despite the central role of writing in study. Because integrated programs utilize course content, students' motivation to participate is high and the learning content is immediately relevant to their needs. Subject content is revised or learned while familiarity with the discourse, modes of communication and distinctive grammatical structures are enhanced.

CASE STUDY 1: INTEGRATING WRITING INTO THE COMPUTING CURRICULUM

The following outlines a teaching program initially developed through a federally-funded project to incorporate writing into the first year Computing curriculum. The project team, consisting of one Computing academic and two Language and Learning academics, consulted with industry professionals, developed teaching materials in collaboration with subject leaders and provided advice on teaching methods to the tutors and lecturers involved in three core first year subjects.[6]

Most undergraduate courses in science and technology-based disciplines offer few opportunities to develop the written communication of students, and there is little or no explicit instruction in the particular language, format, and structural demands of the different types of writing within the discipline. Accordingly, the program seeks to develop students' writing competence through increased exposure to writing tasks involved in the professional and academic computing environments. In so doing, it provides students with greater opportunities to practice writing about computing concepts, thus enhancing their subject knowledge, while at the same time developing students' writing competence through contextualised writing tasks.

The program also seeks to develop students' understanding of the underlying values and rhetorical strategies used in the various writing tasks of their discipline. Examination of a selection of industry documents has revealed a great variety within the generic types, and there appears to be no "standard" format throughout the industry. Therefore, rather than focusing on rigid generic formats, our teaching concentrates on increasing students' awareness of different writing strategies and emphasizes the need to adapt the writing process according to the particular purposes and readerships of different writing tasks. As previously noted, such discipline areas tend to conceive of language as a transparent window on content, and "objectivity" is seen as the predominant feature of the discourse; reports, for example, are seen as simply *recording facts* in a logical order. Our teaching thus analyses the language features and rhetorical strategies creating this impression of objectivity and serving the particular purposes of the author. Our aim is to develop our students' ethnographic abilities so that, as they encounter unfamiliar writing situations in the workplace, they may determine for themselves which linguistic features and strategies are appropriate.

Writing Within the Disciplinary Context

Because computing is a professionally-based discipline, the social setting of its discourse incorporates hypothetical workplace contexts as well as academic contexts. Two of the first-year subjects thus provide opportunities for simulating professional documentation. The main assignment for one subject is an operating systems simulation, which has a small written component incorporating a description of the functionality of the program and a description of where the specifications and functionality vary. To construct this document appropriately, students require an understanding of its purposes and audience. A functionality statement describes *what* a program does, not *how* it does it—its audience is a potential user who needs to determine whether the program will serve his or her needs rather than a programmer who wishes to know how to process a file. Novice student writers commonly confuse the two contexts. The students also need to demonstrate whether or not their program meets the specifications; that is, whether they have been able to achieve the desired outcomes. Analysis of sample documents prior to commencing their assignment facilitates students' understanding of this writing context.[7]

Another subject introduces the system development process and approaches to life cycle models. The first stage of the assignment requires students to simulate interviewing a client and subsequently produce a project brief as the initial contractual arrangement between client and consultant. The second stage involves an analysis of the client's business requirements and the production of a final report incorporating technical diagrams. As no systems are actually developed, a separate exercise in preparing user documentation has been introduced.[8]

The project brief for this subject may be used as an illustration of the students' need to consider the particular values prevailing in the social context of which the written communication is a part. They must develop an understanding of client-consultant relations—consultants depend on the clients for acceptance of proposals and therefore need to project confidence and control in their writing. In this first assignment, often the students' sentences are free from error but do not reflect these dynamics and thus fail to serve their authors' rhetorical purposes. For example, in the brief students are required to set out the expectations of both parties to the business agreement. No doubt due to lack of experience, their phraseology often fails them and does not take into account the impression created. Compare "The consultant should not bother staff" with "The ordinary workings of the library staff will not be disrupted"; and "If you have any problems with the project brief. . ." with "If you have any queries or seek further clarification of terms . . . ." One would not wish to hire a consultant who might be *bothersome* or produce a *problematic* brief. Another example of inexperience with the writing context is the manner in which students often introduce the terms of termination: "If the management finds the computer consultancy inadequate . . . ." A professional seeking to secure a client would not want to even admit the possibility that his/her work might be inadequate. The students have to develop a repertoire of phrases which position themselves as authorities.

It is noteworthy that NESB students in particular misinterpret the discoursal context—for example, "The library's customers will not be harassed or upset in any way," or "Miss X will be faithful in her working hours, not wasting time or increasing the on-site hours," or "The library expects the consultant to be able to do his or her job properly." These difficulties could be seen as not the result of some deficiency in the students' learning but as a reflection of unfamiliarity with the dynamics and power relations inherent in the client/consultant relationship. Initiating students into the discourse in a conscious, explicit fashion will accelerate their development as writers within their discourse community.

In analyzing the systems of a business, a hierarchy of activities must be established, reflecting the order and relationships across these activities. Students' ability in this area often requires development, and this is reflected in the wording and organization of their reports. Many students have difficulty sorting through the great mass of information in the case study to identify main concepts, tending to list the particular details of the client's problems instead of trying to categorize them according to a higher level conception of issues; for example, "They are not sure who their current members are, as their records are inadequate and take too long to retrieve. They do not know how long a person has had a video out for, or which videos they have in stock." Compare these statements with the following:

> The perceived problem areas are management of membership (e.g., keeping accurate membership lists; generating mailing labels; etc.); management of video loans (e.g., the availability of the video and the due date for return, number and type of videos out on loan, etc.); and management of videos (e.g., cataloguing of video titles, date of purchase of video, etc.).[9]

The writer of the latter passage has created a hierarchy through identifying management problems as falling into three areas, membership, video loans, and the videos themselves. Moreover, the student has been able to generate the abstract noun phrase "management of membership" to categorize the type of problem reflected in "they are not sure who their members are." A further examination of this student's work reveals the consistent use of such noun phrases. This is one of the features of academic writing and many professional documents as it allows for abstraction and taxonomy. Once again, drawing students' attention to these features ensures that subsequent reports are more likely to adopt a more professional style and include an appropriate hierarchy of concepts.

While hypothetical workplace contexts are incorporated into the curriculum, much of the disciplinary knowledge is acquired through reading and writing within an academic context; hence there must be appropriate initiation into the conventions of this discourse. Perhaps the most distinguishing features of academic writing are the integration and evaluation of sources, and these activities are often the most difficult for novices to master. The ways in which the writer reports on the literature, simultaneously reflecting the views of various sources yet maintaining a distinguishable position or "voice" in the creation of an argument, are extremely complex and have been the subject of extensive study (Thompson & Yiyun, 1991). In terms of citation, for example, students must not only master the mechanics of convention—positioning, order, punctuation—but more complex aspects such as clearly distinguishing between representation of the author's text and their own evaluation of that text. Moreover, the way in which a student cites information from a text often reveals their attitude to the knowledge presented in the source: the text is an informative text, containing "unequivocal fact"; or the text is interpretive, containing the author's perspective on a subject (Moore, 1994). Compare "An important aspect of C++ is that it is based on the original C language [Joyner, 1992]" with "According to Joyner (1992), the C++ programming language is an adaptation of a traditional programming language C. . ." (Moore, 1994, p. 4). Instruction thus aims to raise awareness of the constructedness of texts, so that students are in a better position to evaluate sources. Analysis and discussion of successful student papers from previous years, together with extracts from expert academic writing (for example, journal articles), facilitate the development of students' understanding of the discourse. Here, subject lecturers may draw on the expertise of language specialists as necessary.

Teaching Strategies

As outlined previously, the teaching methods involve the use of samples of a genre (professional and student), group discussion and analyses of texts, a staged evaluative process which includes opportunities to practice, and explicitly stated teaching objectives and evaluative criteria. Large enrollments and heavy marking loads present challenges to providing appropriate instruction and advice on individual students' writing—hence, we have attempted to introduce avenues for feedback which do not place an excessive strain on the markers. The methods used for the project brief will again serve to illustrate the general approach taken.

The students are first given an opportunity to practice the assignment through a tutorial exercise; a business case study similar to the case study for the assignment. The tutors, posing as clients, are interviewed by the students, who must determine the particular needs of the business and the proposed contractual arrangements for the work to be done. The quality of the project brief will in some measure depend on the students' communicative ability; whether they are able to ask the appropriate questions, listen attentively, and extract the relevant information from the responses. The students are then given general guidelines to follow for writing up the practice project brief. For example, the brief should include the particular problem areas to be investigated, who will be involved in the project, the expected outputs, the financial arrangements, and so on. No prescriptions about the format for the practice brief are given, encouraging students to first consider on their own how they would order the information and format it for readability. The aim is to encourage students to make conscious writing choices, rather than simply providing them with a blueprint to follow unthinkingly.

The subject tutors then read through their students' practice briefs, and the language specialist reads a representative selection from the whole cohort. These practice assignments are not commented on individually, but feedback on common areas of difficulty and success (using concrete examples from student work) is given to the class as a whole in the following lecture. An advantage of group feedback at this early stage is that, instead of receiving a handful of comments individually, the students can benefit from the experiences of their classmates, and have a greater understanding of the quality of work expected. The subject leader then provides a brief for the practice assignment which he himself has written, drawing on his commercial experience and the general tenor of similar industry documents collected. Three successful examples of student briefs are also distributed (anonymously and with the students' permission). The first part of the next tutorial is used to discuss further why they are all successful, comparing the different approaches used, and recommending improvements where necessary. Several examples are used to demonstrate that there is not simply one "correct" way of writing up a brief and to encourage reflection on the different writing strategies which might be employed in different circumstances.

Where possible subject lecturers model the processes involved in assessable work, dividing up and staging assignments to reinforce learning, and providing guidance and feedback at each stage. For example, one subject sets a research paper which incorporates four assessable components: bibliography/library search; summary; essay; oral presentation slides. As each of these components are graded, individual feedback is provided in addition to the group feedback and discussion sessions. Hence, the marking load for this particular subject is high.[10]

For the first component, library staff conduct integrated tutorials on research methodology, developing procedural knowledge and encouraging lateral thinking in the selection of search criteria, as well as introducing the principal information sources of the discipline. A bibliography and list of search terms is then submitted for evaluation by the subject tutors according to set criteria, including breadth and appropriateness of sources used; relevancy, availability, and modernity of publication; and appropriateness of search criteria. This process alerts students to potential weaknesses in their source material and helps to clarify the purpose of the task prior to writing the main piece of assessment. It should be noted here that students are advised of the recursive nature of research; that the bibliography is preliminary, forming the basis for further information searches as they delve deeper into the topic. Teaching instruction for the second component incorporates reading and note-taking strategies in preparation for writing. As with many of the other assignments, a practice tutorial exercise is given prior to the assessed task. Students are assigned a note-taking task using an article related to the research topic. In the subsequent tutorial, small groups are established to compare content and organization of notes, and the strategies employed in the task. A separate article on which the research topic is centered is then assigned for assessment. Writing instruction related to the third component, the research paper itself, uses previous student work to illustrate issues involved in the integration and evaluation of source texts. The fourth assessed component requires students to use a software package to prepare presentation slides based on their research papers. Because of time constraints, the slides are submitted to the tutors without class presentations. This process forces students to consider the main points of their papers—not an easy task for many. It also provides an opportunity to introduce considerations of audience, readability of slides and other matters pertaining to oral presentations.

In all subjects, group discussion is relied on extensively as a means of learning, allowing students to draw on their own experiences and learn from their peers. For example, in the reading strategies component, instead of providing a list of instructions on how to read a text, students are first given the opportunity to reflect on the manner in which they normally approach their reading tasks. In comparing their notes with those of their peers, students' awareness of alternative methods is raised. The tutor then discusses the different reading strategies which might be employed in different reading contexts—for example, reading to find information for an assignment topic, reading for comprehension, reading to remember, reading within different genres and media (i.e., experimental papers or textbook chapters; hypertext). The point is thus made that the notes taken from the same article would vary according to the reading context and the individual purposes of the note-taker. Various approaches to the layout of notes for study purposes are also discussed, as the extensive reading required at the university level is far greater than most students would have experienced previously.

As mentioned earlier, it is important to avoid simply tacking writing assignments onto an existing curriculum. Instead, naturally occurring tasks should be devised. For example, often an article summary exercise is assigned to provide practice in identifying and reporting on salient points, essential skills involved in research paper writing. However, rarely if ever do extended summaries arise out of the actual academic context within which students operate. In terms of the reading and studying process, the writer would be more inclined to take notes from the text. In terms of the final written product, the writer must integrate information from several sources into a small number of paragraphs and must position themselves in terms of the authors of those texts (Moore, 1994). As our aim is to provide contextualized, authentic writing tasks, the second assessment task requires students to summarize an article through note form, a ubiquitous study activity, while the third task incorporates instruction on integrating information from several sources.

Writing may also be employed as a means of enhancing understanding of subject knowledge. In one subject, tutorial questions requiring written responses are assigned each week.[11] The tutors review and select several responses to be used (anonymously) as the basis for discussion during the following tutorial, covering the relevant content as well as expression and organization. The subject leader also posts on an Internet file comments on the overall performance of the student group, including areas of difficulty commonly encountered and sample answers. Writing is thus used as a means of clarifying thought and consolidating subject knowledge. These exercises also provide opportunities to practice writing appropriate responses to exam questions. The subject lecturer has reported a marked increase in the quality of responses (reflected in increased grade averages over previous years) in the written section of the exam, with answers being more focused, better organized and expressed, and containing less irrelevant or contradictory information. It is difficult to make claims as other variables may be operating. However, it seems likely that the increase in grade averages is the result of a combination of the increased rehearsal of subject material through writing (although the content of most questions has not been discussed in tutorials), and the general effect of writing on comprehension.

An alternative to a fully integrated program involving subject specialists teaching in the language specialists' domain is an adjunct program, in which the same close collaboration occurs in terms of the development of teaching materials and team-teaching within the classroom, but the main teaching responsibility lies with the language specialist. The following case study describes an integrated adjunct program for Commercial Law.

CASE STUDY 2: COMMERCIAL LAW LANGUAGE AND LEARNING PROGRAM
Commercial Law is a compulsory subject in the Bachelor of Business degree, usually taken in the first year of study. It poses difficulties for many

students as they confront the peculiarities of the culture of law and legal language while also becoming acquainted with academic culture and its conventions. The program to assist students with the subject, developed because of the number of students seeking help, follows the adjunct model but includes integrated sessions for orientation, assignment writing, and exam strategies, co-taught by subject and language and learning staff. The benefit of such co-operation is that the language and learning academic can emphasize appropriate cognitive processes and literacy expectations while the subject academic can apply these to the law content. The intertwined nature of subject content and discourse is exposed, demonstrating to students that attention to language and writing facilitates understanding of law content.

The students respond well to the language and learning program because, as business students, they are not immersed in legal culture in the same way as students in a law faculty; thus there is less opportunity to absorb this culture tacitly. These problems are compounded for NESB students because law subjects are heavily language-based, and these students most often possess less proficiency in English while also needing to make adjustments to Western academic culture.

Program Objectives and Rationale
The overall objective of the Commercial Law program is to improve students' performance in the subject by focusing on literacy aspects and approaches to study. The program develops strategies for text and case reading and summarizing, analyses writing tasks and models of written responses, and provides practice in writing responses. The aim is to enable students to access and unpack the discourse and discern its embedded assumptions and values. As we have said before, these elements affect the structure of the discourse, the organization of ideas within this structure, and the style and use of grammar. The pedagogical advantage of this approach is that students can discover that there is meaning behind approaches they should employ in their thinking and writing in law subjects. As with the computing subjects discussed earlier, this analytical ability is somewhat ethnographic and its application extends beyond Commercial Law. Students can apply this approach to their studies in other disciplines and to other contexts such as the workplace.

In the mainstream subject, students are assessed through their written responses to case studies or problem questions—sets of facts replicating a realistic situation between two or more parties. They are required to analyze these and, using their knowledge of the law, discern where breaches of the law have occurred. Usually, students are directed to advise a certain party as to their legal rights. In so doing, they need to develop legal arguments both parties could present in court by applying the law to the facts presented in their problem. Finally, they need to summarize and justify their advice.

To produce appropriate writing with acceptable structure for presentation of ideas and appropriate use of resources and techniques (Murphy, Crosling & Webb, 1995), students must consider several key features of the discourse. These include the purpose of the writing tasks, the audience and its expectations and the appropriate position for the writer to adopt. Students are expected to write from the hypothetical position of legal advisers who have been consulted by their clients for advice, and therefore they are expected to communicate lucidly. However, the other element of their audience is their examiner, who is also interested in clear communication but, additionally, wishes to assess the students' analytical abilities; that is, their ability to discern the breaches embedded in the facts, to select and apply the appropriate law and in so doing to demonstrate their cognitive processes.

All these elements are underpinned by an appreciation of the appropriate world view; that is, the values prevailing in the culture of the law which underpin thinking, analysis and writing. Significant values in the legal system are reflected in the adversarial system, wherein both sides of a case are presented and the redress of imbalance occurs through the courts in order to maintain balance and order. Another aspect is the form of argumentation wherein each term of a legal rule has more than one meaning, with no unqualified answer as to the correct meaning, but where final judgment needs to be made (White, 1982). Because legal language in statutes and judges' decisions attempts to cover all situations, it characteristically includes complex sentences with many conditional and relative clauses (Danet, 1980). It also incorporates limited punctuation, noun repetition (Allan & Burridge, 1991) and heavy use of passive voice. Its specialized vocabulary encompasses processes or concepts particular to the discipline. However, while students need to use some specialized vocabulary, they need to bear in mind that their clients need to understand their expression and so complex legal sentences as described above are inappropriate.

The Weekly Program[12]

The weekly program is coordinated with the subject program, drawing on the weekly topics and related material from the course textbook. For example, cases used to demonstrate reading strategies are selected from the topic of study at that time in the mainstream lectures. Thus, the material in the program is relevant to students' needs and student motivation to attend the classes is maintained. Development of reading and writing skills fosters a deeper understanding of subject content and promotes a global rather than segmented view of the discipline and its values. This perspective is also encouraged through guided exercises. The class, facilitated by the language and learning academic, builds a macro structure of topics in the subject in tree diagram form, indicating main themes, topics, sub-topics and sections of these. Such a view is vital if students are to be able to identify issues in their problems; for example, detailed knowledge of "invitation to treat" is of limited value if it cannot be seen within the structure of the elements required for the making of a contract. A global view thus underpins the ability to discern a discipline's values and assumptions.

The teaching of reading strategies is focused on the textbook and case summaries, both of which pose comprehension difficulties for students. These strategies are designed to enable students to cope with the vast amount of required reading and, by focusing on the purpose and organization of content, draw attention to the tacit values in the discourse. For the former, students are encouraged to get an overview of the reading material by previewing headings and sub-headings before reading in more detail, fostering an active rather than passive reading style and providing a framework for the material which follows. At the same time, students discuss in groups their personal reading strategies and consider occasions when the various styles are most appropriate.

Reading and Summarizing the Textbook

Early in their law studies, students often comment that a significant contributor to reading difficulty is the legal vocabulary. It is erroneous to consider comprehension of a discourse solely in terms of "accumulation of a large lexicon" (Shuy & Larkin, 1978, p. 306), because focus on the "organizational principles that determine well-formed sentences and well-formed discourses" is more beneficial. However, it does seem that familiarity with jargon is a confidence-building strategy, especially for NESB students. It provides the tools with which to begin managing the discourse. Thus, the program presents vocabulary by way of "key" terms which are symbolic of investigation in the discipline: the interpretations of these can further clarify the system and its operations. Included here are, for example, nouns representing the significant parties in the legal system such as "plaintiff" and "respondent", and verbs for the significant processes, "to sue," "to revoke," and "to rescind."

The major emphasis, however, is on the structure of the discourse in the text. By objectively determining the function of different sections, students can see how a general statement of a legal rule is made and then a problem or limitation of the general rule posed. A solution to the problem is then presented as a qualified addition to the legal rule. This is followed by a case which forms the precedent for this "new" interpretation. The organization of ideas and the underpinning logic of the text reflects the legal process where the law moves and adjusts to provide precedents and rules for various situations that have been encountered over time. Consideration of case summaries further consolidates students' understanding of the role of cases in the legal system and thus in legal discourse. Implicitly, it provides a model of the appropriate way to use cases in their written legal arguments. This pedagogic strategy of explicating the organization of text material and its significance can be applied in mainstream lectures. From time to time, as material is presented, comments can be made as to how the organization replicates the legal process. For instance, as lecturers introduce an exception to a legal rule, they can comment on the dynamic nature of the law as it attempts to cover all instances that may occur. As they present a case, lecturers can focus on the role of cases as precedents in the common law system, or with legislation, as further interpretations of statutes.

As stated above, students need to include summaries of legal rules in their legal arguments. In the program, students are given authentic summary writing practice; that is, summaries appropriate for legal arguments. First, they are encouraged to discern the key words and phrases, consider alternative ways of expressing these if they are not special legal words, and use these as scaffolding for expressing the rules in their own words. Active learning is catered for as students verbally practice in groups before writing. Especially for NESB students, peer comment allows clarification of misunderstandings, provides feedback on first attempts and further develops English language expertise. It also provides guidance in paraphrasing, for many of these students may use direct quotes for fear of tampering with the written word. By way of examples, the language and learning academic can also outline and demonstrate the position that writers should adopt in relation to written texts in Western academic discourse.

Reading and Summarizing Cases

Cases in texts, that is, summarized versions of law reports, often pose difficulties for students in reading and interpretation. Again, students are encouraged to consider the organizational elements of the case, including the name, the legal principle which has developed from it, the facts leading to the dispute now before the court, the court's decision and the reasons for it. Attention is drawn to the fact that, once again, the adversarial nature of the legal system is replicated in the structure of the case—both parties' versions of the facts are presented before the judge's decision and the reasons are presented. This discoursal structure should be used in students' written responses; that is, they need to identify the issues, provide legal arguments for both parties and select the stronger argument, justifying their choice.

In their assignments and exams, students are required to produce concise summaries of cases, requiring specialized skills. In writing legal arguments, only the material or important facts which influenced the decision and the reasons are required. Therefore, general summarizing techniques which give equal weight to all components are not appropriate. As students practice summary writing and sift the material from the less important facts in the light of the decision and the reasons, they are implicitly deepening their understanding of the legal process. Explication of this procedure can expose the logic underpinning the use of cases in writing and therefore inject meaning into it. This is beneficial for all students, but especially for NESB students who may not be familiar with the adversarial legal system and who need opportunities, with feedback from lecturers and peers, to develop their language and writing expertise. Instruction in appropriate grammar and its formation can also be incorporated at this point; for example, past tense is used with cases which occurred in the past, but present tense is appropriate when citing legal rules because they pertain to the present.

Writing Tasks

The values underpinning appropriate thinking and writing in the subject are further exemplified as the program focuses more directly on writing. The exercises given are authentic tasks of analyzing and writing answers to past examination problem questions. Breaches of law embedded in the problems are similar to those areas under study in the mainstream subject. Through group practice in isolating the problems embedded in the facts and making and justifying judgments as to the stronger case, students are encouraged to develop critical, objective stances. This is sound experience for NESB students whose backgrounds may mean that they adopt subordinate positions in relation to the educational system which may constrain their willingness to make judgments.

Early in the program, students are taken through analysis of a typical problem question and the structure of an appropriate response. As this is modeled, a descriptive rather than prescriptive approach is taken and accompanied by explicit comment concerning the reasons underlying the organization of ideas, engendering meaning. First, the focus is on gaining a clear view of the problem situation. The students take notes and create diagrams of the written problem. NESB students' grammatical knowledge is drawn on and developed at this point. For example, attention is drawn to the use of the conditional tense and its implications for the intentions of the parties, assisting interpretation of legal status.

Importantly, students' attention is focused on the final direction in the problem question, usually to advise a certain party of their legal rights. The hypothetical position and its implications, such as the audience and the writing context, are considered. As legal advisers, students will research and report to their client the legal arguments for both parties before recommending a course of action. The structure of the response reflects this situation and the need for clear explanation. At this point, NESB students may particularly benefit from explanation of the role of law professionals in the Australian legal system underpinning the approach to be taken in their writing.

Disentangling the client/examiner audience emphasizes to students the need to demonstrate their analysis of the facts in relation to the law in their written responses. Experience in the program shows that early in the semester, students can identify the issues in a problem and cite the relevant law but will often conclude without presenting their analysis. This would not satisfy their examiner, who is interested in evaluating cognitive approaches. Thus, explanation of the role of the writer and the need to make critical judgments in the analysis is required. This is useful for NESB students who, because of their cultural backgrounds, may not be disposed to judgment-making. They may also hold different interpretations of the writer's responsibility and so may consider it unnecessary to explain their thought processes to their reader, who after all knows these already as an expert in the discipline.

Next, the problems or the issues in the set of facts need to be isolated. Students draw on their knowledge of the law to ascertain facts where more than one legal interpretation can be made. This is an important point because it exemplifies the adversarial nature of the system to which students' written responses must conform. That is, these are points from which both legal arguments can emanate, requiring final reconciliation as the stronger argument is selected. "Arms" of these arguments may also lead on to further issues where again two arguments can proceed. The structure is like a tree diagram and by demonstrating through concept mapping how arguments flow from one another, students can appreciate the appropriate cognitive approach.

The next stage is where a lecturer's model answer is analyzed in a descriptive rather than prescriptive mode. The emphasis is on the meaning underlying the moves or steps made in the response. Using visual concept mapping, students can see how the structure incorporates both arguments which are balanced in the conclusion. Following such broad analysis of the response, appropriate organization of information within these sections is investigated by taking an objective or functional perspective. For instance, the students can see that an appropriate structure for a legal argument includes stating what is known about the problem situation and therefore does not require investigation, raising the issue, (that is, the differing legal interpretations of an event which could apply), stating the law (legal rules or statutes and appropriate cases), analyzing the relevant facts from the problem question in terms of the law previously stated, and tentatively judging the likely outcome of the legal dispute.

Appropriate formal discourse markers and grammatical forms, that is, words and phrases, are then investigated in terms of their function within the discourse. For example, introduction of the other side of the dispute can occur by the use of a phrase such as " On the other hand, the court may decide . . . ." NESB students may not appreciate the importance of clearly indicating cohesion to the reader when writing in English. Modal verbs (such as "could," "may" and so on) and their function in the discourse are discussed, indicating to students the degree of certainty they should adopt at various stages in the legal argument. For instance, "could" is appropriate when the issue is raised initially, while the more definite "would" is appropriate in the conclusion. The future "will" is inappropriate in the conclusion, given that this includes legal advice only.

Following the analysis described above, students are presented with further typical problems relevant to the area of law under study in the lectures. In groups, active learning is encouraged as students analyze the problem, identify the issues and plan and write responses; students can learn from each other as they discuss the relevant law as well as the structure of responses and appropriate grammatical forms. Following time in or out of the class where students research, plan and write answers to their questions, students are then presented with a model provided by a subject lecturer. It needs to be stressed that responses used are written by various subject lecturers so as to present the variety permissible within the genre. Against these responses, students can evaluate the construction of their legal arguments and whether or not they have addressed appropriate issues.

As the semester progresses, students' attention is directed to various aspects of the different model responses. For example, they can observe the somewhat open nature of the response as the issue to be investigated is first raised. This can be emphasized by attention to—and thus tacit instruction in—the conditional tense in a structure such as "If the response is a counter offer, then ___. However, if it is a ___, then ___." Focus on the structure for the presentation of the alternative legal arguments which both parties could present emphasizes the need for a bilateral approach. Within this structure, the students can appreciate the elements which make up a legal argument and their organization. Their attention can be drawn to the summary of the law pertaining to the issue and integration of the precedent case, reporting only the material facts, the decision and the reasons. They can also note how analysis of these material facts occurs through juxtaposition with the law, forming the basis for the decision as to whether this particular law applies or not. An example of this is the statement: "When Fred said that he would buy the car if *it had new tires, he is adding new terms to the offer because the offer did not mention tires.*" By comparing the problem facts with the italics part in a sentence such as this, students can see the inclusion of the writer's interpretation.

To develop their ability to identify appropriate structure, students are also presented with less developed student responses from previous years. They comment on the successful and less successful features and how they could be improved. For example, a response may be conclusive rather than open initially, may consider only one side of the dispute, may use cases inappropriately, or may conclude that the law does or does not apply without demonstrating the analytical thinking underpinning this conclusion.

Evaluation

Attendance at the adjunct program is voluntary and although there is no formal assessment of students' writing, comparisons of the final results of students who attend the program and the overall cohort of students indicate that participation enhances students' chances of passing or even gaining credits. In addition, useful information about students' difficulties can be gleaned from students' practice examples. Used in a formative way, the language and learning academic can become aware of areas which require further focus and consolidation in the program and this knowledge can also be conveyed to subject staff, indicating areas for comment in lectures and tutorials. For instance, as gauged by students' case summaries written in the program, it may become clear that students do not fully understand that the important information in a case summary is the decision and the reasons, supported by the material facts. In sum, as qualitative evaluations indicate, students appreciate the understandings and skills developed in the program and the benefits to their study of Commercial Law.

CONCLUSION

Through placing instruction within the disciplinary context, integrated programs develop students' writing ability, while promoting understanding of the values, assumptions, and world view underpinning the writing conventions of the discipline involved. Because of the intertwined nature of language and content, attention to writing can enhance students' understanding of their subjects, making discipline-specific writing programs relevant and meaningful. Students are initiated into the disciplinary cultures, which have their own conceptions of knowledge as reflected in the structure, organization, and mode of expression of their discourse. By analyzing texts at the discourse rather than the mechanical level, the integrated programs encourage students to develop a somewhat ethnographic approach which can be transferred across contexts. Making explicit the underpinning assumptions and values of the discourse is of benefit to all students, including NESB students who must adapt to Western academic culture in addition to the disciplinary culture.

The processes involved in writing, including the interdependency with reading, are also addressed, thus promoting a more holistic view of student learning beyond concern with the end written product. Teaching reading strategies for different texts and contexts promotes understanding of the rhetorical structures and cognitive processes implicit in the discourse, providing also a model of the appropriate authorial position to be taken in students' own writing. Students' repertoires of composing strategies are also expanded through peer discussion and group work. Thus, students are exposed to a range of reading and writing strategies to draw on as the writing context shifts. As teachers, we also need to consider the changing learning and working environment and the impact of technological media on reading and writing processes.

A social constructionist approach to integrating writing with subject content requires close collaboration and sharing of respective knowledge areas between subject and writing specialists. The subject specialist may need to develop new teaching methods and become familiar with the knowledge domain of the language specialist, while the language specialist requires induction into the world view and conventions of the discipline. There must be enough time dedicated to this process and the development of appropriate materials. However, academics who do not have the resources to devote to such an extensive application as described here may begin by adopting this approach for one subject only, or even one assignment only. Our experience indicates that, even on a small scale, such an approach encourages students to take a deep level approach to the subject content and writing; moreover, the teaching of both subject and language specialists is enhanced by the sharing of knowledge and expertise.

NOTES

1. Rhetorical structures are the underlying structures which determine the organisation of texts in achieving particular goals. The term text is applied here to any piece of written work, of any type.

2. NESB grammatical error may be attributed to the individual level of language development or the use of a non-standard variety of English and other factors. Within the confines of this paper, however, we address grammatical issues in terms of the context of the discourse, and not in terms of error-correction. For further information on addressing NESB grammatical error see, for example, Leki (1992), Brunton (1989), Smith (1991), Ballard & Clanchy (1991), Clerehan (1995).

3. Perhaps because Australian universities do not have a history of college composition courses, there are few computer labs designed specifically for writing instruction by language specialists. Existing labs are used principally by individual students preparing assignments unassisted, or by computing departments for subject classes.

4. A genre is a type of text, such as a report, essay, letter, brochure, user manual, contract, delivery docket, advertisement, and so on. Within each genre would be sub-genres such as a system specifications report, financial report, psychiatric report. The sub-genres could be further distinguished according to the particular purposes or audiences or institutions involved in their production. A distinction should be made between the different genre approaches currently operating. Our approach draws principally on the work of applied linguists interested in second language acquisition (e.g. Swales, 1990; Swales & Feak, 1994; Bhatia, 1993) and the 'New Rhetoric' of North American genre theorists (e.g. Bazerman & Paradis, 1991; Freedman & Medway, 1994a, 1994b). We are not here referring to the genre theory based on systemic functional linguistics used by language educators in Australia.

5. The idea of subject lecturers teaching writing has been around for some time, most notably in the form of the Writing Across the Curriculum (WAC) movement, begun in the 1970s. In Australia, however, WAC has not taken hold: moreover, such programs have tended to focus on the composition process, using writing-to-learn strategies and often taking a more expressivist approach in the form of free-writing or journal writing exercises. Some recent WAC programs, however, have sought a contextualised approach, emphasising both process and genre approaches, merging

composition strategies and methods of inquiry appropriate to particular disciplines (e.g. Kirscht, Levine & Reiff, 1994; Jones & Comprone, 1993).

6. The project was funded by a federal grant from the Committee for the Advancement of University Teaching (CAUT) in Australia. The project leaders were Nyorie Lindner from the Peninsula School of Computing and Information Technology (PSCIT) and Sheila Vance and Tim Moore from Language and Learning Services (LLS), Monash University, Melbourne, Australia. The subject leaders who developed the curricula for the three subjects are: Nyorie Lindner, Rob Dorling, Phil Steele, Denise Ceddia, and Ewen McPherson, PSCIT.

7. The subject leader who developed these materials is Ewen McPherson, PSCIT, Monash University.

8. The subject leaders who developed this curriculum are Philip Steele and Denise Ceddia, PSCIT, Monash University.

9. The cataloguing of particular problems has been reduced here for the sake of brevity.

10. The subject leaders who developed this curriculum are Nyorie Lindner and Rob Dorling, PSCIT, Monash University.

11. The subject leader who developed these materials is Ewen Mcpherson, PSCIT, Monash University.

12. For further details see Crosling, G., & Murphy, H. (1996). *How to study Business Law: Reading, writing and exams* (2nd ed.). Sydney: Butterworths.

REFERENCES

Allan, K., & Burridge, K. (1991). *Euphemism and dysphemism.* Oxford: Oxford University Press.

Backhouse, R., Dudley-Evans, T. , & Henderson, W. (1993). *Exploring language and rhetoric in Economics.* London: Routledge.

Ballard, B., & Clanchy, J. (1991). *Teaching students From overseas.* Melbourne: Longman Cheshire.

Bazerman, C. (1988). *Shaping written knowledge.* Madison: University of Wisconsin Press.

Bazerman, C., & Paradis, J. (Eds.). (1991). *Textual dynamics of the professions: Studies of writing in professional communities.* Madison: University of Wisconsin Press.

Becher, T. (1981). Towards a definition of disciplinary cultures. *Studies in Higher Education, 6* (2), 109-122.

Berkenkotter, C., Huckin, T., & Ackerman, J. (1991). Social context and socially constructed texts: The initiation of a graduate student into a writing research community. In C. Bazerman, & J. Paradis (Eds.), *Textual dynamics of the professions: Studies of writing in professional communities* (pp. 191-215). Madison: University of Wisconsin Press.

Bhatia, V. (1993). *Analysing genre.* London: Longman.

Biggs, J., & Moore, P. (1993). *The process of learning* (3rd ed.). New York: Prentice-Hall.

Bizzell, P. (1992). *Academic discourse and critical consciousness.* Pittsburgh: University of Pittsburgh Press.

Brinton, D., Snow, M., Wesche, M. (1989). *Content-based second language instruction.* Boston: Heinle & Heinle Publishers.

Bruffee, K. (1986). Social construction, languages and the authority of knowledge: A bibliographical essay. *College English, 48* (8), 773-791

Brunton, D. (1989). *Common English errors in Hong Kong.* Hong Kong: Longman.

Chanock, K. (Ed.). (1994). *Integrating the teaching of academic discourse into courses in the disciplines.* Conference Proceedings. Melbourne: La Trobe University.

Clerehan, R. (1995). Faculty staff assessment of error in the writing of NESB international students. In S. Gill (Ed.), *National and International Challenges and Responses* (pp. 400-409). Conference Proceedings, International English Language Education Conference, Kuala Lumpur, August 1994.

Clifford, J., & Marcus, G. (1986). *Writing culture: The poetics and politics of ethnography.* Berkeley: University of California Press.

Connor, U. (1996). *Contrastive rhetoric: Cross-cultural aspects of second-language writing.* Cambridge: Cambridge University Press.

Connor, U., & Kaplan, R. (Eds.).(1987). *Writing across languages: Analysis of L2 text.* Reading: Addison-Wesley.

Crosling, G,. and Murphy, H. (1996). *How to study Business Law: Reading, writing and exams* (2nd ed.). Sydney: Butterworths.

Danet, B. (1980). Language and the legal process. *Law and Society Review, 14,* 445-564.

Eklundh, K. (1994). Linear and nonlinear strategies in computer-based writing. *Computers and Composition, 11* (3), 203-216.

Farquharson, M. (1988). Ideas for teaching Arab students in a multicultural setting. Paper presented at the Annual Meeting of the Teachers of English to Speakers of Other Languages, Chicago.

Foertsch, J. (1995). The impact of electronic networks on scholarly communication. *Discourse Processes, 19* (2), 301-328.

Foster, D. (1983). *A primer for writing teachers.* New Jersey: Boynton/Cook.

Freedman, A. (1993). Show and tell? The role of explicit teaching in the learning of new genres. *Research in the Teaching of English, 27* (3), 222-251.

Freedman, A., & Medway, P. (Eds.). (1994a). *Genre and the new rhetoric.* London: Taylor and Francis.

Freedman, A., & Medway, P. (Eds.). (1994b). *Learning and teaching genre.* Portsmouth, N.H.: Boynton/Cook, Heinemann.

Fry, K. (1996). Pedagogical issues in effective reading, interacting and writing in technical studies. In R. Pose (Ed.), *Australian Communication Conference: Teaching communication skills in a technological era, Vol. II* (pp. 9-18). Melbourne: Monash University.

Garner, H. (1995). *Teamwork models and experience in education.* Boston: Allyn & Bacon.

Halliday, M. (1978). *Language as social semiotic.* London: Edward Arnold.

Hayes, J., & Flower, L. (1986). Writing research and the writer. *American Psychologist, 41* (10), 1106-1113.

Hinds, J. (1987). Reader versus writer responsibility: A new typology. In U. Connor & R. Kaplan (Eds.), *Writing across languages: Analysis of L2 text* (pp. 141-153). Reading: Addison-Wesley.

Jones, R., & Comprone, J. (1993). Where do we go next in writing across the curriculum? *College Composition and Communication, 44* (1), 59-68.

Kaplan, R. (1966). Cultural thought patterns in intercultural education. *Language and Learning 16,* 1-20.

Kadar-Fulop, J. (1988). Culture, writing and curriculum. In A. Purves (Ed.), *Writing across languages and cultures* (pp. 25-50). Newbury Park: Sage Publications.

Kirsht, J., Levine, R., & Reiff, J. (1994). Evolving paradigms: WAC and the rhetoric of inquiry. *College Composition and Communication, 45* (3), 369-380.

Leki, I. (1992). *Understanding ESL writers: A guide for teachers.* Portsmouth: Boynton-Cook.

Lewins, F. (1992). *Social Science methodology: A brief but critical introduction.* Melbourne: Macmillan.

Lewis, G. (1994). Microsoft MAIL: Facilitating communication in team projects. *Computers and Composition, 11* (1), 59-70.

Love, K. (1996). Unpacking arguments: The need for a metalanguage. *Idiom Special: Responding to students' writing, 1,* 123-139.

Martin, J. (1985). *Factual writing: Exploring and challenging social reality.* Oxford: Oxford University Press.

Martin, E., & Ramsden, P. (1986). Do learning skills courses improve student learning? In J. Bowden (Ed.), *Student learning: Research into practice* (pp. 149-166). Melbourne: University of Melbourne.

Moore, T. (1994). From text to note to text: Attitudes to knowledge in ESB and NESB summarization. Paper presented at RELC Regional Seminar, Singapore.

Murphy, H., Crosling, G., & Webb, J. (1995). Evaluation of language and learning programs: Promoting academic credibility. In M. Garner, K. Chanock, & R. Clerehan (Eds.), *Academic skills advising: Towards a discipline* (pp. 104-113). Melbourne: Victorian Language and Learning Network.

Myers, G. (1991). Stories and styles in two molecular biology review articles. In C. Bazerman, & J. Paradis (Eds.), *Textual dynamics of the professions* (pp. 45-76). Madison: University of Wisconsin Press.

Nystrand, M. (1986). *The structure of written communication.* Orlando: Academic Press.

Osterloh, K. (1986). International differences and communicative approaches to foreign language teaching in the Third World. In J. Valdes (Ed.), *Culture bound: Bridging the cultural gap* (pp. 77-85). Cambridge: Cambridge University Press.

Ostler, S. (1987). English in parallels: A comparison of English and Arabic prose. In U. Connor, & R. Kaplan (Eds.), *Writing across languages: Analysis of L2 text* (pp. 169-185). Reading: Addison Wesley.

Palumbo, P., & Prater, D. (1993). The role of hypermedia in synthesis writing. *Computers and Composition, 10* (2), 59-70.

Parker, O. (1986). Cultural clues to the middle eastern student. In J. Valdes (Ed.), *Culture bound* (pp. 94-102). Cambridge: Cambridge University Press.

Parry, S. (1990). The evaluative writing process: Content and context in harmony. In L. Marshall (Ed.), *Learning from each other* (pp. 49-56). Murdoch, W.A.: Murdoch University.

Pennington, M. (1993). Modeling the student writer's acquisition of word processing skills: The interaction of computer, writing, and language media. *Computers and Composition, 10* (4), 59-80.

Purves, A. (1988). *Writing across languages and cultures.* Newbury Park: Sage Publications.

Radloff, A., & Samson, J. (1993). Promoting deep learning: Using academic writing to change the learner's epistemological stance. Paper presented at the 5th European Conference, European Association for Research on Learning and Instruction, Aix-en-Provence.

Ramsden, P., Beswick, D., & Bowden, J. (1986). Effects of learning skills interventions on first year university students' learning. *Human Learning, 5,* 151-164.

Shuy, R., & Larkin, D. (1978). Linguistic considerations in the simplification/clarification of insurance policy language. *Discourse Processes 1* , 305-321.

Smith, L. (1991). Standards in world Englishes. In M. Tickoo (Ed.), *Languages and standards: Issues, attitudes, case studies*. Anthology Series 26. Singapore: SEAMEO Regional Language Centre.

Swales, J. (1987). Utilising the literatures in teaching the research paper. *TESOL Quarterly, 21* (1), 41-68.

Swales, J. (1990). *Genre analysis: English in academic and research settings*. Cambridge: Cambridge University Press.

Swales, J., & Feak, C. (1994). *Academic writing for graduate students*. Ann Arbor: University of Michigan Press.

Taylor, G. (1986). Errors and explanations. *Applied Linguistics, 7* (2), 144-166.

Taylor, G., Ballard, B., Beasley, V., Bock, H., Clanchy, J., & Nightingale, P. (1988). *Literacy by degrees*. Stony Stratford, U.K.: The Society for Research into Higher Education and Open University Press.

Taylor, G., & Nightingale, P. (1990). Not mechanics but meaning: Error in tertiary students' writing. *Higher Education Research and Development, 9* (2), 161-175.

Thompson, G., & Yiyun Y. (1991). Evaluation in the reporting verbs used in academic papers. *Applied Linguistics, 12* (4), 365-381.

Toulmin, S., Rieke, R., & Janik, A. (1984). *An introduction to reasoning* (2nd ed.). New York: Macmillan.

Valdes, J. (1986). *Culture bound: Bridging the cultural gap*. Cambridge: Cambridge University Press.

van der Geest, T., & Remmers, T. (1994). The computer as a means of communication for peer-review groups. *Computers and Composition, 11* (3), 237-250.

Vance, S. (1995). Writing in context. In M. Garner, K. Chanock, & R. Clerehan (Eds.), *Academic skills advising: Towards a discipline* (pp. 104-113). Melbourne: Victorian Language and Learning Network.

White, J. (1982). The invisible discourse of the law: Reflections on literacy and general education. *Michigan Quarterly Review*, 420-438.

CHAPTER 17

Student Activism and University Teaching in South Korea

Yung Che Kim

This chapter explores an important and unique theme in Korean higher education—student political activism—and its relationship to university classroom learning environments. While several strategies are suggested for college teachers to cope effectively in politically volatile classroom situations, readers are encouraged to develop new approaches to teaching that incorporate appropriate social contexts and political realities.

STUDENT ACTIVISM IN KOREA

For several decades, Korean student activism has symbolized the serious and complex social conflicts within our society. This student activism is largely related to events in Korean history, such as liberation from foreign annexation, the establishment of various political and social systems, and problems of reunification of a nation which is still divided into North and South. An understanding of student activism must thus incorporate an understanding of these political and social events.

Korean Political and Social History

For the first half of this century, a long period of Japanese colonialization (1910-1945) influenced virtually every aspect of social and political development in Korea. Following the country's liberation in 1945, the First Republic—a social democracy—was established, under the leadership of the United Nations and the U.S. military. It is important to note that Korea was at this time (and still remains) divided into South and North Korea. The Korean War, which broke out on June 25, 1950, saw tremendous destruction and heavy loss of life throughout both North and South Korea, although the economic recovery in the South quickly exceeded the North, and has led to an enormous disparity between the two ever since. This chapter is focused mostly on developments in the Republic of Korea (South Korea).

A year later, the Second Republic was overthrown by a military coup d'etat, who then established the Third Republic under the leadership of General Park Chung Hee. In 1971, facing increasing protests on campuses throughout the nation, Park issued an emergency decree of 1971 that threatened to "abolish freedom and autonomy at universities where illegal demonstrations, criticisms, rallies, and sit-ins threaten campus order." Unofficial newspapers, journals, and other publications were outlawed. Thousands of students were expelled. University professors were dismissed—and in some cases sent to jail—for allegedly committing anti-government activities, sometimes as minor as referring to a particular book or author during a lecture. Newspaper reporters and editors who criticized the government were often fired. Yet, despite these repressive measures, student protests spread and become even more aggressive (Lee, 1984).

In 1979, President Park was killed by the chief of the Korean Central Intelligence Agency, leaving the way for Chun Doo Hwan to take power. Although the end of Park's autocratic regime was widely seen as a welcome beginning to a new democratic movement—particularly among students— the new Korean leader suppressed any demonstrations against his military rule. Such suppression culminated in the "Kwangju Incident," in 1980, when a relatively large protest resulted in soldiers beating and shooting hundreds of students and citizens. Although the official death toll was nearly 200, some of those involved insist that about 2,000 were slaughtered (Kim, 1988). This incident resulted in a strong doubt in the legitimacy of the government, not only by students but also the general population of South Korea.

Several successive military governments—also calling themselves "Republics"—came and went in the 1980s, and in 1993, the Sixth Republic—the final military government, even though its president was elected by general voting—ended its presidential term, and a civilian government was established. The new political and social mood in Korea can be characterized by efforts to democratize all economic, social, educational, and cultural institutions in the country, with a particular growing attention towards Korea's place in a "global community."

Organization of Student Activists
Several eminent and notable student movements developed during the Japanese occupation of Korea. However, it is generally recognized that modern student activism in Korea has its roots in the April 19 Student Popular Revolution which developed in 1960. This was a movement for anti-dictatorial democratization and against the First Republic that had formed following

the liberation of Korea. The revolution was organized by students, and was eventually joined by a collection of popular civil representatives. Together, they succeeded in overthrowing the dictatorial government. Thus began a legacy—this revolution laid the foundation for numerous student activist movements, upholding the slogans of the anti-dictatorial democratization, national independence, and the nation's reunification.

Since the early 1970s, university cultures throughout the nation have been driven by study circles. Every university has several of these study circles, which recruit freshmen as new members, and then become the center of their intellectual and social lives. Much like the fraternity system in many universities in the U.S., these groups function as critical organizational units in the campus climate. In South Korea, these study circles also form the basic organizational units of student movements. The study circles adopt programs and topics for debate, usually involving Korean politics and economics. Often, lively debates over ideology ensued. Students who emerge from this underground education share a certain set of basic beliefs (Pilho, 1982).

Goals of Student Activists
There has been a strong sympathy among students and citizens for student activists' insistence on social equality and democracy. Additionally, students are often seen as having a responsibility to the Korean public in preventing social and political corruption. Following the Korean War, student activists focused generally on forming resistance to the military government's rule. These activities continued through the 1960s, '70s, and '80s, and included such notable themes as opposition to the military government's permission of presidential terms without limit, anti-renovation (anti-Yushin) and the democracy restoration movement. During this period, two important developments evolved. One was the linkage of student activism with 'public' or 'civil' movements—for example, the labor movement. During the 1960s and '70s in Korea, intensely rapid industrialization was achieved, which in turn produced a number of difficult problems relating to the severe labor and living conditions of Korean workers, most notably in large metropolitan areas. Laborers organized an independent social movement, which led to wage and labor improvement negotiations. The political underpinnings of this movement meshed evenly with the goals of the student movements of the time.

Another major development of this period involved the rise in support for campus self-ruling, or "campus democratization." Organizers of these movements called for reforming the university governance structures, and campus unrest and boycotting of classes were not infrequent, particularly in the 1980s. However, the core of student activism during this time was not centered in a concern for campus reform, but rather was focused on obtaining the collective moral support from the public. In other words, the student activists' primary goal was to solicit public support for their political movements, by gaining the public's sympathy. Student activism is given a considerable amount of credit for the eventual adoption of the presidential election system by direct voting.

In the late 1970s and early 1980s, industrial workers in Seoul, mostly in their teens and early twenties, from rural areas, suffered from long work hours, meager wages, and generally poor working conditions. Banned from organizing labor unions, they sought and found sympathy from the increasingly powerful student protest movements. Thus, labor problems become one of the top priorities for student activists. Also during the late 1980s, student activism was basically concerned with national problems, using slogans of 'nationalism' and 'anti-foreign power.' The anti-foreign power movement was largely an 'anti-American' movement. Also, many idealistic discussions and activities have involved a refusal to accept the status quo of "the divided country", and many of these activities have become somewhat radical in nature. A number of Korean scholars have expressed concern about the negative effects of an apparent ideological bias and violent radicalism during these years (Kim & Paik, 1991; Cho, 1992). Indeed, student activists of the present days are often considered to be leftist-ideologically biased. Scholars and others are growing concerned that a dogmatic attention to a leftist ideology—or 'ju-che ideology' ('self-reliance doctrine') of North Korean philosophy—may be leading to a loss of support from the general public, which could well lead to their becoming isolated and—of much greater concern—becoming more radical. However, there is another recent development in student movements, in response to recent expansion in Korean higher education.

STRUCTURAL ISSUES IN KOREAN HIGHER EDUCATION
The historical evolution of Korean higher education is only remotely Korean. Until the late 19th century, China had considerable influence in Korea's intellectual and educational leadership. The long period of Japanese colonialization referred to earlier had a substantial impact in the structure, curriculum and administration of Korean universities—even the language of instruction was Japanese. The end of WWII was immediately followed by several decades of Western influence in the Republic of Korea (South Korea), as the United Nations oversaw the establishment of a new, demo-

cratic educational system that came to be based on that of the United States. Today, the predominance of American ideas and practices can be seen in every corner of Korean higher education. (Lee, 1997)

In recent decades, South Korea as a distinct national identity has developed its own economic and social agenda, and the goals of the educational system have reflected an emphasis on teacher education and scientific and technological education. Traditionally, Koreans have viewed higher education as a valuable means for socioeconomic mobility. Indeed, research demonstrates that the rate of economic return from a university education in South Korea is quite high (Economic Planning Board, 1992). Thus, demand for higher education in Korea has always been relatively strong. However, for years the Korean government strictly controlled university enrollments for the purposes of coordinating supply and demand of human resources to meet certain needs of Korean industry.

Recently, successive governmental policies have relaxed the traditionally strict controls on enrollments, resulting in a new era of expansion. In fact, Korean higher education has expanded at a rate unprecedented by any other nation in the world. Unfortunately, according to the Korean Ministry of Education, this phenomenal growth in enrollments has greatly exceeded the rate of institutional expansion. While the student population has increased a thousand percent within the last thirty years, the number of institutions available to accommodate their needs has only doubled (see Table 1).

Table 1

Expansion of Korean Higher Education

Year	Students	4-year Institutions
1965	105,643	70
1975	208,986	72
1985	931,884	100
1995	1,040,166	131

Source: Korean Ministry of Education, 1995. (Note: No data are available for years prior to 1965).

This explosive growth in Korean higher education appears to be the result of many factors, including: (1) a national educational policy that places emphasis on the cultivation of manpower—for the most part intended to compensate for the country's lack of natural resources. (2) a sharp increase in the demand for highly qualified manpower in the wake of industrialization; and (3) Korean society's traditional enthusiasm for education, together with a strong desire for upward social mobility and greater incomes. Particularly, the notion that "education is the key to national development" is widely accepted among many Koreans.

Unfortunately, this rapid expansion of student populations—and the smaller but significant growth in postsecondary institutions—has not been accompanied by a substantial increase in educational resources. The financial plights generally common to most universities and colleges, combined with ever-increasing faculty-student ratios, have resulted in a decline in the overall condition of Korean higher education. One result of constrained resources and bulging classrooms is that professors are overburdened, with little time to conduct preparatory study for instruction. As Lee and Associates (1995) observed, this also may account for the dearth of research activity among Korean professors.

Overall, it is perceived by many that these developments adversely affect the quality of Korean higher education—a perception reflected in the relatively recent focus of Korean student activism on what appears to be governmental inability to meet student demand for a quality higher education experience. However, this is not to say that the government is merely sitting idly by while the higher education system fades.

Responses to New Problems in Korean Higher Education
Until the early 1980s, a particularly salient feature of the Korean system of higher education has been direct government involvement in academic administration, where the government has participated in the accreditation of institutions, faculty, and programs. In recent decades, as the nation embarked on an ambitious agenda of modernization, science and technology were accorded top priority as a critical path to national development. This led to the establishment of research institutes and graduate schools—independent or affiliated with universities. Prominent examples include the Korean Institute of Science and Technology (KIST) and Korea's Advanced Institute of Science (KAIS). In the social sciences and education, the Korean Development Institute (KDI) and the Korea Educational Development Institute (KEDI) are noteworthy for their roles in research, training, and policy development. Another important event during this period of change was the establishment of the Korean Council for University Education (KCUE). Membership of the KCUE is composed of representatives from all 4-year colleges and universities nationwide. The Council was founded with a mission of promoting autonomy and public accountability in university management, as well as improving the quality of university education.

There is now a tremendous interest in finding an effective system to improve instruction, and in the professional development of university and college faculties. Since the establishment of the Presidential Commission for Education Reform (1985), several government-led efforts have been introduced towards implementing practices and programs to address the effectiveness of college teaching. For example, the KCUE sponsors a three-day workshop to help new faculty members develop teaching methods. Each year, these workshops draw more than 100 voluntary participants. However, while ideally one would hope that faculty who really need to improve would be among those most involved in developmental activities (Centra, 1976), this is not often the case. The KCUE is also responsible for gathering model syllabuses across all fields of study, and publishing and distributing these along with related instructional materials (Kwon & Paik, 1993).

The KCUE also launched an accrediting system for individual departments in 1992 and for the comprehensive university system in 1994. The accreditation process is optional in the sense that it is based upon the application of an individual institution, but every university or college is required to have accrediting evaluation every 7 years. Initial accreditation results found that current teaching practices in many of Korea's universities and colleges are not of the quality the government—or the Korean public—would prefer. For example, it was found that while a slight majority of faculty use syllabuses in their courses, many these syllabuses were developed more as an enrollment guide, and with little attention to encouraging effective teaching or learning (Lee, 1994). Concerns over the quality of teaching in Korean colleges and universities are rather frequently manifested in the publication of professional reports and sometimes in the daily newspapers.

Overall, several ideas have been generated for improving instructional quality in higher education (e.g., Joo, 1996; Kim, 1992), focusing on topics such as:

- faculty development, including programs for instructional methods improvement;
- practical orientation sessions for using instructional technology;
- the provision of the opportunity to attend advanced courses and receive supervisory assistance from senior faculty;
- finding better measurement tools for instructional ratings;
- developing better conditions for teaching and learning, such as increasing the number of teaching assistants, providing easy access and availability of media and learning centers;
- reduction of teaching loads and the balanced requirement of teaching and

research in the faculty evaluation; and

- the change of the professors' attitude toward teaching and recognition of importance of good teaching.

In these discussions and ideas, however, one interesting phenomenon seems worth mentioning. Attention towards the improvement of college instruction has focused nearly exclusively on a professor's teaching methods and skills to facilitate student learning, while the development of student study skills and behaviors has been largely neglected. As well, little attention has been given by the government towards involving students in the process of systemic change. Institutional and governmental leaders must explore and come to terms with the historically high levels of student activism in Korea and find ways to use the classroom environment to channel these energies in constructive ways. The remainder of this chapter seeks to engage faculty members and administrators in a conversation along these lines.

DISCUSSION: UNIVERSITY TEACHERS AND TEACHING

The majority of teachers in Korean universities rely on the lecture method, a reflection of Confucianism's powerful hold on education in Asia (Lee, 1996). Confucianism, the philosophical system founded on the teaching of Confucius (551-479 BC), emphasizes benevolence, traditional rituals, filial piety, loyalty, respect for superiors and for the aged, and principled flexibility in advising rulers. This philosophical influence in Korean society may partly explain why the Korean public expects professors to set standards of intellectual excellence and moral thinking and behavior in society. Indeed, a recent international survey of the academic profession revealed that a strong majority of Korean faculty feel that "academics are among the most influential opinion leaders" in their country (Boyer, Altbach, & Whitelaw, 1994).

However, one could argue that students, rather than professors, have been more influential in shaping the social or political agenda. As indicated earlier, during the last thirty years student activism contributed very positively in developing a democratic society by fighting against dictatorial and military regimes. Students in Korea have developed a uniquely active culture of expressing their dissatisfaction towards things in and outside the university classroom. The recent growth in faculty activism is perhaps a reflection of the success of student political activist movements in achieving real policy change. Indeed, in the 1990s, faculty activism appears to be the most important of the new intramural issues at Korean colleges and universities. Professors have begun to organize their own councils and to raise their voices against the governing boards of their institutions (Lee, 1996).

Nonetheless, these student movements have also produced the negative effect of disrupting research and instruction activities on campuses, and contributing to an environment of mistrust and conflict among university members involved. By making the university or college an arena of political struggle, as well as social and ideological debate, student activist movements have in a way furthered the plight that their institutions are already in—their teachers often must struggle against incredible odds to succeed in encouraging student learning and the discovery of knowledge.

College teaching in Korea retains a certain political element, embroiling professors in social and political debate. Indeed, the relatively temporary status that evolved for university teachers under repressive regimes had considerable impact on how they related to their students. Some faculty sympathized with their students' causes to the extent that they helped organize events. Other faculty were so fearful for their jobs that they canceled classes altogether, rather than face potential punishment should a debate break out in class about a certain topic of the day's lecture.

There are several approaches to how professors can cope effectively in classrooms disrupted by student activist agendas. For example, the appropriate use of humor can go miles in handling classroom disruptions. Other suggested strategies include encouraging respect for all students' views and diffusing confrontational exchanges by addressing the points of contention raised, and not the individual students. Another potentially useful perspective is in approaching politically volatile classroom situations as researchers, with the purpose of exploring the social and political implications of ideas in the context of research projects.

It is also important that college teaching methods be varied and offer the flexibility to adapt to the needs of different student groups. Teachers behave as they do partly because of their students—the way students present themselves, and their behavior when in contact with teachers, can influence the instructional environment considerably. Additionally, as Dunkin (1986) and others have observed, characteristics of students—such as previous academic performance, gender, and ethnicity—may affect the way teachers behave in the classroom.

Conversations are taking place around the world which address the topic of student diversity and college teaching practices and cannot be fully addressed within the scope of this chapter. While several papers and articles are available which describe the most prevalent college teaching practices in

Korea (e.g., Joo, 1996; Kim, 1996; Huh, 1996), the remainder of this chapter is concerned with teaching-related issues that can be modified to help faculty better cope with high levels of student activism in the their classrooms. Specifically, the dimensions of curriculum development, faculty training, and teaching evaluation provide three useful and important points of reference along the spectrum of professional activity within which this discussion is framed.

Curriculum Development

How Korean students learn about the legacy of student activism in their country can play an important role in the evolution of student activism in the future. An objective approach to this topic is more preferable than one with idealized student activists as social heroes. As well, how Korean students learn about the dramatically changing world about them, and particularly the interaction between capitalist and socialist nations, will affect the future of Korean student activism (Choi, 1991).

While there can be multiple interpretations of the causes and effects of student activism in Korean higher education, one perspective that stands out as most salient involves a mix between counseling psychology and educational theory (Park, 1988). This perspective views student activism as (1) a symptom of the emotions and pathologies underlying the political, economic, cultural, educational, social structural, and other sectors of a rapidly changing Korean society; or (2) an expression of efforts to construct the "better society" through the pursuit of ideals. Looking at student activism in this manner is useful, as it presents two ways in which education and guidance could be made possible—student activism can be educated (or at least better informed), and student activists can be guided towards constructive means toward achieving their goals.

To achieve this, the content of college teaching must have at least some social relevance, particularly in the fields of social sciences and the humanities. College teaching cannot completely ignore the moral or social realities or conditions that students face. In a rapidly changing political and social environment—such has been the case in Korea for many years—university and college professors must maintain a high level of flexibility in their course design, content, and repertoire of teaching methods. Further, college teachers in such an environment have an additional responsibility of encouraging socially responsible and constructive ways for students to achieve their political agendas. Students must be cognizant of the real situations of society and world which exist parallel to the development of their ideological positions (Choi, 1991).

Teacher Preparation and Development
How are college teachers equipped—in terms of preparation, resources, and support—to cope effectively with learning environments dominated by decades of student activism? The typical Korean orientation program for new faculty members, which usually lasts several hours, covers the organization and government of the university, the academic calendar, the central services providing teaching aids available and others. The portion of these workshops which focus on the development of teaching method is not lengthy, usually only a couple of hours. Generally the program is focused on the administrative purpose, not for improving teaching methods. Further, the program is designed for everyone, despite the particular needs of an individual faculty member.

Other activities involving the preparation and development of faculty include workshops or seminars on teaching, activities that involve new media and technology, and course development meetings (Lee et al., 1994; Huh, 1996). Additionally, grants are often made available for participation in domestic and international academic meetings or sabbatical leaves, although these are mostly oriented toward encouraging research. Typical universities or colleges in Korea hold workshops or seminars every year for all faculty members for one or two days for various purposes. However, even though most faculty members do have only a limited knowledge of how to improve instruction, these workshops do not often focus on developing teaching methods.

In general, university teachers receive little or no training in teaching. As Cox (1994) mentioned, it is usually assumed that the highly qualified academic can easily master sufficiently the rudiments of teaching to satisfy most students. However, some universities or colleges encourage faculties to develop new and demanding courses, and some institutions provide additional points in faculty evaluation scores, if new teaching methods were attempted or new experimental course(s) were developed, as in the case of Ewha Women's University (Paik, 1996). Recently, audiovisual and electronic facilities and devices have been actively incorporated at several institutions, not only for faculty use but also for class use. Increasingly, the effective use of educational technology is emphasized, and thus instructional sessions are frequently available for orientation and helping faculties use these tools.

There are few examples of training or development programs for faculty which might help them perform their duties more effectively in times of high political activism. Certainly, seminars on conflict management and rational negotiation would be useful. In general, there is a definitive need for new approaches to how faculty are prepared to effectively cope with the social contexts of their classroom environments.

Teaching Evaluation

As competition increases for resources distributed among universities and colleges, it is becoming a more common practice to have at least some form of evaluating each faculty member's performance. Teaching evaluation measures are a direct product of various recent government policies which tie differential fiscal support with the performance and efforts of individual institutions and are related to societal pressures and concerns over the perceived declining quality of higher education. Each institution has a slightly different measurement instrument, and the evaluative data collected are usually analyzed by percentile rank among all different courses and provided to faculty members as constructive feedback, although in some cases teaching evaluation scores are used for administrative decision-making on important topics such as promotion (Lee, 1994). Currently, there are no institutional programs that provide annual awards to faculty members for teaching excellence.

The notion of evaluating teaching is relatively new to Korea, a reflection of a traditional belief in Korea that 'the king-master (teacher)-father is the one', and thus should be only respected and not criticized. Recently, when a couple of universities refused promotion for several faculty members on grounds related to their teaching evaluations, several influential domestic newspapers turned this into a highly sensational news item. As well, an emphasis on research throughout the academic profession gives little support for teaching evaluations. As MacKenzie (1970) observed, "whatever the motive which first led [the university teacher] to adopt an academic career, he soon realizes that it is on his achievement as a scholar rather than as a teacher that his advancement in his profession will depend . . . there is certainly little to tempt anyone to give a study of teaching methods time when both inclination and self-interest would lead him to develop his own subject."

Other barriers to the effective widespread use of appropriate teaching evaluation measures include the assumption that teaching is a matter of privacy not be observed, publicized or evaluated. As well, it is widely believed that students are sometimes not fair-minded and usually are not qualified to make judgments about teaching competence, a perception that Cohen (1990) vehemently refutes. Thus, for teaching evaluation to be useful in addressing the challenges posed by student activism, the higher education sector of Korea must become actively involved in changing cultural perceptions and values regarding the academic profession.

Generally speaking, the usefulness of teaching evaluations in addressing the challenges posed by politically active classroom environments should not be ignored. If approached properly, the process of evaluations can be useful for teaching students the importance of targeted, constructive critique, as opposed to emotionally-charged, potentially damaging criticism. Teaching evaluations can and should be used in modifying one's approach to classroom instruction and are more effective when collected periodically throughout the course rather than a summative evaluation at the very end. Feedback from students on the course, if solicited and given appropriately, can lead to a more proactive learning environment, where "hot" issues can be addressed and discussed rationally, without leading the class to a frenzied call for activity in the streets. Current teaching evaluation measures in Korea are not yet used constructively, for this or any other purpose. Thus, departmental or governmental review of this topic is in order.

CONCLUSION

Student activism presents certain challenges for classroom instructors in Korean universities and colleges. There are several issues which the Korean ministry of education—as well as every college and university community in the country—must continue to grapple with in addressing the impact of student activism in higher education. Korea's governmental involvement in higher education enrollment and assessment policies have led to several changes in higher education, but with arguably little collective impact on classroom learning activities. The higher education establishment must encourage—through reward structures as well as by other means—increased attention to appropriate curriculum development and teacher preparation. Faculty must be fully aware of the social contexts of classroom discussions, and be equipped with the skills and resources to effectively cope with politically active students.

Additionally, a government which allows for unbridled expansion in university enrollments, without providing the resources necessary to meet the accompanying growth in needs, encourages a potentially dangerous level of dissatisfaction and disenfranchisement with the system. As indicated earlier, in spite of a marked expansion of enrollment, the number of faculty members has not increased proportionally, and thus, the number of students per professor is currently nearly double that of advanced-industrialized countries. This, coupled with the aforementioned potential for political marginalization of current student movements, promises future challenges to university and college teachers for years to come.

While student activism may seem to pose a barrier to change in higher education, the reality is that both students and faculty are the most vocal ones calling for changes in approaches to classroom teaching and learning. Without doubt, given the history of student activism in Korea, we can expect that responses to the current and evolving condition of higher education will be anything but subtle.

REFERENCES

Beard, R. M. & Hartley, J. (1984). *Teaching and learning in higher education.* Harper & Row.

Boyer, E.L., Altbach, P.G. & Whitelaw, M.J. (1994). *The academic profession in international perspective.* Princeton, NJ: Carnegie Foundation for the Advancement of Teaching.

Centra, J. A. (1976). *Faculty development in the United States: Practice and programs.* Proceedings of the Second International Conference on Improving University Teaching, 98 - 127, Heidelberg, Germany.

Cho, Kun-sang (1992). *Student organization and student activism.* (Korean Council for University Education Report No. 92-9-43). Seoul, Korea: Korean Council for University Education.

Choi, H. (1991). The societal impact of student politics in contemporary South Korea. *Higher Education*, 21, p. 175-188.

Cohen, P. A. (1990). Bridging research into practice. In M. Theall & J. Franklin (eds.), *Student ratings of instruction: Issues for improving practice.* Jossey-Bass.

Cox, B (1994). *Practical points for university teachers.* London: Kogan Page.

Dunkin, M. J. (1986). Research on teaching in higher education. In M. C. Wittrock (ed.), *Handbook of research on teaching.* Macmillan.

Economic Planning Board (1992). *Social indicators in Korea, 1992.* Seoul: Economic Planning Board.

Huh, Hyung (1996). Diverse methods of university teaching method. *Korean Journal of Higher Education*, 80, p. 42-53.

Huh, Suk (1996). Facilitation of the national and international exchanges for professors' academic research. *Korean Journal of Higher Education*, 82, p. 43-49.

Hwang, Jung-kyu, Chang, Un-hyo, Song, In-sup, & Kang, Kyung-seuk (1986). *A study on the development of teaching and learning method of higher education in Korea.* (Korean Council for University Education Report No. 85-6-37). Seoul, Korea: Korean Council for University Education.

Hwang, Jung-kyu, Lee, Hwa-nam, Choi, Hee-sun, Noh, Jong-hee, & Kang, Kyung-suk (1988). *Analysis of instructional system and amount of students' learning in higher education.* (Korean Council for University Education Report No. 88-6-69). Seoul, Korea: Korean Council for University Education.

Joo, Kyung-bok (1996). Curricular content in humanity areas and a reflection of the teaching-learning method. *Korean Journal of Higher Education, 80,* 15-23.

Kang, Moo-sub (1987). An innovative method for improving the quality of university teaching. *Korean Journal of Higher Education, 28,* 105-114.

Kang, Sung-kyu (1992). Teaching and student guidance. *Korean Journal of Higher Education, 59,* 26-33.

Kim, Hyung-kun & Paik, Jung-ha (1991). *Development and guidance of student activism.* (Korean Council for University Education Report No. 91-20-116). Seoul, Korea: Korean Council for University Education.

Kim, Jung-han (1992). Tasks of improving the effectiveness of college teaching. *Korean Journal of Higher Education, 59,* 77-82.

Kim, M. (1988). April Student Revolution as national democratic movement. *History Criticism,* 1 (Summer), p. 31-48 (in Korean).

Kim, Uh-soo (1996). Discussion and writing method in humanity areas. *Korean Journal of Higher Education, 80,* 24-27.

Kwon, Ki-uk (1993). A study on the appropriate teaching load of college professors. *Korean Journal of Higher Education, 5,* 2, 31-55.

Kwon, Ki-uk & Paik, Jung-ha (1993). *Discovering the model syllabuses and their distribution method.* (Korean Council for University Education Research Report No. 93-2-124). Seoul, Korea: Koran Council for University Education.

Lee, Hyun-chung, Park, Jin-kyu, Noh, Min-ju, Chung, Ki-soo, & Sung, Yeul-kwan (1994). *A study on the faculty evaluation and development model.* (Korean Council for University Education Research Report No. 94-5-136). Seoul, Korea: Korean Council for University Education.

Lee, Jae-oh (1984). *A history of Korean student movements after Liberation.* Seoul: Hongsungsa.

Lee, Jong-sung (1995). *A report of comprehensive university evaluation for accreditation.* (Korean Council for University Education Research. Report No. 95-119-624). Seoul, Korea: Korean Council for University Education.

Lee, Sang-joo (1994). *A report of comprehensive university evaluation for accreditation.* (Korean Council for University Education Research. Report No. 94-93-498). Seoul, Korea: Korean Council for University Education.

Lee, Sungho H. (1996). The academic profession in Korea. In Boyer, E.L., Altbach, P.G. & Whitelaw, M.J., *The academic profession in international perspective.* Princeton, NJ: Carnegie Foundation for the Advancement of Teaching.

Lee, Sung-ho (1987). *Daehak kyoyook gwajungron* (Curriculum Development in Korean Universities and Colleges). Seoul: Yonsei University Press.

MacKenzie, N., et al. (1970). *Teaching and learning: An introduction to new methods and researches in higher education.* Paris: UNESCO, International Association of Universities.

Mass, J. B. (1976). Innovations in undergraduate education. *Proceedings of the Second International Conference on Improving University Teaching,* 97-113, Heidelberg, Germany.

Ministry of Education (1995). *Statistical yearbook of education.* Seoul, Korea: Ministry of Education.

Paik, June-woo (1996). The case of faculty evaluation in Ewha Women's University: An exploration for objective faculty rating criteria. *Korean Journal of Higher Education,*

    82, 81-87.
Park, Sung-soo (1988). Guidance problem of the student activism and educational role
    of university. *Korean Journal of Higher Education*, 36, 22-26.
Pilho, H. (1982). Liberation theory in underground college. *Chosun Monthly* (April).
Song, In-sub (1986). Problems of teaching-learning methods and its innovation. *Korean
    Journal of Higher Education*, 23, 68-75.

CHAPTER 18

Accountability Without Tenure

The Impact of Academic Contests on University Teaching at the University of Buenos Aires

Marcela Mollis and Daniel Feldman

INTRODUCTION

Recent years have seen increased attention towards the value of academic tenure in many parts of the world. Some observers have suggested that the tenure system is related to declining faculty orientation towards teaching, through its incumbent rewards for research producitivity, and contributes to poor academic performance among students. It has been argued in several parts of the world that the tenure system places too much emphasis on research activity and too little importance on classroom teaching. We have set out to examine these issues in terms of how they relate to an environment without a tenure system—the University of Buenos Aires. The primary focus of this chapter concerns the impact of academic contests on the quality of university teaching.

Beginning with what is known as the Reform Movement of 1918, a system of contests was introduced in Argentina that is public, open, selective and periodic—each academic post is re-contested every seven years. This system of contests is still in effect in most Argentinean universities. We elected to examine the case of the University of Buenos Aires (UBA) as one adhering closely to the tradition of the Reform Movement, in addition to being the largest of the country's national public universities and the most prestigious in terms of reputation among the sciences.

In this chapter, we will first describe the setting in which these academic contests take place, then examine the structure and process of these contests, and finish with an exploration of their impact on university teaching. Drawing on material from interviews with various university authorities responsible for the machinery of contests, as well as the findings of two research projects, we analyze the influence of these contests—public, open, selective and periodic—in the development of teaching and research activities of faculty as well of the political management of the university. In our study of these influences, we found that this system yields results—in terms of teaching orientation and activity—that are not significantly different from a traditional system of tenure. Thus, the findings of our studies do not support those critics of higher education in various countries who suggest that the abolishment of tenure would lead to improvements in university teaching.

HIGHER EDUCATION IN ARGENTINA

The Argentinean higher education system is complex and heterogeneous, comprised of 82 universities and more than 1,200 third-level non-university establishments. The subsystem of non-university higher education is composed of teacher-training institutes and specialized technical schools. Public universities depend on the Federal Government for their funding, while private institutions are funded by tuition, although many of them also receive public subsidies. Non-university institutions, unlike the universities, are not autonomous from the State but subordinate to central bodies. Although national universities charge no tuition and have been historically autonomous, recently enacted Higher Education Law grants some powers to the Federal Government to supervise and act as a court of appeals in various aspects related to the academic, economic, and political life of the universities.

Beginning in the 1950s, Argentinian higher education entered an era of institutional diversification and differentiation, accompanied by a broadening and massification of post-secondary enrollment. The 7 public universities existing in 1956 grew to 30 public and private institutions by 1970. There was a dynamic push for public education between 1971 and 1974, when 19 national universities were created in different parts of the country. Another wave of expansion began in 1989, and the current heterogeneous and diverse institutional network is comprised of traditional and new universities, public and private, catholic and secular, elite and massive, professionalist and research-oriented. However, the public sector retains the most prominent role in higher education—public universities serve over 700,000 students—more than 85% of total national enrollment—and employ over 100,000 faculty members, generating much of the country's scientific research activity.

At present, the national universities have entered a period of great difficulty, faced with disputes over their autonomy, over independent financial management, and over their ability to receive enough state funding to continue operating. These disputes are made worse by the the central government's present economic policies. Nearly every Latin American country is now involved in a "neoliberal experiment" that has as a central feature the diminished role of the State and increased activity in the private sector (Levy, 1996). Argentina, like Mexico and Brazil, has been influenced and conditioned by an international "agenda of modernization of higher education systems," involving the reduction of state subsidies, the expansion of private institutions and their enrollment, with selective control over the distribution of financial resources, and the promulgation of a Higher Education Law that modifies the system of evaluation and accreditation as well as the traditional concept of university autonomy (Mollis & Hee Bang, 1996; Levy, 1993; Brunner, 1993). In terms of university teaching, this situation has an impact on faculty selection because it restricts the capacity to create new posts and limits the institutional possibilities for investing in the training of personnel for teaching and research.

Expansion has also created new conflicts—while the national universities doubled their enrollment and faculty between 1982 and 1992, the percentage of full-time teachers at the university has been sharply diminished. Currently, there are fewer professors (40%) than docentes auxiliares (instructors and teaching assistants of various sorts), and only 16% of all professors are full-time faculty members, while 58% hold the position of *tiempo parcial*—employed for only ten hours a week. Of the teaching assistants, 8% are full-time, 16% part-time, and 72% have a minimal commitment.

THE UNIVERSITY OF BUENOS AIRES

In the last ten years, because of its size, its human resources, prestige, and geographical location, the University of Buenos Aires (UBA) has been the leader of the university system and has exerted great pressure in the negotiations both within and beyond the university system. Since 1989, negotiations with the central government have become more prominemt (related to the increased degree of conflict) within the context of a "modernization agenda" for higher education that is attuned to globalization through proposals for privatization, diversification, deregulation, and, at the same time, increased State control (Levy, 1993; Mollis, 1995b).

UBA plays a unique and important role in Argentinian higher education. While the average faculty-student ratio for national universities is 13 students per teacher, at UBA there are 27 students for every faculty member. According to the National Ministry of Culture and Education— based on data that the source considers less than reliable (Estadisticas Universitarias, 1992)—in 1992 there were 20 graduates nationwide for every 100 matriculants. In the same year, UBA had a slightly higher rate (24 graduates per 100 matriculants). UBA also has an open-access system of enrollment—it receives any and all Argentinean secondary-school graduates who wish to pursue a university education.

The University of Buenos Aires is also the most important public university center for scientific and technological production in the country. Though there have been fluctuations in its scientific profile over the years, it has produced all three of Argentina's Nobel Prize-winners for Science: Bernardo Houssay (1947), Federico Leloir (1970), and Cesar Milstein (1984). In 1988, 55% of the country's scientific personnel belonged to public universities, and 26% of them worked at UBA. In 1992, UBA boasted 2,700 researchers, 15 % of the country's human resources for science (Mollis, 1995b)[1]. UBA's research mission is part of its institutional ethos, as shaped in the University Statutes (Estatuto Universitario de la UBA, 1966, Capitulo III)—"Research is considered a normal activity inherent in the condition of a faculty member. It is intended that research be increased insofar as adequate budget resources are available" (Art. 8). "Research is undertaken in all the schools and departments" (Art. 9).

History of UBA

The University of Buenos Aires was created during Argentina's Independence period (1821), at a time when the country was striving to shun its colonial past and become a civilized nation. It was born as a secular institution, modern and enlightened, aspiring to continue the French university heritage expressed in the Napoleonic model (Levy, 1986), as opposed to the colonial University of Cordoba, where the only degree granted was in Theology. The decade beginning in 1880 represented a historical turning point for the University of Buenos Aires with respect to its institutional identity. Law Number 1597 (known as the Avellaneda Law), passed in 1885, established the foundational principles of the Argentinean national universities, still in effect today: free education, automonous of governmental control. Any Argentinean student finishing non-compulsory secondary school could enter the university and study there totally free of charge. The law established norms of university government that placed it, fundamentally, in the hands of the faculty members, who were given the power to name new professors, create the syllabuses, and, in general, to give organizational form to the academic mission.

The prosperity enjoyed by Argentina toward the end of the last century was reflected in the University. The libraries grew enormously, and laboratories were developed, although with less intensity than the libraries. The institutional mission of UBA was predominantly professional—the great majority of the students enrolled between 1885 and 1930 chose liberal professions such as law and engineering. Their motivations were often political (training for future leadership)[2] and social (the university diploma positively affected one's chances for social mobility) (Mollis, 1990).

The Reformist Policy (1918–1930): University Government as Democracy
By 1918, Argentina had abandoned the oligarchic and elitist political model of the 1880 regime, adopting universal suffrage, that reflected the interests of the rising middle class and brought Hipolito Yrigoyen, leader of the Radical Civic Union (UCR) to the Presidency. Argentinean universities were not isolated from the process of political democratization taking place in the society as a whole. The national government listened to the students. After 1918, as a result of the University Reform, the Argentinean student movement had vast repercussions in the student movements of other Latin American countries. The achievements of the young Reformists included student participation in the university decision-making process. More broadly, it produced a system of university co-governance in which each of three key groups—professors, students, and graduates—was allotted a fixed representation in the governing bodies.[3] While there had been no change in Argentina's economic model as an exporter of agricultural products and supplier of raw materials to the international market, the University Reform became the expression of the country's political change (Mollis, 1989).[4]

The Reform leaders sought to ensure that the university would remain autonomous; appointment of teaching staff was to be by examination and competition every seven years; open attendance would be allowed at all theoretical courses, and revised teaching methods would be adopted. The Reformist Student Movement thus gave Argentinean universities the peculiar organizational style seen today. In describing university democratization under the Reform, we refer to the quantitative and qualitative incorporation of social sectors traditionally barred from the universities. The wave of student incorporation after 1918 is historically referred to as "the period of the expansion of enrollment." Qualitative democratization, refers not only to the inclusion of social groups from outside the traditional elites but also to the political representation acquired by them. From the quantitative point of view, this period was marked by increased numbers of applicants and graduates at the national universities. One of the principles promoted by the young leaders of the Reform was putting no limits on the number of entrants to the university.

The particularity of the Argentinean University Reform, as regards qualitative "democratization," lies in the increasing university presence of the
middle class—whose inclusion had already been insinuated in the early years
of the century—and, fundamentally, in the political representation they won
in the university's governing bodies. The demands for representation in university government were expressed through the joint will of Argentina's student leaders, oriented toward breaking the monopoly held by the conservative
elite in all university political-administrative decisions. The behavior of the
national universities during this period vividly expressed the intimate relationship that existed between the university and the social changes of its time.

The Golden Decade of the 1960s
In a setting of quantitative and qualitative growth, between 1958 and 1966,
UBA abandoned the exclusiveness of the professionalizing profile inherited
from the foundational Napoleonic model, to pursue the development of research, in science as well as in the humanities—activities that brought it closer
to the Humboldtian university model. In the '60's, an expansion of scientific production allowed the university to project itself at an international
level with the dual role of teaching and research. For the first time, full institutionalization was realized with regard to the reformist principles: autonomy, tripartite government, emphasis on the three university
missions—teaching, research, and external services—open access and no tuition, professors' recruitment by merit (selection by didactic opposition and
professional background), and ideological pluralism.

Authoritarian Crisis: Coups d'Etat
The darkest periods of contemporary Argentinean history—and of the universities in particular—saw university interventions decreed by the National
Executive branch of the government (1930, 1946, 1955, 1966, and 1976).
The common denominator of these decrees was ideological control and the
subjugation of university autonomy, with the resulting proscription and sus-
pension of professors (black lists) and the dissolution of institutional forms
of self-government. The last and most brutal of these interventions (1976-
1983) produced an intemperate dismantling of its cultural and material capital. With reference to the development of scientific investigation during this
period, nearly all the national budget set aside for science and technology
was channeled to CONICET—an agency subordinated to and depending
on the National Executive—thus paralyzing the productive capacity of the

rest of the country's scientific and technological agencies, among them the national universities.

The Present Stage of Democratic Institutionalization

The recovery of democratic institutional life, toward the end of 1983, produced a revived democratization of UBA as well as the rest of the public university system (Decree No. 145/83 and Law 23.068/84), recovering complete autonomy and re-establishing the overturned University Statutes that had been implemented between 1958 and 1966. These Statutes are in force at UBA today. The return to the democratic tradition facilitated the recovery of university scientific activity. Since then, and in accord with changes in national foreign policy goals and in university orientation, the professionalizing mission rules over the scientific and cultural mission. Since then, UBA has made a point of revising its institutional identity, described in the fundamentals of its University Statutes (UBA, 1966): "to promote, transmit and preserve culture through direct contact with universal thought, paying particular attention to Argentinean problems (Base I) and by means of humanist studies, scientific research and artistic creativity" (Base II).

The University of Buenos Aires defines itself as: "a community of professors, students and graduates . . . . It trains original researchers, capable professionals, and career professors, who are socially effective and willing to serve the country; it orients the graduates in their teaching and research tasks, and through them strengthens its relationship with society" (Base III). " . . . It ensures in its premises the most ample freedom of investigation and expression, but does not disengage itself from social, political and ideological problems. On the contrary, it studies them scientifically" (Base IV). " . . . It tries to transmit the benefits of its direct cultural and social action, through university external services" (Base V). "It lends technical assistance to private and state institutions of public interest and participates in undertakings of general interest" (Base V).

This definition of the UBA mission shows that the development of scientific research and the production of knowledge are constitutive activities of its institutional identity, although they do not necessarily determine faculty selection and recruitment. At the time of the "great transformation" that J. J. Brunner (1990) describes as a process of expansion and differentiation that all Latin-American universities have gone through, UBA more than any other Argentinean university has become multi-functional, versatile, highly diversified and therefore a very complex institution (Mollis, 1995a).

A Profile of UBA Faculty Members

The teaching staff at the University of Buenos Aires consists of about 22,000 faculty members (UBA, 1992), of which 54.4% are men and 45.6% women. Many are between 25 and 39 years of age, and 59% (12,500) have been faculty members for less than ten years, while another 2,500 have between 10 and 14 years of experience. At UBA, 30% of the teaching staff have the rank of professor and the rest are auxiliares docentes (assistants). Only 14% of all professors and 7% of the assistants are full-time faculty members, 18% of professors and 11% of assistants work a 20-hour week for the institution, and the rest have a commitment of only 10 hours a week. UBA faculty members are, then, mostly young assistants with a minimum teaching commitment, with a first degree (50% of the staff were licenciados, lawyers, physicians, psychologists, or accountants with five years of university studies).

Fewer than 25% of professors hold doctoral degrees, although 60% have studied or are studying at the postgraduate level (UBA 1992). Professors with doctorates are concentrated in the School of Exact Sciences (29.7%), predictably in accord with the scientific nature of the disciplines in which they teach (Mathematics, Physics, etc.), where research is a priority activity. In contrast, most of the professors in the professional schools—such as Architecture, Engineering and Psychology, where research is most infrequent—went no further than the first university degree. The relatively modest attainment of postgraduate degrees among the Argentinean university teaching staff reflects the fact that completing postgraduate studies has not been an inviolable requisite for reaching high academic rank in Latin American universities, with the notable exception of Brazil (Krotsch and Mollis, 1996). Recent changes implemented within the Higher Education Law address this issue with a new requirement that the possession of a postgraduate degree will be necessary in order to hold the post of professor in national universities.

The predominance of part-time positions, many of which carry a small teaching load, is partly due to limited university budgets, a fact not to be lost sight of in analyzing the selection and evaluation of personnel, the working of the existing institutional mechanisms and the consolidation of academic traditions. The procedures for recruiting and retaining academic personnel result from the combination of a demanding entrance system, scarcity of resources and small academic communities made up of scientists and intellectuals who are leading various occupations to compensate university low salaries. However, to generalize for all faculty is misleading. In Argentina, the schools (facultades) and the set of disciplines taught in each of them seem to determine the orientation of the professor toward research or teaching and the 'professionalizing function', as described by Tony Becher (1987) and Burton Clark (1990).

ACADEMIC CONTESTS: ACCESS AND PERMANENCE IN UNIVERSITY POSITIONS

There are no official figures for the number of faculty members who have the status of *regular* (meaning obtained by contest; others are *interim*). Contests for appointment are to be held every 7 years, and once that interval has elapsed the teacher loses the status of *regular professor* until a new contest is held. With the return to democracy in Argentina (1983), and to meritocratic selection of university personnel, there was a wave of renovation contests, and since 1995 there has been a new wave of contests. At the present time, professorships have generally been contested, while the contesting of lower academic ranks is frequent in some schools and much less so in others.

Tradition at the University of Buenos Aires is based on two foundations. One is the unity of teaching and research (the teacher-researcher), and the other is reflected in university government through collegiate organs, constituted by elected representatives of the three academic constituencies (claustros), with its top executive posts at each level held by contested professors. This combination of requisites for acceding to positions of responsibility—teaching, research, contested merit, representative co-governance—seems to lead in the same direction as some of Rosovsky's conclusions from his experience of institutional leadership at Harvard: "Not everything is improved by making it more democratic . . . . University governance should improve the capacity for teaching and research" (Rosovsky, 1990).

The Organization of Academic Contests

To explain the link between regular professors (contested professors) and the university government, we must describe the governing bodies. The highest body at the University of Buenos Aires is the Supreme Council. It is made up of representatives of each of three key university groups or claustros— the student body, the faculty (contested professors), and the body of UBA graduates—plus the deans of the faculties. The faculties, in turn, are directed by leading Councils made up of representatives of the three claustros. And the faculties are composed of departments that have similar local organs of co-governance. The 1958 Statutes of the University of Buenos Aires instituted the unity between teaching and research, the figure of the professor-researcher as the basic nucleus of its activity. The teaching departments constituted the administrative and academic grouping for the organization of teaching, with the chair as the basic teaching unit.

The chair is constituted by a team of faculty members of various categories—professors and assistants—headed by the senior or titular professor. Basically, the chair has the responsibility for teaching one or more courses in the curriculum. UBA sustains the principle of parallel chairs, meaning that the same course could be given by more than one chair, in which case the students can freely choose between the available options. However, partly for lack of funds and partly due to informal corporative agreements, this practice has not been installed in all schools at the University.

There are differences by faculty. Some of them organize the work of teaching staff along departmental lines that are flexible and rotative. However, the chair (la catedra) is the most traditional form of academic organization in Latin American universities and carries considerable weight for teaching. This fact has led to the university's being called "a bottom-heavy confederation of faculties" (Clark, 1984; Brunner, 1988). The senior professor is responsible for teaching the students and for training the junior assistants, a fact that makes him the highest-ranking decision-maker for setting teaching and training agendas in the department.

The fundamental system of recruitment in Argentinean national universities is the *concurso de antecedentes y oposicion,* a contest based on academic background and competitive performance in a master class. These contests are public and open. Candidates are assessed by a peer group of experts. When funding is sufficient, experts are invited from abroad. However, with present budget tightening, invitation to experts from outside the country have been suspended, with the corresponding loss of international recruiting parameters:

> Regular professors are designated by contest in which full publicity should be assured both as to the academic background of the participants and to the jury's recommendations . . . any ideological or political discrimination, or localistic favoritism is to be excluded . . . and the background the candidates' expertise and their capacity as faculty members and researchers should only be judged by juries of unquestionable authority and impartiality (Estatuto Universitario de la Universidad de Buenos Aires).

The jury is constituted in UBA, composed of three professors of sufficient merit and recognized expertise in the area. Their activity is observed by two overseers—one a graduate of the particular discipline and the other a student—who produce a report on the contest process but take no part in the assessment nor in the discussion of recommendations. In other universities, a graduate and a student are included in the jury itself. The rules do not ban jury members from the same faculty, except when a professor's post is being re-contested, in which case at least two of the jurors must come from outside. However, it is usually considered desirable for some of them to be from other universities. As mentioned above, lack of funding can become a major difficulty in this area.

The call to contest a teaching post is generally a departmental initiative but may be emitted by the faculty government; in any case, it must be approved by the University Supreme Council. There are several variants of this convocation: a call may be issued to contest a post in a chair, in a field of study or by a department. These decisions vary by faculty. However, a call by the chair is most frequent, except in the School of Exact Sciences, where the dominant form is by field of knowledge. This feature shows that academic diversity is reflected in the diversity of calls to contest.

The structure of university co-government is decisively important for the final result of the contest, since the jury's opinions are no more than a recommendation. It is the School Councils that actually propose designations and act as review bodies for appeals against the jury's recommendations.[5] The University Supreme Council makes the final decision. Thus—in the procedure of public contests—administrative, academic, and political forces are combined in the decision-making process.

From beginning to end, the contest process makes mechanisms of appeal and review available to the candidate in every school and at every step: application, jury formation, the jury's recommendation, and the school ruling Council. The Supreme Council, that concentrates power in university government, is the highest body of appeal in the university. However, an appeal beyond the Supreme Council to the public judicial system is not impossible. Although the process is slow, this system of academic appointment through contest is thought to provide a guarantee of transparency through the various controls and supervision and the possibility of objection at different stages.

Criteria for Assessment
The assessment established for the contests is done on the basis of an analysis of the academic and professional background and the formal commit-

ment, full-time or part-time: the candidate presents a research plan and this, too, is considered. Opposition is the name given to an interview and master class on a subject selected by the jury. The positions obtained by contest have a duration of seven years for professors and three for teaching assistants. The Statute is ambiguous regarding the re-contesting of a professor's position: it is not clear whether or not it favors the incumbent. There is no express statement on the subject, but the document does say that recommendations will be made on the basis of performance and, if favorable, a two-thirds majority of the co-governing council has the power to decide for renewal even though there may be another candidate who has shown greater merit.

The rules for contests at UBA grant considerable liberties to the juries regarding assessment criteria. Variations in the call to contest (by chair, field, or department) are directly linked to the schools' different academic traditions (Clark, 1990). Thus, the more research-oriented schools (Exact Sciences, Pharmacy and Biochemistry) give priority to the professor's profile as a researcher, while schools leaning to the holistic education of the students (such as Philosophy and Literature, or Social Sciences) prefer the "integrative professor," to use a term offered by Boyer (1990). UBA authorities who manage contests have observed that in the humanities, the importance of the master class and the erudition that characterizes the good professor seem to be important for winning a contest. In the hard-science schools, the research task takes precedence, so that academic background can almost be taken as a predictor of the result. At any rate, there is no established rule on this. This flexibility of criteria has advantages insofar as it lends dynamism to the machinery, but it has its weak side in that there may be too large a margin of discretion if control over the jury's activities is inadequate.

Expert Judgment and Political Decisions

It may be affirmed that the task of assessing and incorporating faculty members is a two-pronged procedure: (a) assessment by a jury of experts and (b) supervision of the process and of the recommendations by the university's collegiate organs of co-governance. This combination seems to be a determining factor for the legitimation of contests in the academic community.

Prevention of possible bias arising from the flexibility of assessment criteria seems to lie in the control of expert opinion by the representative political bodies that have the final say in the process. In fact, a recent reform in the rules of academic contests grants even more power to the school leading councils and to the Supreme Council for reviewing and modifying expert recommendations. In the opinion of the highest academic authority at UBA, this power of intervention granted to the political bodies tends to prevent flagrant transgressions that might be sanctioned by some academic corporation.

This contradictory relation between the general academic or scientific interest and particular corporate interest is always present in decision-making at UBA, whether it be referred to the assignment of resources or to the policy for contests. There seems to be broad agreement among members of the political leadership at the school and university levels about the need for supervision, control, and regulation by the leading bodies over the management of contests. The departments have the main responsibility for calling an academic post to contest, the first step in the procedure. It is their duty to propose the rank and time commitment of each post as well as jury composition. The reason is that specific knowledge of the disciplines and of competent scholars is to be found in the departments. There is a generalized view that the federative character of many schools leads to difficulty, making the role of the school councils and the Supreme Council a necessary corrective of possible bias. At the same time, the experts' contribution sets clear limits on the discretion enjoyed by the leading political-academic bodies.

The principles underlying teacher recruitment procedures have thus taken shape historically at UBA. Students participated actively in the Reform of 1918 that expanded throughout Latin America from its origins in Cordoba. In the 1960s, a decade of expansion of science production gave the university an international reputation with the concept of "teacher-researcher." There was full institutionalization of the principles of the Reform movement: autonomy, tripartite government (professors, students and graduates), emphasis on the three university missions: teaching, research, and external services, open access and gratuitous education, recruitment of professors on merit (periodic contests with competition in teaching and academic background), and ideological pluralism.

Summary

The introduction of contests responded to the need to break an oligarchic control over the university. The idea of the contest as it actually developed established a means for the entrance of external groups and opened the way for renovation and circulation of personnel. On the other hand, one of the intentions of the contests was to stimulate the production of knowledge and the improvement of training. There are practically no doubts in the university community about the efficacy of the system for fulfilling these goals.

However, these advantages may be diminished if certain conditions are not fulfilled. One of them is the existence or development of an academic tradition based on a practice of assessment, competition, and excellence that meets international standards. These features determine the specific mode of achieving consensus and of debating and working out problematic aspects of contests. The second condition is related to the resources available. In a context of scarce funding—although contests are a useful instrument of selection and recruitment—maintaining equity and retaining valuable researchers is often a difficult matter. The contest process is jeopardized, for example, when a lack of funds hinders the constitution of a good jury.

Contests are the only mode of regular access to teaching and research posts at the University of Buenos Aires. As explained in this chapter, they developed from the early twentieth century, spurred by a political struggle that took shape in the Reform movement. Since that time, contests have had considerable political weight in the institution because representatives of the regular professors make up half of the members of the governing bodies, and only regular professors may aspire to top executive positions at every level in the university. As well, their political importance lies in their potential for conflict with some dimensions of university modernization in the context of structural adjustment and neoliberal policies. Contests provide stability and legitimacy and therefore contrast with some of the requirements of present policies that view the university mission in an entrepreneurial perspective. Contests establish patterns of academic merit and criteria of excellence in individual production that surpass the scope of short-term policy and the establishment of financial goals at the expense of academic excellence.

Contests promote a demanding assessment context for university faculty members. The evaluation is multidimensional and has direct implications for access to and permanence in teaching/research posts. They install an evaluative culture that generates expectations and promotes the development of capabilities for individual competition. Like any assessment process, its effect is permeable to the evaluative perspectives of the experts and of academic institutional politics. The contest, like any other instrument, depends on such decisions and on the institutional framework. Its value is relative to the institutional culture in which it takes place.

Two features characterize the practice of contests. They democratize access procedures, affording an "equal-opportunity base" that is a foundation principle of the Argentinean education system. The contest also installs a criterion that is individual, meritocratic, and dynamic because of its periodic character. It is not always easy to combine these two features. There is a lack of open professoriate positions that blocks career opportunities for younger generations of assistants. As already pointed out, calls to contest are ruled by a fixed structure of posts, defined in the chair teams.

THE IMPACT OF ACADEMIC CONTESTS ON UNIVERSITY TEACHING

In general terms, contests are considered to have had a positive effect on the quality of teaching and research. The requisite of periodic open re-contesting is also esteemed. However, the effects of this periodicity on the contests are hard to assess objectively, given the recurrent interruption of democratic decision-making at UBA as in the country in general over many decades. During the last forty years, coups d'etat have meant the interruption of the normal system of attaining and re-attaining academic positions. The university is now for the first time in the process of re-contesting all the professorships, already granted on democratic terms. The system cannot function without political consensus; most important is the articulation of interests produced in the context of institutional freedom that the autonomy system provides.

Following the Kuhnian metaphor, one could speak of periods of revolution and normal periods. The contests might play a different role in each case. In periods of "revolution," such as the foundational period of the Reform, they facilitated the entry into the profession of members of excluded socioeconomic sectors, and helped to ensure superior scientific and academic merit of the incumbents. Thus a new community of Reformist professors was created. Periodic renovation is also useful because, in most cases, it promotes internal competition. Although this competition does not always become a reality, it is a significant stimulant to production, brings evaluative pressure to bear on the faculty, and legitimates the idea of equal opportunity.

Despite its virtues, contests—like other relatively open assessment systems based on expert opinion—are not immune to criticism. Questioning is most often aimed at the institutional contexts in which they are carried out, at the principles that underlie them, and the mode of regulation.

Case Studies: Academic Contests and the Quality of Teaching in Social Sciences and History

There are actually few studies (Litwin, 1996; Teobaldo, 1996; Mollis & Hee Bang, 1996) that analyze the impact of academic contests on the quality of university teaching. The concept of quality in respect to teaching appears prioritized in the modernizing agendas of higher education of the 90's (Levy, 1993; Brunner, 1993) in the context of neo-liberal policies created for Latin America. In them one recognizes modern educational aims based on the quantitative assessment and evaluation of quality of higher education (Mollis, 1994). In this sense, questions about the quality of teaching are reduced to the question of how much do the students learn. However, very few studies on academic contests show much substantive interest in how the students learn.

In a recent research project conducted at the University of Buenos Aires (Litwin, 1996), different models of "good teaching" produced by regular professors are analyzed (professors who achieved their research and teaching posts through the contests mechanism). A survey was conducted among the School of Philosophy students for them to recognize and describe the best professors in the social sciences field and for them to explain why they chose these as the best teachers. As from the description given by the students, different didactic configurations were reconstructed—in other words, different definitions of "good teaching" were developed according to the selected professors. Among the most relevant types it was found those that refer to the use of pedagogical strategies and to the mentioning of epistemological currents. Most "regular" professors use two types of knowledge that are recognized as the best teaching: (1) they use didactic strategies such as introducing in their lessons attractive, interesting, and practical examples, close to the students everyday reality; and (2) they use theoretical concepts of increasing complexity. Good professors also pose reflective questions that encourage students to discover, through inductive and deductive thought, new and old concepts in each lesson. The study shows that there is a tendency of regular professors to exhibit deep knowledge about theoretical and methodological currents that make their disciplines advance and progress. This characteristic is quite common among regular professors given their research orientation which requires them to be publishing, attending international conferences and seminars, and interacting in academic networks.

One of the objectives sought by Litwin's project was to find for each type of curriculum content the "best way to teach it, free from stereotypes or rituals." Even though the research doesn't analyze the impact of academic contest on the quality of teaching, it was *a priori* considered that "regular" professors are "the best" because of their academic and pedagogic merits. According to this study's author, " good teaching" is understood as:

comprehensive teaching, which has moral and epistemological strength in order to surpass fragile forms of knowledge. The good teaching recovers for the didactic preoccupation moral considerations which had been left aside in the didactic field of the last decade. (Litwin, 1996:60)

The moral aspect of teaching refers to the selection of curriculum contents and methods of evaluation and the exhibition of values which go beyond the curriculum itself. The epistemological aspect refers to the level of comprehensibility, to the quality of explanations and justifications formulated in the frame of the taught discipline, to the solution of problems, to the pre-existing mental images and the construction of new ones based on the former ones. These new approaches to "good teaching" give priority to professors' answers to spontaneous questions by students. Good teaching reflects organized lessons according to analogies or explanations that the students demand:

Responding spontaneity means to respond real questions emerged from an environment for teaching which favors the processes of comprehension . . . . Give time to thinking and worry about generating a rich thinking . . . to be explicative of topics of other fields so that students may discuss about them or solve genuine problems in a disciplinary way. (Litwin, 1996)

Among the main characteristics for being recognized as the "best professor," the study mentions:

Professor gives priority to the discipline contents instead of to activities for students (routines);

Professor worries more about why and how students learn than about teaching;

Teaching generates propositions which refer to problems and practices of professional field;

Provides explanations about how knowledge is being constructed and investigated (explicates the currents of scientific thinking which gives reason to a particular analysis);

Professor shows his experience in the art of teaching through examples of cases solved by himself;

Listening to students interventions and articulates them in a communicational atmosphere, i.e., adapting professor's explanations to students demands (Litwin, 1996,63-64).

In another research project carried out in the School of Philosophy and Letters (Mollis & Hee Bang, 1996), strategies used by regular professors to teach History were investigated. The relevance of this study consists of helping professors of history to better the traditional teaching in secondary schools. Students of secondary schools in general have developed adverse attitudes towards History for considering it "boring, unattractive and far away of reality." This evaluation of the discipline conforms in part, to the fact that it is taught in a very traditional way, which means that a lot of anecdotal information is fed to the student. The teaching of history relies on the memorization of facts not related to the present and student's everyday life.

There is consensus among the experts (Finocchiaro 1989; Entel, 1991) in considering the teaching of history in the secondary school as an act of transmitting definitive truths and facts, presented in a chronological succession from the remote past to the present. Confronted with the question what students do know about history in secondary schools, the answers are

They repeat a lesson from a set text;

They narrate with details of dates, battles and names; and

They organize the information, basically the facts, in a casual and chronological way (e.g., the reasons for the Discovery of America, etc.). (Entel, 1991)

The two predominant features as to what and how the secondary school students learn are: 1) the transmission of definitive truths written in texts prevails over the construction of knowledge; and 2) the accumulation of information prevails over the production of a new learning. This way, when students enter University, they are conditioned by prejudices against history. They suppose that the teaching of that discipline in a higher level will respond to the same tendency of the secondary school. However, given the professionalization and experience of university regular professors, the students find new paradigms which facilitate their learning of the discipline (Mollis & Hee Bang, 1996). In order to recognize an "excellent course of history" run by one of the "best professors" of the School of Education, students describe the following characteristics:

An original syllabus, new curriculum contents;

Updated bibliography (no more than five years old);

A set of didactic activities for students in the shape of Course Work Folders, (these folders represent that professor's plans, and organize his or her classes);

New ways of evaluation (not necessarily easier ones); in general written or oral ways of evaluating which demand activity by the students are appreciated, be it by way of research exercises or practical problems applying theoretical concepts learned in class;

A flexible attitude by the professor, open to questions by the students; Coherent expositions by professor; lessons organized according to the three traditional periods: presentation, development and closure; integration of the taught concepts in a a "conceptual map"; and

Samples of theoretical contents with empirical concepts from the professional field.

It is evident that "good professors" are not only those who have most of their students pass their exams. The quality of professorship is linked to the quality of his or her ethical engagement and epistemological formation, that is to say, it is linked to a complex and integrated professionalization. This new approach to quality of professorship goes beyond the "versus" which confronted the professional training with the scientific formation, or the theoretical orientation versus the practical training.

Nowadays the so-called "didactic configurations" are contextual, they adapt to different contents and disciplines to be taught. One of the most precious qualities of one "good university professor" is his or her capacity to adapt to the spontaneity of students and create a communicational atmosphere which allows students to think, reflect, comprehend, question, and build their own meaning.

These two research projects show that the quality of teaching does not depend on the professor being exclusively a good researcher or a good professional but a *good communicator*. A good teacher adapts his didactic and epistemological strategies to a comprehensive communication so that students will learn. The academic contests promote the conditions and evaluate the academic, scientific, and pedagogical merits of professors, but they don't create "good professors." A good professorship is thus the result of the articulation of three fundamental variables: the disciplines (in which professors are formed), the contents they teach, and the didactic configurations (i.e., the interaction between epistemological contents and the moral duty of helping someone to learn).

CONCLUSION

Academic contests constitute the only strategy in most of the Argentine universities to create teaching and research posts with the category of regular (three years for assistant professors and seven for full and associate professors). As a method for selecting and appointing university professors, the academic contest helps to select "the best" professors, considering the open competition that is promoted and the renovation that takes place every seven or three years according to the hierarchy of the post. However, we have mentioned that academic logic is not the only one that prevails in this mechanism. There is also a political rationality which transforms contests into tools used for purposes related to the proper development of the discipline and the quality of teaching. There are three variables which influence the lack of clarity in the procedures: a) the specific financing of contests, b) the fixed faculty structure c) the academic administration.

For the contests to be legitimate and clear, the jury's convocation is the principal variable. This main step of contests procedure—the jury's convocation—depends on the financing resources to be invested. When there's sufficient financing to invite an international jury, the contest becomes the best selective mechanism for professors, given its impartiality and the expertise of the members of the jury.

As to the rigidity of the faculty of each university, this constitutes one of the most controversial and limiting variables of the mechanism. If the set of research and teaching posts is established previously by way of bureaucratic procedures, then the call to an academic contest will be made not based on the real academic needs but according to administrative parameters. This means that some contests needed from the point of view of the curriculum do not take place because the historical structure of the department didn't contemplate it or isn't flexible to new needs.

Lastly, the academic wish of those responsible of setting forth the mechanism of academic contest influences the results of the contest. The meritocratic rationality is not always dominant in those functionaries who decide. On numerous occasions the contests have privileged the corporate logic of minorities or groups which try to consolidate their organizational power independently from the candidate's merits. This disposition to support certain candidates is consolidated when the members of the jury are named. The legitimacy and clarity of the contest are based fundamentally on the quality, independence and expertise of the jury and that's why its fundamental to maintain the independence of the jury from those who decide to name them. Although these conditions show the limitations of the contests as far as their capacity to select and name the "best professors," so far no other selective mechanism has been put into practice in the Argentine universities which exceeds the advantages of the public, periodic, meritocratic, and political contest.

We have not approached the contest from a policymaking point of view in this paper. We have given priority to examining the system as historically developed and living in the present, through traditions that have shaped our university. Thus, a peculiar combination of academic and political features has emerged, a particular type of teacher-researchers who at the same time are representatives of their academic constituencies (claustros) in the government of the university. Thus, the contest is not merely the road to a post, but an "*initiation rite*" that legitimates the merits of the university professor and makes him or her a potential representative of his peers in university government. Today, a university student or professor can scarcely imagine a university without co-government, without collegiate bodies representing professors, students, and graduates in decision-making, without faculty professors legitimating their rank through competitive public contests based on teaching and academic background. These contests, being public, open, selective and periodic, have installed principles of openness, production, and pluralism that will surely be taken into account in the new guidelines adopted in future faculty recruitment policies.

In the absence of a traditional tenure system in Argentina, one might expect the recruitment and promotion of faculty to look less like the publication-driven scenarios described so often by faculty in Western industrialized countries. However, as this discussion will show, even without a tenure system the situation remains largely unchanged—the search for the "best professor" does not always mean the search for the best teacher but, rather, the best researcher. Indeed, the appointment of "regular" professor—the gold standard in the Argentinian academic profession—often involves publishing, attending international conferences and seminars, and interacting in academic networks, activities similar to that expected from the typical tenure-track junior faculty elsewhere. This example of an academic environment without tenure is most useful for informing the current accountability-driven debate in many countries over whether to abolish or revise tenure, where

several opponents of tenure have presented it as an obstacle to the development of efforts to improve teaching effectiveness. In the case of the University of Buenos Aires, the absence of tenure does not significantly impact the
working conditions under which professors—and their teaching—are evaluated.

NOTES

1. Policies and projects installed since 1990 tend to promote research and the development of human resources and to establish clearer relationships with the economic
   sector and productive enterprise. The strategy for binding the University with the
   social environment has become more clear with the implementation of certain tools
   such as the creation of UBATEC S.A., a tripartite firm in which the University holds
   31.66% of the stock, the State (through the Municipality of Buenos Aires) holds the
   same percentage and the rest is in the hands of the business sector (represented by
   two manufacturers' associations, the Union Industrial Argentina with 25% and the
   Confederacion General de la Industria with 11,68%) (Fanelli, 1993)
2. ". . . the Law School . . . was not merely destined to train lawyers but also, and, perhaps above all, to prepare the future leading groups of our society. In that sense, the
   School, and mainly its body of Professors, identified with the dominant political structures of Argentina . . ." (Halperin, Donghi, T., 1962:142)
3. The collegiate governing bodies are the University Assembly, the Supreme University Council and the School Councils.
4. "The State will guarantee every inhabitant the possibility of entering a university, and
   respect his freedom within it, and for this purpose the gratuitousness of education
   and its secular character is established."
5. At the present time, the school council has the power to adopt a divided jury's recommendation, but it may not modify a unanimous one; it could, however, annul
   the recommendation if it were considered manifestly arbitrary or to contain irredeem-
   able procedural errors. It is now possible, with special majorities, to modify the recommendations.

REFERENCES

Becher, T. (1987). The disciplinary shaping of the profession. In Clark, B., (Ed). *The academic profession: National, disciplinary, and institutional settings*. Berkeley, CA: University of California Press.

Boyer, E. (1990). *Scholarship reconsidered. Priorities of the professoriate*. Princeton, NJ: The
Carnegie Foundation for the Advancement of Teaching.

Brunner, J.J. (1988). *Notas para una teoría del cambio en los sistemas de educación superior*. Documento de Trabajo No 381. FLACSO/CHILE, Santiago de Chile.

Brunner, J.J. (1990). *Educación superior en América Latina. Cambios y desafíos*. Fondo de
Cultura Económica, Santiago de Chile.

Brunner, J.J. (1993). Evaluación y financiamiento de la educación superior en América
Latina. In Courard, H. et al., *Políticas comparadas de educación superior en América
Latina*. FLACSO, Santiago de Chile.

Clark, B. (1984) (ed.). *Perspectives on higher education.* Berkeley, CA: University of California Press.

Clark, B. (1987). *The academic profession: National, disciplinary, and institutional settings.* Berkeley, CA: University of California Press.

Clark, B. (1990) (2nd ed.) *The academic life. Small worlds, different worlds.* Princeton, NJ: The Carnegie Foundation for the Advancement of Teaching.

Caldelari, M., Funes, P. & Associates (1992). *Fragmentos de una memoria: UBA 1821-1991.* UBA, Buenos Aires: Secretaría de Extensión Universitaria.

Entel, A. (1991). *Escuela y conocimiento* (2nd edition). Buenos Aires: Miäno y Dâavila Editores.

Fanelli, A.M. (1993). *La articulación de la Universidad de Buenos Aires con el sector productivo: la experiencia reciente.* (Documento 96) CEDES, Buenos Aires.

Finocchiaro, M.A., (1989) *The Galileo affair : a documentary history.* Berkeley : University of California.

Gil, A.M. (1995). *La diversidad de los academicos.* Universidad Metropolitana de Mexico Press, Mexico.

Halperin, D.T. (1962). *Historia de la Universidad de Buenos Aires.* EUDEBA, Buenos Aires.

Krotsch, P. & Mollis, M. (1996). *Globalization, regional integration and university association: The case of the Asociacion de Universidades, Grupo de Montevideo (AUGM).* Paper presented at the 21st ASHE Conference, Memphis, USA.

Law 23.068/84 (Normalización de las universidades nacionales).

Levy, D. (1996). *Building the third sector : Latin America's rivate research centers and nonprofit development.* Pittsburgh : University of Pittsburgh Press.

Levy, D. (1993). *The New Pluralist Agenda for Latin American Higher Education: Honey I shrunk the State?* Paper introduced to the Seminario sobre Educación Superior en América Latina, Universidad de los Andes, IDE, Banco Mundial, Colombia.

Levy, D. (1986). *Higher education and the state in Latin America: Private challenges to public dominance.* Chicago University Press.

Litwin, E. (1996). Algunas reflexiones en torno a la enseñanza en la Universidad. In *Pensamiento Universitario* , Año 4, No 4-5, Buenos Aires, p.57-67.

Mollis, M. (1989). Argentina. In Altbach, P.G. (Ed.), *Student political activism. An international reference handbook.* Westport, CT: Greenwood Press.

Mollis, M. (1990). *Universidades y estado nacional.* Argentina y Japán, 1885-1930, Editorial Biblios, Buenos Aires.

Mollis, M. (1994). Crisis, calidad, y evalaución de las universidades: tres temas para el debate. In Puiggros & Krotsch (Eds.) *Universidad y Evaluación. Estado del Debate.* Aique, Buenos Aires, p. 211-237.

Mollis, M. (1995a). *Estado, universidades y gestión de políticas científico-tecnológicas en Argentina. Un estudio de casos,* Documento preparado para el Banco Interamericano de Desarrollo (BID), Washington, DC.

Mollis, M. (1995b), En busca de respuestas a la crisis universitaria: Historia y Cultura. *Perfiles Educativos,* Jul-Sep, No 69, Mexico City, p. 34-40

Mollis, M. & Hee Bang, J. (1996). *Que saben de historia los estudiantes que ingresan a la universidad?* Informe de Investigacion, UBACYT FI 049, IICE/UBA.

P.E.N. 1983. Decreto 154 (Declaración del r,gimen provisorio de normalización de las universidades nacionales, hasta que se dicte la ley de fondo).

Rosovsky, H. (1990). *The university. An owner's manual.* New York: W.W.Norton & Company.

Teobaldo, M. (1996). Evaluación de la calidad educativa en el primer año universitario. *La Universidad Ahora*, PESUN, No 9-10, Buenos Aires, p. 94-108.

U.B.A. (1966.) *Estatuto de la Universidad de Buenos Aires.*

U.B.A. (1992.) *La Universidad de Buenos Aires. 170 años.*

Selected Bibliography

Selected Bibliography

Abrami, P.C., & d'Apollonia, S. (1991). Multidimensional students' evaluations of teaching effectiveness: The generalizability of N=1research. *Journal of Educational Psychology*, 83, p. 411-15.

Abrami, P.C. (1989). How should we use student ratings to evaluate teaching. *Research in Higher Education*, 30, p. 221-27.

Abrami, P.C. (1988). SEEQ and ye shall find: A review of Marsh's students' evaluations of university teaching. *Instructional Evaluation*, 9, p. 19-27.

Abu-Lughod, J. (1981). *Engendering knowledge: Women and the university.* Evanston, Ill.: Center for Urban Affairs and Policy Research, Northwestern University.

Altbach, P.G. (ed.) (1997). *The international academic profession: Portraits from 14 countries.* Princeton, NJ: Carnegie Foundation for the Advancement of Teaching.

Aleamoni, L.M., & Yimer, M. (1973). An investigation of the relationship between colleague rating, student rating, research productivity, and academic rank in rating instructional effectiveness. *Journal of Educational Psychology*, 64, p. 274-77.

Andrews, J. Garrison, D.R., & Magnusson, K. (1996). The teaching and learning transaction in higher education: A study of excellent professors and their students. *Teaching in Higher Education*, 1 (1).

Angelo, T.A. (1993). A "teacher's dozen": Fourteen general, research-based principles for improving higher learning in our classrooms. *AAHE Bulletin*, 45 (8).

Angelo, T.A. & Cross, K.P. (1993). *Classroom assessment techniques: A handbook for college teachers.* (2nd. Edition). San Francisco: Jossey-Bass.

Ashcroft, K. & Foreman-Peck, L. (1994). *Managing teaching and learning in further and higher education.* London: The Falmer Press.

Astin, A.W., Korn, W.S., & Dey, E.L. (1991). *The American college teacher.* Los Angeles: Higher Education Research Institute.

Astin, A.W. (1977). *Four critical years: Effects of college beliefs, attitudes and knowledge.* San Francisco: Jossey-Bass.

Austin, A.E. (1990). Faculty cultures, faculty values. In *Assessing academic climates and cultures. New Directions for Institutional Research*, 68, Vol. 17 (4), p. 61-74

Avery, P.B. and Gray, P.L. (1995). Mentoring graduate teaching assistants: Creating an effective mentor/mentee relationship. *The Journal of Graduate Teaching Assistant Development*, Vol. 3, No. 1, p. 9-19.

Ballard, B., & Clanchy, J. (1991). *Teaching students from overseas.* Melbourne: Longman Cheshire.

Banks, T.L. (1988). Gender bias in the classroom. *Journal of Legal Education*, 38, p. 137-46.

Bannister, B.D. (1986). Performance outcome feedback and attributional feedback: Interactive effects on recipient responses. *Journal of Applied Psychology*, 71, p. 203-10.

Barnett, L.T., & Littlepage, G. (1973). Course preferences and evaluations of male and female professors by male and female students." *Psychonomic Society Bulletin,* 13, p. 44-46.

Barr, R.B. & Tagg, J. (1995). From teaching to learning: A new paradigm for undergraduate education. *Change,* 27 (6), p. 12-25.

Basow, S.A., & Silberg, N.T. (1987). Student evaluations of college professors: Are female and male professors rated differently? *Journal of Educational Psychology,* 79, p. 308-14.

Basow, S.A., & Distenfeld, M.S. (1985). Teacher expressiveness: More important for males than females? *Journal of Educational Psychology,* 77, p. 45-52.

Batista, E.E. (1976). The place of colleague evaluation in the appraisal of college teaching: A review of the literature. *Research in Higher Education,* 4, p. 257-71.

Bausell, R.B., & Bausell, C.R. (1979). Student ratings and various instructional variables from a within-instructor perspective. *Research in Higher Education,* 11, p. 167-77.

Baxter-Magolda, M.B. (1992). *Knowing and reasoning in college: Gender-related patterns—students' intellectual development.* San Francisco: Jossey-Bass.

Bayer, A.E. (1973). *Teaching faculty in academe.* American Council on Education, Research Reports, Vol. 8 No. 2.

Beard, R. & Hartley, J. (1984). *Teaching and learning in higher education.* London: Harper & Row.

Beaty, E., Dall'Alba, G. & Marton, F. (1989). Conceptions of learning. *International Journal of Educational Research,* 13.

Beidler, P.G. (Ed.) (1986). *Distinguished teachers on effective teaching: Observations on teaching by college professors recognized by the Council for the Advancement and Support of Education. New Directions for Teaching and Learning,* 28. San Francisco: Jossey-Bass.

Belenky, M.F., Clinchy, B.M., Glodberger, N.R., & Tarule, J.M. (1986). *Women's ways of knowing: The development of self, voice, and mind.* New York: Basic Books.

Benditt, T.M. (1990). The research demands of teaching in modern higher education. In Cahn, S.M., (Ed.) *Morality, responsibility and the university: Studies in academic ethics.* Philadelphia: Temple University Press.

Bennett, S.K. (1982). Student perceptions of and expectations for male and female instructors: Evidence relating to the question of gender bias in teaching evaluations. *Journal of Educational Psychology,* 74, p. 170-79.

Beyer, B. (1987). *Practical strategies for the teaching of thinking.* Needham Heights, MA: Allyn & Bacon Publishing.

Biggs, J. (1987). *Student approaches to learning and studying.* Melbourne: Australian Council for Educational Research.

Biglan, A. (1973). Relationships between subject matter area characteristics and output of university departments. *Journal of Applied Psychology,* 57, p. 204-213.

Blackburn, R.T. & Lawrence, J.H. (1995). *Faculty at work: Motivation, expectation, satisfaction.* Baltimore: The Johns Hopkins University Press.

Blurton, C. (1994). Using the Internet for teaching, learning and research. In Halpern, D.F., et al. *Changing college classrooms: New teaching and learning Strat-*

egies for an increasingly complex world. San Francisco: Jossey-Bass.

Boersma, P.D., Gay, D., Jones, R.A., Morrison, L. & Remick, H.M. (1981). Sex differences in college student-faculty interactions: Fact or fantasy? *Sex Roles,* 7, p. 775-84.

Boice, R. (1991). New faculty as teachers. *Journal of Higher Education,* 62, p. 150-73

Bok, D. (1986). *Higher learning.* Cambridge, MA: Harvard University Press.

Bowden, J. (1988). Achieving change in teaching practices. In Ramsden, P. (Ed.), *Improving learning: New perspectives.* London: Kogan Page.

Bowen, H. & Schuster, J. (1986). *American professors: A national resource imperiled.* New York: Oxford University Press.

Boyer, E.L., Altbach, P.G. & Whitelaw, M.J. (1994). *The academic profession: An international perspective.* Princeton, NJ: Carnegie Foundation for the Advancement of Teaching.

Boyer, E.L. (1990). *Scholarship reconsidered: Priorities of the professoriate.* Princeton, NJ: Carnegie Foundation for the Advancement of Teaching.

Boyer, E. L. (1987). *College: The undergraduate experience in America.* New York: Harper & Row.

Brandenburg, D.C., Slinde, J.A., & Batista, E.E.. (1977). Student ratings of instruction: Validity and normative interpretations. *Research in Higher Education,* 7, p. 67-78.

Braskamp, L.A. & Ory, J.C. (1994). *Assessing faculty work: Enhancing individual and institutional performance.* San Francisco:Jossey-Bass.

Braskamp, L.A., Brandenberg, D.C., & Ory, J.C. (1984). *Evaluating teaching effectiveness.* Beverly Hills, CA: Sage Publications.

Braxton, J.M., Eimers, M.T. & Bayer, A.E. (1996). The implications of teaching norms for the improvement of undergraduate education. *Journal of Higher Education,* 67 (6).

Braxton, J.M., Bayer, A.E., & Finkelstein, M.J. (1992). Teaching performance norms in academia. *Research in Higher Education,* 33 (October), p. 533-569.

Brinckerhoff, L., Shaw, S., & McGuire, J. (1993). *Promoting postsecondary education for students with learning disabilities.* Austin, TX: PRO-ED.

Brinko, K.T. (1993) The practice of giving feedback to improve teaching. *Journal of Higher Education* 64, p. 574-93.

Brinko, K.T. (1990). Instructional consultation with feedback in higher education. *Journal of Higher Education,* 61, p. 65-83.

Brookfield, S.D. (1990). *The skillful teacher: On technique, trust, and responsiveness in the classroom.* San Francisco: Jossey-Bass.

Brooks, V.R. (1982). Sex differences in student dominance behavior in female and male professors' classrooms. *Sex Roles,* 8, p. 683-90.

Brown, D.L. (1976). Faculty ratings and student grades: A university-wide multiple regression analysis. *Journal of Educational Psychology,* 68, p. 573-78.

Brown, G. (1983). *Lecturing and explaining.* London: Methuen.

Brown, G.A., & Atkins, M. (1988). *Effective teaching in higher education.* London:

Methuen.

Brown, G.A., & Atkins, M. (1996). Explaining. In Hargie, O. (Ed.), *Handbook of communication skills.* London: Routledge.

Brown, G.A., & Bahktar, M. (1983). *Styles of lecturing.* Loughborough: Loughborough University Press.

Bruner, J.S. (1966). *Toward a theory of instruction.* Cambridge, MA: Harvard University Press.

Cahn, S.M. (1982). The art of teaching. *American Educator,* 6, p. 36-39.

Centra, J.A. (1993). *Reflective faculty evaluation: Enhancing teaching and determining faculty effectiveness.* San Francisco: Jossey-Bass.

Centra, J.A. (1973). Effectiveness of student feedback in modifying college instruction. *Journal of Educational Psychology,* 65, p. 395-401.

Cerbin, W. (1994). The course portfolio as a tool for continuous improvement of teaching and learning. *Journal of Excellence in College Teaching,* 5(1), p. 95-105.

Chambers, J.A. (1972). *College teachers: Their effect on creativity of students.* National Center for Educational Research and Development, U.S. Department of Health, Education and Welfare.

Chickering, A.W. & Gamson, Z.F. (1987). Seven principles for good practice in undergraduate education. *AAHE Bulletin,* 39, p. 3-7.

Chiodo, J.J. (1989). Professors who fail may be our best teachers. *Teacher Education Quarterly,* 16(1), p. 79-83.

Clark, B. R. (1997). The modern integration of research activities with teaching and learning. *Journal of Higher Education,* 68 (3), p. 241-255.

Clinchy, B.M. (1990). Issues of gender in teaching and learning. *Journal of Excellence in College Teaching,* 1, p. 52-67.

Cochrane, T., Ellis, H.D., & Johnston, S.L. (1992). *Computer based education in Australian higher education: A case study at the Queensland University of Technology.* Canberra, Australia: Australian Government Publishing Service.

Cohen, E.G. (1986). *Designing group work.* New York: Teachers College Press.

Cohen, P.A. (1980). Effectiveness of student-rating feedback for improving college instruction: A meta-analysis of findings. *Research in Higher Education,* 13, p. 321-41.

Cohen, P.A., & McKeachie, W.J. (1980). The role of colleges in the evaluation of teaching. *Improving College and University Teaching,* 28, p. 147-54.

Cooper, B. & Foy, J.M. (1967). Evaluating the effectiveness of lectures. *Universities Quarterly,* 21.

Cooper, C.R. (1982). Getting inside the instructional process: A collaborative diagnostic process for improving college teaching. *Journal of Instructional Development,* 5, p. 2-10.

Cooper, J. (1990). *Cooperative learning and college instruction: Effective use of student learning teams.* Long Beach: California State University Press.

Cornelius, R.R., Gray, J.M., & Constantinople, A.P. (1990). Student-faculty interaction in the college classroom. *Journal of Research and Development in Education,* 23, p. 189-97.

Crawford, M., & MacLeod, M. (1990). Gender in the college classroom: An assessment of the "chilly climate" for women. *Sex Roles,* 23, p. 101-22.

Creswell, J.W., & Roskens, R.W. (1981). The biglan studies of differences among academic areas." *Review of Higher Education,* 4, p. 1-16.

Cross, K.P. & Angelo, T.A. (1988). *Classroom assessment techniques: A handbook for faculty.* Ann Arbor, MI: National Center for Research to Improve Postsecondary Teaching and Learning.

Cross, K.P. (1977). Not can, but will college teaching be improved? *New Directions for Higher Education,* 17, p. 1-15.

Dahlgren, L.O. (1984). Outcomes of learning. In Marton, F., Hounsell, D., & Entwistle, N. (Eds.), *The experience of learning.* Edinburgh: Scottish Academic Press.

Davis, B.G. (1993). *Tools for teaching.* San Francisco: Jossey-Bass.

Davis, C.A. (1992). *Handbook for new college teachers and teaching assistants.* Kalamazoo, MI: Davis & Associates.

Davis, J.R. (1993). *Better teaching, more learning: Strategies for success in postsecondary settings.* Phoenix, AZ: Oryx Press.

Davis, R.B., Maher, C.A., & Noddings, N. (Eds.) (1990). Constructivist views on the teaching and learning of mathematics. *Journal for Research in Mathematics Education.* National Council of Teachers of Mathematics.

Davis, T.M. & Murrell, P.H. (1993). *Turning teaching into learning: The role of student responsibility in the collegiate experience.* ASHE-ERIC Higher Education Report No. 8. Washington, DC: The George Washington University.

Dechant, K., Marsick, V., & Kasl, E. (1993). Towards a model of team learning. *Studies in Continuing Education,* 15(1), p. 1-14.

Deci, E.L. (1975). *Intrinsic motivation.* New York: Plenum Press.

Dey, E.L., Ramirez, C.E., Korn, W.S., & Astin, A.W. (1993). *The American college teacher: National norms for the 1992-93 HERI faculty survey.* Los Angeles: Higher Education Research Institute.

DeZure, D. (1996). Closer to the disciplines: A model for improving teaching within departments. *AAHE Bulletin,* 48 (February), p. 9-12.

Diamond, R.M. & Wilbur, F.P. (1990). Developing teaching skills during graduate education. *To Improve the Academy,* 9, p. 199-216.

Dilts, D.A., Haber, L.J., & Bailik, D. (1994). *Assessing what professors do: An introduction to academic performance appraisal in higher education.* Westport, CT: Greenwood Press.

Donald, J.G. & Sullivan, A.M. (1985). *Using research to improve teaching. New Directions for Teaching and Learning,* 23. San Francisco: Jossey-Bass.

Dougherty, T.J. (1992). Multimedia on campus. *Syllabus,* 22, p. 17.

Doyle, W.E. (1981). An outdoor-challenge experience and the effective development of college students. (Doctoral dissertation, University of Massachusetts, 1981). *Dissertations Abstracts International,* 42 (3), 1022A-1023A.

DuBois, G. (1993). Hidden characteristics of effective community college teachers. *Community College Journal of Research and Practice,* 17, p. 459-71.

Dunkin, M.J. (1995). Concepts of teaching and teaching excellence in higher education. *Higher Education Research and Development,* 14(1), p. 21-33.

Dunkin, M.J. (1994). Award winning university teachers' beliefs about teaching. *Higher Education Research and Development,* 13(1), p. 85-92.

Dwyer, W.C. (1996). Student evaluations: The final form. *Thought and Action: The NEA Higher Education Journal.*Washington, DC: NEA Publishing.

Eaton, J.S. (1994). *Strengthening collegiate education in community colleges.* San Francisco: Jossey-Bass.

Eble, K. (1988). *The craft of teaching.* San Francisco: Jossey-Bass.

Eble, K.E., & McKeachie, W.J. (1985). *Improving undergraduate education through faculty development.* San Francisco: Jossey-Bass.

Edgerton, R., Hutchings, P. & Quinlan, K. (1991). *The teaching portfolio: Capturing the scholarship of teaching.* Washington, DC: American Association for Higher Education

Eells, W.C. (1957). *College teachers and college teaching: An annotated bibliography on college and university faculty members and instructional methods.* Atlanta, GA: Southern Region Educational Board.

Eison, J. (1990). Confidence in the classroom: Ten maxims for new teachers. *College Teaching,* 38(1), p. 78-83.

El-Khawas, E. (1991). Senior faculty in academe: Active, committed to the teaching role. *Research Briefs,* 2(5). Washington, D.C.: American Council on Education, Division of Policy Analysis and Research.

Elmore, P.B., & Pohlman, J.T. (1978). Effect of teacher, student, and class characteristics on the evaluation of college instructors. *Journal of Educational Psychology,* 70, p. 187-92.

Entwistle, N.J. (1992). *The impact of teaching on learning outcomes in higher education.* Sheffield: Universities' and Colleges' Staff Development Unit.

Entwistle, N.J., & Tait, H. (1990). Approaches to learning, evaluations of teaching, and preferences for contrasting academic environments. *Higher Education,* 19, p. 169-194.

Entwistle, N.J. (1988). *Styles of learning and teaching.* London: David Fulton.

Entwistle, N.J., & Ramsden, P. (1983). *Understanding student learning.* London: Croom Helm.

Entwistle, N.J. & Hounsell, D. (1975). *How students learn.* Lancaster: University of Lancaster Press.

Ericksen, B.L. & Strommer, D.W. (1991). *Teaching college freshmen.* San Francisco: Jossey-Bass.

Erickson, G.R., & Erickson, B.L. (1979). Improving college teaching: An evaluation of a teaching consultation procedure. *Journal of Higher Education,* 50, p. 670-83.

Fairweather, J.S. & Rhoads, R.A. (1995). Teaching and the faculty role: Enhancing the commitment to instruction in American colleges and universities. *Educational Evaluation and Policy Analysis,* 17(2), p. 179-194.

Fairweather, J.S. (1993). *Teaching, research and faculty rewards, A summary of the re-*

search findings of the Faculty Profile Project. Penn State University: NCTLA.

Falk, G. (1986). *The life of the academic professional in America: An inventory of tasks, tensions and achievements.* Lewiston, MD: Edwin Mellen Press.

Farrell, M. P. (1973). The effects of comparative feedback and interpersonal evaluation on the teaching effectiveness of college professors. *Dissertation Abstracts International,* 34, 1609A. (University Microfilms No. 73-23, 559).

Farquharson, M. (1988). Ideas for teaching Arab students in a multicultural setting. Paper presented at the Annual Meeting of the Teachers of English to Speakers of Other Languages, Chicago.

Fassinger. P.A. (1995). Understanding classroom interaction: Students' and professors' contributions to students' silence. *Journal of Higher Education,* 66 (1).

Feldman, K.A. & Newcomb, T.M. (1994). *The impact of college on students.* New Brunswick, NJ: Transaction Publishers.

Feldman, K.A. (1993). College students' views of male and female college teachers: Part I—evidence from the social laboratory and experiments. *Research in Higher Education,* 33, p. 317-75.

Feldman, K.A. (1993). College students' view of male and female college teachers: Part II—evidence from students' evaluations of their classroom teachers. *Research in Higher Education,* 34, p. 151-211.

Feldman, K.A. (1988). Effective college teaching from the students' and faculty's view: Matched or mismatched priorities? *Research in Higher Education,* 28, p. 291-344.

Feldman, K.A. (1987). Research productivity and scholarly accomplishment of college teachers as related to their instructional effectiveness: A review and exploration. *Research in Higher Education,* 26, p. 227-98.

Feldman, K.A. (1986). The perceived instructional effectiveness of college teachers as related to their personality and attitudinal characteristics: A review and synthesis. *Research in Higher Education,* 24(2).

Feldman, K.A. (1983). Seniority and experience of college teachers as related to evaluations they receive from students. *Research in Higher Education,* 18, p. 3-124.

Feldman, K.A. (1976). The superior college teacher from the students' view. *Research in Higher Education* 5, p. 243-88.

Finkelstein, M.J. (1995). College faculty as teachers. In *The NEA 1995 Almanac of Higher Education.* Washington, DC: NEA Publishing. p. 33-47.

Forest, J.J.F. (1997). Teaching and ambiguity. *Teaching in Higher Education* 2(2).

Forest, J.J.F. (1995). Turning the mirror on ourselves: Research on teaching in postsecondary education. *International Higher Education,* 2 (Summer). Boston College Center for International Higher Education.

Fox, D. (1983). Personal theories of teaching. *Studies in Higher Education* 8, p. 151-163.

Fransson, A. (1977). On qualitative differences in learning. IV—effects of motivation and test anxiety on process and outcome. *British Journal of Educational Psychology,* 47, p. 244-57.

Freire, Paulo (1970). *Pedagogy of the oppressed.* New York: The Seabury Press.

Frey, P.W. (1978). A two-dimensional analysis of student ratings of instruction. *Research in Higher Education,* 9, p. 69-91.

Furhmann, B.S. & Grasha, A.F. (1983). *A practical handbook for college teachers.* Boston, MA: Little & Brown

Gaff, J.G. (1991). *New life for the college curriculum.* San Francisco: Jossey-Bass.

Gaff, J.G. (Ed.) (1978). Institutional renewal through the improvement of teaching. *New Directions for Higher Education,* No. 4. San Francisco: Jossey-Bass.

Gaff, J.G. (1975). *Toward faculty renewal: Advances in faculty, instructional and organizational development.* San Francisco: Jossey-Bass.

Gaff, J.G. & Wilson, R.C. (1971). *The teaching environment: A study of optimum working conditions for effective college teaching.* Berkeley: Center for Research and Development in Higher Education, University of California.

Gage, N.L. (Ed.) (1963). *Handbook of research on teaching.* Chicago: Rand McNally.

Gardner, H. (1993). *Multiple intelligences.* New York: Basic Books.

Geisinger, K.F., & Abedor, A.J. (1985) Organizational change and the development of faculty evaluation systems. *Journal of Instructional Development,* 8, p. 22-25.

Getzels, J.W. & Jackson, P.W. (1963). The teacher's personality and characteristics. In N.L. Gage (Ed.) *Handbook of research on teaching.* Chicago: Rand McNally.

Gibbs, G. (Ed.) (1994). *Improving student learning: Theory and practice.* Oxford: Oxford Brookes University, Oxford Center for Staff Development.

Gibbs, G. & Jenkins, A. (1992). *Teaching large classes in higher education: How to mantain quality with reduced resources.* London: Kogan Page.

Gibbs, G., Habeshaw, S. & Habeshaw, T. (1988). *53 interesting ways to appraise your teaching.* Bristol: Technical and Educational Services.

Gibbs, G. (1981). *Teaching students to learn: A student-centered approach.* Milton Keynes: Open University Press.

Gilmore, G.M., Kane, M.T. & Smith, M.L. (1981). The generalizability of student ratings of instruction: Estimates of teacher and course components. *Journal of Educational Measurement,* 15, p. 1-13.

Goldschmid, M.L. (1978). The evaluation and improvement of teaching in higher education. *Higher Education,* 7, p. 221-245.

Goodman, N.R. (1994). Intercultural education at the university level: Teacher-student interaction. In Brislin, R.W. & Yoshida, T. (Eds.), *Improving intercultural interactions: Modules for cross-cultural training programs.* Thousand Oaks, CA: Sage.

Goodwin, L.D. & Stevens, E.A. (1993). The influence of gender on university faculty members' perceptions of "good" teaching. *Journal of Higher Education,* 64(2).

Gow, L., & Kember, D. (1993). Conceptions of teaching and their relationship to student learning. *British Journal of Educational Psychology,* 63, p. 20-33.

Gow, L., Kember, D. & Sivan, A. (1992). Lecturer's views of their teaching practices: Implications for staff development needs. *Higher Education Research and Development,* 11(2), p. 135-149.

Gow, L., & Kember, D. (1990). Does higher education promote independent learning? *Higher Education,* 19, p. 307-22.

Green, M.F. (1997). *Transforming higher education: Views from leaders around the world.* American Council of Education, Series on Higher Education: Oryx Press.

Greenwood, G.E., & Ramagli, Jr., H.J. (1980). Alternatives to student ratings of college teaching. *Journal of Higher Education,* 51, p. 673-84.

Halpern, D.F. (Ed.) (1994). *Changing college classrooms: New teaching and learning strategies for an increasingly complex world.* San Francisco: Jossey-Bass.

Hauerwaus, S.M. (1988). The morality of teaching. In Deneef, A.L. Goodwin, C.D., & McCrate, E.S. (Eds.), *The academic's handbook.* Durham, N.C.: Duke Press.

Haller, E.P., Child, D.A., & Walberg H.J. (1988). Can comprehension be taught? A quantitative synthesis of metacognitive studies. *Educational Researcher,* 17(9), p.5-8.

Hartley, J. (1985). *Designing instructional text* (2nd Edition). London: Kogan Page.

Heath, R. (1964). *The reasonable adventurer.* Pittsburgh: University of Pittsburgh Press.

Heller, J.F., Puff, R.C. & Mills, C.J. (1985). Assessment of the chilly college climate for women. *Journal of Higher Education,* 56 (July/August), p. 446-61.

Higgins, C.S., Hawthorne, E.M., Cape, J.A., & Bell, L. (1993). The successful community college instructor: A profile for recruitment. *Community College Review,* 21, p. 27-36.

Hodgson, V. (1997). Lectures and the experience of relevance. In Marton, F., Hounsell, D.J. & Entwistle, N.J. (Eds.), *The experience of learning* (2nd Edition). Edinburgh: Scottish Academic Press.

Hofer, B.K. & Pintrich, P.R. (1997). The development of epistemological theories: Beliefs about knowledge and knowing and their relation to learning. *Review of Education Research,* 67 (1), p. 88-140

hooks, b. (1994). *Teaching to transgress: Education as the practice of freedom.* New York: Routledge.

Hoover, K.H. (1980). *College teaching today: A handbook for postsecondary instruction.* Boston, MA: Allyn & Bacon.

Hounsell, D.J. (1997). Understanding teaching and teaching for understanding. In Marton, F., Hounsell, D.J. & Entwistle, N.J. (Eds.), *The experience of learning* (2nd Edition). Edinburgh: Scottish Academic Press.

House, E. R. (1993). *Professional evaluation: Social impact and political consequences.* Newbury Park, Calif.: Sage.

Howard, G.S. (1977). A program to improve university instruction: A promising area for psychologists. *Professional Psychology,* 8, p. 316-27.

Inkeles, A. & Sasaki, M. (1996). *Comparing nations and cultures: Readings in a cross-disciplinary perspective.* Englewood Cliffs, NJ: Prentice Hall.

Institute for International Education (1997). *Towards transnational competence: Rethinking international education: A U.S.-Japan case study.* New York: IIE Research Report 28.

Jacobs, L.C. & Chase, C.I. (1992). *Developing and using tests effectively: A guide for faculty.* San Francisco: Jossey-Bass.

Jansen, J. (Ed.) (1991). *Knowledge and power in South Africa: Critical perspectives across the disciplines.* Johannesburg: Skotaville.

Johnson, G.R. (1995). *First steps to excellence in college teaching.* (Third Edition). Madison, WI: Magna Publications.

Karp, D.A., & Yoels, W.C. (1976). The college classroom: Some observations on the meanings of student participation. *Sociology and Social Research,* 60, p. 421-39.

Kaschak, E. (1978). Sex bias in student evaluations of college professors. *Psychology of Women Quarterly,* 2, p. 235-43.

Katz, J. (1985). Teaching based on knowledge of students. *New Directions for Teaching and Learning,* 21, p. 3-11.

Kember, D. & Gow, L. (1994). Orientations to teaching and their effect on the quality of student learning. *Journal of Higher Education,* 65(1), p. 58-74.

Kember, D., & Gow, L. (1991). A challenge to the anecdotal stereotype of the Asian student. *Studies in Higher Education,* 16, p. 117-28.

Kember, D., & Gow, L. (1990). Cultural specificity of approaches to study. *British Journal of Educational Psychology,* 60, p. 356-63.

Kember, D., & Gow, L. (1989). A model of student approaches to learning encompassing ways to influence and change approaches. *Instructional Science,* 18, p. 263-88.

Kerry T. & Tollitt-Evans J. (1992). *Teaching in further education.* Oxford: Blackwell.

King, A. (1992). From sage on the stage to guide on the side. *College Teaching,* 41(1), p. 30-35.

Knoedler, A.S. & Shea, M.A. (1992). Conducting discussions in the diverse classroom. *To Improve the Academy,* 11, p. 123-135.

Knox, A. (1993). *Strengthening adult and continuing education: A global perspective on synergistic leadership.* San Francisco: Jossey-Bass.

Kolb, D.A. (1976). *Learning style inventory.* Boston: McBer.

Kotula, J.R. (1975) Affecting community college teaching behavior through feedback. *Journal of Applied Psychology,* 36.

Kugel, P. (1993). How professors develop as teachers. *Studies in Higher Education,* 18(3), p. 315-328.

Kulik, J.A., & Kulik, C. (1974). Student ratings of instruction. *Teaching of Psychology,* 1 p. 51-57.

Landbeck, R.C., & Mugler, F. (1996). The transition from high school to university at the University of the South Pacific. In Gibbs, G. (Ed.), *Improving student learning: Using research to improve student learning.* Oxford: Oxford Centre for Staff Development.

Langford G. (1978). *Teaching as a profession.* Manchester, UK: Manchester University Press

Laurillard, D. (1993). *Rethinking university teaching.* London: Routledge.

Leinhardt, G., & Greeno, J. (1986). The cognitive skill of teaching. *Journal of Educational Psychology,* 78(2), p. 75-95.

Levine, A. (Ed.) (1993). *The higher learning in America.* Baltimore: Johns Hopkins University Press.

Levinson-Rose, J., & Menges, R.J. (1981). Improving college teaching: A critical review of research. *Review of Educational Research,* 51, p. 403-34.

Lewis, K.G. (Ed.) (1988). *Face to face: A sourcebook of individual consultation techniques for faculty/instructional developers.* Stillwater, Okla.: New Forums Press.

Lewis, L. (1996). *Marginal worth: Teaching and the academic labor market.* New Brunswick, NJ: Transaction Publishers.

Lomperis, A.M.T. (1990). Are women changing the nature of the academic profession? *Journal of Higher Education,* Vol. 61, No. 6., p. 643-677.

Lowman, J. (1984). *Mastering the techniques of teaching.* San Francisco: Jossey-Bass.

McCaughey, R. (1993). But can they teach? In praise of college professors who publish. *Teachers' College Record,* 95 (Winter), 242-257.

McKeachie W.J. (Ed.) (1994) *Teaching tips: Strategies, research and theory for college and university teachers.* Lexington, MA: D.C.Heath Co. (9th ed.).

McKeachie, W.J. (1990). Research on college teaching: The historical background. *Journal of Educational Psychology* Vol. 82, No. 2, pp.189-200.

McKeachie, W.J., Pintrich, P.R., Lin, Y. & Smith, D.A. (1986). *Teaching and learning in the college classroom: A review of the research literature.* Ann Arbor, MI: National Center for Research to Improve Postsecondary Teaching and Learning.

McKeachie, W.J., Lin, Y.G., Daugherty, M., Moffett, M.M., Neigler, C., Nork, J., Walz, M., & Baldwin, R. (1980). Using student ratings consultation to improve instruction. *British Journal of Educational Psychology,* 50, pp. 168-74

McKeachie, W.J., & Lin, Y.G. (1975). Multiple discriminant analysis of student ratings of college teachers. *Journal of Educational Research,* 68, p. 300-305.

Mangieri, J.N. & Block, C.C. (Eds.) (1994). *Creating powerful thinking teachers and students: Diverse perspectives.* New York: Harcourt Brace.

Mann, R.D., Ringwald, B.E., Arnold, S., Binder, J., Cytrynbaum, S., & Rosenwein, J.W. (1970). *Conflict and style in the college classroom.* New York: Wiley.

Mansfield, D.L. & Murrell, P. (1991). The use of student learning styles in teaching world politics. *Innovative Higher Education,* 15 (2), pp. 127-136.

Markie, P.J. (1994). *A professor's duties: Ethical issues in college teaching.* Lanham, MD: Rowman and Littlefield Publishers, Inc.

Marsh, H.W. (1991). A multidimensional perspective to students' evaluations of teaching effectiveness: A response to Abrami and d'Apollonia (1991). *Journal of Educational Psychology,* 83, p. 416-21.

Marsh, H.W. (1987). Students' evaluations of university teaching: Research findings, methodological issues, directions for future research. *International Journal of Educational Research,* 11 (3).

Marsh, H.W. (1983). Multidimensional ratings of teaching effectiveness by students from different academic settings and their relation to student/course/instructor characteristics. *Journal of Educational Psychology,* 75, p. 150-66.

Marsh, H.W. (1982). SEEQ: A reliable, valid, and useful instrument for collecting students' evaluations of university teaching. *British Journal of Educational Psychology,* 52, p. 77-95.

Marsh, H.W. & Bailey, M. (1993). Multidimensional students' evaluations of teaching effectiveness: A profile analysis. *Journal of Higher Education*, 64(1).

Marsh, H.W., & Dunkin, M.J. (1992). Students' evaluations of university teaching: A multidimensional perspective. In Smart, J. (Ed.) *Higher education: Handbook of theory and research*. New York: Agathon.

Marsh, H.W., & Hocevar, D. (1991). The multidimensionality of students' evaluations of teaching effectiveness: The generality of factor structures across academic discipline, instructor level, and course level. *Teaching and Teacher Education*, 7, p. 9-18.

Marsh, H.W. & Roche, L. (1994). *The use of students' evaluation of university teaching to improve teaching effectiveness*. Canberra: Australian Government & Publishing Service.

Marton, F., et al. (1997) *The experience of learning* (2nd edition). Edinburgh Scotland: Scottish Academic Press.

Marton, F., Dall'Alba, G. & Beaty, E. (1994). Conceptions of learning, *International Journal of Educational Research*, 19, p. 277-300.

Marton, F., & Saljö, R. (1976). On qualitative differences in learning, outcome, and process. *British Journal of Educational Psychology*, 46, p. 4-11.

Matiru, B. & Mwangi, A. (Eds.) (1995). *Teach your best: a handbook for university lecturers*. (2nd ed.) Bonn: Deutsche Stiftung für internationale Entwicklung.

Menges, R.J. & Svinicki, M.D. (Ed.) (1991). College teaching: From theory to practice. *New Directions for Teaching and Learning*, 45. San Francisco: Jossey-Bass.

Menges, R.J., Weimer, M. & Associates (1997). *Teaching on solid ground: Using scholarship to improve practice*. San Francisco: Jossey-Bass.

Mezirow, J. (1990). A critical theory of adult learning and teaching. In Tight, M. (Ed.), *Adult learning and teaching*. London: Routledge.

Miller, R. (1987). *Evaluating faculty for promotion and tenure*. San Francisco: Jossey-Bass.

Miller, R. (1972). *Evaluating faculty performance*. San Francisco: Jossey-Bass.

Millman, J. (Ed.) (1981). *Handbook of teacher evaluation*. Beverly Hills,CA: Sage.

Mills, B.J. (1991). Putting the teaching portfolio in context. *To improve the academy*, 10, pp. 215-9.

Milton, O., Pollio, H.R., & Eison, J. (1986). *Making sense of college grades*. San Francisco: Jossey-Bass.

Miron, M. (1985). The "good professor" as perceived by university instructors. *Higher Education*, 14, p. 211-15.

Morris, S. & Hudson, W. (1995). International education and innovative approaches to university teaching. *Australian Universities' Review*, 38(2) p.70-74.

Morris, W.H. (Ed.) (1970). Effective college teaching; the quest for relevance. Washington, DC: American Association for Higher Education by American Council on Education.

Murphy, Jr., R. (1993). *The calculus of intimacy: A teaching life*. Columbus: Ohio State University Press.

Murray, H.G. (1987). Classroom teaching behaviors related to college teaching effectiveness. In Aleamoni, L.M., *Techniques for evaluating and improving instruc-*

tion. New Directions for Teaching and Learning 31. San Francisco, CA: Jossey-Bass. p. 9-24.

Murray, H.G., Rushton, J.P. & Paunonen, S.V. (1990). Teacher personality traits and student instructional ratings in six types of university courses. *Journal of Educational Psychology,* 82 (2). American Psychological Assocation. p. 250-261.

Murray, J.P. (1995). *Successful faculty development and evaluation: The complete teaching portfolio.* ASHE-ERIC Higher Education Report No. 8. Washington, DC: The George Washington University.

Murray, J.P. (1994) Why teaching portfolios? *Community College Review,* 22, pp. 33-43.

Myers, C. & Jones, T.B. (1993). *Promoting active learning: Strategies for the college classroom.* San Francisco: Jossey-Bass.

National Center for Education Statistics (1994). *NCES Survey Report, 1993 National Study of Postsecondary Faculty.* Washington, DC: U.S. Department of Education, Office of Research and Improvement.

Neer, M.R. (1987). The development of an instrument to measure classroom apprehension. *Communication Education,* 36, p. 154-166.

Neff, R.A. & Weimer, M. (1989). *Classroom communication: Collected readings for effective discussion and questioning.* Madison, WI: Magna Publications.

Newble, D. & Cannon, R. (1991). *A hanbook for teachers of universities and colleges: A guide for improving teaching methods.* London: Kogan Page.

Oldfather, P. (1994). *When students do not feel motivated for literacy learning: How a responsive classroom culture helps.* Reading Research Report No. 8. Athens, GA: National Reading Research Center, University of Georgia.

Ornstein, A.C. (1995). The new paradigm in research on teaching. *Educational Forum,* 59 (Winter), p. 124-129

Oser, F.K., Dick, A. & Patry, J. (1992). *Effective and responsible teaching: A new synthesis.* San Francisco: Jossey-Bass.

Osterloh, K. (1986). International differences and communicative approaches to foreign language teaching in the Third World. In Valdes, J. (Ed.), *Culture bound: Bridging the cultural gap.* Cambridge: Cambridge University Press.

Otten, K.K. (1991). *How do universities in the UNC System identify and reward excellent teaching?* Raleigh, NC: North Carolina Center for Public Policy Research.

Parker, O. (1986). Cultural clues to the Middle Eastern student. In J. Valdes (Ed.), *Culture bound: Bridging the cultural gap.* Cambridge: Cambridge University Press.

Pearson, C.S., Shavlik, D.L. & Touchton, J.G. (Eds) (1989). *Educating the majority.* San Francisco: Jossey-Bass.

Penner, J.G. (1984). *Why many college teachers cannot lecture.* Springfield, IL: Charles C. Thomas.

Perlberg, A. (1983). When professors confront themselves: Towards a theoretical conceptualization of video self-confrontation in higher education. *Higher Education,* 12, p. 633-63.

Perry, R.P. (1991). Perceived control in college students: Implications for instruction in higher education. In Smart, J. (Ed.), *Higher education: Handbook of theory and research* (Vol. 7). New York: Agathon Press. pp. 1-56.

Perry, R.P. (1990). Introduction to the special section on instruction in higher education. *Journal of Educational Psychology,* 82(2), p. 183-188

Perry, W.G. (1985). Different worlds in the same classroom: Students' evolution in their vision of knowledge and their expectations of teachers. In Gullette, M.M. (Ed.), *On teaching and learning.* Cambridge, MA: Harvard-Danforth Center for Teaching and Learning.

Perry, W.G. (1970). *Forms of intellectul and ethical development in the college years: A scheme.* New York: Holt, Rinehart & Winston.

Pintrich, P.R. & Garcia, T. (1991). Student goal orientation and self-regulation in the college classroom. In Maher, M. & Pintrich, P.R. (Eds.), *Advances in motivation and achievement: Goals and self-regulatory processes* (Vol. 7, pp. 371-401). Greenwich, CT: JAI Press.

Pintrich, P. (1988). Student learning and college teaching. In Young, R.E. and Eble, K.E. (Eds.) *College teaching and learning: Preparing for new commitments. New Directions for Teaching and Learning,* 33 (Spring). San Francisco: Jossey-Bass.

Piper, D.W. (1994). *Are professors professional? The organization of university examinations.* London: Jessica Kingsley Publishers, Ltd.

Platt, G., Parsons, T., & Kirshstein, R. (1978). Undergraduate teaching environments: Normative orientations to teaching among faculty in the higher education system. *Sociological Inquiry,* 43, p. 3-21.

Pratt, D.D., & Associates (1997). *Five perspectives on teaching in adult and higher education.* Melbourne, FL: Krieger Publishing.

Pratt, D.D. (1992). Conceptions of teaching. *Adult Education Quarterly,* 42, p. 203-20.

Prégent, R. (1994). *Charting your course: How to prepare to teach more effectively.* Madison, WI: Magna Publications.

Prichard, K.W. & Sawyer, R.M. (Eds.) (1994). *Handbook of college teaching: Theory and applications.* Westport, CT: Greenwood Press.

Ramsden, P. (1992). *Learning to teach in higher education.* London: Routledge.

Ramsden, P. (1988). *Improving learning: New perspectives.* London: Kogan Page.

Ramsden, P., Margetson, D., Martin, E. & Clarke, S. (1995). *Recognising and rewarding good teaching in Australian higher education.* Canberra: Australian Government Publishing Service.

Ramsden, P., & Entwistle, N.J. (1981). Effects of academic departments on students' approaches to studying. *British Journal of Educational Psychology,* 51, p. 368-83.

Richardson, J.T.E. (1994). Cultural specifity of approaches to studying higher education: A literature survey. *Higher Education,* 27(4).

Robertson, E., & Grant, G. (1982). Teaching and ethics: An epilogue. *Journal of Higher Education,* 53 (May/June), p. 345-357.

Rose, C. & Nicholl, M.J. (1997). *Accelerated learning for the 21st Century.* New York: Delacorte Press.

Rosenshine, B. (1971). Teaching behaviors related to student achievement. In Vestbury, L. (Ed.), *Research into classroom processes: Recent developments and next steps.* New York: Teachers College Press.

Rowland, Stephen. (1996). Relationships between teaching and research. *Teaching in Higher Education,* 1(1).

Runyan, M.K. (1991). The effect of extra time on reading comprehension scores for university students with and without learning disabilities. *Journal of Learning Disabilities,* (February).

Ruth, D. (1996). Teaching at a South African university. *Teaching in Higher Education,* 1(1).

Ryan, M.P. & Martens, G.G. (1989). *Planning a college course: A guidebook for the graduate teaching assistant.* Ann Arbor, MI: The National Center for Research to Improve Postsecondary Teaching and Learning.

Sacks, P. (1996). *Generation X goes to college: An eye-opening account of teaching in postmodern America.* Chicago: Open Press.

Sadler, D.R. (1983). Evaluation and the improvement of academic learning. *Journal of Higher Education,* 54 (January/February), p. 60-79.

Saljö, R. (1979). Learning in the learner's perspective, I—some commonsense conceptions." *Reports from the Institute of Education,*University of Gothenburg, Sweden, No. 77.

Samuelowicz, K. & Bain, J. (1992). Conceptions of teaching held by academic teachers. *Higher Education,* 22, p. 229-249.

Sawyer, R.M., Prichard, K.W. & Hostetler, K.D. (1992). *The art and politics of college teaching: A practical guide for the beginning professor.* New York: Peter Lang Publishing.

Schmier, L. (1995). *Random thoughts: The humanity of teaching.* Madison, WI: Magna Publications.

Schön, D. (1983). *The reflective practitioner: How professionals think in action.* New York: Basic Books.

Scratz, M. (1992). Researching while teaching: An action research approach in higher education. *Studies in Higher Education,* 17, p. 81-95.

Seldin, P. (1993). *Successful use of teaching portfolios.* Bolton, Mass: Anker Publishing

Seldin, P. (1991). *The teaching portfolio: A practical guide to improved performance and promotion/tenure decisions.* Bolton, MA: Anker Publishing.

Seldin, P. & Associates (1989). *How administrators can improve teaching.* San Francisco: Jossey-Bass.

Shavelson, R. & Stern, P. (1981). Research on teachers' pedagogical thoughts, judgements, divisions, and behavior. *Review of Educational Research,* 51, p. 455-498.

Sherman, B.R. & Blackburn, R.T. (1975). Personal characteristics and teaching effectiveness of college faculty. *Journal of Educational Psychology,* 67(1), p. 124-131.

Sherman, T.M., Armistead, L.P., Fowler, F., Barksdale, M.A., & Reif, G. (1987). The quest for excellence in university teaching. *Journal of Higher Education,* 48, p. 66-84.

Shulman, L. (1993). Teaching as community property: Putting an end to pedagogical solitude. *Change.* (November/December).

Slaughter, S. (1985). From serving students to serving the economy: Changing expectations of faculty role performance. *Higher Education,* 14, p. 41-56.

Slavin, R.E. (1990). *Cooperative learning: Theory, research and practice.* Englewood Cliffs, NJ: Prentice Hall.

Slavin, R.E., Leavey, M.B., & Madden, N.A. (1986). *Team accelerated instruction.* Watertown, MA: Charlesbridge.

Smith, B. & Brown, S. (Eds.) (1995). *Research and teaching in higher education.* London: Kogan Page.

Smith, D.G. (1977). College classroom interactions and critical thinking. *Journal of Educational Psychology,* 69, p. 180-90.

Sorcinelli, M.D. (1984). An approach to colleague evaluation of classroom instruction. *Journal of Instructional Development,* 7, p. 11-17.

Stark, J.S., Shaw, K.M., & Lowther, M.A. (1989). *Student goals for college and courses: A missing link in assessing and improving academic achievement.* ASHE-ERIC Higher Education Report No. 6. Washington, DC: George Washington University.

Statham, K.A., Richardson, L., & Cook, J. (1991). *Gender and university teaching: A negotiated difference.* Albany, N.Y.: State University of New York Press.

Stevens, E. (1988). Tinkering with teaching. *Review of Higher Education,*12, p. 63-78.

Stevens, E., Goodwin, L., & Goodwin, W. (1991). How are we different? Attitudes and perceptions of teaching across three institutions. *Journal of Staff, Program, and Organizational Development,* 9, p. 1-12.

Strike, K.A., & Posner, G.J. (1985). A conceptual change view of learning and understanding. In West, L.H.T. & Pines, A.L. (Eds.), *Cognitive structure and conceptual change.* New York: Academic Press.

Svinicki, M. (Ed.) (1990). *The changing face of college teaching. New Directions for Teaching and Learning* 42. San Francisco: Jossey-Bass.

Tiberius, R. & Billson, J. (1991). The social context of teaching and learning. In *College teaching: From theory to practice. New Directions for Teaching and Learning* 45 (Spring). San Francisco, CA: Jossey-Bass.

Tierney, W.G. & Bensimon, E.M. (1996). *Promotion and tenure: Community and socialization in academe.* Albany, NY: SUNY Press.

Tierney, W.G. & Rhoads, R.A. (1993). *Enhancing promotion, tenure, and beyond: Faculty socialization as a cultural process.* ASHE-ERIC Higher Education Report No. 6. Washington, DC: George Washington University.

Timpson, W.M. & Bendel-Simso, P. (1996). *Concepts and choices for teaching: Meeting the challenges in higher education.* Madison, WI: Magna Publications.

Timpson, W.M., Burgoyne, S., Jones, C., & Jones, W. (1996). *Teaching and performing: Ideas for energizing your classes.* Madison, WI: Magna Publications.

Travers, R.M.W. (1981). Criteria of good teaching. In Millman, J. (Ed.), *Handbook of teacher evaluation.* Beverly Hills,CA: Sage.

Trigwell, K., & Prosser, M. (1996). Changing approaches to teaching: A relational perspective. *Studies in Higher Education,* 21, p. 275-284

University of California (1980). *Report of the Task Force on Teaching Evaluation.* Berkeley, CA

U.S. Department of Education (1994). *Integrating research on faculty: Seeking new ways to communicate about the academic life of faculty.* (Conference Report) Results from the 1994 Forum. Washington, DC: U.S. Department of Education.

Valdes, J. (Ed.) (1986). *Culture bound: Bridging the cultural gap.* Cambridge: Cambridge University Press.

Van Rossum, E.J., & Schenk, S.M. (1984). The relationship between learning conception, study strategy, and learning outcomes. *British Journal of Educational Psychology,* 54, p. 73-83.

Verdugo, R.R. (1995). Racial stratification and the use of Hispanic faculty as role models: Theory, policy, and practice. *Journal of Higher Education,* 66(6).

Ware, J.E. & Williams, R.G. (1975). The Doctor Fox effect: A study of lecturer effectiveness and rating of instruction. *Journal of Medical Education,* 50, p. 149-156.

Warren, J.R. (1972). *Varieties of Academic performance.* Oakland, CA: Western College Association.

Warton, P.M. (1995). What parts of teaching do academics see as feasible to delegate? *Higher Education* 29, p. 129-141.

Watkins, D. & Biggs, J.B. (Eds.) (1996). *The Chinese learner: Cultural, psychological, and contextual influences.* Hong Kong/Melbourne: Comparative Education Research Centre/Australian Council for Educational Research.

Watkins, D. & Regmi, M. (1992). How universal are student conceptions of learning? A Nepalese investigation. *Psychologia,* 35, p. 101-110.

Weimer, M.E. (Ed.) (1993). *Faculty as teachers.* University Park: Pennsylvania State University

Weimer, M.E. (1991). *Improving college teaching.* San Francisco, Ca: Jossey-Bass.

Weimer, M. & Lenze, L.F. (1991). Instructional interventions: A review of the literature on efforts to improve instruction. In Smart, J.S. (Ed.), *Higher education: Handbook of theory and practice,* Vol. 7. New York: Agathon Press.

Weimer, M. (1990). *Improving college teaching: Strategies for developing instructional effectiveness.* San Francisco: Jossey-Bass.

Weimer, M. & Neff, R.A. (1989). *Teaching college: Collected readings for effective discussion and reading.* Madison, WI: Magna Publications.

Weimer, M., Parret, J. & Kerns, M.M. (1988). *How am I teaching? Forms and activities for acquiring instructional input.* Madison, WI: Magna Publications.

Weimer, M. (1987). Translating evaluation results into teaching improvements. *AAHE Bulletin,* 39(8), 8-11.

Weimer, M., Parrett, J.L., & Kerns, M.M. (1988). *How am I teaching?* Madison, WI: Magna Publications.

Weiss, L. (1985). Faculty perspectives and practice in and urban community college. *Higher Education* 14, p. 553-574.

Wilson, E.K. (1982). Power, pretense, and piggybacking: Some ethical issues in teaching. *Journal of Higher Education,* 53 (May/June), p. 268-281.

Wilson, R.C. (1987). Toward excellence in teaching. In Aleamoni, L.M. (Ed.) *Techniques for evaluating and improving instruction. New Directions for Teaching and Learning* 31. San Francisco: Jossey-Bass.

Wilson, R.C. (1986). Improving faculty teaching: Effective use of student evaluations and consultants. *Journal of Higher Education,* 57 (March/April 1986), p. 196-211.

Wittrock, M. (Ed.) (1986). *Handbook of research on teaching* (3rd Edition). New York: Macmillan.

Wright, W.A., & O'Neil, M.C. (1995). Perspectives on improving teaching in Canadian universities. *The Canadian Journal of Higher Education,* 24(3), p. 26-57.

Wright, W.A., & O'Neil, M.C. (1994). Teaching improvement practices: New perspectives. *To Improve the Academy,* 13, 1-37.

Wright, W.A. & Herteis, E.M. (1993). *University teaching and learning: An instructional resource guide for teaching assistants.* Halifax, Nova Scotia: Dalhousie University Press.

Zuriff, G.E. (1997). Learning disabilities in the academy: A professor's guide. *Academic Questions,* 10(1), p. 53-65

RECOMMENDED PERIODICALS

AAHE Bulletin. Washington, DC: American Association of Higher Education.

Academic Questions. Princeton, NJ: National Association of Scholars.

Assessment and Evaluation in Higher Education. London: Carfax Publishers.

ASHE-ERIC Higher Education Reports. Washington, DC: George Washington University.

British Journal of Sociology. Boston, MA: Routledge & Kegan Paul.

British Journal of Sociology of Education. Oxfordshire: Carfax Publishing.

Campus Review (weekly Australasian newspaper for higher education).

Change: The Magazine of Higher Learning. Washington, DC: American Association of Higher Education.

Chronicle of Higher Education (weekly newspaper for higher education). Washington, DC.

College Teaching. Washington, DC: Heldref Publications.

Community College Review. North Carolina State University.

Community College Social Science Journal. El Cajon, CA: Community College Social Science Association.

Contents Pages in Education. Oxfordshire, UK: Carfax Publishing.

Cooperative Learning and College Teaching. Carson, CA: California State University, Dominguez Hills.

Education, Research and Perspectives. Nedlands: University of Western Australia, Dept. of Education.

European Journal of Education. Oxfordshire, UK: Carfax Publishing.

Focus on Law Studies: Teaching About Law in the Liberal Arts. Chicago, IL: American Bar Association.

Higher Education. Amsterdam, the Netherlands: Kluwer Publishers.

Higher Education in Europe. Bucharest, Romania: UNESCO European Center for Higher Education.

Improving College and University Teaching. Corvallis: Graduate School, Oregon State College.

Innovative Higher Education. Athens: University of Georgia.

Interchange. Toronto: Ontario Institute for Studies in Education.

International Journal of Innovative Higher Education. West Yorkshire, UK: University Without Walls International Council.

International Journal of Qualitative Studies in Education. London: Taylor & Francis.

International Higher Education. Chestnut Hill, MA: Boston College Center for International Higher Education.

Issues & Inquiry in College Learning and Teaching. Ypsilanti, MI: Faculty Center for Instructional Excellence, Eastern Michigan University.

Journal of the Association for the Improvement of Community College Teaching. Washington, DC: AICCT.

Journal of College Science Teaching. Washington, DC: National Science Teachers Association.

Journal of Higher Education. Ohio State University Press.

Journal of Professional Studies. Fort Collins, CO: College of Professional Studies, Colorado State University.

Journal of Studies in International Education. New York: Council on International Educational Exchange.

Journal of Teaching and Learning. Grand Forks, ND: Center for Teaching and Learning, University of North Dakota.

Journal on Excellence in College Teaching. Oxford, OH: Miami University.

Le Monde de L'Education. Paris: S.A.R.L. Le Monde.

Lingua Franca: The Review of Academic Life. New York: Ingram Periodicals.

Logos (a quarterly journal of the world book community).

New Directions for Higher Education (series). San Francisco, CA: Jossey-Bass.

New Directions for Teaching and Learning (series). San Francisco, CA: Jossey-Bass.

On Teaching and Learning. Boston, MA: Harvard-Danforth Center, Harvard University.

On the Horizon. San Francisco, CA: Jossey-Bass.

Prospects. Paris: UNESCO.

Review of Higher Education. Baltimore, MD: Johns Hopkins University Press.

Revista caribeäna de educaciâon bilingèue (Caribbean Review of Bilingual Education). Rio Piedras, Puerto Rico: Centro de Servici.

Russian Education and Society. Armonk, NY: M.E. Sharpe, Inc.

Suid-Afrikaanse tydskrif vir hoèer onderwys (South African Journal of Higher Education). Committee of University Principals of South Africa.

Teaching English in the Two-Year College. Urbana IL: National Council of Teachers of English.

Teaching in Higher Education. London: Carfax Publishers.

The Teaching Professor. Madison, WI: Magna Publications.

Teaching Resource Bulletin. Chicago: the American Bar Association, Commission on College and University Nonprofessional Legal Studies.

The Times Higher Education Supplement (a weekly newspaper on higher education). London.

Index

faculty and diversity 39, 40–43. *See also* diversity: of faculty; diversity: of students

Fairweather, J. 49. *See also* faculty: reward systems

feedback 120, 131, 131–135. *See also* student learning: feedback

Feldman, K. 40, 46, 102

Fiji 113, 118

Finland 223, 234

Forest, J.J.F. 35–69

Fox, D. 48, 89

Freire, P. 347

G

Gao, L.B. 22

Gardiner, L. 76, 93, 97, 99, 102

Gardner, H. 75

gender and faculty issues 40–43. *See also* faculty: women and minority

Germany 38

Gibbs, G. 97, 99, 223–235

Glass & Smith 64

group discussion 377. *See also* collaborative learning

Guam 204–219

H

Heath, R. 78. *See also* reasonable adventurer

Herrick, M. 237

Hispanic
  faculty 41.
    See also diversity: of faculty
  students 41.
    See also diversity: of students

Hong Kong 22, 24–33, 38, 206

Hounsell, D. 98

Hudson, L. 75, 79

Hyland, T. 305–319

I

individuality 365. *See also* cross-cultural psychology: individualistic

instruction
  classroom methods 39, 50–56, 191, 375–379
  issues of language in 39, 43–45, 116, 364–365

International Consortium for Educational Development 223–235

Internet 56–59, 131, 289–293, 298, 367. *See also* technology: in teaching

Israel 38, 137–159

J

Jamaica 345, 350

Japan 22, 38, 45, 206, 365, 396

Jessup, G. 312

jig saw method 214. *See* collaborative learning: jig saw method

Johnson, Johnson & Holubec 161, 183

K

Kember & Gow 22, 254, 255

Kember & McKay 29

Kenya 241

Kerr, C. 67

Kim, Y.C. 393–397

Kiribati 113, 115

knowledge 20.
  construction 67, 75, 105, 367, 378.
    See also cognitive psychology

Kohn, M.L. 38

Korea 38, 393

Kulik & Kulik 183

Kwangju Incident 394

L

Latin America 410–411, 416

Laurillard, D. 100

teaching assistants 260, 260–268, 269–270
teaching awards 269–270
teaching dossier. *See* portfolios
teaching practicum 259–268
  York University handbook 271–273
teaching routines 50–56
technology
  in teaching 39, 56–59, 100, 289–293, 350–359, 366, 403. *See also* Internet
Teichler, U. 325, 341
tenure 6, 10, 238, 410, 429
Thomas & Bain 97
Tierney and Bensimon 40, 42. *See also* faculty: reward systems
Tokelau 113
Tonga 113
Trigwell, K. 92
Trigwell, Prosser & Taylor 20
Trinidad 346, 349
Trow, M. 326
tutorials 115
  by teleconferencing 354
  tutorial support 129, 131–135, 369
  UWI Resident Tutors 346–359
Tuvalu 113

U
United Kingdom 4, 19, 24–28, 38, 223, 224, 225, 227, 248, 275, 287, 305, 319
United States 4, 19, 24–28, 38, 40, 48, 103, 116, 223, 225, 229–231, 287, 397
University of Botswana 241–257
  Higher Education Development Unit 243–257
University of Buenos Aires 409–430
University of Copenhagen 327, 331
University of Guam 204–219
University of Malawi 241

University of Manitoba 240
University of Nottingham 347
University of Queensland 228
University of South Australia 285
University of the South Pacific 113–133
University of Utrecht 225, 231
University of the West Indies 345

V
Vance and Crossling 361–388
Vanuatu 113, 115
Vygotsky, L.S. 138

W
Watkins & Biggs 22
Watkins, D. 19–33
Western
  versus non-Western 19–33, 203–204, 364–365. *See also* cross-cultural psychology
Western Samoa 113, 115
Wheeler & Schuster 239, 254
Witkin, H. 78, 79
women. *See* Caplan, P.; faculty: women and minority
Wright, W.A. 3–16, 256, 339
writing
  ability of students 361
  for enhancing subject understanding 378
  evaluation of 380, 386–392
  and reading 366–368
writing instruction 361–388
  theoretical framework for 362

Y
York University 259–268

Z
Zambia 241
Zimbabwe 241